Urban Lives

Urban Lives

An Industrial City and Its People During the Twentieth Century

Edited by
MARTIN DRIBE, THERESE NILSSON, AND
ANNA TEGUNIMATAKA

OXFORD
UNIVERSITY PRESS

Oxford University Press is a department of the University of Oxford. It furthers
the University's objective of excellence in research, scholarship, and education
by publishing worldwide. Oxford is a registered trade mark of Oxford University
Press in the UK and certain other countries.

Published in the United States of America by Oxford University Press
198 Madison Avenue, New York, NY 10016, United States of America.

© Oxford University Press 2024

Some rights reserved. No part of this publication may be reproduced, stored in
a retrieval system, or transmitted, in any form or by any means, for commercial purposes,
without the prior permission in writing of Oxford University Press, or as expressly
permitted by law, by licence or under terms agreed with the appropriate
reprographics rights organization.

This is an open access publication, available online and distributed under the terms of a
Creative Commons Attribution – Non Commercial – No Derivatives 4.0
International licence (CC BY-NC-ND 4.0), a copy of which is available at
http://creativecommons.org/licenses/by-nc-nd/4.0/.

You must not circulate this work in any other form
and you must impose this same condition on any acquirer.

Library of Congress Cataloging-in-Publication Data
Names: Dribe, Martin, editor. | Nilsson, Therese, editor. |
Tegunimataka, Anna, editor.
Title: Urban lives : an industrial city and its people during the twentieth
century / [edited by Martin Dribe, Therese Nilsson, Anna Tegunimataka]
Description: New York, NY : Oxford University Press, [2024] | Includes
bibliographical references and index.
Identifiers: LCCN 2023057106 (print) | LCCN 2023057107 (ebook) |
ISBN 9780197761090 (hardback) | ISBN 9780197761113 (epub)
Subjects: LCSH: Landskrona (Sweden)—Economic conditions. | Landskrona
(Sweden)—Social conditions. | Urbanization—Sweden. |
Industrialization—Sweden.
Classification: LCC HT145.S8 U73 2024 (print) | LCC HT145.S8 (ebook) |
DDC 330.9485—dc23/eng/20240116
LC record available at https://lccn.loc.gov/2023057106
LC ebook record available at https://lccn.loc.gov/2023057107

DOI: 10.1093/oso/9780197761090.001.0001

Printed by Integrated Books International, United States of America

Contents

List of Illustrations	vii
Acknowledgments	xv
Contributors	xvii

1. Urban Lives: A Micro-Level Approach to Economic and Demographic Change in the Twentieth Century — 1
   Martin Dribe, Therese Nilsson, and Anna Tegunimataka

2. Landskrona: The Industrial City — 26
   Martin Dribe and Patrick Svensson

3. Economic Inequality and Social Mobility — 82
   Gabriel Brea-Martinez and Martin Dribe

4. Migration in Times of Economic Growth and Recession — 115
   Finn Hedefalk, Patrick Svensson, and Anna Tegunimataka

5. Social Class Segregation in Landskrona — 146
   Gabriel Brea-Martinez, Finn Hedefalk, Therese Nilsson, and Vinicius de Souza Maia

6. The Gender Revolution: Marriage, Fertility, and Divorce in the Industrial City — 170
   Luciana Quaranta and Maria Stanfors

7. A Healthy Marriage? Marital Status and Adult Mortality — 213
   Ingrid K. van Dijk and Martin Dribe

8. Maternal and Infant Health: Understanding the Role of Institutions and Medical Innovations — 243
   Ingrid K. van Dijk, Volha Lazuka, and Luciana Quaranta

9. The Late Emergence of the Socioeconomic Gradient in Adult Mortality: An Urban Phenomenon? — 281
   Tommy Bengtsson, Martin Dribe, and Jonas Helgertz

10. Income, Inequality, and Geography: Disparities in Age at Death — 307
    Gabriel Brea-Martinez, Finn Hedefalk, and Therese Nilsson

11. The Industrial City and Its People: Summary and Conclusion — 339
    Martin Dribe, Therese Nilsson, and Anna Tegunimataka

Index — 353

Illustrations

Boxes

8.1	Reforms and medical innovations related to maternal and child health in Sweden, 1900–Present.	249
8.2	Institutional developments in Landskrona related to maternal and child health.	255

Figures

2.1	The mean population of Landskrona, 1910–2017.	29
2.2	The mean population of the eleven cities, 1911–2017.	30
2.3	Net in-migration (per 1,000 population) to the eleven cities, 1911–2017.	33
2.4	Share of workers in industry of all workers, 1900–2000, in the eleven cities.	36
2.5	Industrial structure of the eleven cities (shares of workers per sector).	38
2.6	Women as share of total industrial workforce in the eleven cities, 1911 and 1990.	47
2.7	Mean income (1970-constant prices), 1970–2010, in the eleven cities.	49
2.8	Crude death rates (per 1,000 population) in the eleven cities, 1911–2017.	55
2.9	Infant mortality (IMR, per 1,000 births) in the eleven cities, 1875–1935.	56
2.10	Child mortality (age 1–4, per 1,000 population) in the eleven cities, 1875–1935.	57
2.11	Adult mortality (40–59 years, per 1,000 population) in the eleven cities, 1875–1935.	58
2.12	Old-age mortality (60+ years, per 1,000 population) in the eleven cities, 1875–1935.	59
2.13	Crude birth rates (per 1,000 population) in the eleven cities, 1911–2017.	60

2.14	General fertility rate (per 1,000 population, women 15–49 years) in the eleven cities, 1910–1990.	61
2.15	Crude marriage rates (per 1,000 population) in the eleven cities, 1911–2017.	62
2.16	Proportions married of men and women all ages, in the eleven cities, 1910–1970.	63
2.17	Proportions of the population 20–64 with at least two years of post-secondary education, in the eleven cities, 1970–2010.	67
2.18	Voter share for the Social Democratic party, in the eleven cities, 1919–2018.	68
2.19	Share of seats in city board for parties reaching representation in Landskrona, 1919–2018.	69
2.20	Elected women (share of all elected) in municipality elections in the eleven cities, 1919–2018.	70
3.1	Distribution of social class for men and women respectively, 1905–2015.	85
3.2	Gini coefficients for total income for men (A) and women (B) age 20–64, 1905–2015.	93
3.3	Share of income earned by the top 1 percent in Landskrona, 1905–2015.	95
3.4	Gender gap in lifetime income by quintile and decadal birth cohort. Men and women born 1920–1969.	95
3.5	Income gap for social classes in relation to higher white-collar for men (A) and women (B) in Landskrona, 1905–2015.	97
3.6	Income gap for Swedish-born and foreign-born by gender in Landskrona, 1905–2015.	98
3.7	Income gap between Landskrona and the five parishes by social class, 1905–2015.	98
3.8	Proportion of children attaining a higher lifetime income than their fathers in Landskrona, by gender and cohort (1920–1965).	103
A3.1	Fraction of children attaining a higher lifetime income than their fathers in Landskrona by fathers' deciles and decade of birth (1920–1965).	109
A3.2	Fraction of children attaining post-secondary education by fathers' income deciles and decade of birth (1940–1965).	110
4.1	In-migration to Landskrona by birth region, 1905–2014 (absolute numbers).	124
4.2	Out-migration from Landskrona by birth region, 1905–2014 (absolute numbers).	124
4.3	In- and out-migration and total migration (per 1,000 population), Landskrona, 1905–2014.	125

4.4	Net migration (per 1,000), Landskrona, 1905–2014.	128
5.1	Mean family size in Landskrona by block in 1920, 1940, and 1960.	154
5.2	Mean age of the family head (FH) in Landskrona by block in 1920, 1940, and 1960.	155
5.3	Share of children (<18 years old) in Landskrona by block in 1920, 1940, and 1960.	156
5.4	Share of families headed by women in Landskrona by block in 1920, 1940, and 1960.	157
5.5	Share of families headed by a medium-skilled worker family head in Landskrona by block in 1920, 1940, and 1960.	158
5.6	Share of families headed by a lower white-collar family head in Landskrona by block in 1920, 1940, and 1960.	158
5.7	Share of families headed by a lower-skilled worker family head in Landskrona by block in 1920, 1940, and 1960.	159
5.8	Share of families headed by an unskilled worker family head in Landskrona by block in 1920, 1940, and 1960.	159
5.9	Share of families headed by a higher white-collar family head in Landskrona by block in 1920, 1940, and 1960.	160
5.10	Adjusted isolation index ($\eta 2$) in Landskrona by year and social class (1905–1967).	161
5.11	Adjusted isolation index ($\eta 2$) in Landskrona for higher white-collar workers by the age of the family head (1905–1967).	162
6.1	Civil status among men and women in Landskrona and the five parishes, 1905–2015.	179
6.2	Crude marriage rates in Landskrona and the five parishes, 1905–2015.	181
6.3	Crude marriage rates by social class in Landskrona and the five parishes, 1905–2015.	182
6.4	Average age at first marriage by gender in Landskrona and the five parishes, 1905–2015.	183
6.5	Total fertility rates in Landskrona and the five parishes, 1905–2015.	190
6.6	Total fertility rates by social class in Landskrona and the five parishes, 1905–2015.	191
6.7	Average age at first birth among women aged 18–49 in Landskrona and the five parishes, 1905–2015.	192
6.8	Average birth intervals in years (trends) by parity among women aged 18–49 in Landskrona and the five parishes, 1905–2015.	194
6.9	Relative risk ratios of divorce and widowhood among women and men in their first marriages in Landskrona and the five parishes, 1905–2015.	202

6.10	Relative risk ratios of divorce and widowhood among women and men in their first marriages in Landskrona and the five parishes, 1905–2015.	203
7.1	Marital status in Landskrona and the five parishes, ages 30–79.	220
7.2	Marriage and divorce rates in Sweden and Landskrona and the five parishes.	221
7.3	Proportion of women and men newly bereaved (bereaved in the past year) in Landskrona and the five parishes.	223
7.4	Kaplan-Meier survivor functions by gender and period.	224
8.1	Percentage of births in maternity wards by area, 1912–1947.	256
8.2	Maternal mortality ratio and female crude death rates at age 15–49 by decade in the study area.	259
8.3	Stillbirths rate by year and area, 1905–1967.	260
8.4	Sex ratio at birth by year and area, 1905–2015.	262
8.5	Infant, post-neonatal, late neonatal, and early neonatal mortality rates in the study area by year, 1905–2015.	263
8.6	Developments in infant mortality by infant age in the study area by year, 1905–2015.	265
8.7	Medical and healthcare interventions included in the analyses (shares of affected children).	267
9.1	Age-standardized death rates, 30–89 years (per 1,000).	289
10.1	Population in Landskrona by 250 m^2 grids in six different years (1940–1965).	317
10.2	Mean family income in Landskrona by 250 m^2 grids in six different years (1940–1965).	318
10.3	Gini index in Landskrona by 250 m^2 grids in six different years (1940–1965).	319

Maps

1.1	The study area in western Scania, southern Sweden.	13
2.1	The location of the eleven cities in Sweden.	28
2.2	Landskrona of 1918, with industries marked with circles and housing projects with squares.	51

Tables

2.1	Share of the population younger than 15 years (percent) in the eleven cities and Sweden as a whole.	31

2.2	Share of the population 65 and older (percent) in the eleven cities and Sweden as a whole.	32
2.3	Sex ratios (M/F) in the eleven cities and Sweden as a whole.	33
2.4	Distribution of foreign-born in Landskrona.	34
2.5	Mean income for employed men in the eleven cities in 1920 and 1930.	48
2.6	Share of population subject to poor relief, ten cities as compared to the level in Landskrona, 1910, 1920, 1950, and 1960.	65
A2.1	Number of workers in the shipyard industry in Landskrona, 1875–1983.	73
A2.2	Number of workers in the sugar industry in Landskrona, 1865–1965.	73
A2.3	Industrial structure of Landskrona 1910–1990 (shares of workers per sector), percent.	74
A2.4	Net in-migration (per 1,000 population) to Landskrona, 1910–2017.	75
A2.5	Age-specific mortality rates (per 1,000 population) 1875–1935.	76
3.1	Top three occupational titles by social class for men (A) and women (B) in Landskrona, 1905–2015.	87
3.2	Intergenerational rank-rank associations of income between fathers and children.	100
3.3	Intergenerational rank-rank associations of income between paternal grandfathers and grandchildren.	101
3.4	Intergenerational rank-rank associations of income between maternal grandfathers and grandchildren.	102
A.3.1	Mean income by social class for men and women in Landskrona, 1905–2015 (SEK).	107
A3.2	Mean income by social class for men and women in the five parishes, 1905–2015 (SEK).	108
4.1	In-migration to Landskrona 1905–2014 by period and previous residence (percent).	129
4.2	Out-migration from Landskrona 1905–2014 by period and destination (percent).	130
4.3	Net migration, Landskrona 1905–2014, by period and origin and destination (number of migrants).	130
4.4	Odds ratios of in-migration (staying at least five years).	133
4.5	Odds ratios of out-migration (staying away at least five years).	135
4.6	Odds ratios of in-migration from Malmö, Lund, Helsingborg (staying at least five years).	137
4.7	Odds ratios of out-migration to Malmö, Lund, Helsingborg (staying away at least five years).	138

4.8	Odds ratios of in-migration from rural areas <10 km from Landskrona (staying at least five years).	140
4.9	Odds ratios of out-migration to rural areas <10 km from Landskrona (staying away at least five years).	141
6.1	Cox proportional hazard estimates of first marriage in ages 18–49 in Landskrona and the five parishes.	185
6.2	Cox proportional hazard estimates of first birth among women in ages 18–49 in Landskrona and the five parishes.	196
6.3	Cox proportional hazard estimates of second and higher-order births among women in ages 18–49 in Landskrona.	197
6.4	Cox proportional hazard estimates of second and higher-order births among women in ages 18–49 in the five parishes.	198
6.5	Average age at first marriage and duration of marriage for married, divorced, and widowed women and men in Landskrona and the five parishes, 1905–2015.	201
6.6	Results from multinomial logistic regressions: the relative risk of divorce and death (of either spouse) compared to remaining married among first marriages in Landskrona and the five parishes, 1905–2015.	204
7.1	Descriptive statistics, men and women aged 30–79, by person-year, Landskrona and the five parishes.	218
7.2	Marital status and mortality (hazard ratios) by gender and period, age 30–79.	225
7.3	Timing of widowhood and mortality (hazard ratios) by gender and period, age 30–79. Landskrona and the five parishes.	228
7.4	Marital status and mortality (hazard ratios) by social class gender and period, age 30–79. Landskrona and the five parishes.	229
7.5	Marital status and mortality (hazard ratios) by gender, age and period. Landskrona and the five parishes.	230
A7.1	Marital status and mortality (hazard ratios) by gender and period, age 30–79. Landskrona and the five parishes.	236
A7.2	Timing of widowhood and mortality (hazard ratios) by gender and period, age 30–79. Landskrona and the five parishes.	237
A7.3	Individual social class, marital status, and mortality (hazard ratios) by gender and period, age 30–79. Landskrona and the five parishes.	238
A7.4	Marital status, timing of widowhood mortality (hazard ratios) by gender, age 30–79. Landskrona and the five parishes. Cohabitors (after 1990) excluded from the single group. 1975–2015.	239

8.1	Share of infant deaths by cause in Landskrona and the five parishes by period, 1905–2015.	264
8.2	Intervention effects of the expansion of maternity wards and neonatal intensive care units (NICUs) as interventions, Landskrona and the five parishes, 1905–2015.	269
8.3	Intervention effects of the opening of the infant healthcare center, Landskrona, 1905–2015.	271
8.4	Intervention effects of the introduction of antibiotics, Landskrona and the five parishes, 1905–2015.	272
A8.1	Results for the unit root tests for the demographic outcomes, Landskrona and the five parishes.	275
9.1	Hazard ratios of mortality, age 30–89, Landskrona and the five parishes (percent).	291
9.2	Hazard ratios of mortality by social class, ages 30–89, by urbanity.	293
9.3	Hazard ratios of mortality by social class and age group. Landskrona and the five parishes.	294
A9.1	Relative frequencies of the variables included in the analysis.	298
A9.2	Hazard ratios of mortality, age 30–89. Individual social class. Landskrona and the five parishes.	302
10.1	Descriptive statistics of the variables used in the logistic regressions.	315
10.2	Marginal effects for variables of interest from all models.	322
A10.1	Full model marginal effects for the probability of dying before age 50.	327
A10.2	Marginal effects of the full logistic regression models on the probability of dying before the age 70 in Landskrona, 1939–1967.	328
A10.3	Marginal effects of the full logistic regression models on the probability of dying before age 50 with exposure measured on ages 40–50 in Landskrona, 1939–1967.	329
A10.4	Marginal effects of the full logistic regression models on the probability of dying before age 70 with exposure measured on ages 60–70 in Landskrona, 1939–1967.	330
A10.5	Marginal effects of the full logistic regression models on the probability of dying before age 50 in Landskrona, 1939–1967, by gender.	331
A10.6	Marginal effects of the full logistic regression models on the probability of dying before age 70 in Landskrona, 1939–1967, by gender.	332

A10.7 Marginal effects of the full logistic regression models on the probability of dying before age 50 and 70 without HISCLASS in Landskrona, 1939–1967. 333

A10.8 Marginal effects of the full logistic regression models on the probability of dying before age 50 and 70 in Landskrona, 1939–1967, adding Gini and squared Gini terms for controlling for nonlinear associations. 334

Acknowledgments

This volume presents findings from the research program "The Rise and Fall of the Industrial City: Landskrona Population Study" (PI: Martin Dribe), which was generously funded by Riksbankens Jubileumsfond (RJ) 2016–2023 (grant number: M15-0173:1). The aim of the research program was to analyze long-term demographic processes connected to industrialization, modern economic growth, and the profound societal transformations of the twentieth century. We studied these vital economic and demographic changes in Sweden through the lens of an industrial city—Landskrona in southern Sweden—which has experienced this transformation. The different chapters of this volume are good examples of this research, and together they provide a coherent analysis of these long-term processes and patterns. All the contributors have been involved in the program and are or have been based at the Center for Economic Demography at Lund University in Sweden. We as editors thank all authors for a good and fruitful collaboration within the program and in the writing of this volume.

Most of the research presented in this volume is based on the Scanian Economic-Demographic Database (SEDD), which is the result of a long-term collaboration between Lund University and the National Archives in Lund, initiated by Tommy Bengtsson in 1983. We are most grateful to the current head of the National Archives in Lund, Göran Kristiansson, for an excellent collaboration over the years. A group of research assistants has been working with data entry, quality control, record linkage, and coding of variables. This group has included Erik Andersson, Mats Andersson, Sofia Brasjö, Markus Isaksson, Per Johansson, and Rolf Nilsson. Clas Andersson has been our data manager, structuring and maintaining the database and serving researchers with data extractions. Finn Hedefalk and Luciana Quaranta have been instrumental in developing the database; Finn through the geocoding of blocks and addresses and Luciana in contributing to structure the database and produce datasets for statistical analysis to the benefit of the entire research group.

The development of the database has been an integral part of the national infrastructure SwedPop, which is a partnership between the University of Gothenburg, Lund University, Umeå University, the National Archives, and Stockholm City Archives with equal funding from the partner institutions and the Swedish Research Council (grant numbers: RFI 2017-00666 and 2021-00183). We thank our collaborators in SwedPop and especially the principal investigator, Elisabeth Engberg at Umeå University.

Finally, we thank research secretary Madeleine Jarl who has assisted in preparing the volume for publication. The funding for Open Access was provided by the Lund University Library.

—Martin Dribe, Therese Nilsson, and Anna Tegunimataka

Contributors

Tommy Bengtsson is Professor Emeritus of Economic History and Demography at Lund University. His main research concerns longevity, aging, migration, and integration, past and present. Over the years he has made several contributions to the literature on the effects of short-term economic stress on demographic behavior and on how conditions in early life affect socioeconomic performance and health in later life.

Gabriel Brea-Martinez is a Researcher in Economic History at Lund University. His research centers on the interplay between social mobility, socioeconomic inequality, and various dimensions of demographic behavior, favoring a long-term approach examining historical and contemporary periods.

Ingrid K. van Dijk is Associate Professor of Economic History at Lund University and affiliated with the Radboud Group for Family History and Historical Demography, Radboud University. Her research interests are long-term changes in population health, the role of families, changing disease environments, and the social gradient in health.

Martin Dribe is Professor of Economic History and Director of the Centre for Economic Demography at Lund University. He is the principal investigator of the Scanian Economic-Demographic Database and led the research program, "The Rise and Fall of the Industrial City: The Landskrona Population Study (2016–2023)." Dribe's research focuses on historical and contemporary economic demography covering mortality, fertility, migration, marriage, and social mobility. His work has been published in the leading journals of demography and economic history.

Finn Hedefalk is a Researcher in Economic History at Lund University. He has a background in geography and specializes in geographic information systems and spatial analysis. His research focuses on neighborhood conditions and their long-term effects, and he has participated in several projects involving the geocoding of micro-level data.

Jonas Helgertz is Associate Professor of Economic History at Lund University and affiliated with the ISRDI and the Minnesota Population Center, University of Minnesota. His research concerns life-course determinants of demographic, socioeconomic, and health outcomes. Helgertz uses historical micro-data to understand how decisions and events in early life influence longevity and the socioeconomic and contextual determinants of mortality.

Volha Lazuka is Associate Professor of Economics at the University of Southern Denmark, with affiliations at IZA and the Centre of Economic Demography. Her research primarily focuses on how historical public health interventions and various social reforms causally affect the health and economic well-being of individuals.

Vinicius de Souza Maia is a PhD student in Economic History at Lund University. He holds a master's degree in demography from the State University of Campinas, and his PhD project focuses on neighborhood effects on fertility and family formation.

Therese Nilsson is Professor of Economics at Lund University and Research at the Institute of Industrial Economics. Her research is in applied microeconomics and has been published in top-tier journals in economics. By exploiting historical policy reforms in the domains of health and education her research seeks to uncover the causal impact of human capital investments across the life course. Nilsson's research also focuses on cultural and institutional economics.

Luciana Quaranta is Associate Professor of Economic History at Lund University. Her research focuses on historical demography and examines period and early-life determinants of living standards, health, and well-being using detailed micro-level data. She has also contributed to the development of the Scanian Economic-Demographic Database and the Intermediate Data Structure.

Maria Stanfors is Professor of Economic History at Lund University. Her research is applied and focuses on the economic histories of female labor force participation, housework, caregiving, and family formation, as well as the interrelationships between them. Typically, her research uses individual-level data and focuses on gender differences using a long-term perspective.

Patrick Svensson is Professor of Agrarian History at the Swedish University of Agricultural Sciences. His main research area concerns the workings of the pre-industrial economy and the transition to modern economic growth. Svensson's most recent research projects focus on long-term studies of inequality in Sweden and the everyday life in a rural society during the Agricultural and Industrial Revolutions.

Anna Tegunimataka is Associate Professor of Economic History at Lund University. Her research focuses on economic demography, with a specialization in migration. She has contributed to the literature on the role of citizenship status by examining individual-level effects of naturalization for immigrants. She also works on the income and intergenerational effects of intermarriage.

1
Urban Lives

A Micro-Level Approach to Economic and Demographic Change in the Twentieth Century

Martin Dribe, Therese Nilsson, and Anna Tegunimataka

The Big Picture

The past 200 years have witnessed revolutionary changes in living conditions for most people in the Western world. Nutrition, consumption, and overall quality of life improved dramatically, and the demographic constraints and behaviors that shape people's everyday lives were entirely transformed (Broadberry and O'Rourke 2010; Deaton 2013; Fogel 2004; Galor 2011; Goldin 2021). While the broad outline of these processes is well known through extensive research at the macro level, we still know very little about their micro-level foundations, largely because of the scarcity of appropriate data in most countries. This volume addresses highly relevant research questions using a unique data infrastructure that allows a detailed investigation at the micro level, covering most of the twentieth century and the beginning of the twenty-first.

Industrialization led to dramatic improvements in living standards by bringing in completely new ways of organizing society, wider access to high-quality consumer goods, a secure food supply, comfortable and hygienic housing, expeditious and inexpensive transportation, greater representation in political processes, and many other changes that have shaped the society we take for granted today (Broadberry and O'Rourke 2010). One of the most significant and enduring effects of industrial growth in the nineteenth and twentieth centuries was the rapid urbanization that accompanied it (Bairoch 1988). The relocation of the rural population to the cities was a common trend across Europe and North America, and it ushered in the most profound changes in normal working life since the Neolithic Revolution. For the first time in history, a majority of the working population was not relegated to manual farm labor but was instead given work in factories and offices in urban settings. The transition from a rural to an urban society not only had significant economic implications but also was a catalyst for sociopolitical change directly related to the great labor movements of the era and crucial in securing many of the fundamental conditions enjoyed in modern welfare states, such as access to high-quality healthcare, childcare, and schooling, as well security in old age or in cases of disability (e.g., Baldwin 1990; Magnusson 2007; Olsson 1990).

In conjunction with these enormous societal transformations, more understated but nonetheless radical changes also emerged. These were changes in individual life courses, particularly in the ways individuals experienced basic demographic events: birth, death, marriage, and migration (Davis 1945; Demeny 1968; Notestein 1945). Improvements in health and declining mortality at all ages have considerably prolonged human life (Oeppen and Vaupel 2002). The mortality of infants and young children, once an anticipated reality, has become a nearly incomprehensible rarity in only three generations (see, e.g., Viazzo and Corsini 1993). Adults of all ages have experienced persistent increases in longevity and nowadays remain active and healthy up to and beyond retirement. Methods of preventing, diagnosing, and treating disease have made tremendous progress thanks to the scientific, social, and institutional breakthroughs of the industrial era and thereafter, and have all contributed to great improvements in life expectancy (Easterlin 1999; Kunitz 2006). The reduction in the number of births per woman and the transition to smaller families also changed living conditions, especially for women and young children, and had important ramifications for the age structure of the population (Lee 2003). This in turn has had far-reaching modern-day implications for public spending, labor supply, savings, and, ultimately, economic growth (Lindert 2004). Following the decline of fertility, family forms and formation changed and new life course patterns emerged, especially because married women were entering the labor force at an accelerating pace (Goldin 2021; Stanfors and Goldscheider 2017). The role of marriage has gradually become more marginalized as nonmarital cohabitation has become an increasingly important route toward family formation and as divorce has received ever greater social and institutional acceptance and support (Lesthaeghe 1983, 2010; Stanfors et al. 2020; Van de Kaa 1987). These changes have provided entirely new conditions for labor supply, educational investment, and economic decision-making within families.

Changes in the direction and volume of the flow of people also characterized Western countries in the twentieth century. Many transitioned from being emigrant countries to immigrant countries, and Sweden exemplifies this phenomenon. Industrialization gave people their first opportunity to travel further to seek work and a better life, and about 1 million Swedes did so by going to North America (Hatton and Williamson 1998; Runblom and Norman 1976). Then, as living standards improved and converged with those in North America, emigration flows slowed to a trickle (Taylor and Williamson 1997), and, in the 1950s and 1960s, the golden age of Swedish economic performance, the tide turned and attracted workers from the rest of Europe. Stagnation in the 1970s saw this strong pull factor disappear, and, at the same time, immigration laws became stricter, but immigrants continued to arrive in even greater numbers as refugees and family reunification migrants (Lundh and Ohlsson 1999). This posed new challenges to society in terms of the labor market and social integration of these immigrants, but it offered opportunities, too (Bevelander and Lundh 2007; Lundborg 2013).

Migration can have significant economic impacts on the countries and regions that attract these individuals, including enhanced innovation (Hunt and Gauthier-Loiselle 2010; Moser et al. 2014; Sequeira et al. 2020), lower consumer prices (Bound et al. 2017; Cortes 2008), increased trade (Burchardi et al. 2019), and greater specialization in the labor market (Foged and Peri 2016). International migration also has important implications for the origin countries through, for example, remittances (Gibson et al. 2018), the transmission of know-how (Khanna and Morales, 2017; Khanna et al. 2022), and the transfer of cultural and political values that promote better governance (Docquier et al., 2016; Tuccio et al. 2019).

The most recent chapter in this long-term development has been the erosion of the traditional industrial society that served as the engine for these transformations. In recent decades, the relative importance of the manufacturing sector has declined, giving way to the rise of the service and knowledge economy. While this new development has generally been beneficial, it has placed a strain on many cities whose economies were dependent on manufacturing. Previously wealthy cities fell into stagnation, while others were able to leverage their position by creating a more modern, service-based economy.

Despite extensive previous research, these processes are still poorly understood due to a lack of suitable micro-level data. Even though we know the basic outline of these fundamental societal changes in the twentieth century, we lack a detailed picture of much of the process, especially for the pre-1970 period.

Aim and Scope

In this volume, we look at economic and demographic change at the micro level of individuals and families to contribute to a better understanding of the societal transformations that profoundly changed people's lives during the twentieth century. We study these vital transformations in Sweden through the lens of an industrial city—Landskrona—and its rural hinterland. Landskrona, founded in 1413, evolved from being a port and military town in the pre-industrial period to becoming a medium-sized industrial city (Jönsson 1993, 1995) that later experienced serious deindustrialization (Jönsson 1997). Sweden was a country with limited urbanization, and its cities were small by international comparison.

Landskrona had a population of 14,000 in 1900, which grew to about 40,000 in the 1970s, reaching 45,000 in 2015, after a period of both stagnation and decline and, after the year 2000, growth. As well as being subject to the fundamental demographic processes occurring everywhere else, Landskrona experienced considerable immigration and bears evidence of many of the present-day societal challenges of both economic stagnation and transformation as well as immigrant integration.

The research presented in this volume is based on a unique data infrastructure, the Scanian Economic-Demographic Database (SEDD), which contains economic and demographic longitudinal data at the individual level for the entire twentieth century. Each chapter answers research questions related to health, family, migration, and residential segregation, combining demographic and socioeconomic information for all individuals who were born in or moved to Landskrona. Individuals present in the historical population registers have been linked to the complete national population registers in Sweden for the period 1968–2015. Thus, the book offers a concise, yet comprehensive, examination of economic and demographic processes connected to modern economic growth and profound societal transformation in a city transitioning from the industrial to the post-industrial era.

The unique data have given us entirely new opportunities to study individuals and families from a long-term historical perspective, to follow individuals across individual life courses and generations, and to situate individuals and families in their social, institutional, and environmental contexts. The volume provides novel insights into the micro-level foundations of economic-demographic processes over the long run. A conceptual advantage of using individual-level instead of aggregate data is that the patterns correspond more closely to individual-level decision-making, and a micro-level perspective allows for an improved understanding of underlying mechanisms regarding the relationships studied. More importantly, a micro-level approach does not suffer from the confounding from compositional differences over time inherent to aggregated data.

Another approach common to several of the chapters is to view the findings identified for individuals and their household members residing in the city in relation to those in nearby rural settings. These comparisons are relevant not least for understanding urban–rural divides and potential shifts therein during the transition from a rural to an urban society. The different chapters unite around four main economic-demographic processes: inequality in health and mortality, changing family patterns and gender relations, social and economic mobility, and migration. Each chapter addresses research questions connected to the research frontier in these respective fields to improve our understanding of these fundamental societal processes. The analyses in the chapters are based on a common periodization reflecting the long-term social, economic, and demographic development of Swedish society.

Periodization: The Rise and Fall of the Industrial City

The "rise of the industrial city" began as early as the nineteenth century and continued until the 1950s. Rationalization in industry in the 1960s led to continued rapid growth in some sectors (e.g., the shipyard industry) but to a downturn in others (e.g., sugar production and, to some degree, textiles and clothing manufacturing). In the 1970s, this development resulted in a structural crisis and ultimately in the "fall of the industrial city," which culminated in the 1980s. From the 1990s onward, there has been renewed expansion in many industrial cities in terms of innovation and sectors (hi-tech, knowledge-intensive, services, etc.). This has fundamentally changed the old industrial cities, including Landskrona, even though the upturn here has been somewhat weaker than in some of its counterparts such as nearby Malmö, the third largest city in Sweden. We identify four broad periods of "rise" (1905–1949), "culmination" (1950–1974), "fall" (1975–1994), and a "new rise" (1995–2015). The first period can be subdivided around 1930, demarcated by the deep economic crisis connected to the Great Depression. The first period also covers the two world wars. Sweden was neutral and nonparticipating in both World War I and World War II, but, given the importance of international trade in a small open economy, ongoing war and related blockades meant shortages and rationing together with increased price levels (Torregrosa-Hetland and Sabaté 2022). This periodization fits well with the periodization of Swedish industrial history as outlined by economic historian Lennart Schön (e.g., 2010), and it also fits with major elements of Sweden's social and political development during the twentieth century (e.g., Magnusson 2007; Olofsson 2007; Stanfors 2007). Below, we characterize the different periods in terms of economic, social, and political development and also look at the national and international developments in relation to Landskrona specifically (see also Chapter 2).

1905–1929

The period 1890–1930 saw rapid economic growth following the real breakthrough of Swedish industrialization. During 1910–1930, gross domestic product (GDP) per capita grew by about 2 percent per year, which was the fastest in the Western world. The new development blocks created around manufacturing, textile, paper, transportation, and mass media (newspapers) were linked to electricity and electric power. The transformation phase lasted until about 1915 and was followed by structural rationalization and a structural crisis in the early 1930s. The period saw growth in real wages and an expansion of services related to industrialization (e.g., banking), while employment in agriculture declined, from 58 percent in 1890 to 34 percent in 1930 (Schön 2010). This was similar to developments in other industrial economies during this Second Industrial Revolution, when growth and rapid technological change were increasingly connected to electrification and oil (the combustion engine) (Landes 1969), as well as to new organizational forms of the market and businesses (Chandler 1977). This phase of industrialization began in the late nineteenth century and continued well into the next period as well.

In Landskrona, industrial expansion lasted until the early 1920s, when a crisis hit the shipyard, although expansion continued in the other industries. The share of industrial workers increased until 1920, and then declined somewhat between 1920 and 1930. Industrial expansion led to continued urbanization and city growth both in Sweden and elsewhere. In the United States, the share of population in urban areas grew from around 35 percent in 1900 to more than 50 percent in 1930 (Boustan et al. 2018). The investment in urban infrastructures such as water and sewerage culminated in this period (e.g., Helgertz and Önnerfors 2019), but there were still the considerable problems of poverty and poor living conditions among the working class (Elmér 1971). Access to higher education beyond the basic seven years of schooling remained highly selective.

This period saw the establishment of the male breadwinner model, whereby most married women did not participate in the labor force (Stanfors and Goldscheider 2017). As in many other countries in Europe, fertility decline started around 1880 and continued until the early 1930s, when it reached a below-replacement level (Coale and Watkins 1986; for Sweden, see Hofsten and Lundström 1976). Mortality had declined since the late eighteenth century, and, in the early twentieth century, it dropped sharply in the case of infectious diseases following improved knowledge about disease transmission and the development of new vaccines and, subsequently, effective medical drugs (Easterlin 1999). Quite possibly, improved diet and nutrition also contributed to the decline in mortality in this period (see Dribe and Karlsson 2022; Molitoris and Dribe 2016). Emigration to North America was still significant in the first decades of the twentieth century but diminished at the end of the 1920s.

Universal suffrage for men and women was only fully implemented in 1921, after decades of gradual expansion and a raging political conflict around the issue (e.g., Lewin 1989, Chapter 3). This was a period of weak governments and frequently shifting majorities in parliament. The working class was mobilized politically through both the Social Democratic Party, founded in 1889, and the nationwide trade union for blue-collar workers, Landsorganisationen (LO), founded in 1898. Social policy was also expanded, with reforms in both social insurance and pensions (Elmér 1971; Olsson 1990). In Landskrona, the Social Democrats gained a majority of the city council in 1919, which they maintained until 1991 (see Chapter 2).

1930–1949

The 1930s began with an economic crisis (including the "Kreuger Crash" in 1932[1]), a knock-on effect of the international crisis of the Great Depression. The turbulence of the latter had a strong negative impact on the Swedish economy, with a sharp decline in real income, industrial production, employment, and prices. Yet compared to the United States and many other European countries, the recession in Sweden, which brought about minor disruption and failures in the banking sector, was milder and of shorter duration, and this was of importance to the industrial sector and investment in general (Jonung 1981). Until 1950, Swedish economic growth was faster than in other industrial countries: productivity grew by 2.5 percent yearly between 1931 and 1935 and between 1951 and 1955 (Schön 2010). The crisis was followed by a new transformation period, one based on previous innovations related to electricity and the motor vehicle. As in other industrial nations, production was now geared toward standardized mass production and increased specialization ("Fordism") and toward creating a mass market for consumer products. Meanwhile, in Landskrona, the share of industrial workers in the workforce continued to increase.

Investment in improved housing continued in alignment with functionalism, but the problems of inadequate housing and low living standards in the poorer segments of the population remained. After the culmination of the fertility decline in the early 1930s, marriage and fertility rates increased sharply in the mid-1940s during the baby boom (e.g., Stanfors 2003). This was not a specifically Swedish phenomenon; similar increases in marriage and fertility took place in most Western countries at about the same time (Easterlin 1961; Van Bavel and Reher 2013). The increase in marriage and family building spurred the demand for new housing. The labor market saw a major institutional change in the form of the establishment of the "Swedish Model" through the so-called Saltsjöbaden Agreement. This set a new standard for centralized negotiations between the national blue-collar trade union, LO, and the Swedish Federation of Employers (Svenska arbetsgivareföreningen) in an effort to reduce the level of conflict in the labor market and create favorable conditions for the development of Swedish industry (Lundh 2009). In Landskrona, there was a net in-migration from other parts of Sweden during this period of industrial expansion.

Politically, the 1930s meant the emergence of social democratic hegemony at the national level. The Social Democrats led the governments in power between 1932 and 1976, except for one short spell in 1936. In this period, early family policy was introduced, such as the extension of unpaid maternity leave from 6 weeks to 6 months, an allowance for mothers with small children, and a universal child allowance in 1948 (Stanfors 2003, appx. 2). A new Keynesian economic policy was introduced to address the development and crisis of capitalism. It gave the government a greater role in the economy but without the socialization of private enterprise, and it led to short-term budget deficits, public work programs, and the abandonment of the gold standard (Schön 2010).

As already mentioned, the Social Democrats had governed Landskrona since 1919. Municipal government had the main responsibility for social welfare, childcare, and basic education—areas that also saw the first significant reform activity in this period. Programs targeting young children's health involved trained health workers who provided information, support, and monitoring through home visits and local clinics, with a particular emphasis on nutrition and sanitation (Bhalotra et al. 2017, 2022). These initiatives were part of a broader international infant welfare movement at the time (Fildes et al. 2013), one fueled by concerns about population decline and exacerbated by World War I (Davis 2011). This period also saw major reforms in primary education. In 1842, the first statute of compulsory education provided a foundation for a thoroughly organized school system whereby every parish had to offer six years of schooling by an approved teacher to all children (Slunga 2000).[2] Yet, in the 1920s, there were large differences across urban and rural areas in terms of school quality and total period of instruction. When benchmarking with other Western European countries, which offered seven or eight years of compulsory education, politicians and teacher organizations were also concerned that Sweden was lagging behind regarding the amount of time children spent in school. As a response, compulsory education was extended by one year and school terms were extended and also harmonized across the country (cf. Fischer et al. 2020, 2021). These different social reforms constituted a significant first step in the development of the modern welfare state.

1950–1974

The period after the end of World War II has been labeled the "golden years" of the Swedish economy, a time of stable economic growth with no major downturns. Real wages and living standards improved dramatically—for the working class, too—and this included the introduction of new consumer goods such as television and various household appliances. A similar development took place throughout the Western world (see, e.g., Crafts and Toniolo 2010; Gordon 2016). Several large investment programs in housing, electric power, and infrastructure were launched with strong government backing. Energy use (oil and electricity) increased sharply, and there was large-scale mechanization and automation of production processes as well as the rationalization of distribution and trade. At the same time, there were early signs of difficulties in the textile and clothing industries in the face of increased competition from abroad. In agriculture, further rationalization led to a drastic fall in employment.

In Landskrona, rationalization of the sugar industry led to the closing of the sugar refinery in 1960, followed by the closure of the sugar factory in 1962. Despite this, manufacturing increased for most of the period, but the textile industry was severely affected by the national crisis and most factories closed either during this period or shortly after 1975. The shipyard grew during the 1950s and 1960s, but the number of employees was reduced during the 1970s. The share of industrial workers increased until 1960, but then declined for the rest of the period (see Chapter 2).

There were, moreover, major investments in housing throughout the period, which culminated in the "million homes program" (*miljonprogrammet*) in 1965–1975. Investment in housing was driven by ongoing urbanization through large-scale in-migration to cities from rural areas, and homes were built using public funding, with the overall goal of combating housing shortages and modernizing the housing stock. Sweden was the only Western country to carry out a public building program on this scale in the post-war period,[3] and, in most cities, including Landskrona, this program resulted in new housing estates being added to the built-up areas on the urban periphery (Andersson et al. 2010). In 1950, for the first time in history, half of the Swedish population lived in urban areas, although many of the places defined as urban were quite small and based on town privileges dating far back. In 1950, only three cities had a population of more than 100,000, with the most densely populated being the capital city of Stockholm with 750,000 residents. Increased labor migration from Finland and southern Europe further contributed to this development. The public sector expanded greatly following investment in education, healthcare, and social provision, an expansion which also meant increased bureaucratization that provided employment in white-collar jobs in this sector. One landmark reform was the introduction of a new and more generous pension system in 1959 (e.g., Elmér 1971; Olofsson 2007). In this period, the traditional male breadwinner model began to erode as a result of the increasing labor force participation of married women in the first phase of the "gender revolution" (Goldscheider et al. 2015; Stanfors and Goldscheider 2017). These developments affected Landskrona, too, in terms of educational expansion, such as the establishment of compulsory nine-year basic comprehensive schooling in 1962 and the construction of several large new housing areas on the outskirts of the old city.

During this post-war boom, the Social Democrats ruled without interruption and with the same Prime Minister, Tage Erlander, serving between 1946 and 1969. State involvement in the economy increased and social policy expanded. Important reforms where Sweden was clearly a forerunner compared to many other Western countries included paid maternity leave (3 months in 1955, extended to 6 months in 1963), parental leave (1974), and the separate taxation of spouses (1971).

1975–1994

The oil crisis of 1973 set off a long period of industrial decline and economic crisis which hit energy, industry, and public finances at the same time and affected the entire industrial world, Sweden included (see, e.g., Crafts and Toniolo 2010; Schön 2010). Despite strong rationalization during the 1960s, the Swedish economy expanded until 1973, when the oil crisis led to higher energy prices. However, even without the oil crisis there would have been a structural crisis followed by a new period of structural transformation. From the second half of the 1970s onward, the transformation of industrial society was connected to electronic technology (the "Third Industrial Revolution"), the rise of the knowledge economy, and the increased importance of skills and education (Schön 2010; see also Goldin and Katz 2010).

The crisis in the steel and shipyard industries continued until the early 1980s, when they were all but closed down. From the mid-1980s, there was an economic boom following economic "liberalization" (removal of regulations and tax reforms) and expansive monetary policy, including several devaluations of the Swedish krona. As in other countries across Europe, productivity growth was slower than before (Crafts and Toniolo 2010), but, over the period as a whole, the Swedish economy grew by 1.8 percent per year (Schön 2010). Due in part to previous deregulations and expansive monetary policies, Sweden was hit by a financial crisis in the early 1990s that spilled over to the economy at large in the form of a crisis in the real estate and housing markets and high unemployment in both construction and other sectors. This crisis had severe effects on the economy and employment in Landskrona, where most of the jobs in textile production and ship manufacturing disappeared. By the end of the period, the deindustrialization of the city was more or less complete, and the share of its industrial workers was in continuous decline.

Economic difficulties and new dominant political ideologies (neo-liberalism) meant that this period also saw the culmination of the expansion of the public sector and the welfare state. Nationally, the Social Democrats lost power to a center-right coalition in 1976, but there were frequent changes in government until the Social Democrats regained power in 1982 and ruled thereafter until 1991, when a new center-right coalition government was formed which lasted until 1994. Economic policy took a new direction, with a less Keynesian orientation and the deregulation of financial markets and tax cuts. During the financial crisis of the early 1990s, the fixed currency regime was abandoned for a free-floating exchange rate, which in effect led to a further devaluation of the krona. Large-scale government support to industry was terminated in the second half of the 1980s, forcing a restructuring of the economy. In 1995, Sweden joined the European Union, which led to a further convergence of Swedish economic development and economic policy with that in the rest of Europe, as well as to new conditions for the movement of goods, capital, and labor (Schön 2010).

Married women's labor force participation continued to increase, and important family policy reforms were enacted to facilitate the combination of family life and work for both men and women. These reforms concerned both the expansion of parental leave and more affordable and universally available preschool childcare (Stanfors 2003, 2007). Together with the other Nordic countries, Sweden was a forerunner in this development, as well as in changes in family demography that have been labeled "the Second Demographic Transition" (Lesthaeghe 1983, 2010; van de Kaa 1987). This transformation had its roots in the preceding period, and it gained speed and prominence in the 1970s and 1980s (Stanfors and Goldscheider 2017).

1995–2015

The crisis of the early 1990s was followed by a new period of economic growth in the industrial world. This development was linked to the increasing importance of services, the increasing demand for higher education, and also to the expansion of lower-grade occupations in services. Technological change involving electronics—especially the computer and the internet—was important in this period, and continued globalization brought with it a more pronounced division of labor between different parts of the world and an increase in trade flows (Crafts and Toniolo 2010; Gordon 2016; Schön 2010).

Landskrona saw some improvement in the early 2000s in terms of labor market and population development. This was especially visible in the transportation and welfare sectors at a time when industrial activity and employment continued to decline. However, the service sector did not expand as much as in several other former industrial cities, thus leaving Landskrona with higher unemployment, a lower education level among its workforce, and lower productivity than in the rest of Sweden. Migration to the city increased and so did the population, but the problems of segregation and low income, especially among the city's foreign-born inhabitants, remained throughout the period (see Chapter 2).

This period also saw the beginning of the second phase of the gender revolution, in the form of a government subsidy for childcare for families and increasing male involvement in the private sphere. There was an almost full transition to a two-earner model, even though there were still more women with small children in part-time work than there were men (Stanfors and Goldscheider 2017).

After twelve years of Social Democratic government at the national level, a center-right coalition government came to power in 2006 and remained in office until 2014. The same happened in Landskrona, which has been governed by a Liberal-led coalition since 2006. While there has been expansion in some parts of the welfare sector, such as programs related to family and gender equality, there have been cutbacks in other areas such as pensions and levels of compensation in various social security programs.

Area, Data, and Methods

The empirical analyses presented in this volume are based on data for an area in western Scania in southern Sweden, consisting of the port town of Landskrona and five rural or semi-urban parishes: Hög, Kävlinge, Halmstad, Sireköpinge, and Kågeröd (see Map 1.1.). The localities are in relative proximity to each other and still show considerable variations in historical landownership, production structure, and geographical conditions.

This study design offers the advantage of examining economic-demographic interactions while minimizing the introduction of confounding factors related to regional or cultural differences. While the population of the study area is not statistically representative of Sweden or Europe as a whole, it is not atypical either, and it shows long-term patterns of economic and demographic development similar to those in other contexts (see, e.g., Bengtsson and Dribe 2021 for a review of previous research on the same area in the context of the more general historical development).

Taken together, the five parishes had a population of about 6,000 at the beginning of the twentieth century, 5,000 mid-century, and 9,000 at the end of the century (Dribe and Quaranta 2020). Over the entire twentieth century, the population declined in the four largely rural parishes while it increased in the semi-urban area of Kävlinge and in Landskrona. In 1900, Kävlinge made up 30 percent of the population of the five parishes, and, in 1990, this was 66 percent. The population of Landskrona increased from 14,000 in 1900 to 45,000 in 2015, but part

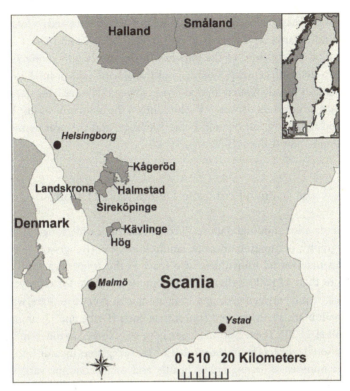

Map 1.1 The study area in western Scania, southern Sweden.
Source: Map by Finn Hedefalk, Lund University. This material is not covered by the terms of the Creative Commons license of this publication. For permission to, reuse please contact the rights holder

of that expansion was related to the inclusion of surrounding parishes into the municipality (see Chapter 2).

The main focus of this volume is on the city of Landskrona and a comparison between the city dwellers and those living in Landskrona's rural hinterland. Chapter 2 provides a detailed description of its social, economic, demographic, and political development over the twentieth century and compares this development with that of other cities in Sweden.

The five parishes, located 20–30 kilometers east/southeast of Landskrona, were originally all rural with different geographical conditions and ownership structures. Halmstad, Sireköpinge, and Kågeröd are neighboring parishes located in the transition area between the agricultural plains and more forested areas. They were dominated historically by land owned by the nobility and farmed by noble tenants or agricultural laborers working for the estates. Hög and Kävlinge are neighboring parishes about 20 kilometers south of the other three parishes. They are located on the plains and were dominated by freeholding peasants and tenants on Crown land (see Bengtsson 2004 and Dribe 2000 for more detailed descriptions of the parishes in the nineteenth century). At the end of the nineteenth century, Kävlinge was transformed into a small town with small industries mostly related to food processing and textiles. This transformation was to a large extent driven by the building of the main railway line between Malmö and Göteborg, one station being Kävlinge, and this was connected to other regional railway lines (Hellborg 2017).

The Scanian Economic-Demographic Database

The SEDD is a longitudinal data resource including a wide range of variables on demography, occupation, income, landholding, etc. (Bengtsson et al. 2021). It contains data for all individuals who lived in the study area from 1905 to 1967: more than 175,000 individuals. Income is available for each year from 1946 onward, and between 1905 and 1945 for at least every five years, while data on occupation are available on a continuous basis (Dribe and Quaranta 2020, Helgertz et al. 2020). These historical data have been linked to different contemporary national registers from 1968 to 2015.[4] These registers include information on a large number of demographic, health, and socioeconomic variables. The links made were based on unique personal identification numbers which were introduced in 1947 and are available for all individuals present in the historical registers after this date. Individuals originating in the study area and for whom we have their unique personal identification number, as well as their children and grandchildren, were followed in the national registers regardless of place of residence in Sweden. The linked data make it possible to study socioeconomic and demographic outcomes from a full life-course perspective at the individual level between 1905 and 2015. This is a unique feature of the data and hence of the research presented in this volume.

An additional significant contribution is that the longitudinal micro-data have been geocoded at the address level, providing the residential histories of the full population (Hedefalk and Dribe 2020). This allows us to take a long-term perspective of the importance of nearby neighbors as well as employing spatial perspectives and analyses related to economic-demographic change and to life in a city undergoing transformation.

The core data come from the continuous population registers, which have their origin in the nineteenth-century catechetical examination registers (see Dribe 2000, Dribe and Quaranta 2020 for a more detailed description of this source material). Individuals are entered in these registers according to place of residence, indicated either by a housing unit, farm or similar, or with an explicit address. Nuclear families are grouped together with husband, wife, sons, and daughters declared in the source. Usually, the individuals from different nuclear families living together in one household can also be identified (e.g., servants and lodgers). For all individuals in the registers, there is information on name, date of birth, place of birth, occupation, time of in-migration (including moves within the parish), place of previous residence, date of marriage, date of death, date of out-migration, place of out-migration, and father's occupation at birth of the individual. Data from the population registers have been cross-checked with data from vital event registers (births, deaths, and marriages).

Information on different sources of income as well as occupation has been retrieved from income and taxation registers. For the period 1905–1946, income for husbands and wives is usually merged, meaning that only family income can be calculated. From 1947 onward, income is reported separately for husbands and wives even though there was joint taxation of spouses until 1971 (see Helgertz et al. 2020). The incomes reported in the registers are based on individual tax returns (see Chapter 3 for a more detailed description of the income data).

Occupation and Social Class

Several chapters of this volume use social class to measure socioeconomic status. These social classes consist of people with similar opportunities in life in terms of economic well-being and social status. We measured social class based on occupation as noted in the sources. Occupations are registered in the vital events registers (births, deaths, and marriages), the population registers, the poll-tax registers, and the income and taxation registers. Information from all these records was used to create a time-varying indicator of social class.

For the period before 1968, information about occupation is available on a regular (and often annual) basis in different sources, meaning that an individual could have more than one occupation registered for the same year, in which case the occupation with the highest status was chosen. For the period after 1967, occupational information is available in the censuses of 1970, 1975, 1980, 1985, and 1990. We interpolated occupational status for the years between censuses.[5] From 2001 onward, occupation has been recorded annually in the occupation registers based on information from employers, which means that the unemployed and the self-employed who had no employees are not included.

Occupational notations have been coded in an internationally comparable coding scheme for historical occupations using the Historical International Standard Classification of Occupations (HISCO; Van Leeuwen et al. 2002). HISCO is an adaptation of the 1968 version of ISCO, developed by the

International Labor Organization (ILO). The coding system distinguishes 1,675 different occupational categories and categorizes these using a five-digit hierarchical code, describing sector and more specific tasks. HISCO has been applied to occupational titles from different sources in a large number of countries, spanning the period from the late sixteenth to the twentieth century (Van Leeuwen 2020). In addition to the occupational codes, there are two variables defined on the basis of the occupational titles to reflect status (e.g., noble titles) and relation (e.g., wife, retired).[6]

While occupational notations in SEDD (before 1968) were coded directly into HISCO, data from 1968 onward in the censuses and occupational registers from Statistics Sweden (SCB) were available in two different occupational schemes, the NYK[7] and SSYK.[8] These codes were transcoded using different crosswalks, being converted first into ISCO-88, then into ISCO-68, and finally into HISCO (see Dribe and Helgertz 2016).

These standardized occupations in HISCO have subsequently been coded into the Historical International Social Class Scheme (HISCLASS), a 12-category occupational classification scheme based on skill level, degree of supervision, whether manual or nonmanual, and whether urban or rural (Van Leeuwen and Maas 2011). In our analyses, we mostly used a six-class version of the scheme. It includes the following classes:

- Higher white-collar workers (HISCLASS 1–2)
- Lower white-collar workers (HISCLASS 3–5)
- Skilled workers (HISCLASS 6–7)
- Lower-skilled workers (HISCLASS 9–10)
- Unskilled workers (HISCLASS 11–12)
- Farmers (HISCLASS 8)
- NA

The NA category consists of individuals without a registered occupation, a very heterogeneous group that varied substantially over time. Farmers are also a heterogeneous group, including large-scale farmers, the workers employed on their farms, and also small-scale farmers working on other farms. This is why it is problematic to fit farmers into the class scheme at any time, a problem exacerbated by the dataset encompassing such a long period. Furthermore, this group was already tiny by the 1950s, and it is practically absent in Landskrona.

The remaining five classes, which we focus on, broadly reflect a status hierarchy from lowest (unskilled workers) to highest (higher white-collar workers). HISCLASS is frequently used in historical studies of social stratification and is very similar to other commonly used class schemes in the stratification literature (e.g., the Erikson, Goldthorpe, and Portocarero [EGP] scheme (see Erikson and Goldthorpe 1992).

For married women, their own social class is unlikely to be a valid indicator of their actual social position since the share of those in gainful employment outside the family business was very low well into the twentieth century. Consequently, we sometimes used the highest class within the couple to indicate social class, taking what has sometimes been called a "dominance approach" (Erikson 1984).

Social class was measured at both the individual and family levels (occupation of family head, usually the father/husband). In some analyses, we also used information about the social class of husband and wife. In addition, we used information from all different sources in giving priority to current observations and then choosing the highest social class (lowest HISCLASS) to represent the social class for the observation.

Statistical Methods

The SEDD is structured according to the Intermediate Data Structure (IDS), developed by George Alter and Kees Mandemakers for historical longitudinal micro-data (Alter and Mandemakers 2014; see Dribe and Quaranta 2020 for a more detailed description of the data structure of the SEDD). The information in the IDS version of SEDD has been used to construct a number of more specific analytical variables (e.g., occupation of family head and number of children in the family; Quaranta 2015) and to produce an extraction of all events and variables which could be transformed into an episode file used for statistical analysis (Quaranta 2016). This episode file contains time spans for each individual, during which the values of all variables are constant. It includes start date, end date, individual ID number (a simple running number to protect the identity of the research person when analyzing the data), birth date, and values of all variables in the data reflecting individual, family, and household contexts. Most of the analyses in this book are based on this data file.

The longitudinal nature of the data makes them highly suitable for event-history analysis, where the likelihood of an event is modeled as a function of a set of explanatory variables. There are several statistical models which can be used, but in this book most chapters use either the continuous-time Cox proportional hazards model or the discrete-time logit model, depending on the nature of the analysis.

In Cox regression, the hazard rate of an event for an individual (e.g., death) is modeled as a function of a set of variables, or covariates, assuming a constant multiplicative (proportional) difference over the duration time of the hazard rate between individuals with different values on the covariates.[9] Results are presented as hazard ratios, which are the exponentiated parameter estimates. The hazard ratio expresses the hazard rate of an event in the group under consideration relative to the reference category. For example, a hazard ratio of 1.2 means that the hazard rate of an event for the category is 20 percent higher than that for the reference category.

The data in the discrete-time analyses are annualized to include one observation per individual and year. Hence, instead of comparing risks at exact time points, there is only one observation each year for an individual. Results can be presented as odds ratios, which are defined as the exponentiated parameter estimates. They are similar to the hazard ratios in the Cox regressions but indicate the odds[10] of an event in the group under consideration relative to those in the reference category. An odds ratio of 1.2 means that the odds in the category are 20 percent higher than in the reference category. As well as odds ratios, the estimates can be presented as marginal effects and thus indicate the impact of the variable on the probability of the event, evaluated at the means of the other variables in the model.

Outline of the Volume

This volume is organized into nine substantive chapters, discussing various important aspects of the social, economic, and demographic development of the industrial city over the period 1905–2015.

Chapter 2 provides core insights regarding overall advancements in twentieth-century Sweden and in the study setting of Landskrona. It delves into the question of how generalizable the developments in the city are, and, specifically, it provides a comparative analysis of the economic, demographic, and political development of the city over 100 years compared to ten other cities of a different character in Sweden, and the chapter also provides details regarding the city's economic history.

Chapter 3 analyzes the development of economic inequality and social mobility in the city and makes comparisons with the development in Sweden as a whole, as well as with the more general development of other Western societies in this period.

Chapter 4 focuses on the inflow and outflow of people to and from the city over the course of 100 years, examining migrant heterogeneities as well as the interrelationship between migration, economic growth, and recession, respectively. The chapter also provides descriptive evidence regarding the role of economic conditions as an important factor in internal and international migration.

Chapter 5 examines how residential segregation developed in Landskrona over the twentieth century, with the aim of understanding where certain social classes resided and how residential patterns developed over time and whether the city's present-day segregation emerged during the study period. The analysis in this chapter is based on a detailed geocoding of all individuals living in Landskrona from 1905 to 1967.

Chapter 6 adds a gender frame to the ongoing story of industrialization and family change. It describes trends in family demographic behavior against the backdrop of economic structural change and welfare state expansion, important not least when it comes to gender relations and female independence.

Chapter 7 adopts a long-term perspective in an analysis of the relationship between marital status and health, focusing on differences in adult mortality between never married, currently married, and previously married during a period when marriage patterns underwent substantial changes at the same time as health improved and the welfare state evolved.

Chapter 8 examines the development of maternal and infant health during the twentieth century and how it is interrelated with institutional and medical changes, such as the expansion of hospital facilities, infant care, and the availability of antibiotics.

Chapter 9 provides insights into the socioeconomic health differences across rural and urban areas, adding to recent research on the emergence of the health gradient.

Chapter 10 focuses on the relationship between income, income inequality, and health in the city, with a specific focus on the role of long-term exposure to economic conditions for individual longevity.

Chapter 11 summarizes the findings of the chapters and discusses overall conclusions.

Notes

1. The Kreuger Crash refers to a financial collapse in the early 1930s, which was tied to the fraudulent activities of Swedish industrialist Ivar Kreuger, known as the "Swedish Match King."
2. Compared to other European countries, the Swedish population was remarkably literate right from the early nineteenth century (Sandberg 1979), as a result of regular home visits made by the local priest to test parishioners on their knowledge of the Bible (Lindmark 2011; Paulsson 1946). However, primary education was only formalized in 1842.
3. Public building programs of comparable size were only implemented in the socialist countries in Eastern Europe where there were no private construction companies.

4. The collection of personal data and linkage to the contemporary registers were both made within the project "Economic Demography in a Multigenerational Perspective," approved by the Regional Ethical Review Board in Lund (2010/627) in accordance with the EU's General Data Protection Regulation (GDPR) and the Swedish Law on the Ethical Review of Research on Humans (*Lagen om etikprövning av forskning som avser människor*).
5. For example, the occupational information available in the 1980 census was used for 1978, 1979, 1980, 1981, 1982, and the same applies to the 1985 census, which was used for 1983, 1984, 1985, 1986, 1987.
6. The coding of occupations in SEDD has been harmonized with other historical databases in the Swedish infrastructure project SwedPop (www.swedpop.se).
7. *Näringslivets yrkesklassifikation.*
8. *Standard för svensk yrkesklassificering.*
9. The hazard rate is the instantaneous probability of an event as the time interval approaches zero. It is used in survival analysis to model the probability of events in a continuous time scale.
10. The odds are defined as $p_i/(1 - p_i)$, where p_i is the probability of the event under consideration.

References

Andersson, R., T. Bråmå, and E. Holmqvist. 2010. "Counteracting Segregation: Swedish Policies and Experiences." *Housing Studies* 25 (2): 237–256.

Alter, G., and K. Mandemakers. 2014. "The Intermediate Data Structure (IDS) for Longitudinal Microdata, Version 4." *Historical Life Course Studies* 1 (1): 1–29.

Bairoch, P. 1988. *Cities and Economic Development: From the Dawn of History to the Present.* Chicago: University of Chicago Press.

Baldwin, P. 1990. *The Politics of Social Solidarity: Class Bases of the European Welfare State, 1875–1975.* Cambridge: Cambridge University Press.

Bengtsson, T. 2004. "Mortality and Social Class in Four Scanian Parishes." In *Life Under Pressure: Mortality and Living Standards in Europe and Asia 1700–1900*, edited by T. Bengtsson, C. Campbell, and J. Z. Lee, 37–41. Cambridge, MA: MIT Press.

Bengtsson, T., and M. Dribe. 2021. "The Long Road to Health and Prosperity, Southern Sweden, 1765–2015. Research Contributions From the Scanian Economic-Demographic Database (SEDD)." *Historical Life Course Studies* 11: 74–96.

Bengtsson, T., M. Dribe, L. Quaranta, and P. Svensson. 2021. The Scanian Economic Demographic Database: Version 7.2 (Machine-readable Database). Lund: Lund University, Centre for Economic Demography.

Bevelander, P., and C. Lundh. 2007. "Employment Integration of Refugees: The Influence of Local Factors on Refugee Job Opportunities in Sweden." IZA Discussion Paper no. 2551.

Bhalotra, S., M. Karlsson, and T. Nilsson. 2017. "Infant Health and Longevity: Evidence from a Historical Intervention in Sweden." *Journal of the European Economic Association* 15 (5): 1101–1157.

Bhalotra, S., M. Karlsson, T. Nilsson, and N. Schwarz. 2022. "Infant Health, Cognitive Performance and Earnings: Evidence from Inception of the Welfare State in Sweden." *Review of Economics and Statistics* 104 (6): 1138–1156.

Bound, J., G. Khanna, and N. Morales. 2017. "Understanding the Economic Impact of the H-1B Program on the U.S." NBER Working Paper 2017: 23153.

Boustan, L. P., D. M. Bunten, and O. Hearey. 2018. "Urbanization in the United States, 1800–2000." In *The Oxford Handbook of American Economic History. Vol. 2*, edited by L. P. Cain, P. V. Fishback, and P. W. Rhode, 75–99. Oxford: Oxford University Press.

Broadberry, S., and K. H. O'Rourke. 2010. *The Cambridge Economic History of Modern Europe, Vol. 1 & 2*. Cambridge: Cambridge University Press.

Burchardi, K. B., T. Chaney, and T. A. Hassan. 2019. "Migrants, Ancestors, and Foreign Investments." *Review of Economic Studies* 86 (4): 1448–1486.

Chandler, A. D. 1977. *The Visible Hand: The Managerial Revolution in American Business*. Cambridge, MA: Harvard University Press, Belknap.

Coale, A. J., and S. C. Watkins (eds.). 1986. *The Decline of Fertility in Europe*. Princeton: Princeton University Press.

Cortes, P. 2008. "The Effect of Low-Skilled Immigration on U.S. prices: Evidence from CPI Data." *Journal of Political Economy* 116 (3): 381–422.

Crafts, N. F. R., and G. Toniolo. 2010. "Aggregate Growth, 1950–2005." In *The Cambridge Economic History of Modern Europe, Vol. 2*, edited by S. Broadberry and K. H. O'Rourke, 296–332. Cambridge: Cambridge University Press.

Davis, K. 1945. "The World Demographic Transition." *The Annals of the American Academy of Political and Social Science* 237 (1): 1–11.

Davis, A. 2011. "A Revolution in Maternity Care? Women and the Maternity Services, Oxfordshire c. 1948-1974." *Social History of Medicine* 24: 389–406

Deaton, A. 2013. *The Great Escape. Health, Wealth, and the Origins of Inequality*. Princeton: Princeton University Press.

Demeny, P. 1968. "Early Fertility Decline in Austria-Hungary: A Lesson in Demographic Transition." *Daedalus* 97 (2): 502–522.

Docquier, F., E., Lodigiani, H. Rapoport, and M. Schiff. 2016. "Emigration and Democracy." *Journal of Development Economics* 120 (1): 209–223.

Dribe, M. 2000. *Leaving Home in a Peasant Society. Economic Fluctuations, Household Dynamics and Youth Migration in Southern Sweden, 1829-1866*. Södertälje: Almqvist & Wiksell International.

Dribe, M., and J. Helgertz. 2016. "The Lasting Impact of Grandfathers: Class, Occupational Status, and Earnings over Three Generations in Sweden 1815-2011." *Journal of Economic History* 76 (4): 969–1000.

Dribe, M., and O. Karlsson. 2022. "Inequality in Early Life: Social Class Differences in Childhood Mortality in Southern Sweden, 1815-1967." *Economic History Review* 75 (2): 475–502.

Dribe, M., and L. Quaranta. 2020. "The Scanian Economic-Demographic Database (SEDD)." *Historical Life Course Studies* 9: 158–172.

Easterlin, R. A. 1961. "The American Baby Boom in Historical Perspective." *American Economic Review* 51 (5): 869–911.

Easterlin, R. A. 1999. "How Beneficent Is the Market? A Look at the Modern History of Mortality." *European Review of Economic History* 3 (3): 257–294.

Elmér, Å. 1971. *Svensk socialpolitik* [Swedish Social Policy]. Lund: Gleerups.

Erikson, R. 1984. "Social Class of Men, Women and Families." *Sociology* 18 (4): 500–514.

Erikson, R., and J. H. Goldthorpe. 1992. *The Constant Flux: A Study of Class Mobility in Industrial Societies*. Oxford: Oxford University Press.

Fildes, V., L. Marks, and H. Marland. 2013. *Women and Children First: International Maternal and Infant Welfare, 1870–1945*. London: Routledge.

Fischer, M., U. G. Gerdtham, G. Heckley, M. Karlsson, G. Kjelsson, and T. Nilsson. 2021. "Education and Health: Long-Run Effects of Peers, Tracking and Years." *Economic Policy* 36 (105): 3–49.

Fischer, M., M. Karlsson, T. Nilsson, and N. Schwarz. 2020. "The Long-Term Effects of Long Terms: Compulsory Schooling Reforms in Sweden." *Journal of the European Economic Association* 18 (6): 2776–2823.

Foged, M., and G. Peri. 2016. "Immigrants' Effect on Native Workers: New Analysis on Longitudinal Data." *American Economic Journal: Applied Economics* 8 (2): 1–34.

Fogel, R. W. 2004. *The Escape from Hunger and Premature Death, 1700–2100. Europe, America, and the Third World*. Cambridge: Cambridge University Press.

Galor, O. 2011. *Unified Growth Theory*. Princeton: Princeton University Press.

Gibson, J., R. Halahingano, and S. Stillman. 2018. "The Long-Term Impacts of International Migration: Evidence from a Lottery." *World Bank Economic Review* 32 (1): 127–147.

Goldin, C. 2021. *Career and Family: Women's Century-Long Journey Toward Equity*. Princeton: Princeton University Press.

Goldin, C., and L. F. Katz. 2010. *The Race Between Education and Technology*. Cambridge, MA: Harvard University Press.

Goldscheider, F., E. Bernhardt, and T. Lappegård. 2015. "The Gender Revolution: A Framework for Understanding Changing Family and Demographic Behavior." *Population and Development Review* 41 (2): 207–223.

Gordon, R. J. 2016. *The Rise and Fall of American Growth. The U.S. Standard of Living Since the Civil War*. Princeton: Princeton University Press.

Hatton, T. J., and J. G. Williamson. 1998. *The Age of Mass Migration: Causes and Economic Impact*. Oxford: Oxford University Press.

Hedefalk, F., and M. Dribe. 2020. "The Social Context of Nearest Neighbors Shape Educational Attainment Regardless of Class Origin." *Proceedings of the National Academy of Sciences* 117 (26): 14918–14925.

Helgertz, J., T. Bengtsson, and M. Dribe. 2020. "Income Data in the Scanian Economic-Demographic Database (SEDD)." Lund Papers in Economic Demography 2020: 6. Lund University: Centre for Economic Demography.

Helgertz, J., and M. Önnerfors. 2019. "Public Water and Sewerage Investments and the Urban Mortality Decline in Sweden 1875–1930." *History of the Family* 24 (2): 307–338.

Hellborg, R. 2017. *Kävlinges historia II. Järnvägarna i Kävlinge* [The History of Kävlinge II. The Railroads in Kävlinge]. Kävlinge: Harjagers härads fornminnes- och hembygdsförening.

Hofsten, E., and H. Lundström. 1976. *Swedish Population History: Main Trends from 1750 to 1970*. Stockholm: SCB.

Hunt, J., and M. Gauthier-Loiselle. 2010. "How Much Does Immigration Boost Innovation?" *American Economic Journal: Macroeconomics* 2 (2): 31–56.

Jönsson, Å. 1993. *Historien om en stad. Del 1: Landskrona 1413–1804* [The History of a Town. Part 1: Landskrona 1413–1804]. Landskrona: Landskrona kommun.

Jönsson, Å. 1995. *Historien om en stad. Del 2: Landskrona 1805–1899* [The History of a Town. Part 1: Landskrona 1805–1899]. Landskrona: Landskrona kommun.

Jönsson, Å. 1997. *Historien om en stad. Del 3: Landskrona 1900-1997* [The History of a Town. Part 1: Landskrona 1900-1997]. Landskrona: Landskrona kommun.

Jonung, L. 1981. "The Depression in Sweden and the United States. A Comparison of Causes and Policies." In *The Great Depression Revisited*, edited by K. Brunner, 286-315. Boston, MA: Kluwer-Nijhoff Publishing.

Khanna, G., and N. Morales. 2017. "The IT Boom and Other Unintended Consequences of Chasing the American Dream." *Center for Global Development Working Paper* 2017: 460.

Khanna, G., E. Murathanoglu, C. B. Theoharides, and D. Yang. 2022. "Abundance From Abroad: Migrant Income and Long-Run Economic Development." NBER Working Paper 2022: 29862.

Kunitz, S. J. 2006. *The Health of Populations: General Theories and Particular Realities*. Oxford: Oxford University Press.

Landes, D. S. 1969. *The Unbound Prometheus: Technological Change and Industrial Development in Western Europe from 1750 to the Present*. Cambridge: Cambridge University Press.

Lee, R. 2003. "The Demographic Transition: Three Centuries of Fundamental Change." *Journal of Economic Perspectives* 17 (4): 167-190.

Lesthaeghe, R. 1983. "A Century of Demographic and Cultural Change in Western Europe." *Population and Development Review* 9 (3): 411-435.

Lesthaeghe, R. 2010. "The Unfolding Story of the Second Demographic Transition." *Population and Development Review* 36 (2): 211-251.

Lewin, L. 1989. *Ideologi och strategi. Svensk politik under 100 år* [Ideology and Strategy. Swedish Politics during 100 Years]. Stockholm: Norstedts.

Lindert, P. 2004. *Growing Public: Social Spending and Economic Growth Since the Eighteenth Century*. Cambridge: Cambridge University Press.

Lindmark, D. 2011. "Hemundervisning och läskunnighet [Home Schooling and Literacy]." In *Utbildningshistoria* [History of Education], edited by E. Larsson and J. Westberg, 69-82. Studentlitteratur, Lund.

Lundborg, P. 2013. "Refugees' Employment Integration in Sweden: Cultural Distance and Labor Market Performance." *Review of International Economics* 21 (2): 219-232.

Lundh, C. (ed.) 2009. *Nya perspektiv på Saltsjöbadsavtalet* [New Perspectives on the Saltsjöbad Agreement]. Stockholm: SNS.

Lundh, C., and R. Ohlsson. 1999. *Från arbetskraftsimport till flyktinginvandring* [From Labor Import to Refugee Migration]. Stockholm: SNS.

Magnusson, L. 2007. *An Economic History of Sweden*. London: Routledge.

Molitoris, J., and M. Dribe. 2016. "Industrialization and Inequality Revisited: Mortality Differentials and Vulnerability to Economic Stress in Stockholm, 1878-1926." *European Review of Economic History* 20 (2): 176-197.

Moser, P., A. Voena, and F. Waldinger 2014. "German Jewish Émigres and US Invention." *American Economic Review* 104 (10): 3222-3255.

Notestein, F. W. 1945. "Population: The Long View." In *Food for the World*, edited by T. W. Schultz, 36-57. Chicago: University of Chicago Press.

Oeppen, J., and J. W. Vaupel. 2002. "Broken Limits to Life Expectancy." *Science* 296 (5570): 1029-1031.

Olofsson, J. 2007. *Socialpolitik. Varför, hur och till vilken nytta?* [Social Policy: Why, How, and To What Use?]. Stockholm: SNS Förlag.

Olsson, S-E. 1990. *Social Policy and Welfare State in Sweden*. Lund: Arkiv förlag.

Paulsson, E. 1946. *Om folkskoleväsendets tillstånd och utveckling i Sverige under 1920- och 1930-talen (till omkring år 1938)* [About the State and Development of Primary Schooling in Sweden During the 1920s and 1930s (until 1938)]. Jönköping, Sweden: Länstryckeriaktiebolaget.

Quaranta, L. 2015. "Using the Intermediate Data Structure (IDS) to Construct Files for Statistical Analysis." *Historical Life Course Studies* 2: 86–107.

Quaranta, L. 2016. "STATA Programs for Using the Intermediate Data Structure (IDS) to Construct Files for Statistical Analysis." *Historical Life Course Studies* 3: 1–19.

Runblom, H., and H. Norman (eds.). 1976. *From Sweden to America. A History of the Migration*. Minneapolis: University of Minnesota Press.

Sandberg, L. 1979. "The Case of the Impoverished Sophisticate: Human Capital and Swedish Economic Growth Before World War I." *Journal of Economic History* 39 (1): 225–241.

Schön, L. 2010. *Sweden's Road to Modernity. An Economic History*. Stockholm: SNS.

Sequeira, S., N. Nunn, and N. Qian. 2020. "Immigrants and the Making of America." *Review of Economic Studies* 87 (1): 382–419.

Slunga, N. 2000. *Arbetsstugorna i norra Sverige: ett filantropiskt företag i skolans tjänst* [The Work Houses in Northern Sweden: A Philanthropic Enterprise in the Service of Education]. Uppsala, Sweden: Föreningen för svensk undervisningshistoria.

Stanfors, M. 2003. *Education, Labor Force Participation and Changing Fertility Patterns. A Study of Women and Socioeconomic Change in Twentieth Century Sweden*. Stockholm: Almqvist & Wiksell International.

Stanfors, M. 2007. *Mellan arbete och familj. Ett dilemma för kvinnor i 1900-talets Sverige* [Between Work and Family: A Dilemma for Women in Twentieth-Century Sweden]. Stockholm: SNS.

Stanfors, M., F. N. G. Andersson, and G. Sandström. 2020. "A Century of Divorce: Long-Term Socioeconomic Restructuring and the Divorce Rate in Sweden, 1915–2010." Lund Papers in Economic Demography 2020: 2.

Stanfors, M., and F. Goldscheider. 2017. "The Forest and the Trees: Industrialization, Demographic Change, and the Ongoing Gender Revolution in Sweden and the United States, 1870–2010." *Demographic Research* 36 (6): 173–226.

Taylor, A. M., and J. G. Williamson. 1997. "Convergence in the Age of Mass Migration." *European Review of Economic History* 1 (1): 27–63.

Torregrosa-Hetland, S., and O. Sabaté. 2022. "Income Tax Progressivity and Inflation During the World Wars." *European Review of Economic History* 26 (3): 311–339.

Tuccio, M., J. Wahba, and B. Hamdouch. 2019. "International Migration as a Driver of Political and Social Change: Evidence from Morocco." *Journal of Population Economics* 32 (4): 1171–1203.

Van Bavel, J., and D. S. Reher. 2013. "The Baby Boom and Its Causes: What We Know and What We Need to Know." *Population and Development Review* 39 (2): 257–288.

Van de Kaa, D. J. 1987. "Europe's Second Demographic Transition." *Population Bulletin* 42: 1–59.

Van Leeuwen M. H. D. 2020. "Studying Long-Term Changes in the Economy and Society Using the HISCO Family of Occupational Measures." *Oxford Research Encyclopedias: Economics and Finance*. Oxford: Oxford University Press.

Van Leeuwen, M. H. D., and I. Maas. 2011. *HISCLASS: A Historical International Social Class Scheme*. Leuven: Leuven University Press.

Van Leeuwen, M. H. D., I. Maas, and A. Miles. 2002. *HISCO. Historical International Standard Classification of Occupations*. Leuven: Leuven University Press.

Viazzo, P. P., and C. A. Corsini. 1993. *The Decline of Infant Mortality in Europe, 1800–1950: Four National Case Studies*. Florence: International Child Development Centre.

2
Landskrona
The Industrial City

Martin Dribe and Patrick Svensson

Introduction

Landskrona was founded in 1413, as a mercantile port town with a deep natural harbor (Jönsson 1993). Later in the sixteenth century it also became an important fortified military town, a role it mostly lost after Sweden gained control of the province of Scania (*Skåne*) in 1658. In 1700, the town had barely 500 inhabitants, but this number increased to almost 3,300 in 1800, making Landskrona second only to Malmö in population size among the Scanian towns. As of the mid-nineteenth century factories and financial institutions began appearing (Jönsson 1995). The city was a pioneer in the new sugar (beet) industry. Its development was similar to that of other cities, as exemplified by the emergence of newspapers, schools, a hospital, institutional poor relief and old-age care, a municipal board and governance, and a railway line. The port was used for shipping grain from its hinterland, supporting the region's role as the country's breadbasket. The last quarter of the nineteenth century saw the founding of mechanical factories and a shipyard; the latter would come to play an important role in the city's economy and also for its identity for nearly a century. These developments together transformed Landskrona from a military and agriculturally based town to a modern industrial city. New factories and companies were established, and the number of industrial workers increased considerably.

In 1863, during the formation of the Swedish municipality system, Landskrona became a separate unit consisting of the town itself (*Landskrona stad*). This unit remained unchanged until 1959, when the rural municipality of Sankt Ibb (the island of Ven) was incorporated into it, and expansion continued from 1967 to 1974 by incorporating further parts of the surrounding rural municipalities (*landskommmuner*). In 1971, the City of Landskrona was formally renamed Landskrona Municipality (*Landskrona kommun*), although since 2009 the two terms have been used interchangeably.

During the early twentieth century, the town's transition into an industrial city continued (Jönsson 1997), and investments in infrastructure and services provided an increasingly better quality of life for the inhabitants. In 1900, the municipality acquired the first regular bus service in the country, saw the building of a new county hospital, and became a pioneer in sickness insurance when a number of small insurance associations joined together to form a central association in 1910. Educational support was provided by the founding of the first municipal high school in Sweden. To secure housing for the wave of new industrial workers, large-scale construction plans were laid out by the municipality during the first half of the twentieth century.

As well as undergoing economic transformation, Landskrona took part in the early foundation of the socialist movement, and, in 1894, the local Social Democratic party (*Landskrona arbetarekommun*) was formed. The city was ruled by the Social Democrats for 72 years, from the first democratic election (universal suffrage) in 1919 until 1991, reflecting the strong presence of industry and the clout of the working-class movement. As in much of industrial Sweden, the post-World War II period was a time of expansion and progress that witnessed the establishment of several new factories in Landskrona. The high demand for labor in the local economy made the city an attractive destination for immigrants and also enabled women to enter the labor force.

After the recession of the 1970s following the oil crises, Landskrona experienced widespread deindustrialization. Some factories were rationalized and reduced their workforces while others closed altogether. Industrial closures resulted not only in unemployment but also in out-migration and an oversupply of housing. The earlier influx of labor migrants came to be supplanted by the in-migration of refugees from the Balkan Wars in the early 1990s. The negative economic and social development following deindustrialization has been difficult to stop and has led to persistently high levels of unemployment, fiscal strain, and cuts in public spending as well as social problems which arose around the year 2000. The city has also become increasingly segregated along ethnic lines, with negative sentiments being shown toward immigrants in parts of the population (Wallengren 2014).

In this chapter, we analyze the demographic, economic, social, and political development of Landskrona and compare this with the development of ten other Swedish cities that vary in character. These are Stockholm, Göteborg, and Malmö, the three largest cities; Borås, Gävle, and Norrköping, other Swedish industrial cities larger than Landskrona; and Halmstad (Halland),[1] Sundsvall, Trelleborg, and Uddevalla, which are of a similar size. These cities are spread throughout the country and have different initial industrial profiles. The location of the cities are shown in Map 2.1.

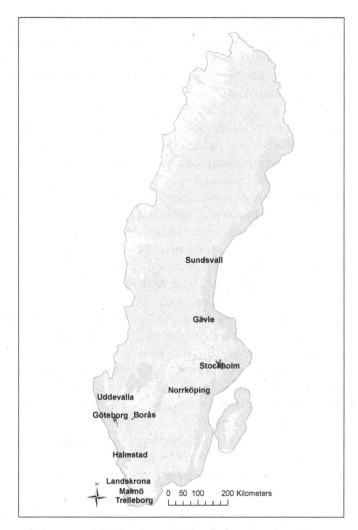

Map 2.1 The location of the eleven cities in Sweden.
Source: Map by Finn Hedefalk, Lund University. This material is not covered by the terms of the Creative Commons license of this publication. For permission to, reuse please contact the rights holder

Population Development

In 1900, Landskrona had a population of about 14,000. It grew rapidly up to about 1920, when it reached the 20,000 mark, followed by a decline during the 1920s and then an increase again between 1930 and 1960, reaching almost 30,000. Administrative changes meant the population jumped to 37,000 in just a few years, after which followed a long period of stagnation and even decline during the 1970s and 1980s in conjunction with a period of major industrial crisis. Not

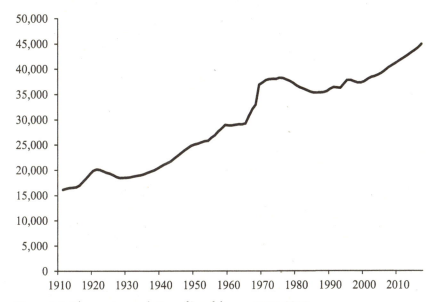

Figure 2.1 The mean population of Landskrona, 1910–2017.
Source: Swedish Official Statistics (SOS) Befolkningsrörelsen 1911–2017. 1911–1961 is the city of Landskrona, from 1962, it is Landskrona municipality.

until the early 2000s did the population start to increase again, reaching 45,000 in 2015 (see Figure 2.1). This development is a good illustration of the rise and fall of Landskrona as an industrial city.

A comparison of the population development to that in other Swedish cities (Figure 2.2) reveals considerable similarities, indicating that Landskrona was not alone in experiencing first an expansion and then a contraction of its population. Most cities saw growth for much of the period up to 1970, after which followed a period of stagnation and, in some cases, considerable decline. Since then, from the late 1990s onward, a new period of urban growth has taken place. There are also some cases that are exceptions. Stockholm, the largest city in Sweden, peaked as early as around 1960 and then saw a sharp decline in its population until the mid-1970s, after which a new period of expansion began. The decline in the 1960s and 1970s was connected to the expansion of the Stockholm metro area, which, to a large extent, took place in the adjacent towns and municipalities that grew at the expense of the city. A similar process of suburbanization took place in Göteborg and Malmö, second and third in terms of population size, but not to the same extent. More urban construction took place within their city limits than was the case in Stockholm.

The population development in Gävle, Sundsvall, and Halmstad also differed somewhat from the general picture. It stagnated in Gävle and Sundsvall in

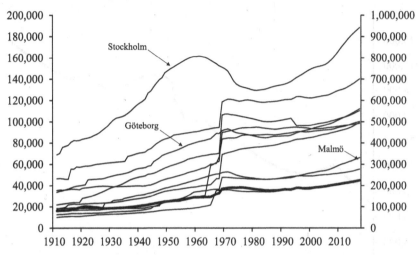

Figure 2.2 The mean population of the eleven cities, 1911–2017. Landskrona is represented by the thick line.
Stockholm, Göteborg, and Malmö are plotted on the right-hand scale. 1911–1961 refers to the towns, from 1962 to the municipality.
Source: Swedish Official Statistics (SOS) Befolkningsrörelsen 1911–2017. 1911–1961 is the city of Landskrona, from 1962, it is Landskrona municipality.

the early twentieth century due to problems facing the main industries and to low fertility and increasing migration south to Stockholm (*Statens offentliga utredningar* [SOU] 1949, 7). The population in these towns showed no substantial growth until after World War II. Gävle and Halmstad experienced little stagnation in the 1970s and 1980s.

Age and Sex Structure of the Population

We now turn to the age structure of the population, which is intimately connected to the development of population growth and its components: mortality, fertility, and migration (to which we return below). A population that is growing at a moderate rate because fertility exceeds mortality (natural growth) will have an age structure resembling a pyramid as more people are added at the base. Very high rates of growth (about 3 percent per year) mean that the age structure will start to resemble a Christmas tree. Conversely, when the population stagnates the age structure will become more rectangular.

Table 2.1 displays the proportion of children (younger than age 15) in the population, starting at 16 percent in 1910, when fertility was still in decline. As a

Table 2.1 Share of the population younger than 15 years (percent) in the eleven cities and Sweden as a whole.

	1910	1930	1945	1950	1960	1970	1980	1990
Borås	16.4	11.5	10.6	14.3	22.1	19.6	15.3	13.8
Gävle	16.0	10.7	9.4	11.0	21.8	20.3	17.5	15.8
Göteborg	14.6	10.8	9.7	10.7	20.9	18.2	15.1	14.8
Halmstad	15.7	10.7	10.4	11.4	21.5	19.1	16.5	14.6
Landskrona	**15.6**	**11.3**	**10.3**	**11.5**	**20.9**	**18.5**	**15.5**	**14.6**
Malmö	15.1	10.0	9.9	11.0	20.8	18.3	13.6	13.9
Norrköping	13.7	10.4	10.0	11.1	20.6	19.1	16.6	15.6
Stockholm	10.8	7.6	8.6	10.1	19.0	14.5	12.5	14.4
Sundsvall	13.6	10.5	9.9	11.1	21.1	21.3	16.8	14.6
Trelleborg	NA	12.5	10.4	11.4	21.2	21.6	17.6	16.3
Uddevalla	16.6	11.1	10.1	11.3	24.5	22.1	15.9	14.8
Sweden	31.7	24.8	21.6	23.4	23.7	22.0	20.6	19.1

Source: SOS Folkräkningen 1910–1960 and Folk och Bostadsräkningen 1970, 1980, 1990.

comparison, the proportion younger than 15 in Sweden as a whole was 32 percent in 1910. The lower share of children in Landskrona and other cities is explained by the high proportion of young adults and lower fertility, at least partly because rural areas lagged in the fertility decline (Dribe 2009). Over time, the proportion of children further declined to 10 percent in 1945 and then increased rapidly to 21 percent in 1960, before returning to levels around 15 percent in the 1980s. In relation to other cities, Landskrona was at neither extreme but positioned in the middle. Compared to Sweden as a whole, the cities continued to have lower shares of young people, but the differences were smaller than in the beginning of the century.

If we now look at the proportion of those older than 65 in Table 2.2, this increased dramatically over the twentieth century, reflecting the general aging process of the Swedish population. Starting at 3 percent in 1910, it increased to 24 percent in the 1990s. From being a rarity in 1910, those older than 65 constituted a quarter of the population in 1990. Initially this was due to falling fertility, but, from the mid-twentieth century onward, decreasing mortality among the elderly was the main factor, and the same development took place in other cities with some variation in magnitude. Also, when we look at Sweden as a

Table 2.2 Share of the population 65 and older (percent) in the eleven cities and Sweden as a whole.

	1910	1930	1945	1950	1960	1970	1980	1990
Borås	2.4	3.1	3.5	4.6	8.8	12.5	19.9	22.6
Gävle	2.9	4.0	4.8	4.6	10.3	12.9	16.0	18.2
Göteborg	2.8	3.4	3.8	4.2	10.8	13.5	18.2	19.7
Halmstad	3.1	4.1	4.4	4.4	10.8	14.0	18.5	21.4
Landskrona	3.0	4.2	4.3	4.5	11.3	14.5	20.9	24.0
Malmö	2.2	3.3	4.2	4.6	10.8	13.0	20.1	22.7
Norrköping	3.7	4.3	4.8	4.9	11.9	14.9	19.6	21.5
Stockholm	2.9	3.6	4.1	4.6	11.9	16.1	21.5	21.3
Sundsvall	2.8	3.9	3.6	4.0	10.3	11.2	15.2	18.4
Trelleborg	NA	3.5	4.4	4.5	9.8	11.7	17.4	20.4
Uddevalla	3.8	4.5	4.4	4.1	7.8	10.8	17.7	21.6
Sweden	8.4	9.2	9.9	10.2	12.0	13.9	16.6	17.9

Source: SOS Folkräkningen 1910–1960 and Folk och Bostadsräkningen 1970, 1980, 1990.

whole, the share of those older than 65 increased sharply from 8 percent in 1910 to 18 percent in 1990.

Table 2.3 shows the sex ratios in the different cities (men vs. women, all ages). As well as Trelleborg and, in certain years, Uddevalla and Gävle, Landskrona had a fairly high sex ratio even though it was lower than for the country as a whole (96 percent in 1910 and 98 percent in 1990).

Migration

Net in-migration rates to Landskrona in 1910–2016 (in-migrants minus out-migrants divided by the mean population) contain two periods when there was a distinctly positive migration balance: 1930–1950 and the 2000s (see Appendix, Table A2.4). These were also periods of considerable population growth, while the 1960s and 1970s saw population stagnation, if we discount the artificial increase due to boundary changes (see Figure 2.1). In Figure 2.3, net in-migration to Landskrona is compared to that for the other cities. The expansion periods 1930–1950 and the 2000s can be seen in most cases but to a varying extent. In

Table 2.3 Sex ratios (M/F) in the eleven cities and Sweden as a whole.

	1910	1930	1945	1950	1960	1970	1980	1990
Borås	80.9	83.4	88.1	89.6	88.2	89.1	88.5	87.9
Gävle	90.3	88.3	89.4	87.5	93.6	96.1	94.3	94.0
Göteborg	86.4	88.9	91.7	93.5	95.1	97.4	94.0	93.6
Halmstad	91.6	88.0	91.8	92.3	92.9	92.8	91.6	91.4
Landskrona	**92.4**	**89.5**	**95.1**	**94.7**	**99.8**	**99.5**	**94.4**	**93.3**
Malmö	87.0	84.8	88.3	89.8	92.9	93.9	90.4	89.5
Norrköping	80.9	84.3	89.7	91.4	92.4	94.0	91.1	91.5
Stockholm	81.8	80.4	83.0	85.9	87.9	88.1	87.0	88.1
Sundsvall	86.0	83.5	88.7	89.2	91.7	97.8	94.8	94.0
Trelleborg	NA	96.9	99.3	99.3	99.9	102.2	96.7	95.2
Uddevalla	82.9	82.9	91.3	95.2	98.6	95.8	94.5	92.7
Sweden	95.6	96.8	99.0	99.2	99.5	99.8	98.2	97.6

Source: SOS Folkräkningen 1910–1960 and Folk och Bostadsräkningen 1970, 1980, 1990.

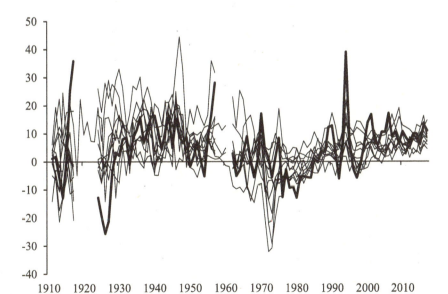

Figure 2.3 Net in-migration (per 1,000 population) to the eleven cities, 1911–2017. Landskrona is represented by the thick line.

Source: Swedish Official Statistics (SOS) Befolkningsrörelsen 1911–2017. 1911–1961 is the city of Landskrona, from 1962, it is Landskrona municipality.

Table 2.4 Distribution of foreign-born in Landskrona (percent).
A. 1946–1965

Country of origin	1946	1950	1955	1960	1965
Denmark	33.0	33.6	32.8	36.4	28.4
Estonia	15.6	6.8	4.1	3.1	2.6
Finland	4.0	3.8	5.2	9.7	20.6
Italy	0.5	0.4	0.2	3.0	2.0
Yugoslavia	0.2	0.0	0.1	1.0	6.7
Norway	7.2	5.9	6.0	4.6	3.4
Poland	8.6	15.6	6.5	2.7	3.0
Czechoslovakia	1.1	4.9	4.0	3.4	2.8
Germany	16.8	16.1	31.6	21.7	18.5
Hungary	0.2	0.9	0.1	5.3	3.9
Austria	0.9	1.1	1.5	2.5	1.9
Other	12.0	10.8	8.0	6.6	6.1
Total	100	100	100	100	100
N	649	1,301	1,378	1,752	2,209

B. 1970–2015 (country groups)

Country of origin	1970	1975	1980	1985	1990	1995	2000	2005	2010	2015
Africa	0.3	0.5	0.5	0.5	0.8	2.2	2.1	2.4	3.0	3.1
Asia	0.7	1.0	3.1	5.4	11.4	11.8	12.1	15.5	20.8	27.7
EU28 excl. Nordic countries	30.4	29.0	29.5	30.7	29.6	19.4	17.7	16.4	19.6	18.3
Europe excl. EU28 and Nordic	16.5	16.9	18.9	17.9	16.4	38.2	45.7	44.0	38.8	35.7
North America	1.1	0.9	1.2	1.2	1.1	0.9	0.7	0.7	0.8	0.8
Nordic	50.3	50.7	45.3	42.6	38.7	25.9	20.2	19.6	15.4	13.0
Oceania	0.1	0.2	0.1	0.0	0.1	0.1	0.1	0.1	0.1	0.1
USSR	0.5	0.5	0.6	0.5	0.5	0.4	0.4	0.2	0.2	0.2
South America	0.1	0.2	0.9	1.1	1.4	1.1	1.0	1.0	1.2	1.1
Total	100	100	100	100	100	100	100	100	100	100
N	3,386	4,197	3,846	3,613	4,281	6,540	6,958	8,250	10,082	11,412

Note: Panel A is based on data from population registers, panel B on data on country of birth (grouped) from Statistics Sweden.
Source: The Scanian Economic-Demographic Database (Bengtsson et al. 2018).

the first of these, Landskrona's position comes in the middle, but, during both the 1995 peak (connected to the flow of refugees from former Yugoslavia) and the 2000s, it experienced comparatively high rates of in-migration. It is also clear that the stagnation period in the 1960s and 1970s affected Landskrona more than the other cities, showing the highest net out-migration at this time. Immigration (in-migration of foreign-born) to Landskrona began in earnest after World War II, although a number of Jewish refugees came during the war as well. During 1945, about 2,800 refugees mainly from Poland, Czechoslovakia, Hungary, and Romania came with "the white buses" (a relief effort organized by the Red Cross under Count Folke Bernadotte (see, e.g., Jönsson 1997). Over the coming years, a large number of refugees entered Sweden in Landskrona, to be moved on to other places at a later date. In total, 20,000 refugees were housed at the old fortress between 1945 and 1949.

Table 2.4 panel A shows the distribution of the foreign-born population in 1946–1965 in Landskrona. In the 1940s and early 1950s, immigrants from Denmark predominated together with refugees from Germany, Poland, and Estonia. The crisis in Hungary in 1956 created the next major flow of immigrants, as this was a time of high demand for labor. After the instruction in 1954 allowing free movement of persons in the Nordic countries, immigration from Denmark and Finland increased, and, as of the mid-1960s, the flow of labor migrants from southern Europe (especially Yugoslavia) and also Finland increased.

Panel B shows the distribution of foreign-born by country groups between 1970 and 2015. In 1970, those from the Nordic countries predominated in the foreign-born population, but their numbers have fallen dramatically since then. Instead, the proportion of immigrants from other parts of Europe has increased, as has the share coming from outside Europe, especially from Asia but also from Africa. In the mid-1970s, Syrians from Turkey and Lebanon came as refugees. The oversupply of housing at the time made it attractive for the municipality to welcome immigrants to fill the empty apartments. Then, in the early 1990s, the Balkan Wars produced a great influx of refugees, especially from Bosnia and Kosovo. During 1994 and 1995, 2,000 refugees arrived in the city. In 1996, the municipality had 4,300 foreign citizens, about 2,000 of whom were from former Yugoslavia, 800 from Denmark, and 200 from Finland. In addition, there were also foreign-born who had become naturalized and obtained Swedish citizenship (Jönsson 1997).

Industrial Development

A first characteristic of an industrial city is that a substantial share of the working population works in manufacturing. Looking at our sample of eleven cities, it is

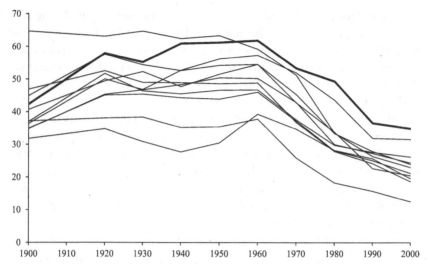

Figure 2.4 Share of workers in industry of all workers, 1900–2000, in the eleven cities (percent). Landskrona is represented by the thick line.
1910 is interpolated using the mean of 1900 and 1920.
Sources: SOS Folkräkningen 1910–1960 and Folk och Bostadsräkningen 1970, 1980, 1990. For 2000: Registerbaserad arbetsmarknadsstatistik (RAMS).

clear that most of them show an increasing share of industrial workers during the early twentieth century (except Borås, which already had a very high share by 1900; see Figure 2.4). The highest shares appeared during the golden age of Swedish industry in the 1950s and 1960s, and the general trend shows that these increased until the 1960s and then decreased. Landskrona fits the overall pattern but is at the high end of the distribution peak in 1960, by which time it had the highest shares of those cities where more than 60 percent of the workforce were in industry. Even after undergoing deindustrialization, as all the cities did, Landskrona still had a higher share employed in manufacturing in 2000 than did the others.

Employment in Landskrona was thus dominated by industry all through the twentieth century. Even so, in an industrial city, people also worked in other professions, although many of them were of course related to the industrial sector. In the early 1900s, the transport sector was the second largest, together with services (BiSOS A: Befolkningsstatistik 1900). Transports encompassed the railways but above all the port and the shipping of both goods and passengers. In the 1930s, Landskrona had the eighth largest port in Sweden (Jönsson 1997, 49). Industrial products and food were shipped, and passenger ferries to Denmark, Germany, and Norway went on a regular basis. However, due to competition with surrounding larger cities, the transport sector never succeeded in developing into the leading Scanian hub, although short periods of success existed. Instead, over time the commercial sector and retail and public services grew faster than transports. In the final decade of the twentieth century, the public sector alone accounted for more than a third of all employment. Still the industrial sector was the largest also by that time (Folk och bostadsräkningen 1990).

Sweden's early industrialization was characterized by a relatively high degree of rural industry. A large real wage gap between urban and rural areas was potentially an important factor behind this (Lundh 2012). Even so, at the same time as the wage gap increased there was an increasing tendency for manufacturing to be located in urban areas. This trend speaks in favor of other factors being more important. The location of industry during late nineteenth-century industrialization depended on a number of factors such as human capital, natural resources, and geographies of trade and communication. Furthermore, some branches of industry grew rapidly at the beginning of the second half of the nineteenth century and constituted an important part of overall industrial production—these branches were directed toward the domestic market and particularly those within food production and processing (Schön 2010, 143).

This implies that, in general, Swedish industrial production relied on both the traditional industries of the Industrial Revolution, textiles and iron workshops, and on industries producing foodstuffs and other items directed toward the growing internal demand that came from the middle class and, as of the 1860s, the working class as well. It also suggests that the nature of early industrialization could differ between towns and cities depending on location, communications, and proximity to natural resources.

In 1910, our eleven cities do indeed show a variety of ways in which industries predominated. However, as industrialization matured and transportation and communications improved, access to resources and markets became more uniform, which also reduced the differences between the cities in terms of their industrial structure. By 1990, Borås, with its textiles, and Trelleborg, with its rubber industry, formed outliers in a general structure where the metal/machine and paper/pulp industries were predominant (see Figure 2.5).

So how well did Landskrona fit into this picture? Since Landskrona was a port town with a natural harbor surrounded by some of the best soils in Sweden, we would expect it to be based on its geographical advantages, with its food and metal industries directed toward agriculture and with shipping forming its base, and indeed it was.

In 1850, there were thirteen recorded factories in Landskrona. According to the factory statistics, the largest workplace was a textile factory with 105 employees, which depended on a workforce consisting of inmates serving life sentences at the local prison. The second largest workplace was the sugar factory, which based its production on locally produced sugar beet. It employed only

38 URBAN LIVES

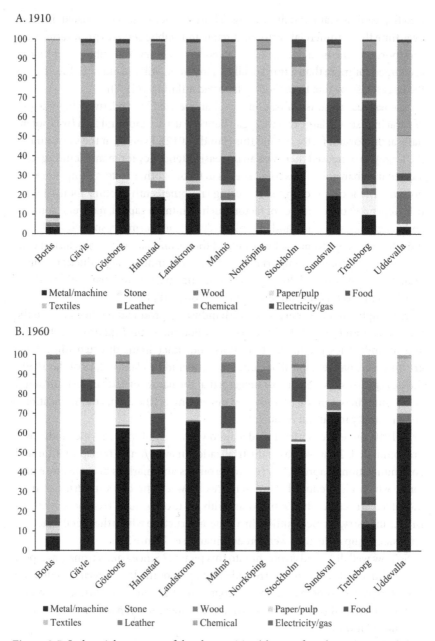

Figure 2.5 Industrial structure of the eleven cities (shares of workers per sector).
Sources: For 1910 and 1960, SOS Industri; for 1990, Folk- och Bostadsräkningen, part 5, table 22.

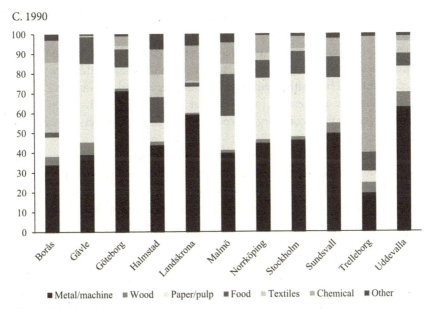

Figure 2.5 Continued

twenty-six workers but had a much higher production value than the textile factory. The remaining factories had fewer than ten employees each and consisted of a shipyard, a rope-maker, a number of tanning factories, and a dyeing factory, all with a connection to the natural harbor and the supply of inputs; in addition, there was a factory that made musical (brass) instruments and a clock-making "factory" with two employees. That industrialization was in its early phase is shown by the fact that the number of people engaged in work at artisan shops was substantially larger than those engaged in the factories.

Twenty years later, a new element seen in the industrialization of Landskrona was the foundries and mechanical workshops. These workshops melted pig iron and metal scrap to produce iron suited for different specialized purposes. Thus, these can be seen as alternatives to the massive iron foundries located in central Sweden, and these city foundries were often directly linked to a mechanical workshop (Schön 2010, 88). The foundries and workshops in Landskrona produced ovens, agricultural tools, and machines.

In 1890, the industrial structure of Landskrona relied on the sugar refinery, the mechanical workshops, and a brush factory. Together these employed around

75 percent of the town's industrial workers. In addition to these four factories, there were eighteen others recorded for this year, including a coke factory, five chemical-technical factories (producing fertilizers, mineral water, soda, and sulfuric acid), a shipyard, a brick factory, two breweries, a cloth factory, a tobacco plant, and two leather tanneries. The number of workers was small within these industries, and, except for the leather tanneries—an industry in which Landskrona was the second largest producer in Sweden—production was rather limited in Swedish terms.

Thus, from 1850 to 1890, the number of factories had grown from thirteen to twenty-two and the number of workers from 145 to more than 900. This period constitutes the early industrialization phase of Landskrona. From then on, the town turned into an industrial city. This is shown not only by the domination of industry in providing an occupation for the inhabitants but also by the way this domination is reflected in the town structure.

The new series published by Statistics Sweden and starting with the year 1911 provides the grouping of industries by goods produced. In Landskrona, the chief industries in this year were food (e.g., sugar) and tobacco followed by textiles, the mechanical industry, the leather tanneries, and the chemical industry. The number of factories had almost tripled to fifty-seven since 1890, the number of workers had more than doubled, and, apart from the establishment of a new large textile factory with 233 workers and a large number of recently started small industries, the industrial structure rested on the same businesses that formed the core of the town's early industrialization. The sugar refinery was still the largest with 385 workers, followed by three mechanical workshops (in all, 365 workers), two brush factories (100), two tobacco plants (97), and five foundries (94 workers). Artisan shops still existed but their share of the workers was only around 19 percent.

Over time, the metal/machine sector increased and became predominant as early as in the 1940s and onward. Other sectors that increased their share of the industrial workforce in Landskrona were the paper/pulp and chemical industries, and these replaced food and textiles as the main employers of industrial workers.

Overall, major changes took place in the period around 1920 and in the 1970s and 1980s. The first period saw the establishment of the shipyard and its closure in 1922, while the second saw a major industrial crisis whereby the textile factory, shipyard, and largest mechanical workshop all closed down within a period of fifteen years. Moreover, the decline of the share of workers in the food industry was partly related to the sugar mill closing down in 1960. In the next section, we look at this development in more detail.

Landskrona's Main Industrial Employers

In 1900, Landskrona was the twelfth largest industrial town in Sweden in terms of the absolute number of industrial workers. Over time it fell to thirteenth place in 1920, fifteenth in 1930, seventeenth in 1950, and twenty-first in 1960. Looking at the census years, the number of workers in industry increased continuously from 1910 to 1980, except for in 1930. Thereafter the absolute number declined. The relative and absolute development of industry was connected to certain large companies and their expansion and demise.

The Shipyard Industry

The shipyard industry shaped much of Landskrona's industrial development, particularly from the 1910s right up to the early 1980s. However, since Landskrona was an important port, the shipyard industry had a prehistory before the 1910s. As early as 1850, the factory registers note the existence of a shipyard with nine people engaged in the business. It was clearly stated that the work of the shipyard (Landskrona Warfsaktiebolag) was to repair ships rather than build them, and the total cost that year amounted to 1,000 *riksdaler banko*, indicating a very small business.[2]

The real breakthrough for the shipyard industry came in 1915, with the foundation of the shipyard Öresundsvarvet. Its establishment meant there was an imminent need of labor and housing for the workers and their families (Varvshistoriska föreningen i Landskrona). That same year, the shipyard estimated that an influx to the city of 1,000–2,000 workers was needed for the shipyard to fulfill its production goals. In both 1920 and 1921, there were repeated concerns over the scarcity of labor, particularly skilled labor. The immigration of German workers covered some of the needs to a degree, but far from all of them. In 1920, the shipyard was the largest in the Nordic countries, and the total workforce amounted to more than 1,100 workers.

The establishment of Öresundsvarvet in Landskrona in the 1910s was part of a general trend in shipyard expansion in Sweden which also encompassed shipyards in cities such as Göteborg and Malmö (Schön 2010, 269). In contrast to the development of the shipyards in these two cities, which had several new orders coming in during the late 1910s, Öresundsvarvet was severely hit by the economic crisis of the early 1920s. This crisis had already started in 1920 and was at its most severe in 1921, when gross domestic product (GDP) fell 5 percent in Sweden and production volumes in industry around 15 percent. The crisis was international in scale and the result of new capacity being built after the war at a time of falling demand (Schön 2010, 246–248). With large outstanding debts incurred by investment in the new shipyard and with no new orders for ships, Öresundsvarvet had started cutting the number of workers as well as their wages during 1921. In early 1922, after the construction and delivery of a large steamer had been completed, the lack of new orders meant all the staff and workers had to be laid off, which necessitated a reconstruction of the company. A month later it went bankrupt.

The bankruptcy of the shipyard was a major setback for the city of Landskrona in terms of its industrial development and also its substantial investment in the shipyard area and the general measures taken to invest in the town's infrastructure. Furthermore, laying off a large part of the industrial working class had far-reaching effects on the city as a whole in terms of supplying food, clothing, and housing for them and their families.

Already in 1923, a new shipyard was established, Nya Varvsaktiebolaget Öresund, but this was significantly smaller than the previous one, employing less than a third of the workforce in 1925 as compared to the number employed in 1920. It was renamed Öresundsvarvet in 1935, and from then on it expanded, bringing the workforce back to the 1920 level in the early 1950s.

In 1940, Götaverken, a shipyard in Göteborg, took over the ownership of Öresundsvarvet. The 1950s saw a new period of expansion including extending the area for the plant, building new production facilities, and establishing a three-year workshop school for training skilled workers for the shipyard. Swedish shipyards saw their highest level of production in 1967, and, in 1975, Öresundsvarvet employed around 3,500 workers.

Increased international competition during the 1970s led to fewer orders, and this together with large interest payments put the Swedish shipyards in a precarious position. The Swedish state took over control of Götaverken and thereby Öresundsvarvet as well in 1976. It came up with a number of propositions to solve the shipyard crisis: cuts in the number of employees, state loans for production costs, and eventually the closing down of at least one of the major shipyards.

In the late 1970s, the number of workers at Öresundsvarvet was reduced, and, in 1980, the state-owned company Svenska varv decided to close down the shipyard. Large-scale protests against the decision took place in Landskrona, with the local factory management on the same side as the workers. Even though a majority in the Swedish Parliament voted against the closure, Svenska varv stood firm and the shipyard eventually closed its doors in 1983 (see Sources, Öresundsvarvet).

After this, attempts were made to use the premises for similar business purposes. Small firms whose main business was repairing ships were located there, including Cityvarvet AB with around 200 workers and Bruces shipyard with approximately the same number.

The Sugar Industry

In 1850, the sugar industry boasted the second largest factory in Landskrona, employing twenty-six laborers and based on the production of sugar beet in the surrounding rural areas. Twenty years later, the old sugar factory had been replaced by a new one and had more than thirteen times as many employees as in 1850. The production process used eight steam engines, and a large part of the workforce—205 out of 341 employees—were seasonal laborers employed during the 4 months of autumn and early winter when the cropping of the sugar beet took place.

The combined sugar factory and refinery in Landskrona was destroyed by a fire in 1875, and the refinery was rebuilt close to where the old factory had been located and where it started up again with 164 workers as soon as 1877. The sugar refinery was one of a total of seven in Sweden. In 1883, a new sugar factory was built at Säbyholm, outside the town, where the company had already established its sugar beet farm by 1853. Thus, from then on there was a refinery inside the town and a sugar factory right outside it.

The company was part of a larger company, Skånska sockerfabriksaktiebolaget, and during this period some industries started forming cartels to prevent competition from new companies. This was most common among industries with large investments in fixed capital, where production was directed toward the domestic market and, in many cases including the sugar industry, protected from international competition (Schön 2010, 227–228). In 1907, twenty-one sugar factories and eleven refineries merged into one company, Svenska sockerfabriks AB.

The first half of the twentieth century saw an expansion of the sugar industry in terms of area devoted to sugar beet, total sugar production, and workers employed by the industry. Still, a large part of the workforce—up to 40 percent—consisted of seasonal labor. Nationally there was a slight decline during the 1930s, but for Landskrona there was a sustained increase in workers until 1940, when their number reached 775.

The sugar industry in Sweden underwent a major rationalization after World War II. Between 1948 and 1963, four of the five existing sugar refineries closed and twelve of the nineteen sugar factories went the same way (Kuuse 1982, 192). There were multiple reasons for this rationalization. After the war prices abroad fell below those in Sweden, forcing producers down this route to meet competition from abroad on the rather restricted Swedish market. Moreover, Swedish production facilities were underused in the sense that the sugar beet season was quite short, and prolonging it required fewer facilities. The seasonal aspect was supplemented by the increased use of cars and tractors to transport the beets, making rail access from producer to facility less important. Finally, the rationalization of the sugar industry was one small aspect in an overall government strategy to rationalize both agriculture and industry in the post-World War II period. One important reason for this strategy was the need for more workers in high-productivity sectors facing a shortage of labor (Kuuse 1982, 188–191).

For Landskrona, rationalization meant that the sugar refinery closed in 1960, followed two years later by the sugar factory in Säbyholm, the fourth largest in Sweden at the time.

The Metal Industry

Small workshops and foundries played an important role in the early industrialization of Landskrona (see above). Over time they became fewer, and the general development of the sector can be studied by looking at one of the largest firms: AB Landsverk.

The 1911 statistics show that five different firms were engaged in the metal industry. By far the largest was Landskrona Nya Mekaniska Verkstad with 317 workers. The firm was founded by two industrialists in 1872 as Petterson & Ohlsen but changed its name in 1876. Its main business was manufacturing agricultural tools, ovens, and railway coaches. It was hit hard by the crisis of the early 1920, and half of its shares were sold to a German company, GHH. The German influence became a major factor in its development during the 1920s and '30s. It changed its name to Landsverk, and, in addition to making railway coaches and harbor cranes, it started on the research and development of military tanks. This was one way for the German military to sidestep the ban in Germany, introduced after World War I, on developing tank technology.

After World War II German interests were replaced by Swedish ownership, and, from 1947, Landsverk was owned by Kockums, a major shipyard and a railway coach manufacturer in Malmö. Landsverk gradually replaced its previous production, now focusing on excavators and dump trucks. In 1965, the company had 1,300 employees.

The foundry was closed in 1967 and during the 1970s the company, owned as it was by Kockums, was hit by the shipyard crisis. The state took over ownership and the number of workers was gradually reduced. In 1991, the new owner, VME Industries, decided to close the factory and laid off the remaining 117 workers.

The Textile Industry

Landskrona became home to Sweden's first clothing industry when Schlasbergs factory for men's clothing was established in 1896 (Jönsson 1995, 237). The firm started out as a domestic industry (see Marx 1887, ch. 15, section 8) with one tailor and a dozen seamstresses working from home but then successively expanded and transformed into a factory with 250 employees around the time of World War I and 400 in the 1950s. Its first location in the city center was supplemented by another at the old aircraft factory during the expansion. After World War II the company recruited workers among refugees and also from

Denmark, and, in 1950, a new factory was built close to the new housing area of Sandvången in the east. In the 1970s, Schlasbergs was one of Sweden's leading clothing companies.

In the 1920s, two other clothing companies were formed (Carl Emond and Emil Emond), making various items of clothing for not only men but also women (suspenders, stockings, dresses, etc.). They placed their factories in the southern industrial district on the site of the former aircraft factory. However, their textile production was exposed to the emissions from Supra, a major chemical plant situated next door. The workers were affected, too, and both they and the company protested against this during the 1950s. Carl Emond moved its production to the northern part of the city in the 1950s, while Emil Emond remained in the southern part. The two companies expanded from the 1930s onward and employed more than 800 workers, mostly women.

A fourth company, Stinson, made bathrobes, braces/suspenders, etc. It was smaller than the previous three but expanded production from its founding in the 1940s to the 1960s and built its factory in the northwestern part of the city in 1958.

International competition, first from Eastern Europe and subsequently from Asia, became a major challenge to Sweden's textile industries from the 1950s onward. It hit the major textile cities of Borås and Norrköping hard and severely affected the industry in other cities as well. All the companies in Landskrona closed one after another during the crisis: Carl Emond in 1970, Emil Emond in 1974, and Schlasbergs in 1978 (Jönsson 1997, 403–410), while Stinson moved its production elsewhere. This was the third of several industrial crises to hit Landskrona in the 1970s, and, whereas the closing down of the shipyard and metal industries mainly affected men, the textile crises affected women.

Other Industries

As we have discerned from Figure 2.4, the manufacturing industry in Landskrona was, in common with other Swedish industrial cities, fairly diversified in the early part of the twentieth century, and, while the industries mentioned above formed its core, other industries came and went during the century.

As regards the metal workshops, one important business was Thulinverken. The pilot and pioneer Enoch Thulin developed the aircraft factory, which at its peak had 800 employees and built about 100 airplanes and 700 engines between 1915 and 1919. Thulin died in a plane crash over Landskrona in 1919, and, in 1920, the company went bankrupt. It was reconstructed to build automobiles but faced too stiff competition from both newly started Volvo and foreign cars. It began making automobile parts instead, such as brakes, but also made mechanized weaving machines (Jönsson 1997).

Other companies combined metal with electrical goods, one such being Järnkonst, which was founded in 1946. It produced electric light fittings and had around 1,000 employees when it was sold to ASEA in 1969. The company still exists, now under the name of CEBE. Another company in a similar field is BESAM, founded in 1962. It produces automatic doors, has around 300 employees, and is part of ASSA ABLOY.

A third industry, the chemical sector, had already appeared in the early stages of industrialization with soda and fertilizers as its main products. A fertilizer factory was built on the reef Gråen outside Landskrona harbor in the 1880s. The company also built housing for its workers on the premises. Their tasks included handling phosphate, which meant poor working and living conditions. Production increased, and, in the early twentieth century, there were more than 100 workers and a new factory was built in the southern industrial area close to the railway. A major fire burned down the factory in 1924 and also damaged Thulinverken and Öresundsvarvet. The factory was rebuilt, and production increased further. In 1931, the leading fertilizer companies throughout Sweden were merged into one company, AB Förenade Superfosfatfabriker. The 1950s saw further expansion and the Landskrona factory became one of the largest in Europe with more than 400 workers. In the 1970s, it changed its name to Supra, and in 1981, there were 525 workers in the factory and 175 employed at the head office. The company is now named Yara; it moved to Malmö in 2016.

Finally, other companies related to agriculture were established in Landskrona and its outskirts as well, such as Weibull seeds and plant breeding. Landskrona is also home to Bergsöe, which specializes in the recycling of lead from car batteries. This company is the only one of its kind in the Nordic countries.

The Industrial Workers

The factory statistics enable us to study the employment of men and women in Landskrona during early industrialization. In 1870, 15 percent of its factory workers were women. Almost all of these worked in the sugar factory, with a few in the tile and chalk factory and the salt refinery. The largest employer by far of men was the sugar factory but a substantial number also worked in the textile factory, all of them convicts serving life sentences.

Of the 903 factory workers in Landskrona in 1890, 164 (18 percent) were women. The biggest employers of women were the sugar refinery and the brush factory; 92 percent of the women worked here, with an almost even split. The two biggest employers of men were the foundries and the sugar refinery. In addition to the foundries, the coke, fertilizer, leather, and brick factories and the shipyard

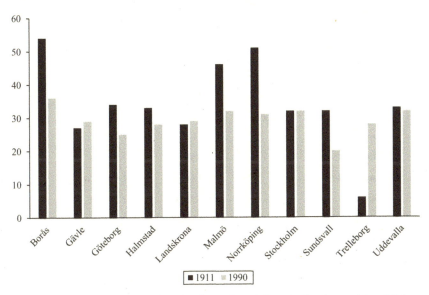

Figure 2.6 Women as share of total industrial workforce in the eleven cities, 1911 and 1990.

Sources: For 1911, Kommerskollegium, Avdelningen för näringsstatistik, Hiaaa: 210; for 1990, SCB, Folk- och bostadsräkningen, part 5, table 22.

and gasworks had only male workers. The small textile and tobacco factories employed men and women to almost the same extent.

For 1911, we can compare Landskrona to the other cities and see that at that time around 28 percent of its workers were women (Figure 2.6). This is close to the average for our eleven cities. Three cities have much higher shares whereas the one for Trelleborg is extremely low. Overall, the textile industry was important for the employment of women, an indication of this being that the share of women workers in the industry in 1911 was highest in Borås (54 percent) and Norrköping (50 percent) where textiles predominated in both. Another industry with a high share of women was the tobacco industry (Eriksson and Stanfors 2015).

In 1990, the share of women employed in the industry was evenly spread across the eleven cities, including Landskrona at around 30 percent. In Landskrona, this was at the same level as seventy-nine years earlier: 29 percent as compared to 28 percent in 1911. The textile cities showed the largest decrease in the share of women employed during this period after Swedish textiles were forced out of business from the 1950s onward. In addition, the outlier Trelleborg had now come in line, with women constituting around 30 percent of its workers.

Table 2.5 Mean income for employed men in the eleven cities in 1920 and 1930. Landskrona = 1.

	1920	1930
Borås	1.00	1.03
Gävle	1.04	1.09
Göteborg	1.28	1.30
Halmstad	0.99	1.03
Landskrona	**1.00**	**1.00**
Malmö	1.12	1.19
Norrköping	0.92	0.98
Stockholm	1.38	1.68
Sundsvall	1.14	1.21
Trelleborg	1.05	1.07
Uddevalla	0.95	0.97

Source: SOS Folkräkningen, 1920, 1930.

Looking in greater detail at Landskrona in 1911, the largest employer of women was Schlasbergs, which manufactured clothing and mainly employed seamstresses (in total 179 women), the sugar refinery (72), the brush factory (64), and a cigar and tobacco factory (58). All the textile factories and tobacco producers employed more women than men.[3] The largest employers of men were Landskrona Nya Mekaniska Verkstad (a metal workshop with 317 men), the sugar refinery (313), another metal workshop (99), and the fertilizer factory (94) (BiSOS D).

Eighty years later, in 1990, the largest industrial employer of women in Landskrona was the mechanical workshops with more than 55 percent of the total number of women in industry. In second and third place came the chemical and the pulp industries, with the same ranking as for the employment of men in the city. This pattern, showing that large industries employing women were the same as for men in absolute terms, is apparent across the eleven cities.

However, the share of women in the total workforce followed another pattern and was highest in textiles. In eight of the eleven cities (including Landskrona), women constituted more than half of the workforce in this industry, which is also the only one where women constituted more than 50 percent of the workforce in any city except in the wood sector in Trelleborg. Other sectors employing a relatively high share of women in 1990 were food and pulp.

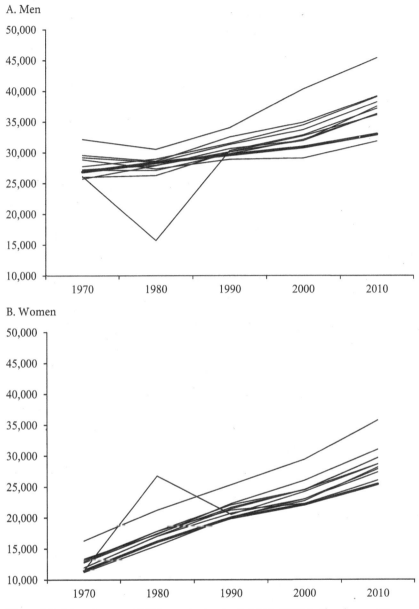

Figure 2.7 Mean income (1970–constant prices), 1970–2010, in the eleven cities. Landskrona is represented by the thick line.

Calculations based on micro-level register data from municipalities (*kommuner*) for cohorts born 1930–1980, age 20–64.

Source: Statistics Sweden, The Swedish Interdisciplinary Panel, Centre for Economic Demography, Lund University.

Turning to earnings, Table 2.5 shows mean income for men in our sample of cities relative to Landskrona in 1920 and 1930. In both years, Landskrona was clearly at the bottom, together with Borås, Halmstad, Norrköping, and Uddevalla. In 1920, average earnings for men was 38 percent higher in Stockholm than in Landskrona, while the corresponding figure in 1930 was no less than 68 percent. In Göteborg, men earned about 30 percent more than those in Landskrona, and in Malmö 12–19 percent more.

There are several different factors explaining these results. Comparing income within the same industry, Stockholm stood out with higher annual incomes than in other Swedish cities in, for example, the metal and mechanical workshop sector and in the tobacco factories. Differences between Landskrona and, for example, Malmö and Göteborg were on the other hand small and, if anything, incomes were higher in Landskrona in these branches (Arbetsstatistik, A:2, 119; Arbetsstatistik, A:3, 136). Generally, besides the higher income level in Stockholm, it was income differences between branches that were large rather than between cities (SOS: Lönestatistisk årsbok 1930, 90). This points to the industrial structure being one important cause for different income levels. Another factor affecting the mean income of the employed was the overall employment structure in the cities. Over the period 1900 to 1960, Landskrona had, together with Borås, the highest share of the population employed in industry of the eleven cities. Having a large share of industrial workers and thereby a large group of unskilled or lower skilled workers was another explanation for the relatively low mean income.

From 1970, we can look at income using micro-level register data. Figure 2.7 shows mean income for men (panel A) and women (panel B) in 1970 at constant prices at the municipality level. Throughout the period Landskrona is among those cities with the lowest mean income for both men and women, showing that the differences observed early in the twentieth century persisted into the twenty-first.

Industrial Location

In the late nineteenth century, the city of Landskrona was quite small and most factories were located within the city center. Starting with the harbor, the shipyard was strategically located immediately opposite its entrance beside the toll offices. Located not far from there, in the inner harbor, was the sugar refinery with its own quay. The same block housed the brush factory. In the very center of the city, we find mechanical workshops and a steam mill. And further east, north of the railway line which entered the city from the east and ended immediately south of the harbor, we also find a concentration of industries: the leather factories, a wool spinning factory, and a steam saw. South of the railway were

Map 2.2 Landskrona of 1918, with industries marked with circles and housing projects with squares.

Source: Karta över Landskrona stad upprättad år 1918 av stadsingenjören, Göteborgs Litografiska AB. Stadsbyggnadsförvaltningen, Landskrona stad. This material is not covered by the terms of the Creative Commons license of this publication. For permission to, reuse please contact the rights holder

several blocks not yet named, where a soda factory was located. The general picture this gives us is that during the early industrialization phase of the late nineteenth century most factories were located at the heart of the towns and therefore close to where people lived.

The 1918 map reveals that a few years later industries had moved out of Landskrona's city center and were mainly located in the newly developed area south of the railway (Map 2.2). Here we find the mechanical workshop, fertilizer factory, a new aircraft factory, a rubber factory, and an oil factory. Further east along the south side of the railway track were the city's gas and electricity works.

South of these newly occupied industrial districts and right by the sea was the new shipyard, Öresundsvarvet, which covered a large area including a dry dock. Still, some industries remained at their old locations, such as the sugar refinery and the old, smaller shipyard.

Social Development

Housing

The industrial expansion of the early twentieth century led to a shortage of housing, meaning that many workers had very poor-quality accommodation. Already in 1915 the city council brought up the question of housing in connection with the establishment of Öresundsvarvet, and, in 1916, the shipyard started to plan the construction of four apartment houses for their workers and families east of the city center. In 1917, the shipyard asked for permission to build more housing nearby, and a year later the persistent demand for more labor meant the shipyard had sought to attract workers by building housing for almost 600 families. In 1920, the shipyard established a health insurance fund and was poised to build six large new apartment houses. All this housing meant that the workers lived in the city close to the industrial part of the town but still had quite a long way to go to the shipyard at its southwestern location (see the squares in Map 2.2). By now the shipyard owned housing for 600 workers, and construction was under way for a further 200. In 1922, when Öresundsvarvet went bankrupt, it owned sixty-eight buildings worth more than 1.3 million SEK.

As in most other Swedish cities, there were periods of marked expansion in construction in the 1920s, 1940s, and 1960s. The 1920s saw, for example, the building of 1.5-storey family homes for people of limited means under the so-called Own Home movement (*Egnahemsrörelsen*). There was also a severe shortage of small one- or two-room apartments at the time, which prompted the municipality to speed up the building of new apartment houses. Landskrona was, together with Nyköping and Västerås, a pioneer in municipality-led housing construction. In 1917, a rental association (*hyresgästförening*) was formed to safeguard the interests (including rent control) of the tenants in these apartments. Such associations were later to become an important part of the Social Democratic labor movement.

During the 1920s and 1930s, most apartment houses were built in the central parts of town. In 1933, the first HSB association (a cooperative housing association) was formed, but it ran into problems initially with unsold apartments. Not until 1939 were thirty-two apartments ready.

During World War II a municipal housing company was formed, Landskronahem, which built a large number of houses between 1950 and 1970 to address the pressing problem of mostly very poor-quality housing or no housing at all in the early 1940s.

In the 1950s, a new and large housing area, Sandvången, was built, offering a total of 810 apartments and other amenities including central laundry facilities with washing machines, ninety-nine garages, and a facility with sixty-eight freezers. There were also local shops and facilities for organizations and hobby purposes. Other similar though smaller areas were developed, too. During this period, some of the industries previously located in the industrial district, such as the textile factories, were moved closer to the homes of their workers in the northeastern part of the town.

In the central parts of the city, many old houses were demolished to make room for new construction and a new city, a movement which ultimately met with resistance. Despite these changes, the sugar refinery would remain located in the city center until 1960.

The 1960s saw the construction of even larger housing projects during the "million homes program" (*Miljonprogrammet*), a plan to build 1 million new apartments in Sweden during the period 1965–1975 to alleviate the housing shortage. In 1965, there were 2,400 individuals queuing for an apartment in Landskrona. There were still the problems of cramped housing, too, with families of five children living in two-room apartments and families of two to four children living in one-room apartments. This was also a period when the industry faced a shortage of labor and promoted both immigration and in-migration from throughout Sweden. By the second half of the 1970s, times had changed, and there was now an excess supply of housing, leaving empty many apartments in areas of new development. There was also increasing criticism of the new residential areas and the destruction of the old city. Many of these "million homes program" areas would face increasing segregation and social problems in the period to come, in both Landskrona and elsewhere.

Health and Mortality

In 1900, a county hospital (Länslasarettet) was opened in Landskrona. There was also a nursing home (*sjukhem*) which took care of the elderly and the chronically ill who could not be cared for in the county hospital, and this had room for seventy-six patients. The capacity of the county hospital gradually increased from 60 beds when it opened to about 120 in the late 1920s. In 1900, the hospital provided 6,600 care days with an average stay of 32 days (!). By 1910, this number had increased to 18,600, while the average stay had been shortened to 24 days.

In 1950, the county hospital provided 54,500 care days, with an average hospitalization time of 14 days (Jönsson 1997, 15). Its expansion had continued with a maternity ward in the 1930s and a children's hospital in the 1940s, and now came further expansion through the 1960s, '70s, and '80s. In 1972, the maternity ward was closed, but the antenatal unit remained open for a time until it, too, was closed in 1981.

The city was considered by the Swedish medical authority (Medicinalstyrelsen) to have the healthiest (i.e., least sick) population among the larger cities (with a population of more than 10,000), and, in 1910, the sickness and burial fund Solidar was founded, establishing Landskrona as one of the country's pioneers in sickness insurance (Jönsson 1997, 9).

The first known water pipe system in the city was made of wood and connected to open freshwater in the city. In 1868, it was 4 kilometers long and provided 131 wells with water (Jönsson 1997, 55). This water was not really suitable for drinking, however; drinking water was collected from wells on the outskirts of town. In the 1870s, the water system was further developed with iron pipes and new wells. Pipes were drawn under all the streets in the city and were connected in some cases directly to houses and in other cases to outdoor water pumps. At the beginning Landskrona was the only city in Sweden that relied exclusively on groundwater, hence the city had drinking water of very high quality. Toward the end of the nineteenth century the increased demand for water and lack of pressure in the system required the construction of a water tower, which was ready in 1904. In 1883, heated public baths were built but were soon deemed to be insufficient, and, in the first decade of the twentieth century, they were expanded. In 1913, a newly built public bathhouse was opened. These baths were important because they were not mainly used for recreational swimming but for washing.

During World War I there were food shortages and rationing in Landskrona as in other Swedish towns, despite the fact that Sweden was neutral and did not take active part in the war. The fact that the town had professional fishermen meant its population of 17,000 had access to local produce, which was quite an advantage over some other cities. Even so, in April 1917, the so-called "hunger demonstrations" meant that 3,000–4,000 protestors converged here as well.

The mortality development as measured by the crude death rate (CDR) was fairly uniform across the cities (Figure 2.8).[4] The peak in 1918 was caused by the Spanish flu and is the last epidemic that can be clearly detected in aggregate mortality statistics. The Spanish flu hit Landskrona in August of that year, and the spread of the epidemic accelerated from September onward. To stop it spreading the decision was taken to close the cinemas and the theater as well as forbid lectures and dance events in places where people congregated. Later in the fall, a further decision was taken to close the schools. The epidemic had weakened

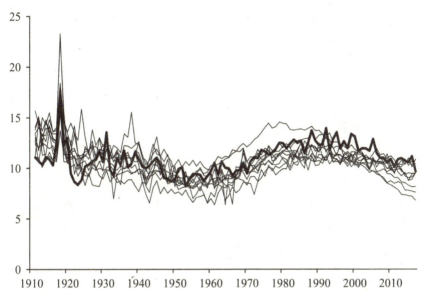

Figure 2.8 Crude death rates (per 1,000 population) in the eleven cities, 1911–2017. Landskrona is represented by the thick line.

Source: Swedish Official Statistics (SOS) Befolkningsrörelsen 1911–2017. 1911–1961 is the city of Landskrona, from 1962, it is Landskrona municipality.

considerably by the end of October, and, in early November, the restrictions were lifted. In early December, it looked as though it had completely vanished, only to reemerge shortly before Christmas of 1918. After early February 1919, it finally disappeared (Jönsson 1997, 122–124).

After the end of the pandemic total mortality declined until about 1960, when it began to increase again—a result of the population growing older, not of an increase in age-specific mortality. A particular feature in Landskrona's case was a peak in mortality in 1931.

If we look at infant mortality (the number of children younger than 1 year dying divided by the number of births), there is a more or less continuous decline throughout the period 1875–1935, and this pattern is also fairly uniform across cities (Figure 2.9). The series is slightly erratic due to the small number of child deaths, which creates some random fluctuations in the measure. The series begins as early as in 1875, when infant mortality in Landskrona was about 15 percent. In the early 1880s, it peaked at 25 percent, the prevailing level for Sweden as a whole a hundred years earlier (Statistics Sweden 1999). This peak appears to be related to epidemic outbreaks in measles and diphtheria, but also in outbreaks in diarrhea.[5] In 1935, the figure was down to 3 percent. There are no city-level data after this time, but for the country as a whole infant mortality

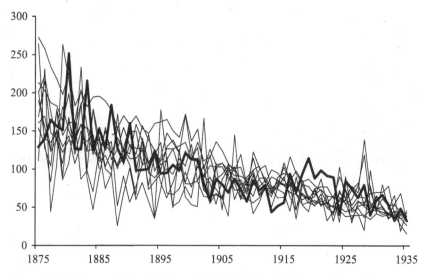

Figure 2.9 Infant mortality (IMR, per 1,000 births) in the eleven cities, 1875–1935. Landskrona is represented by the thick line.

Source: BiSOS A Befolkningsstatistik, BiSOS K Hälso- och sjukvården (1875–1910), SOS Befolkningsrörelsen, Allmän hälso- och sjukvård (1911–1935). See Helgertz and Önnerfors (2019).

around 2000 was roughly 3 or 4 per thousand (Statistics Sweden 1999), a spectacular improvement in life expectancy over the course of the twentieth century.

Child mortality (age 1–4) shows a similar improvement from 1875 to 1935 (Figure 2.10), and also in this case the development is fairly uniform across cities. We also see a reduction in the variability of mortality, which in itself is an important sign of improvement in the well-being of the population. The pattern in Landskrona does not deviate much. The development for boys and girls, respectively, in Landskrona is also highly similar, with no noticeable difference in the mortality level between the sexes either.

Figures 2.11 and 2.12 show adult and old-age mortality for men and women separately for the period 1875–1935. For adult men (age 40–59) there is a decline from around 20 per thousand to 10 per thousand over this period. Except for the quite high mortality rate in Stockholm, the patterns are quite similar across the cities, placing Landskrona in the middle or the lower half. For women, mortality in this age group declined from around 15 to 5–10 per thousand. Looking at the gender differences in mortality in Landskrona, male adult mortality was somewhat higher than female for most of the period up until 1935, but after the 1890s the difference is quite small (Appendix, Table A2.5).

LANDSKRONA: THE INDUSTRIAL CITY 57

A. Men

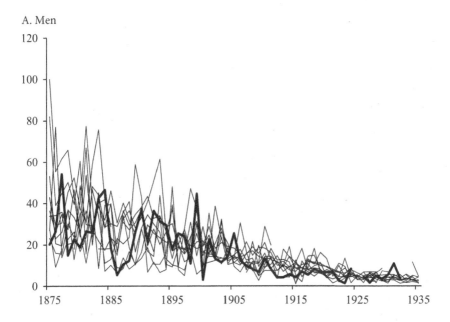

B. Women

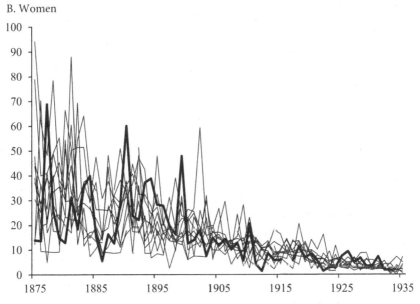

Figure 2.10 Child mortality (age 1–4, per 1,000 population) in the eleven cities, 1875–1935. Landskrona is represented by the thick line.

Source: BiSOS A Befolkningsstatistik, BiSOS K Hälso- och sjukvården (1875–1910), SOS Befolkningsrörelsen, Allmän hälso- och sjukvård (1911–1935). See Helgertz and Önnerfors (2019).

A. Men

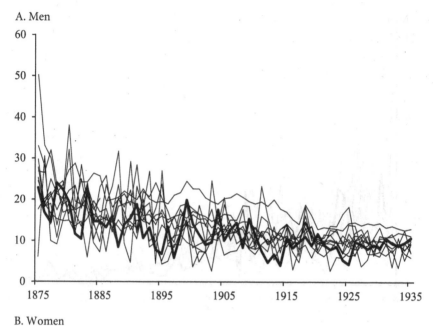

B. Women

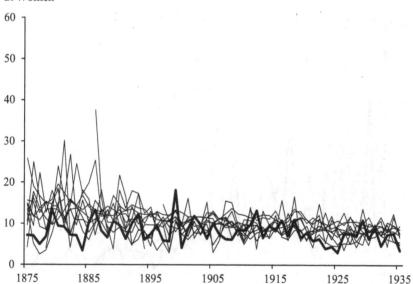

Figure 2.11 Adult mortality (40–59 years, per 1,000 population) in the eleven cities, 1875–1935. Landskrona is represented by the thick line.

Source: BiSOS A Befolkningsstatistik, BiSOS K Hälso- och sjukvården (1875–1910), SOS Befolkningsrörelsen, Allmän hälso- och sjukvård (1911–1935). See Helgertz and Önnerfors (2019).

LANDSKRONA: THE INDUSTRIAL CITY 59

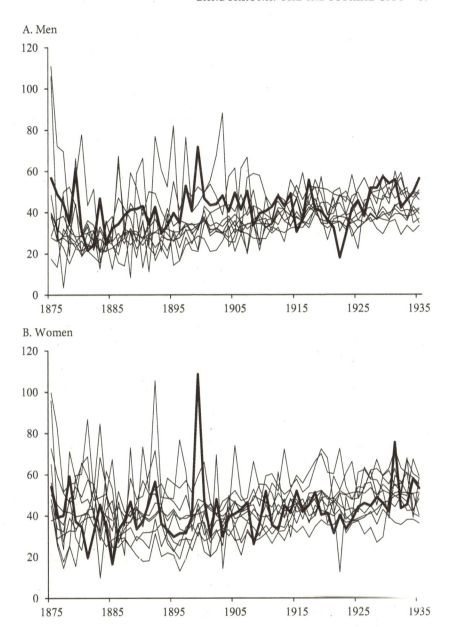

Figure 2.12 Old-age mortality (60+ years, per 1,000 population) in the eleven cities, 1875–1935. Landskrona is represented by the thick line.

Source: BiSOS A Befolkningsstatistik, BiSOS K Hälso- och sjukvården (1875–1910), SOS Befolkningsrörelsen, Allmän hälso- och sjukvård (1911–1935). See Helgertz and Önnerfors (2019).

Family Patterns

Looking first at childbearing, the crude birth rate (CBR) gives a summary picture of the number of births in relation to the size of the population.[6] Figure 2.13 shows the CBR for the selected cities. Overall, it is clear that fertility followed a similar development in all cities. From 1910 to about 1930, it declined in the final phase of the fertility transition, during which time the total fertility rate in Sweden declined from more than 4 children per woman before 1880 to fewer than 2 in the 1930s. This development was part of the demographic transition taking place throughout the Western world during the nineteenth and early twentieth centuries. Landskrona did not deviate from the general trend except to show somewhat lower fertility in the late 1980s and early 1990s, when the population of the city had aged quite a lot as a result of its earlier decline, and then it showed somewhat higher fertility in the early 2000s following its recovery. The three biggest cities had a much higher fertility level after 1995; this was connected to their demographic expansion, with a greater number of younger people moving in and having families.

Fertility, as measured by the CBR, also shows strong short-term variations, which is a well-known phenomenon in Swedish fertility history (e.g., Stanfors

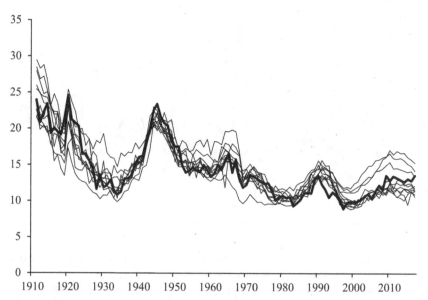

Figure 2.13 Crude birth rates (per 1,000 population) in the eleven cities, 1911–2017. Landskrona is represented by the thick line.

Source: Swedish Official Statistics (SOS) Befolkningsrörelsen 1911–2017. 1911–1961 refer to the towns, from 1962 to the municipalities.

2003). Soon after the end of its decline in the 1930s, fertility rebounded, creating what is commonly known as the baby boom of the 1940s. This boom is also clearly visible in Landskrona, with 1945 as the top year. After the baby boom, fertility declined slightly although it did not go down to the previously low levels. In the second half of the 1960s, it increased again, creating a second baby boom before the real baby bust of the 1970s and 1980s. Around 1990 came a further increase, followed by a decline and historic low levels of fertility in 1999. In the 2000s, fertility began increasing again, more so in Landskrona than in the country as a whole, but it should also be noted that the CBRs are sensitive to rapid changes in the population age structure, such as the large-scale immigration of those of childbearing age.

Figure 2.14 shows the general fertility rate for the census years 1910–1990 (births per 1,000 women aged 15–49 years), a rate less sensitive to changes in population age structure. It corroborates the previous picture of a decline in fertility up to 1930, then an increase up to 1950, a slight decline up to 1960, and another increase up to 1970. Of course, most of the short-term variations are lost when one looks only at the census years. It is also clear that Landskrona had quite high fertility until 1950, but since then it has been at a more average level.

In 1867, daycare for young children aged 2–6 years was established through an institution called Asylen. It was open 14 hours per day on weekdays. Fourteen

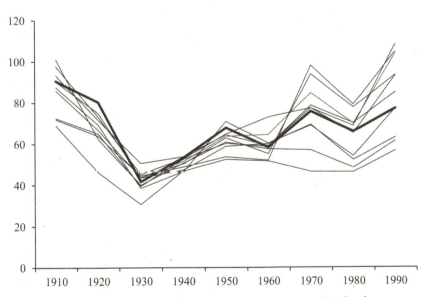

Figure 2.14 General fertility rate (per 1,000 women 15–49 years) in the eleven cities, 1910–1990. Landskrona is represented by the thick line.

Source: SOS Folkräkningen 1910–1960 and Folk och Bostadsräkningen 1970, 1980, 1990.

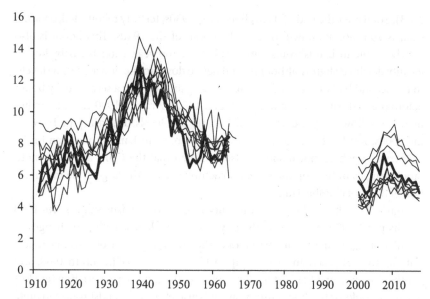

Figure 2.15 Crude marriage rates (per 1,000 population) in the eleven cities, 1911–2017. Landskrona is represented by the thick line.

Source: Swedish Official Statistics (SOS) Befolkningsrörelsen 1911–2017. 1911–1961 refer to the towns, from 1962 to the municipalities.

years later, in 1891, 111 children were cared for there, and food was included. The facility was run by the Landskrona Women's Organization (*Landskronas fruntimmersförening*). It was expanded in 1909 and 1937; ten years later the municipality took over, and the facility was still active in the late 1990s (Jönsson 1997).

In 1918, Annie Weibull opened a school for homemakers (housewives). She was also part of the establishment of Vita Bandets Mjölkdroppe in Landskrona, in 1916, which aimed to promote breastfeeding and child and maternal health. In the same year, she started a childcare facility (*barnkrubba*) with room for six children initially. In 1943, there were twelve children and an additional eighteen in the kindergarten (*barnträdgårdsavdelningen*).

Family formation in the late 1990s and early 2000s was higher in both Landskrona and the three biggest cities, and, in Figure 2.15, the crude marriage rate (number of marriages divided by the mean population) is shown. In the period before 1965, Landskrona was much in line with other cities in terms of marriage. Unfortunately, there are no city-level data on marriages between 1965 and 2000. Nonetheless, the increasing propensity to marry during the baby boom is clearly visible in all cities. It is an often-cited fact that the baby boom was to

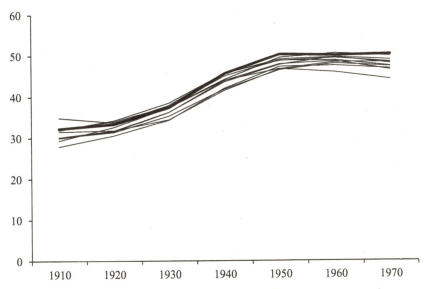

Figure 2.16 Proportions married (percent) of men and women all ages, in the eleven cities, 1910–1970. Landskrona is represented by the thick line.
Source: SOS Folkräkningen 1910–1960 and Folk och Bostadsräkningen 1970, 1980, 1990.

a large extent a marriage boom even though marital fertility increased as well (Sandström 2014; Van Bavel and Reher 2013).

Figure 2.16 displays the proportion of married individuals of all ages for both sexes. It clearly shows the increase in the proportion of the population in Landskrona who were married from 1910 to 1970. Between 1940 and 1970, Landskrona was also the city with the highest proportion of married people in the population.

Poor Relief

Swedish industrialization led to a sharp social transformation, and for poor relief new challenges appeared. A growing number of poor and increasing municipal costs led to a new poor relief act, in 1871, introducing a stricter definition of poverty than previously (Engberg 2005, 65). Over time, the reform met criticism from many social layers, and, in 1918, requirements were eased, support became larger, and some of the old forms of support were prohibited, such as auctioning out of poor children and rotational boarding (Gerger 1992, 31). The poor houses would be transformed into homes for the elderly, and support was also given to people in their homes. However, although the old requirement of having to work to receive support was eased, workhouses still existed.

The new Act had a direct impact on the poor relief system. Already in 1925, the people in workhouses constituted less than 1 percent of those who received poor support in Sweden. From 1925 to 1937, further changes took place: the share of people receiving aid through indoor relief in poor houses decreased from 13 percent to 8 percent of all poor support receivers, while outdoor relief to people in their own homes increased at almost the same rate (from 59 to 70 percent of the total receivers of poor support). Poor people in need of healthcare, in hospitals or other facilities, also introduced in the 1918 Act, increased slightly, from around 12 percent to 15 percent (Bonniers konversationslexikon 1949, 1114). With the extension of the welfare state all elderly had a right to a place at an elderly home, so this was no longer seen as part of poor relief although some of the residents could receive pecuniary support. In 1948, poor houses still existed although people admitted to these facilities were few. Most of the support came through home support. In 1960, almost all poverty relief was in the form of direct support to families or individuals, in cash and in kind, a model still applied (SOS: Fattigvården 1918–1956 and SOS: Socialhjälpen 1957–1960).

In 1910, the city of Landskrona had one poor house that could keep up to 180 individuals. In addition, there was a smaller one for nine people (BiSOS U: Kommunernas fattigvård och finanser, 1910–1914, 1). Because 1918 was a difficult year given the shortage of food (the result of a bad harvest in 1917 combined with the war preventing trade), Öresundsvarvet started a small food court, the "root crops restaurant." In 1920, the town still had one poor house for 180 people and a smaller one for six people.

In 1910, a total of 1,394 people received poor relief in the city, and these constituted 8.7 percent of the total population in Landskrona. The average for ninety-four Swedish cities was 6.5 percent, and, of the eleven cities in our study, Norrköping had the highest share with 9.2 percent, followed by Halmstad, Sundsvall, and Landskrona. We are able to compare the development in the cities for 1920, 1950, and 1960 as well (see Table 2.6). Generally, Landskrona was at the higher end until 1960, when the shares between the cities were fairly equal.

Education

Schools, either privately funded or maintained by the local community, existed in Sweden long before the twentieth century. During the nineteenth century, their organization began to be regulated by the state but was run by the local municipalities, starting with the 1842 act decreeing mandatory primary schools in every parish. This was followed by the establishment of pre-primary schools

Table 2.6 Share of population subject to poor relief, ten cities as compared to the level in Landskrona, 1910, 1920, 1950, and 1960.

	1910	1920	1950	1960
Borås	79	88	70	115
Gävle	58	68	64	91
Göteborg	73	55	82	100
Halmstad	103	112	49	99
Landskrona	100	100	100	100
Malmö	73	79	73	98
Norrköping	106	125	97	109
Stockholm	95	79	100	114
Sundsvall	102	80	64	61
Trelleborg	35	35	na	Na
Uddevalla	77	87	na	112
Landskrona (level %)	8.7	8.1	6.0	4.9

Sources: BiSOS U: Kommunernas fattigvård och finanser, 1910–1914: 1 for 1910; SOS Fattigvården 1918–1956 for 1920 and 1950; and SOS Socialhjälpen 1957–1960 for 1960.

(*småskolor*, encompassing the first two years of the primary school) in the 1880s. At the same time secondary education and vocational training were on the rise.

As for primary education, in 1900, Landskrona had four primary schools (*folkskolor*) and three pre-primary ones (*småskolor*), with teaching taking place in five schoolhouses. All the teachers in the pre-primary schools were women, whereas those in primary schools were both women and men (thirteen vs. seventeen, respectively) (BiSOS P: Undervisningsväsendet: Berättelse om folkskolorna för år 1900).

In 1897, a new middle (secondary) school (*realskola/femklassigt läroverk*) was built in Landskrona, and its pupils did five years of study. In the autumn term of 1900, a total of 124 pupils attended the school (eighty in the first three grades which followed a common curriculum, and forty-four in the final two grades). The teachers were the headmaster, five adjunct teachers, and three other teachers (drawing, music, gymnastics, and handicrafts) (BiSOS P: Undervisningsväsendet. Berättelse om statens allmänna läroverk för gossar. Läsåret 1900–1901). In 1910, there were 149 students spread relatively evenly across what were now six grades. As of 1880, Landskrona also had a technical school (crafts and engineering) and, from 1900 to 1970, a seminar course (post-high school education for elementary school teachers).

In 1900, there were 1,345 pupils in primary schools and 584 in pre-primary schools (aged 7–14 years, the compulsory schooling age stated in the 1882 Primary School Act). Adding those who were in secondary education and vocational schools (249), those in private schools (43), students from outside the district, and those in "schools for backward children" and home education brings the total to 2,261 pupils aged 7–14 years. The total number of children recorded in the statistics was 2,319, the difference taking into account that forty-four had finished the school after passing the final tests, ten were absent because of illness, one for another reason, and information on three children was missing. This total number represented 1,181 boys and 1,138 girls (BiSOS P 1900, table 7).

In 1907, the first municipal high school (*kommunalt gymnasium*) in the country opened, and, in 1911, the first five (!) students graduated. Four years later, a common schoolhouse for the secondary *realskola* and the high school was built, in effect providing an equivalent to the state-run high schools (*högre allmänt läroverk*) available in other cities. At its start, the municipal high school was only open to boys but in 1921, it also accepted girls, the first of whom graduated in 1923. This extended opportunities for girls to acquire a higher education than that offered by the high school for girls that had been in existence since 1871 and lasted until 1971.

From the early 1930s, the municipal high school was transformed into a standard state-run high school (Jönsson 1997, 65–76). As in the rest of the country, high school education gradually became more widespread with increasingly larger cohorts of children entering at this level. This required a steady increase in the number of schoolhouses, and, in the early 1970s, a completely new high school was opened.

Figure 2.17 shows the proportion of the population with a minimum of two years of post-secondary education (university or professional post-high school) from 1970 to 2010. In 1970, this only applied to about 5 percent of men and an even smaller percentage of women (individuals born after 1930, aged 20–64). In 2010, the figure in Landskrona was around 20 percent for men and 30 percent for women. It is quite clear that the educational level in Landskrona was low compared to other cities.

Political Development

In 1866, the centuries-old Diet of the Four Estates (*Ståndsriksdagen*) was replaced by a two-chamber parliament. The organization of municipalities changed about the same time, and, in both national and local elections, voting was restricted by

LANDSKRONA: THE INDUSTRIAL CITY   67

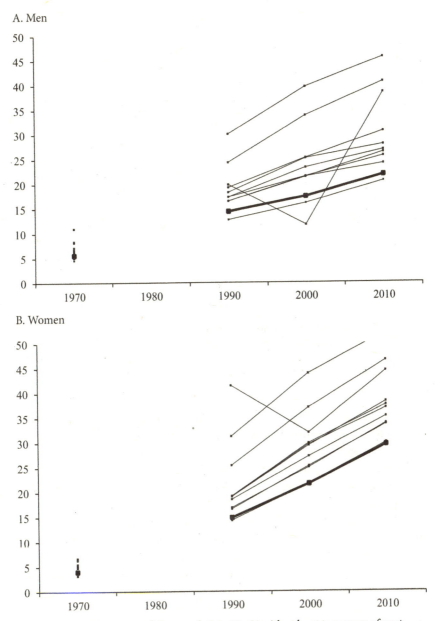

Figure 2.17 Proportions of the population 20–64 with at least two years of post-secondary education, in the eleven cities, 1970–2010. Landskrona is represented by the thick line.
Calculations based on micro-level register data from municipalities (*kommuner*) for cohorts born 1930–1980, age 20–64.
Source: Statistics Sweden, The Swedish Interdisciplinary Panel, Centre for Economic Demography, Lund University.

68 URBAN LIVES

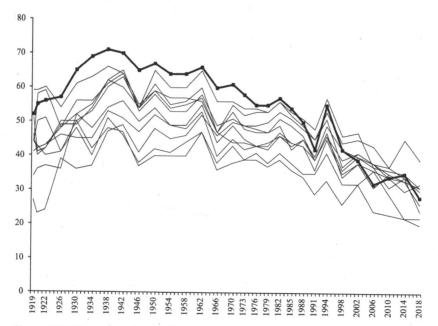

Figure 2.18 Voter share for the Social Democratic party, in the eleven cities, 1919–2018 (percent). Landskrona is represented by the thick line.

Sources: SOS Kommunala valen, 1919–1966 and SOS Allmänna valen, del 2: Kommunala valen, 1970–1998; Valmyndigheten, valresultat kommunala valen 2002–2018.

income; only around 20 percent of men older than 21 had voting rights while women had none (Nationalencyklopedin: rösträttsrörelsen). Furthermore, the number of votes per person depended on income or wealth. During the early twentieth century reforms eased voting restrictions for men, but the law granting one vote per person and voting rights for both men and women was not passed until 1918.

The first election with the new extended franchise took place at city and municipality levels in March 1919, when the Social Democratic party made substantial gains. It became the dominant political party in Sweden from then on, and in all eleven cities there is a common trend and variations in the voter share of the Social Democrats (see Figure 2.18). In Landskrona, the Social Democrats gained twenty-two of the forty seats on the city council in the 1919 election, creating their own majority (see Figure 2.19). Overall, the party had the highest share of votes among the cities until 1982, reaching a peak in the 1930s, when they held 75 percent of the city council seats. The Social Democrats kept a majority of elected seats until the 1991 election, needing no other party's support to retain this position.

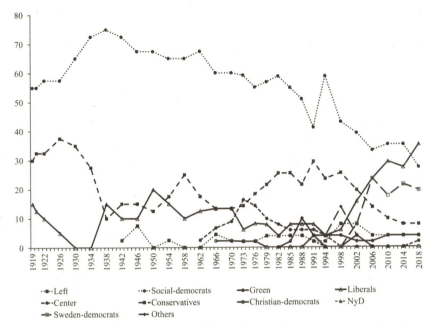

Figure 2.19 Share of seats in city board for parties reaching representation in Landskrona, 1919–2018.

Sources: SOS Kommunala valen, 1919–1966 and SOS Allmänna valen, del 2: Kommunala valen, 1970–1998; Valmyndigheten, valresultat kommunala valen 2002–2018.

In 1991, a coalition of the Liberals, Conservatives (*Moderaterna*), Center Party, and Christian Democrats ruled the city, but, in 1994, the Social Democrats regained power with 59 percent of the seats. During the period 1998–2002, they formed a coalition with the Left Party to create a political majority. From 2006 onward, the ruling coalition has consisted of the Liberals, the Green Party, and the Conservatives.

Recently the voting patterns in Landskrona have been different from those in the other cities through the rise of the Liberal Party during the twenty-first century. This has been mirrored by a large fall in votes for the Conservatives in Landskrona during the same period. Another important feature of the city has been the rise of the Sweden Democrats, a right-wing nationalist party, in the 2002 and 2006 elections. Their emergence and rise have mirrored that in many other Scanian municipalities, though it has taken place later in the rest of Sweden.

The new voting franchise of 1918 not only gave women suffrage but also implied that women could be elected. In the elections of 1919, between 6 and 20 percent of all elected politicians in the eleven cities were women (see Figure 2.20). This share increased during the 1940s, but it was not until the 1970s

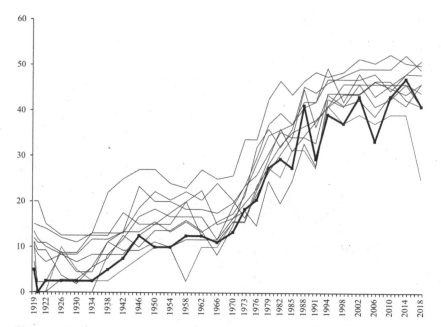

Figure 2.20 Elected women (share of all elected) in municipality elections in the eleven cities, 1919–2018 (percent). Landskrona is represented by the thick line.

Sources: SOS Kommunala valen, 1919–1966 and SOS Allmänna valen, del 2: Kommunala valen, 1970–1998; Valmyndigheten, valresultat kommunala valen 2002–2018.

and 1980s that it exceeded 40 percent. The trend was similar across the cities, with Stockholm being a forerunner. Landskrona followed the general trend and variations, although in the lower bound from 1991 onward. The lower shares for Landskrona and Trelleborg thereafter have partly been due to the rise of right-wing parties with low levels of female representatives.

Voter turnout (in the municipal elections) generally increased in Sweden from 81 percent in 1962 to around 90 percent in the 1970s and early 1980s. After 1985, it dropped to 84 percent, reaching a low point in 2002 with 78 percent, and increased again thereafter, reaching 84 percent in 2018. However, the cities studied have shown considerable variations; some had a decreasing relative voter turnout during the period compared to the national average, while others were closer to the overall national trend. Landskrona belonged to the cities showing a lower turnout than average and decreasing over time. A decline after the 1998 election was particularly noticeable with a 3 percentage points lower turnout than nationally, reaching a low of 5 percentage points below the average in 2014. This was matched by only one of the other cities: its southern neighbor of Malmö, whose turnout fell from 5.5 percentage points to

7.6 percentage points below the national average for the same period. Göteborg had a 3–4 percentage points lower turnout than average but the decrease had started as far back as the 1970s.

Conclusion

In the second half of the nineteenth century, Landskrona was transformed from a small administrative town into an industrial city. Early industrialization rested on the classical components of metal and textiles in combination with specific sectors based on Landskrona's geographical position (i.e., its food industry, which was based on the surrounding fertile agricultural lands, and the shipyard industries based on its natural harbor).

Around 1910, the population was more than 15,000, and the demographic structure of the city was in line with other emerging industrial cities in Sweden. Except for the mortality peak in connection with the Spanish flu in 1918, demographic and industrial growth continued during the 1910s. Around 1915, industrial development took a leap forward with the establishment of a new shipyard and an aircraft factory to supplement the existing textile and metal industries and fertilizer factories. Early twentieth-century development also included investment in schools, housing for the in-migrating workers and their families, and a new area south of the city devoted to industry.

The economic crises of the early 1920s hit Landskrona hard—above all the bankruptcy of the shipyard. This affected the city in several ways: in-migration was replaced by considerable out-migration and the city's population decreased. The 1920s also meant that the Social Democratic party took political power, which they retained until the election in the early 1990s.

Industrial expansion and population growth gained speed again after 1930 and kept up the pace until the late 1960s. The industrial expansion rested on the reopening of the shipyard, new companies in textile manufacturing, and long-established companies in the chemical and metal sectors. Apart from the sugar mill closing down in 1960, this was a golden age of industry in Landskrona as in the rest of Sweden. New housing areas were built for the workers, and refugees and labor force immigrants supplemented the internal labor force.

From the late 1960s, the city's fortunes changed again. Several industries faced increased competition from abroad and expansion leveled off. Population growth stagnated and was eventually replaced by a decline. Net in-migration turned into net out-migration, and, in the 1970s, the leading textile firms closed one after the other. Both the shipyard and the largest metal workshop reduced their staff. The culmination of the crisis came in the early 1980s, when the largest industrial employer, the shipyard, closed. This crisis had long-term effects on the city's development and, although the population is now growing again and new firms have been established during the 1990s and 2000s, social and economic problems remain.

The overall development of Landskrona has mostly been similar to the general development of Swedish industrial cities in both economic and demographic terms. Fluctuations in population development during a trend of growth have mirrored the expansion and stagnation of employment, particularly in industry. Industrial specialization based on local natural assets and location lost out when major branches of Swedish industry appeared in many cities; cities which in many cases faced the same problems during the 1970s recession. Although Landskrona is in this way a good illustration of a Swedish industrial city, it also has characteristics peculiar to itself, as do the other cities. It follows the same trends and variations as the other cities but is in some cases at the lower end of the distribution, such as in earnings and education. To understand its development, we therefore need knowledge of both its general economic development and the specific contexts.

Acknowledgments

We thank Karolina Pantazatou for her excellent research assistance, and Martin Önnerfors, Jonas Helgertz, Finn Hedefalk, Kirk Scott, and Chris Smith for providing data, maps, and tabulations. A previous version of this chapter appeared as a working paper, Dribe and Svensson (2019), and a shorter version was previously published in Swedish in Dribe and Svensson (2020).

Appendix
Landskrona-Specific Tables and Figures

Table A2.1 Number of workers in the shipyard industry in Landskrona, 1875–1983.

Year	N	Year	N	Year	N
1875	47	1915	44	1955	1,197
1880	74	1920	1,128	1960	1,667
1885	30	1925	354	1965	1,539
1890	28	1930	543	1970	c. 2,400
1895	11	1935	443	1975	c. 3,500
1900	24	1940	913	1979	3,043
1905	31	1945	952	1982	1,788
1910	25	1950	965	1983	c. 400

Sources: For 1875–1910, BiSOS (D) Fabriker och manufakturer; for 1915–1965, SOS Industri; and for 1970–1983 Jönsson (1997), and Varvshistoriska föreningen.

Table A2.2 Number of workers in the sugar industry in Landskrona, 1865–1965.

Year	N	Year	N	Year	N
1865	103	1900	362	1935	606
1870	150	1905	379	1940	775
1875	149	1910	436	1945	618
1880	286	1915	428	1950	443
1885	449	1920	474	1955	273
1890	592	1925	525	1960	173
1895	685	1930	565	1965	0

Sources: For 1865–1910, BiSOS (D) Fabriker och manufakturer; and for 1915–1965: SOS Industri.

Table A2.3 Industrial structure of Landskrona 1910–1990 (shares of workers per sector), percent.

	Metal/machine	Stone	Wood	Paper/pulp	Food	Textiles/leather	Chemical	Electricity	Other
1910	20.8	1.5	3.1	2.1	37.8	28.3	4.9	1.6	0.0
1915	32.6	1.4	5.5	2.4	34.1	15.3	6.2	2.5	0.0
1920	58.2	0.6	4.5	1.8	16.0	10.1	7.4	1.4	0.0
1925	32.0	1.3	2.7	2.8	31.1	16.0	11.6	2.4	0.0
1930	37.7	0.9	2.2	2.5	26.2	17.4	11.1	2.0	0.0
1935	32.9	0.5	3.2	2.1	21.4	28.2	10.1	1.5	0.0
1940	37.8	0.2	2.1	2.1	20.5	27.6	8.4	1.4	0.0
1945	46.7	0.3	1.0	3.2	17.3	16.8	13.0	1.7	0.0
1950	46.3	0.1	1.0	4.0	13.3	21.5	12.1	1.7	0.0
1955	57.8	0.1	0.8	4.6	10.1	15.1	9.8	1.7	0.0
1960	65.7	0.1	0.6	6.0	6.0	12.7	9.0	0.0	0.0
1965	63.8	0.1	0.7	7.7	2.2	16.2	9.4	0.0	0.0
1970	65.1	0.0	0.9	7.4	3.9	11.8	10.8	0.0	0.0
1975	66.6	0.0	0.7	7.6	3.2	7.3	12.3	0.0	2.3
1980	68.1	0.0	0.4	8.4	3.4	2.5	13.8	0.0	3.4
1985	55.6	0.0	1.8	12.9	4.7	1.7	19.3	0.0	4.1
1990	59.2	0.0	0.8	13.3	1.9	0.9	17.9	0.0	5.9

Sources: For 1910–1960, SOS Industri; for 1970–1990, SOS Folk- och Bostadsräkningen.

Table A2.4 Net in-migration (per 1,000 population) to Landskrona, 1910–2017.

	Net in-mig		Net in-mig		Net in-mig
1910		1950	−1.72	1990	12.75
1911	1.18	1951	1.82	1991	3.35
1912	1.83	1952	6.71	1992	−6.11
1913	−5.69	1953	0.35	1993	6.32
1914	−12.86	1954	−5.2	1994	38.89
1915	0.6	1955	8.33	1995	6.8
1916	25.28	1956	16.66	1996	−2.54
1917	35.85	1957	28.05	1997	−5.81
1918		1958		1998	−1.13
1919		1959		1999	5.74
1920		1960		2000	13.77
1921		1961		2001	16.71
1922		1962	2.86	2002	6.51
1923		1963	−5.05	2003	6.07
1924	−12.81	1964	−2.92	2004	10.48
1925	−19.66	1965	3.25	2005	10.49
1926	−25.62	1966	9	2006	17.14
1927	−21.18	1967	−0.06	2007	8.78
1928	−3.68	1968	−5.59	2008	10.46
1929	3.25	1969	0.81	2009	6.46
1930	2.21	1970	17.01	2010	10.63
1931	7.96	1971	4.63	2011	8.37
1932	8.58	1972	1.47	2012	6.51
1933	−1.01	1973	−5.6	2013	9.83
1934	8.53	1974	1.6	2014	9.83
1935	11.27	1975	8.4	2015	6.08
1936	15.84	1976	−12.65	2016	13.1
1937	6.85	1977	−2.8	2017	10.92
1938	10.93	1978	−9.35		
1939	16.03	1979	−9.05		
1940	16.33	1980	−12.84		

(continued)

Table A2.4 Continued

	Net in-mig		Net in-mig		Net in-mig
1941	10.67	1981	−5.33		
1942	4.39	1982	−5.21		
1943	10.71	1983	−5.58		
1944	16.38	1984	−5.77		
1945	4.91	1985	1.02		
1946	15.27	1986	−0.28		
1947	9.13	1987	3.74		
1948	6.65	1988	3.42		
1949	8.63	1989	12.24		

Sources: SOS Befolkningsrörelsen 1911–2017.

Table A2.5 Age-specific mortality rates (per 1,000 population) 1875–1935. Men and women in Landskrona.

	Age 1–4 years		Age 40–59 years		Age 60+ years	
	Men	Women	Men	Women	Men	Women
1875	20.28	13.89	22.84	7.13	56.75	54.05
1876	26.50	13.60	16.86	7.02	48.93	39.21
1877	54.14	68.81	14.40	4.94	44.42	40.07
1878	14.86	26.07	24.00	6.81	34.79	59.16
1879	22.71	14.78	22.39	13.30	61.45	37.21
1880	18.82	12.85	19.46	9.41	30.61	34.56
1881	26.47	31.24	11.63	9.20	21.49	19.53
1882	25.89	18.31	10.39	7.23	24.44	32.06
1883	42.68	35.63	22.38	7.07	46.82	45.33
1884	46.56	39.86	14.72	3.41	25.51	34.36
1885	18.36	15.14	14.59	10.26	32.33	16.54
1886	5.32	5.48	13.22	13.27	34.33	32.99
1887	10.54	16.26	15.97	8.25	38.71	37.84
1888	12.22	12.55	8.44	6.59	41.26	46.73

Table A2.5 Continued

	Age 1–4 years		Age 40–59 years		Age 60+ years	
	Men	Women	Men	Women	Men	Women
1889	25.82	28.25	13.94	10.60	41.69	33.45
1890	36.85	60.05	15.44	9.56	43.09	37.26
1891	21.54	23.79	18.78	6.27	34.16	46.30
1892	36.35	22.06	10.65	10.11	42.65	56.49
1893	31.23	37.19	13.18	12.31	29.81	36.09
1894	29.47	38.79	7.84	6.10	33.60	33.03
1895	17.74	28.28	6.83	7.47	39.63	29.74
1896	25.44	27.90	13.39	9.52	34.72	31.44
1897	24.02	19.85	5.86	5.86	52.90	31.54
1898	10.95	16.18	11.39	5.70	40.63	39.47
1899	44.66	47.82	19.90	18.12	71.64	108.55
1900	3.04	12.58	14.04	4.10	46.86	47.48
1901	22.39	13.91	11.48	8.71	43.48	30.03
1902	13.23	18.27	9.03	11.86	44.06	47.84
1903	11.56	7.48	9.60	9.70	48.20	29.94
1904	14.30	14.80	17.50	6.39	40.33	39.43
1905	25.43	11.70	10.07	10.08	49.48	40.83
1906	12.46	14.35	12.71	7.42	41.38	42.87
1907	9.82	10.19	14.33	6.29	50.33	46.37
1908	8.16	12.73	8.35	6.11	33.69	26.23
1909	6.79	5.66	15.30	8.56	39.43	36.49
1910	13.19	20.62	11.49	8.33	40.52	51.78
1911	8.21	4.28	7.59	9.74	42.65	35.37
1912	4.11	1.43	4.76	13.23	47.89	33.15
1913	4.14	8.62	6.74	6.57	43.09	44.90
1914	5.60	5.83	4.04	9.56	48.84	41.31
1915	4.22	5.85	10.64	8.28	30.41	51.91
1916	6.97		8.29	10.84	36.77	41.98

(continued)

Table A2.5 Continued

	Age 1–4 years		Age 40–59 years		Age 60+ years	
	Men	Women	Men	Women	Men	Women
1917	5.48	5.70	9.71	7.10	55.62	45.01
1918	8.12	11.27	11.04	11.04	41.45	51.13
1919	6.66	6.93	8.86	6.54	40.46	40.39
1920	6.62	8.27	11.72	7.79	36.25	41.12
1921	6.67	5.56	9.01	5.83	32.43	31.45
1922	2.70	1.41	7.93	6.32	17.95	40.18
1923	1.39	2.89	8.59	3.96	29.13	33.40
1924	8.43	2.92	5.35	4.46	41.74	37.81
1925		7.44	4.31	3.00	45.58	44.05
1926	4.55	9.36	9.75	7.55	38.02	45.91
1927	1.60	4.89	9.23	7.58	51.72	44.56
1928	5.00	6.71	8.05	7.00	51.69	48.81
1929	3.46	3.44	8.98	10.86	57.14	45.86
1930	5.36	3.51	8.29	6.29	53.86	41.85
1931	10.90	7.22	10.67	9.03	55.76	75.44
1932	3.67	1.85	9.42	4.64	42.07	43.43
1933		1.91	8.80	7.33	46.07	45.27
1934			9.57	7.63	49.62	57.86
1935	1.92	2.00	10.74	3.51	56.29	53.09

Source: Swedish Official Statistics (SOS) Befolkningsrörelsen 1911–2017. 1911–1961 is the city of Landskrona, from 1962, it is Landskrona municipality.

Notes

1. Halmstad is a town in Halland county and should not be confused with Halmstad in Malmöhus county, which is one of the five parishes, see Chapter 1.
2. The company seems to have had rather fluctuating fortunes: it was not listed in the 1870 registers; in 1875, it had seventy-one employees and a production value of almost 78,000 kronor with 148 ships undergoing repairs; in 1890, thirty workers were employed at the shipyard, which repaired 155 ships during the year for a total production value of 55,000 kronor.
3. It is possible that the share of women is underrecorded given that some women performed industrial work at home, particularly in textiles. However, for at least one factory producing gloves, the records explicitly mention that half of the registered female workforce worked from home.
4. The CDR is the total number of deaths divided by the mean population in the year.
5. BiSOS A 1880, part I, tab. 16, causes of death under age 10 for towns in Malmöhus county.
6. The CBR is the total number births divided by the mean population in the year. We do not have access to age-specific data at the city level, and we can therefore not derive total fertility rates.

Sources

Arbetsstatistik utgiven av K. Kommerskollegii afdelning för arbetsstatistik, 1899–1913 https://www.scb.se/hitta-statistik/aldre-statistik/innehall/annan-historisk-statistik/arbetsstatistik-utgifven-af-k.-kommerskollegii-afdelning-for-arbetsstatistik-18991913/
    A:2 Undersökning av tobaksindustrin (1899).
    A:3 Undersökning af den mekaniska verkstadsindustrien i Sverige. Större egentliga mekaniska verkstäder (1901).

Bidrag till Sveriges Officiella Statistik (BiSOS).
    A: *Befolkningsstatistik* (1875–1910).
    D: *Fabriker och manufakturer* (1865–1910).
    K: *Hälso och sjukvården* (1875–1910).
    P: *Undervisningsväsendet* (1900–1910), *Folkskolorna*.
    P: *Undervisningsväsendet* (1900–1910). *Allm. Läroverken*.
    U: *Kommunernas fattigvård och finanser* (1910–1914: 1).

Registerbaserad arbetsmarknadsstatistik (RAMS), https://www.scb.se/hitta-statistik/statistik-efter-amne/arbetsmarknad/sysselsattning-forvarvsarbete-och-arbetstider/registerbaserad-arbetsmarknadsstatistik-rams/

Förvärvsarbetande 16+ år med arbetsplats i regionen (dagbefolkning) (RAMS) efter region, näringsgren SNI92 och kön, år 1990–2003.

Sveriges Officiella Statistik (SOS) https://www.scb.se/sv_/Hitta-statistik/ Historisk-statistik/Digitaliserat—Statistik-efter-serie/Sveriges-officiella-statistik-SOS-utg-1912-/
    Allmän hälso-och sjukvård (1911–1935).
    Befolkningsrörelsen (1911–2017).
    Folkräkningen (1910–1960).
    Folk och bostadsräkningen (1970–1990).
    Industri och bergshantering (1911–1968).
    Löner (1929–2003).
        Lönestatistisk årsbok för Sverige (1929–1951).
    Socialtjänst (1918–1996).
        Fattigvården (1918–1956).
        Socialhjälpen (1957–1960).
    Valstatistik (1871–1999).
        Kommunala valen (1919–1966).
        Allmänna valen, del 2: Kommunala valen (1970–1998).

Statens offentliga utredningar (SOU) 1949: 2, *Norrlandskommitténs principbetänkande, Andra delen. Särskilda utredningar,* Stockholm 1949.

Valmyndigheten, valresultat kommunala valen 2002–2018: https://www.val.se/valresultat.html, accessed May 6, 2019.

Varvshistoriska föreningen i Landskrona: http://www.varvshistoriska.com/?p=visa-nyhetartikel&n=oresundsvarvet-1915, accessed April 1, 2019.

Öresundsvarvet, https://varv100.se/nedlaeggningen.html, accessed May 28, 2019.

References

Bengtsson, T., M. Dribe, L. Quaranta, and P. Svensson. 2018. "The Scanian Economic Demographic Database. Version 6.2 (Machine-readable database)." Lund: Lund University, Centre for Economic Demography.

Bonniers konversationslexikon (1937–1949). [Bonnier's Conversation Dictionary (1937–1949]. Stockholm: Alb. Bonniers bokförlag.

Dribe, M. 2009. "Demand and Supply Factors in the Fertility Transition: A County Level Analysis of Age-Specific Marital Fertility in Sweden 1880–1930." *European Review of Economic History* 13 (1): 65–94.

Dribe, M. and P. Svensson. 2019. "Landskrona 1900–2000: A Comparative Analysis of the Economic and Demographic Development." Lund Papers in Economic Demography 2019: 3. Lund University: Centre for Economic Demography.
Dribe, M., and P. Svensson. 2020. "Den industrialiserade staden. [The Industrialized City]." In *RJ:s årsbox 2020*. Staden [RJ's Year Box 2020], edited by J. Björkman and P. Hadenius. Göteborg and Stockholm: Makadam förlag.
Engberg, E. 2005. *I fattiga omständigheter. Fattigvårdens former och understödstagare i Skellefteå socken under 1800-talet* [In Poor Circumstances. Poor Relief Policy and Paupers in Skellefteå Parish, Sweden, in the Nineteenth Century]. Umeå: Department of Historical Studies.
Eriksson, B., and M. Stanfors. 2015. "A Winning Strategy? The Employment of Women and Firm Longevity during Industrialization." *Business History* 57 (7): 988–1004.
Gerger, C. 1992. *Där nöden var som störst. En studie av fattigdom och fattigvård i en småländsk landsbygdssocken 1835–1915* [Poverty in Locknevi: A Country Parish in Småland, 1835–1915]. Stockholm: Kulturgeografiska institutionen.
Helgertz, J., and M. Önnerfors. 2019. "Public Water and Sewerage Investments and the Urban Mortality Decline in Sweden 1875–1930." *The History of the Family* 24 (2): 307–333.
Jönsson, Å. 1993. *Historien om en stad. Del 1: Landskrona 1413–1804* [The History of a Town. Part 1: Landskrona 1413–1804]. Landskrona: Landskrona kommun.
Jönsson, Å. 1995. *Historien om en stad. Del 2: Landskrona 1805–1899* [The History of a Town. Part 1: Landskrona 1805–1899]. Landskrona: Landskrona kommun.
Jönsson, Å. 1997. *Historien om en stad. Del 3: Landskrona 1900–1997* [The History of a Town. Part 1: Landskrona 1900–1997]. Landskrona: Landskrona kommun.
Kuuse, J. 1982. *Sockerbolaget Cardo, 1907–1982* [The Sugar Company Cardo, 1907–1982]. Malmö: Sockerbolaget Cardo.
Lundh, C. 2012. "Wage Forms, Cost of Living and the Urban-Rural Wage Gap: Southern Sweden, 1881–1930." *Scandinavian Economic History Review* 60 (2): 123–145.
Marx, K. 1887. *Capital: A Critique of Political Economy. Volume I. The Process of Production of Capital*. Moscow: Progress Publishers.
Nationalencyklopedin. 1989–1996. Höganäs: Bra Böcker AB.
Sandström, G. 2014. "The Mid-Twentieth Century Baby Boom in Sweden: Changes in the Educational Gradient of Fertility for Women Born 1915–1950." *The History of the Family* 19 (1): 120–140.
Schön, L. 2010. *Sweden's Road to Modernity. An Economic History*. Stockholm: SNS.
Stanfors, M. 2003. *Education, Labor Force Participation and Changing Fertility Patterns: A Study of Women and Socioeconomic Change in Twentieth Century Sweden*. Stockholm: Almqvist & Wiksell International.
Statistics Sweden. 1999. *Befolkningsutvecklingen under 250 år. Historisk statistik för Sverige* [Population Development in Sweden in a 250-Year Perspective: Historical Statistics of Sweden]. Stockholm: SCB.
Van Bavel, J., and D. S. Reher. 2013. "The Baby Boom and Its Causes: What We Know and What We Need to Know." *Population and Development Review* 39 (2): 257–288.
Wallengren, H. 2014. *Socialdemokrater möter invandrare. Arbetarrörelsen, invandrarna och främlingsfientligheten i Landskrona under efterkrigstiden* [Social Democrats Meet Immigrants: The Labor Movement, the Immigrants, and Xenophobia]. Lund: Nordic Academic Press.

3
Economic Inequality and Social Mobility

Gabriel Brea-Martinez and Martin Dribe

Introduction

The industrialization and development of capitalist societies have historically been connected to changes in social and economic inequality and to social mobility. Industrialization thoroughly transformed occupational structure. Occupations related to manufacturing and services increased, while those in agriculture declined, first in relative terms and then, ultimately, also in absolute terms. At the same time, managerial, administrative, and highly qualified technical occupations increased in importance, leading to an expansion of the white-collar middle class. The development of this new middle class was particularly strong in urban areas, while the old middle class of artisans and tradesmen connected to rural areas and small towns declined in importance (Dribe et al. 2015).

The new conditions brought about by industrialization led to changing patterns of social mobility. Compared with preindustrial times, industrial society saw higher social mobility as a result of increasing downward mobility at first, as people went from farms to factories, and of mainly upward mobility thereafter, as the new middle class recruited workers born in the working class (Grusky and Hauser 1984; Lipset and Zetterberg 1956). The expansion of new higher-status positions almost automatically increased absolute social mobility, but it did not necessarily mean that society became more open by increasing social mobility in a relative sense net of the changes in occupational structure. Several influential studies have found rather similar levels of openness (relative mobility) in different industrial societies at different levels of economic development and economic growth (Erikson and Goldthorpe 1992; Featherman et al. 1975), thus questioning a universal connection between industrial development and social mobility.

Despite these empirical findings, it has been argued that labor recruitment became increasingly based on personal achievement rather than inherited assets (ascription), thus limiting occupational and social inheritance and promoting social mobility (Treiman 1970). This process gained strength with the dramatic expansion of higher education around the middle of the twentieth century.

However, there were also other barriers to upward social mobility as high-status parents turned to means other than bequests to try to maintain the status of their children. Pierre Bourdieu, for example, argued the importance of the role of transmission of social and cultural capital in creating such barriers (Bourdieu and Passeron 1999).

A previous study of five rural parishes near Landskrona found that both absolute and relative mobility increased from the late nineteenth century to 1970, mainly as a result of increasing upward mobility (Dribe et al. 2015). Formal education and meritocracy became more important over time for entering the middle class, but this process was related more to the maturing of an industrial economy than to the early stages of industrialization.

Seen from a cross-country perspective, higher socioeconomic mobility is related to lower levels of economic inequality—what American economist Alan Kreuger labeled "the Great Gatsby curve" after F. Scott Fitzgerald's 1925 novel (see Corak 2013). Empirical research has also shown that economic inequality (income and/or wealth) decreased during the maturation of industrial society in most Western countries, including Sweden (Piketty 2018; Roine and Waldenström 2008). Inequality, as measured by the share of total income earned by the top 1 or top 10 percent, declined from the early twentieth century until about 1980. Since 1980, it has increased in most countries, including Sweden. In a broad sense, income inequality reflects how resources and opportunities are distributed among individuals. When seen in combination with social and economic transformations in society, income inequality provides insights into the nature of opportunities for, and barriers to, social mobility.

This chapter describes and discusses the long-term trends in socioeconomic disparity in Landskrona over the entire twentieth century. We analyze income inequality and intergenerational income mobility and relate these outcomes to the development of the industrial economy of the city and its immediate environs, and we compare this development to that in Sweden in general for the period when such a comparison is possible.

We analyze income inequality using the Gini coefficient and the share of total income of top earners (top 1 percent). This gives an indication of the level of income concentration and the nature of its development from industrialization to deindustrialization. To better understand the likely mechanisms underlying the changes in inequality, we study the development of disparity by gender and social class. Finally, we analyze the long-term development of intergenerational income mobility in Landskrona by both measuring its persistence and calculating the magnitude of upward income mobility. Besides providing a necessary background to the socioeconomic development of Landskrona in the twentieth century, this chapter also contributes to research on inequality and social mobility more generally by offering a more detailed analysis than is possible to conduct at the national level.

Occupation, Social Class, and Income

The data from the Scanian Economic-Demographic Database (SEDD; Bengtsson et al. 2021) and the linked national registers (see Chapter 1) enabled us to follow an individual's income and occupation over time and across generations during the entire period of study. We measured social class based on occupation using the Historical International Social Class Scheme (HISCLASS; Van Leeuwen and Maas 2011; see Chapter 1 for a more detailed description).

Information on income came from the income and taxation registers based on individual tax returns (see Helgertz et al. 2020). Income was defined as the total income from sources related to labor (including self-employment but excluding income from capital and real estate). All income data were inflation-adjusted using the consumer price index (Statistics Sweden 2020). In the registers, income was reported in accordance with the tax law, which established different thresholds for tax exemption (see Helgertz et al. 2020 for a detailed description). The share of individuals without a registered income due to fiscal exemption in Landskrona varied over time and was higher during the early periods. For instance, in 1905–1929 an average of 12 percent of men of working age had an income below the threshold, a figure which decreased to only 6 percent between 1930 and 1949, and finally to less than 3–4 percent from the 1950s onward (Debiasi et al. 2023).

We had annual income for the five parishes for the entire period but for Landskrona only from 1947. Before this year, we had information at five-year intervals and imputed data for the missing years. In the imputation, we used available income information (from the previous and next closest years) and occupational information from the Historical International Standard Classification of Occupations (HISCO; Van Leeuwen et al. 2002) for men of working age (18–64) and single women within the same age range.[1]

Social Stratification in Landskrona

The social structure changed markedly in this area during the study period. Figure 3.1, panel A, shows that medium-skilled workers constituted the largest social class for men in Landskrona during the first three-quarters of the twentieth century (1905–1974). Together with the lower-skilled workers, they constituted almost 50 percent of the male labor force. Unskilled workers represented the third

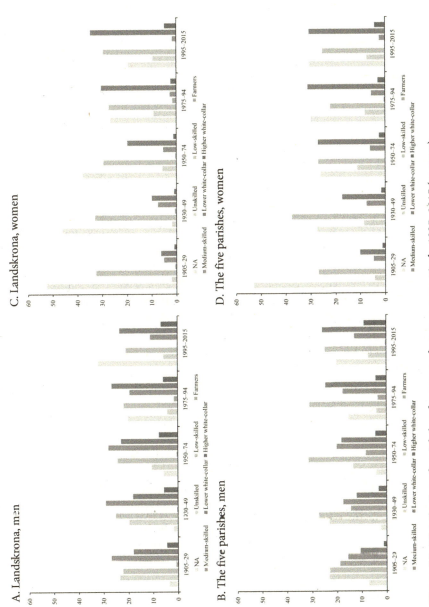

Figure 3.1 Distribution of social class for men and women respectively, 1905–2015 (percent). Income data for women available from 1947.

Source: Scanian Economic-Demographic Database (SEDD; Bengtsson et al. 2021).

largest social class at the beginning of the century but declined, especially after 1975. This decline is in line with both the city's general economic development and Sweden as a whole, whereby the importance of unskilled labor decreased and the importance of skilled and educated labor increased. We see the opposite trends for the white-collar classes, especially the lower white-collar workers, who progressively increased to become the largest social class after 1975.

Landskrona's economic and occupational change is in line with Sweden's national and regional development. Figure 3.1, panel B, shows the social structure for men in the five parishes. Until the mid-1970s, the occupational structure differed markedly from that in Landskrona, mainly due to a higher share of farmers and unskilled workers. The increase in the importance of white-collar workers (lower white-collar) from 1975 onward is then similar to that in Landskrona.

Moreover, Figure 3.1 shows that the social structure of women changed in both Landskrona (panel C) and the five parishes (panel D), an observation based on their own recorded occupations. However, we should bear in mind some specific characteristics regarding the female labor force. First, up until the 1950s, women with a registered occupation were usually single and relatively young and often working in lower-skilled jobs. Not until the 1960s was there an expansion in the gainful employment of married women (Stanfors and Goldscheider 2017).

It is also important to note the high share of women with missing occupations (NA) during the first three-quarters of the twentieth century. This is mainly due to the low participation rates of married women (Silenstam 1970) but could also be due in part to poor-quality recording of women's occupations, as has been the case in other historical contexts (Humphries and Sarasúa 2012). Overall, women's occupational structure in Landskrona and in the five parishes followed a similar path over much of the period studied. It is noticeable that the distribution of occupations was concentrated mainly on low-skilled workers and lower white-collar workers from the 1970s onward.

To better understand the change in the social structure over time and its differences by gender, Table 3.1 depicts the three most common occupations in each social class across periods. At the top of the table, we can see the main occupations held by higher white-collar workers. For men (panel A) in the period 1905–1974, this class was dominated by engineers and industrial managers, indicating the importance of industry in Landskrona, most notably the shipyard (see Chapter 2). For women in this class (panel B), occupations connected to education (e.g., teachers) were the most common. However, from the 1970s onward, men and women in the highest class had more similar occupations, these being in education, public administration, computer systems, and financial management. The lower white-collar workers saw the fewest changes in occupational composition across time and by gender. This social class was made up

Table 3.1 Top three occupational titles by social class and period for men (A) and women (B) in Landskrona, 1905–2015.

A. Men

HISCLASS	1905–1929	%	1930–1949	%	1950–1974	%	1975–1994	%	1995–2015	%
Higher status white-collar	Engineer	25	Engineer	28	Engineer	30	Manager retail	14	Computer system designer	9
	Military officer	11	Industry manager	13	Industry manager	13	Sec. educ teacher	11	Manager retail	8
	Industry manager	9	Accountant	6	Accountant	6	Manager finance	7	Sec. educ teacher	8
Lower status white-collar	Clerk	16	Clerk	15	Clerk	10	Mechanical technician	16	Stock clerk	10
	Lower military officer	9	Retailer	11	Retailer	9	Stock clerk	11	Salesperson	9
	Retailer	8	Clerical supervision	7	Clerical supervision	9	Commercial rep.	10	Building caretaker	8
Medium-skilled	Carpenter	14	Carpenter	11	Sheet-metal worker	14	Sheet-metal worker	19	Metal assembler	12
	Blacksmith	8	Sheet-metal worker	10	Carpenter	10	Machinery assembler	17	Carpenter	11
	Tailor	7	Lathe setter-operator	5	Machinery assembler	8	Electrician	10	Car mechanics	11

(continued)

Table 3.1 Continued

HISCLASS	1905–1929	%	1930–1949	%	1950–1974	%	1975–1994	%	1995–2015	%
Lower-skilled	Soldier	20	Welder	8	Driver	11	Machine-tool operator	15	Machine-tool operator	15
	Welder	9	Driver	8	Gas-pipe fitter	10	Welder	14	Printing-machine operator	12
	Building painter	8	Sugar refiner	7	Construction worker	8	Truck driver	12	Truck driver	12
Unskilled	Seaman	30	Laborer	33	Factory worker	30	Gardener	37	Cleaner	20
	Laborer	23	Factory worker	24	Laborer	27	Ship's deck crew	21	Laborer manufacturing	20
	Factory worker	16	Warehouse porter	13	Warehouse porter	19	Cleaner	17	Gardener	16

B. Women

HISCLASS	1905–1929	%	1930–1949	%	1950–1974	%	1975–1994	%	1995–2015	%
Higher status white-collar	Teacher	25	Teacher	19	Journalist	18	Sec. educ. teacher	24	Sec. educ. teacher	16
	Tech. educ. teacher	6	Journalist	7	Sec. educ. teacher	9	Manager retail	16	Public serv. admin.	8
	General nursing teacher	6	Tech. educ. teacher	6	Teacher	5	Manager finance	6	Manager retail	8
Lower status white-collar	Retail trade	27	Retail trade	32	Clerk	28	Office clerk	28	Salesperson	15
	Clerk	15	Clerk	23	Retail trade	26	Salesperson	16	Office clerk	12
	Other retail trade	11	Other retail trade	6	Prim. educ. teacher	5	Book-keeping clerk	6	Pre-primary teacher	9
Medium-skilled	Housekeeper (supervision)	56	Housekeeper (supervision)	57	Housekeeper (supervision)	44	Machinery assembler	27	Metal assembler	26
	Cook	10	Cook	5	Bookbinder	15	Sewing-machine operator	18	Cook	21
	Milliner	8	Baker	11	Cook	8	Cook	8	Electrical mechanic	12

(*continued*)

Table 3.1 Continued

HISCLASS	1905–1929	%	1930–1949	%	1950–1974	%	1975–1994	%	1995–2015	%
Lower-skilled	House servant	44	House servant	32	Seamstress	31	Personal care	30	Home-based personal care	31
	Personal maid	21	Seamstress	25	House servant	15	Child-care	14	Personal care	26
	Sewer	16	Personal maid	11	Nursing aid	7	Home-based personal care	12	Child-care	13
Unskilled	Factory worker	63	Factory worker	35	Char worker	33	Office cleaner	83	Office cleaner	78
	Char worker	20	Char worker	22	Factory worker	25	Gardener	11	Manufacturing worker	7
	Cook aid	5	Warehouse porter	19	Warehouse porter	25	Messenger	3	Gardener	4

Source: Scanian Economic-Demographic Database (SEDD; Bengtsson et al. 2021).

mainly of different kinds of clerks and office workers and occupations related to commerce.

Among skilled workers, carpentry was one of the most common occupations for men in all periods. Similarly, occupations connected to industry and factory production were also common in several periods (e.g., metal sheet workers and machine assemblers). Until the 1970s, in Landskrona the most important skilled occupations for women were related to services such as food or housekeeping supervision. It is only from the mid-1970s that occupations related to machinery and mechanics became as important for women as for men in this social class.

For lower-skilled workers, men show the most radical change in occupational composition over time. While during the first three decades of the twentieth century work as welders, building painters, and soldiers was important for these classes, occupations related to transportation and factory work (drivers, truck drivers, and machine operators) were more important in the final periods. For women, there were fewer changes in the lower-skilled occupations, these being mostly related to domestic services and caretaking.

Finally, among male unskilled workers there was an important transformation over time. For instance, while "seaman" was the most common occupation in this group in the first period, factory workers and unspecified laborers became predominant by mid-century. Today, gardeners and cleaners are among the most common unskilled occupations. For women, factory workers and warehouse porters were typical choices in the first three-quarters of the century, and, as with men, gardeners and cleaners have been important occupations since the mid-1970s.

Overall, there was remarkable occupational diversification in the white-collar classes during the period of our analysis. Before 1950, the top three occupations in each class constituted almost 50 percent of all occupations, but, since the 1970s, these have only made up 30–35 percent. Moreover, all social classes benefited from a significant rise in mean income (Appendix, Tables A3.1 and A3.2). However, simply looking at the overall trend hides important differences by class, location, and gender, which we study in more detail in the next section.

Income Inequality

We turn now to an analysis of income inequality between individuals. To do this we used Gini coefficients, basing our calculations on individual-level total labor income. The Gini coefficient ranges from 0 (complete equality) to 1 (complete inequality).[2] In addition to the Gini coefficient, we also measured income inequality between individuals using the share of income earned by the top

1 percent. The purpose is to chart the way economic accumulation influenced disparity in Landskrona in the long run.

In addition, we identified economic disparity by social class and gender by measuring different sets of median income gaps to describe the relative disparity between classes in the different periods analyzed. This measure informs us, for instance, about how much more in percentage terms the occupational group with the highest status (e.g., higher white-collar workers) earned than other groups in a given period.

Figure 3.2 shows the Gini coefficients for those age 20–64 in Landskrona for men and women separately. We can distinguish three main phases with marked income inequality patterns from these figures. From 1905 to 1929, there were substantial fluctuations in income inequality. The Gini coefficient increased and decreased for short spells during the period of economic growth but was also affected by the brief recession in the 1920s. During this period the yearly percentage change shows a widely fluctuating pattern. In fact, if we average the annual percentage changes for the entire period, there is no trend at all. Similarly high volatility is found in wealth inequality at the national level, especially for the time around World War I (Roine and Waldenström 2008). Moreover, one should take into account that, prior to the 1920s, the first industrial expansion to take place in Landskrona was related to its shipyard, which attracted both specialized and unskilled workers, contributing to high levels of income disparity (see Chapter 2).

There was a remarkable decline in the Gini coefficient from 0.46 in 1930 to 0.26 in 1949, showing for the first time lower levels of inequality than in the five parishes. Overall, the average yearly percentage changes between 1930 and 1939 show a clear decrease in inequality of about 2.4 percentage points. Again, this pattern of decline is in line with the development at the national level regarding the decline in inequality, the emergence of the welfare state, and an overall equalization of economic growth between Swedish regions (Henning et al. 2011; Roine and Waldenström 2009).

Between 1950 and the early 1990s, Sweden experienced an initial period of rapid economic growth followed from the 1970s onward by a deindustrialization process and weak economic growth (Schön 2010). The period of economic downturn in particular had a major effect on Landskrona. However, economic inequality did not change much in this period. Despite a degree of change during the oil crisis of the early 1970s, inequality in Landskrona only declined slightly until the mid-1980s, coinciding with national levels (Domeij and Flodén 2010). However, the overall trend was relatively flat, with an average annual increase in the Gini coefficient of 0.5 percentage points. This relatively flat pattern in

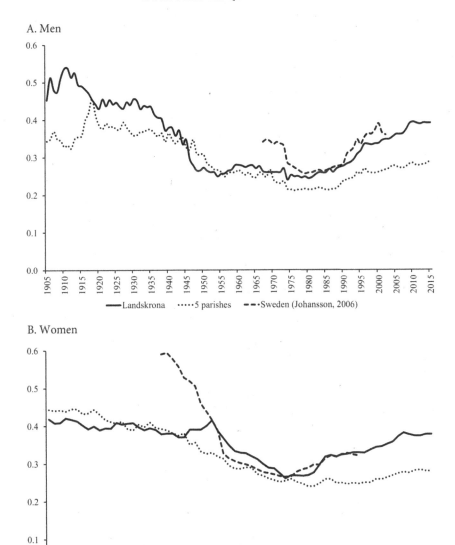

Figure 3.2 Gini coefficients for total income for men (A) and women (B) age 20–64, 1905–2015.

Source: Scanian Economic-Demographic Database (SEDD; Bengtsson et al. 2021).

economic disparity was also seen nationally as income concentration remained fairly constant between 1950 and 1975 (Roine and Waldenström 2008).

Finally, in the last period from 1990, income inequality increased monotonically with an average annual increase of 1.4 percentage points. This development is similar to that in Sweden as a whole and in most other developed countries (Alvaredo et al. 2013; Johansson 2006; Nielsen and Alderson 1997). As a result, the Gini coefficient in 2010 reached the same levels as before World War II.

The temporal change in inequality over time in Landskrona is highly similar to the level and development for Sweden as a whole for the period when data are available (see Figure 3.2). These similar patterns highlight the contribution of our historical analysis for Landskrona, showing how income inequality between individuals evolved in Sweden before 1968, when national-level data become available.

Figure 3.3 shows the share of income earned by the economic elites (top 1 percent) and helps us to understand the driving forces behind the high inequality observed in the first half of the twentieth century and its progressive decline until the 1970s, after which the share remained fairly stable at around 5 percent. Until about 1940, the income concentration of the top 1 percent accounted for much of the income disparity in Landskrona, with around 15 percent of income earned by this group. This concentration of income among the economic elites was similar at the national level (Roine and Waldenström 2008). Interestingly, the first years of the 1920s showed the highest levels of inequality, coinciding with the first shipyard crisis in Landskrona, which led to increasing unemployment rates and severely affected the city's economy (see Chapter 2).

A number of factors accounted for and characterized the patterns of inequality in Landskrona across the twentieth century. Among these, gender differences in income radically changed during the 1960s. Figure 3.4 displays the gender gap in lifetime income for cohorts of men and women born between 1920 and 1969 (average income at ages 40–49). Overall, the total gender gap (the dashed black line) decreased monotonically from around 70 percent for the 1920–1929 cohort to 22 percent for those born in 1960–1969. These trends align with empirical findings at the national level since the 1980s (Edin and Richardson 2002).

However, the changes were not equal across the entire income distribution. A breakdown of the information by income quintiles shows an unequal development of the gender gap. The change in the gender gap was due to shrinking differences in the poorest half of the income distribution (the first three quintiles). Conversely, among individuals with the highest incomes (Q5) the differences between men and women have been quite constant for the 1930–1939 cohort and those born thereafter. These income differentials have been interpreted as proof of the existence of a glass ceiling in Sweden, especially as seen in the upper tail of the income distribution (Albrecht et al. 2003).

ECONOMIC INEQUALITY AND SOCIAL MOBILITY   95

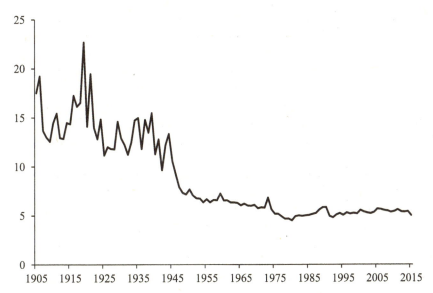

Figure 3.3 Share of income earned by the top 1 percent in Landskrona, 1905–2015.
Source: Scanian Economic-Demographic Database (SEDD; Bengtsson et al. 2021).

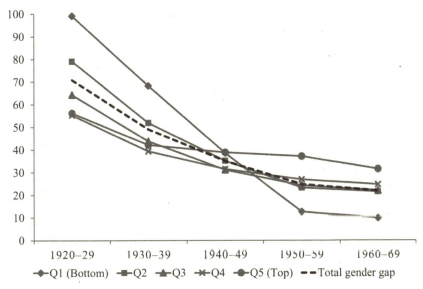

Figure 3.4 Gender gap in lifetime income by income quintile and decadal birth cohort. Men and women born 1920–1969.
Median lifetime income gap between men and women born in the same decade and by income quintile (separately by gender). Higher numbers indicate a larger gap. The cohorts born 1920–1969 were aged 40–49 (45 for the last cohort) during the period 1960–2015.
Source: Scanian Economic-Demographic Database (SEDD; Bengtsson et al. 2021).

Next, a look at inequality across social classes reinforces the argument that the general decline in inequality in Landskrona in 1905–1949 was due mainly to the shrinking impact of income shares for the economic elites. Figure 3.5 displays the median income gap between the highest class (higher white-collar) and all other classes. Between 1905 and 1949, men (Figure 3.5, panel A) in the higher white-collar class had an income 40–80 percent higher than the average for other classes, with a marked gradient ranging from lower white-collar workers to unskilled workers. From 1950 to 1994, the income gaps shrank remarkably to only 10 percent for lower white-collar workers, 20 percent for skilled and lower-skilled workers, and 40 percent for unskilled workers. In the last period, 1995–2015, the gaps increased slightly again. In the case of women (Figure 3.5, panel B), for whom we know the incomes of both married and single women since 1947, the pattern is similar to that of men in 1950–2015.

Conversely, if we repeat the same exercise, comparing Swedish-born and foreign-born in Figure 3.6, we see patterns that are the total opposite of those for social class. During most of the twentieth century, place of birth did not affect income differences. However, since the 1990s, with increasing immigration from countries such as the former Yugoslavia, income inequality by place of birth has increased dramatically for both men and women. The main reason behind this was the significantly low income of new immigrants arriving since the 1990s, in comparison to the rest of the population.

As shown in Figure 3.5, inequality decreased markedly over time, mainly due to smaller differences in income between the higher white-collar class and other classes. This equalizing process, which took place during the period 1940–1970, could be explained by the city's industrial and economic consolidation and the increase in income for the working class, which nuanced the impact of the economic elites. In addition, we observe that occupational differences in the contribution to inequality and the weight of the economic elites tend to be marginal from the 1970s onward, which indicates that the main factors driving inequality changed. These changing patterns also had a geographic component. Figure 3.7 shows the income gap between social classes in Landskrona and the five parishes. Higher positive values denote higher average incomes in the city than in the five parishes. In 1905–1949, occupations were on average better paid in Landskrona. Overall, the gap ranged from 30 to 40 percent higher incomes in the urban area than in the rural.

Interestingly, the gap among the unskilled workers in 1930–1949 was almost 50 percent higher in Landskrona. This was a period of ongoing industrialization and points to a considerable urban premium attracting unskilled workers from the rural areas to the city. However, from the 1950s onward, the differences between the two settings disappeared with a period of solid homogenization of economic growth in geographic terms in Sweden (Henning et al. 2011). Moreover,

ECONOMIC INEQUALITY AND SOCIAL MOBILITY 97

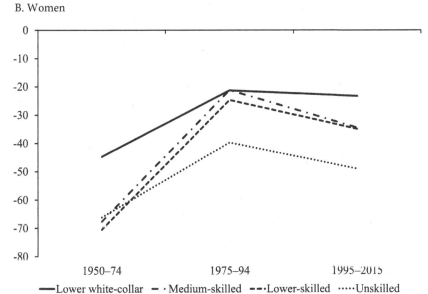

Figure 3.5 Income gap for social classes in relation to higher white-collar for men (A) and women (B) in Landskrona, 1905–2015.
Measured as the median income gap between higher white-collar workers and the other classes. More negative values indicate a larger gap.
Source: Scanian Economic-Demographic Database (SEDD; Bengtsson et al. 2021).

98 URBAN LIVES

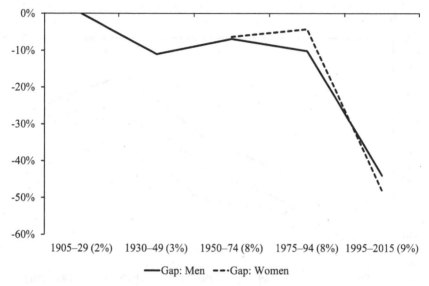

Figure 3.6 Income gap for Swedish-born and foreign-born by gender in Landskrona, 1905–2015.
Median income gap between Swedish-born and foreign-born. Larger values indicate a larger gap. The x-axis indicates different periods and in parentheses the share of foreign-born among those with a registered income.
Source: Scanian Economic-Demographic Database (SEDD; Bengtsson et al. 2021).

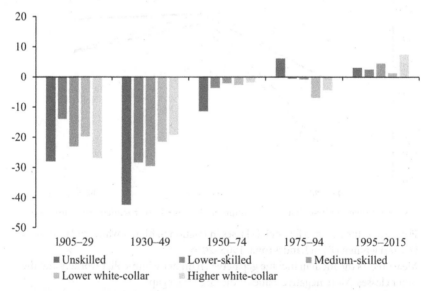

Figure 3.7 Income gap between Landskrona and the five parishes by social class, 1905–2015.
Negative values indicate higher incomes in Landskrona and positive values higher median incomes in the five parishes.
Source: Scanian Economic-Demographic Database (SEDD; Bengtsson et al. 2021).

from 1995, the gaps are switched round, showing slightly higher incomes in the five parishes, a change that is at least in part related to suburbanization.

Intergenerational Income Mobility

We measured intergenerational income mobility by focusing on the earnings of fathers and grandfathers (both paternal and maternal) and on their association with the earnings of sons and daughters by decadal birth cohorts (from the 1920s to the 1960s).

The calculations are based on a proxy for lifetime income, which is the average income at ages 40–49 for grandfathers, fathers, sons, and daughters, respectively (see Mazumder 2016). Basing our calculations on mean income, we created the percentile rank position of each individual's lifetime income by gender and year of birth and did the same for the fathers and grandfathers grouped by year of birth of (grand)sons and (grand)daughters, following the same methodology as other studies on income mobility (see Chetty et al. 2014).

Hence, social mobility was measured in two different ways. First, we computed the intergenerational rank-rank association by regressing father's and grandfather's income percentile on ego's percentile, which measured the extent to which the lifetime income of an individual was associated with the income of their ancestors, and which, in other words, captured how strong income persistence was. We display results from the regressions for the intergenerational rank-rank associations by decadal cohorts in both the full SEDD sample[3] and Landskrona. The βs are the associations, and the higher the value the lower the intergenerational income mobility.

$$y(ego)_i = \alpha + \beta_1 y(father)_i + \varepsilon_i$$

$$y(ego)_i = \alpha + \beta_1 y(father)_i + \beta_2 y(paternal\ grandfather)_i + \varepsilon_i$$

$$y(ego)_i = \alpha + \beta_1 y(father)_i + \beta_2 y(maternal\ grandfather)_i + \varepsilon_i$$

Finally, we also computed a measure of absolute upward income mobility based on inflation-adjusted lifetime income for fathers and children, which indicates the fraction of individuals who attained a higher income than their fathers.

Table 3.2 shows the results for father-son and father-daughter rank-rank associations. Overall, the association between fathers' and sons' permanent income varies little across cohorts, showing a slightly U-shaped pattern with higher

Table 3.2 Intergenerational rank-rank associations of income between fathers and children.

	Sons		Daughters	
	Full sample	Landskrona	Full sample	Landskrona
Cohort 1920–1929	0.296***	0.310***	0.117**	0.0969
N	693	504	627	470
Cohort 1930–1939	0.157***	0.111*	0.135***	0.133**
N	791	498	879	519
Cohort 1940–1949	0.200***	0.197***	0.130***	0.111**
N	4,381	1,061	4,245	929
Cohort 1950–1959	0.233***	0.240***	0.192***	0.172***
N	9,935	1,140	10,151	1,040
Cohort 1960–1965	0.265***	0.221***	0.208***	0.186***
N	15,780	1,432	15,449	1,361

Notes: ***$p < 0.01$; **$p < 0.05$; *$p < 0.1$. The coefficients displayed for each cohort correspond to a different model, and the N informs about the number of individuals analyzed at each regression model.
Source: Scanian Economic-Demographic Database (SEDD; Bengtsson et al. 2021).

values (less mobility) for the older and younger cohorts. Income elasticities were relatively low, ranging from 0.15 to 0.29. The levels and patterns over time for sons are quite similar to previous findings for Sweden and other Nordic countries over the long term (Modalsli 2017). For instance, studies of Sweden that looked at cohorts born from the 1950s onward found estimates of 0.27 (Nybom and Stuhler 2016), 0.21, and 0.23 (Björklund and Jäntti 1997; Heidrich 2017). Most of the previous research has found lower income persistence between fathers and daughters than between fathers and sons (Fortin and Lefebvre 1998; Heidrich 2017; Österberg 2000; Pascual 2009). Similarly, in Landskrona, we find slightly lower persistence for daughters than for sons, ranging from 0.12 to a maximum of 0.2. However, the intergenerational associations increased monotonically across cohorts for daughters, which was not the case for sons. Far from implying a decline in social mobility, this signifies that women (daughters) acquired an income closer to their fathers' as they increasingly entered the labor market. Interestingly, for both men and women, some members of the youngest cohorts (born 1950–1965) were in their 40s during the economic crisis of the early 1990s. Therefore we cannot ascertain if the decline in social mobility

Table 3.3 Intergenerational rank-rank associations of income between paternal grandfathers and grandchildren.

	Grandsons		Granddaughters	
	Full sample	Landskrona	Full sample	Landskrona
Cohort 1940–1949				
Father	0.172**	0.194**	0.187**	0.150*
Paternal GF	0.0485	0.0285	0.0528	0.0577
N	436	344	411	304
Cohort 1950–1959				
Father	0.248***	0.258***	0.123*	0.148*
Paternal GF	-0.00842	0.00977	0.0329	0.0503
N	389	272	372	234
Cohort 1960–1965				
Father	0.245***	0.195***	0.214***	0.241***
Paternal GF	0.0287	0.0708	-0.0116	0.046
N	1,398	357	1,319	350

Note: ***p < 0.01; **p < 0.05; *p < 0.1. See Table 3.2.
Source: Scanian Economic-Demographic Database (SEDD; Bengtsson et al. 2021).

(higher associations) was due to this crisis. Tables 3.3 and 3.4 display the rank-rank associations between men and women and their paternal and maternal grandfathers. Alongside grandfathers, we also regress the father's rank in the same regressions to capture the grandparental generation's net effect. Overall, most estimates for grandfather status are small and not statistically significant, with associations never surpassing 0.08. Such low levels are in line with other studies of multigenerational social mobility both in Sweden and internationally (Anderson et al. 2018; Dribe and Helgertz 2016; Engzell et al. 2020; Hällsten and Kolk 2023; Helgertz and Dribe 2022).

Next, we turn to the analysis of intergenerational mobility focusing on absolute upward income mobility, as indicated by the share of men and women who had a higher lifetime income than their fathers (see Chetty et al. 2017). Figure 3.8 shows the absolute income mobility for sons and daughters by birth year (1920–1965). About 90 percent of sons born between the 1920s and 1940s had a higher lifetime income than their fathers. The pattern is similar for those born in the

Table 3.4 Intergenerational rank-rank associations of income between maternal grandfathers and grandchildren.

	Grandsons		Granddaughters	
	Full sample	Landskrona	Full sample	Landskrona
Cohort 1940–1949				
Father	0.171**	0.179**	0.198***	0.115
Maternal GF	0.0357	-0.0162	-0.00514	0.0000573
N	398	325	365	274
Cohort 1950–1959				
Father	0.256***	0.275***	0.194***	0.205**
Maternal GF	-0.0172	-0.0311	0.0352	0.0474
N	429	280	393	227
Cohort 1960–1965				
Father	0.245***	0.190***	0.188***	0.226***
Maternal GF	0.0503*	0.0384	0.0493	0.0434
N	1,462	434	1,390	406

Note: ***p < 0.01; **p < 0.05; *p < 0.1. See Table 3.2.
Source: Scanian Economic-Demographic Database (SEDD; Bengtsson et al. 2021).

1960s, with about 80 percent absolute mobility. The cohorts born in the 1950s have somewhat lower levels, which is likely connected to the fact that many were 40–49 years old during the crisis of the early 1990s. That said, the corresponding estimates for women are lower than for men, never more than 60 percent higher than their fathers' income. Overall, the levels are in line with other estimates of absolute income mobility for sons in Sweden, estimates which are usually much higher than in the United States (Chetty et al. 2017; Liss et al. 2019).

If we break down the measure of absolute mobility by the income position of fathers we get a more detailed picture of how the pattern of upward income mobility changed across cohorts and by gender. Ninety percent of sons born 1920–1939 (up to decile 9) earned more than their fathers, a figure which dropped for the cohorts born in 1940–1965, especially among fathers' deciles 5–9, when the proportions were around 20–40 percent. Conversely, for daughters the decline in upward mobility across fathers' deciles is more linear than for sons. Moreover, the levels between cohorts differ. While the 1940–1959 cohorts experienced far

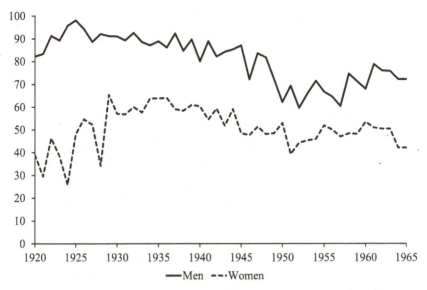

Figure 3.8 Proportion of children attaining a higher lifetime income than their fathers in Landskrona, by gender and cohort (1920–1965).
Source: Scanian Economic-Demographic Database (SEDD; Bengtsson et al. 2021).

less upward mobility than the older cohorts, the 1960s cohorts had similar levels to the 1920s and 1930s cohorts, indicating that at least women experienced an increase in social mobility in the latter part of the study period (see Appendix, Figure A3.1, panel A for sons, and panel B for daughters).

One possible explanation for the decline in income mobility for women born after 1960 is their entry into higher education and participation in the labor force both before and after marriage. Overall, the likelihood of achieving a post-secondary degree increased substantially and almost linearly from income deciles 6 and upwards jumping from 50 to 80 percent (see Appendix, Figure A3.2, panel A for sons, and panel B for daughters). Conversely, the changes below decile 5 were lower than 50 percent. There were no changes between cohorts for men, and even the sons of fathers in the bottom half of the income distribution saw lower attainment in the youngest cohorts. However, there was a substantial increase for women born in the 1960s. Accordingly, the youngest cohort of daughters had a 20 percent higher likelihood of attaining a post-secondary education. This significant catch-up of younger generations in education, especially among women, has arguably been the main channel of equalization through which the Swedish welfare state has operated (Breen and Jonsson 2007).

Conclusion

Throughout the 110 years of occupational and income data analyzed in this chapter, Landskrona underwent a tremendous socioeconomic transformation that shaped economic inequality and social mobility, and occupational and gender characteristics were further determinants in this process. Overall, we can identify three main phases in the development of socioeconomic disparities in the city which reflect development also at the national level.

In the first phase, from 1905 to 1930, we see high and fluctuating levels of economic inequality in the city. Such trends were driven mainly by the country's rapid economic growth and industrialization followed by economic downturns (e.g., the post-World War I crisis). At local level, too, the culmination of Landskrona's first industrialization, characterized by the importance of the shipyard, was followed by stagnation toward the end of the 1920s. During this period, Landskrona attracted unskilled and low-skilled workers due mainly to the higher wages it offered compared to those in the rural and semi-rural areas nearby. In this regard, the high levels of inequality were driven more than anything by an important accumulation on the part of the economic elites (e.g., top 1 percent), which can also be seen in the income gap between occupations in the higher status white-collar class and other classes.

The second phase in Landskrona's development was characterized by a substantial decline in inequality from 1930 to 1950 and the stabilization (a Gini coefficient below 0.3) of its levels over a long time (from 1950 to the 1970s). Between 1930 and 1950, Sweden went from a severe economic crisis, one related to both the Great Depression worldwide and national events such as the "Kreuger crash," to a period of rapid recovery and substantial economic growth (e.g., Schön 2010). This development affected particular industrial cities such as Landskrona, which saw their occupational structure radically transformed with an increase in industrial workers and the adoption of new production processes (e.g., Fordism). In addition, this period saw the implementation of new social policies. Reform activities had started earlier but accelerated after World War II, with a strong orientation toward equality, redistribution of social risks, and economic efficiency. The Swedish government and local authorities made large investments in education, primary care, housing, and urban infrastructure. This period also featured important social policy initiatives, such as pension reforms and more support for families. (e.g., Olofsson 2007). In only 20 years, income inequality in Landskrona declined by 10 Gini points while there was a continued decline in the share of income earned by the top earners as well as in the income differential between occupational groups.

The last part of this second phase (1950–1970s) saw the culmination of economic growth and welfare expansion in Sweden. Real income increased significantly, and the government stimulated the economy through major investment in public infrastructure and housing. Overall, income inequality in both Landskrona and Sweden as a whole remained relatively low (Gini = 0.25–0.30), with only small fluctuations during the oil crisis of the early 1970s. Landskrona was severely affected by the industrial crisis, which was characterized by the demise of the local textile industry and the reduction of employment at the shipyard. As well as this, regional disparities in income (Landskrona compared to the five parishes) disappeared during this period.

Finally, during the last phase—the period after the end of the 1970s—Landskrona experienced further deindustrialization marked by an increase in unemployment in the industrial sector and a negative migratory balance. However, the degree of public investment and socioeconomic transformation seen decades before during the rise in skilled and white-collar occupations and in the growth of women's labor force participation was now seen once again, helping to continue the redistributive process. This limited the increase in inequality until the end of the 1980s. It was only when the whole country was affected by new economic policies and a financial crisis in the early 1990s that the levels of inequality started to increase steadily until the 2010s, when they reached the same level as before World War II.

We observed a clear U-shaped long-term trend in inequality in Landskrona. This trend broadly coincided with development in Sweden as a whole and justifies a detailed analysis of Landskrona as way to understand inequality in the country as a whole for the period before we have ready access to national-level data on income at the individual level. The main determinants driving inequality at the beginning of the twentieth century were not the same as in the period following the 1990s. The economic disparity until the 1930s was mainly due to large income differences between social groups, a marked rural-urban gap, and substantial gender disparities. Since then, and especially since World War II, Landskrona has seen greater equality. The decline in economic inequality between the main social groups resulted from both absolute and relative changes. First, the share of workers belonging to white-collar groups increased in importance as demand for skilled and educated labor increased due to technological change during the Third Industrial Revolution (see Goldin and Katz 2008). As well as this, the progressive expansion of the Swedish economy meant reduced income differences in the economic attainment of the higher and lower social classes.

Another remarkable feature driving disparities to lower levels across the twentieth century was the narrowing gender gap in income (see Stanfors 2007; Stanfors and Goldscheider 2017). Among its main determinants was the increase in the labor force participation of women—first single women and then married as well—as part of the transition from the male breadwinner model to dual-earner families. Moreover, gender differences also diminished primarily through educational expansion which benefited women. However, it must be taken into account that decreasing gender differences in income were observed only within the lower half of the income distribution since differences at higher levels of income have remained almost unchanged, indicating the existence of a "glass ceiling." Therefore, the determinants of disparity in Landskrona's past cannot be used to understand why levels of inequality are rising in the twenty-first century. In this regard, new divergences such as the one observed between Swedish-born and foreign-born individuals might partly explain income inequality, as seen, for instance, in the challenges of ensuring the economic integration of migrants (see also Chapter 4).

Our long-term historical analysis of inequality is also useful in understanding the future implications of rising disparities in income. Interestingly, the intergenerational income persistence also showed a U-shaped pattern over time. Such a pattern coincided with Landskrona's inequality trends over the long term. For instance, income persistence was much higher for individuals born in 1920–1929 than for those born afterward (1930–1949). Hence, people born in 1920–1929 grew up in a time of greater inequality than did younger generations, which brings to mind the association between inequality and social mobility as envisaged by the Great Gatsby curve. Moreover, intergenerational income persistence was higher for the generations born in the 1950s and 1960s, again coinciding with the renewed increase in inequality since the 1970s.

Nevertheless, even though the cohorts of the 1920s and 1960s experienced similar patterns in the inequality–income persistence relationship (relative social mobility), the rates of absolute upward economic mobility among them (those earning more than their fathers) still differed. In terms of relative mobility, and given higher income persistence, the oldest cohorts faced greater barriers in attaining a relatively higher position (income percentile) than did their fathers in comparison to other individuals in the income distribution. Still, they could easily acquire a higher income than their fathers. Conversely, the younger generations in our analysis followed a pattern increasingly similar to their fathers in relative terms and earned less than them in absolute terms. This combination of higher income inequality and a smaller fraction of children earning more than their fathers poses a challenge for the future because growing inequality might be an obstacle to equal opportunities.

Appendix

Table A3.1 Mean income by social class for men and women in Landskrona, 1905–2015 (SEK).

Men	1905–1929	1930–1949	1950–1974	1975–1994	1995–2015
Higher white-collar	82,761	82,549	98,647	108,891	138,971
Lower white-collar	29,604	35,486	58,538	86,358	101,319
Medium-skilled	16,686	26,047	44,671	70,003	86,628
Farmers	10,840	18,679	44,023	51,198	62,985
Lower-skilled	14,967	24,056	44,448	67,116	81,432
Unskilled	13,221	21,180	33,642	60,486	68,048
Women	**1905–1929**	**1930–1949**	**1950–1974**	**1975–1994**	**1995–2015**
Higher white-collar	22,526	33,335	43,378	66,704	103,159
Lower white collar	13,103	15,604	24,024	52,359	75,615
Medium-skilled	6,108	7,483	17,721	50,238	65,823
Farmers	2,438	3,678	20,590	29,121	37,302
Lower-skilled	5,739	8,573	15,428	48,410	62,169
Unskilled	6,618	9,299	15,064	40,160	50,121

Note: All incomes adjusted for CPI at 1980 SEK level.

Source: See Figure 3.1. Source: Scanian Economic-Demographic Database (SEDD; Bengtsson et al. 2021).

Table A3.2 Mean income by social class for men and women in the five parishes, 1905–2015 (SEK).

Men	1905–1929	1930–1949	1950–1974	1975–1994	1995–2015
Higher white-collar	54,516	66,314	94,237	97,792	145,326
Lower white collar	24,144	30,536	56,138	80,648	102,004
Medium-skilled	13,913	20,549	45,760	70,594	91,671
Farmers	6,236	17,012	43,383	49,465	59,276
Lower-skilled	13,355	18,952	43,737	67,044	83,803
Unskilled	11,039	14,629	30,745	64,494	72,524
Women	1905–1929	1930–1949	1950–1974	1975–1994	1995–2015
Higher white-collar	16,793	24,748	39,954	61,411	105,087
Lower white-collar	12,519	14,845	25,091	50,458	75,421
Medium-skilled	7,498	6,648	16,763	47,268	60,372
Farmers	8,362	7,786	23,119	32,976	41,761
Lower-skilled	8,099	8,224	15,703	47,431	63,506
Unskilled	6,996	6,721	19,675	41,239	52,348

Source: Scanian Economic-Demographic Database (SEDD; Bengtsson et al. 2021). Note: All incomes adjusted for CPI at 1980 SEK level.

ECONOMIC INEQUALITY AND SOCIAL MOBILITY 109

A. Sons

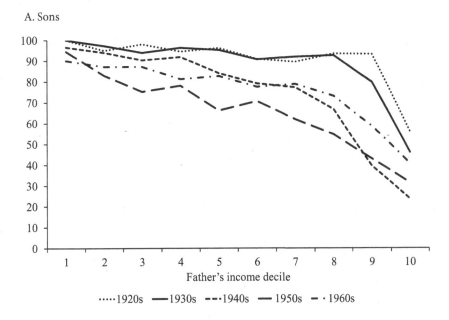

B. Daughters

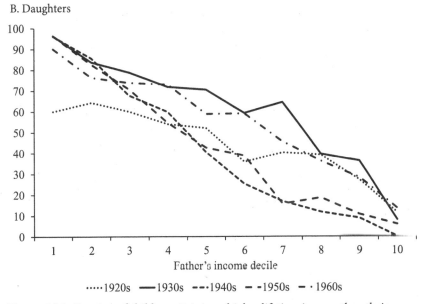

Figure A3.1 Fraction of children attaining a higher lifetime income than their fathers in Landskrona by fathers' income deciles and decade of birth (1920–1965).
Source: Scanian Economic-Demographic Database (SEDD; Bengtsson et al. 2021).

A. Sons

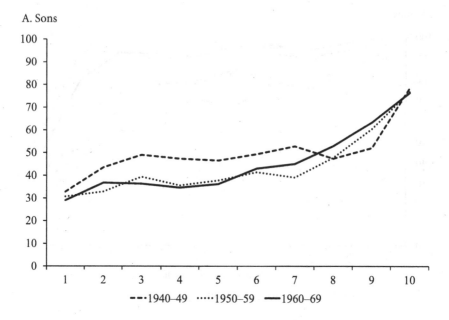

B. Daughters

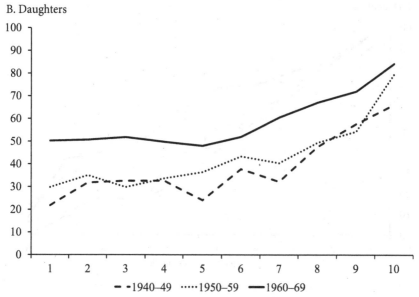

Figure A3.2 Fraction of children attaining post-secondary education by fathers' income deciles and decade of birth (1940–1965).

Source: Scanian Economic-Demographic Database (SEDD; Bengtsson et al. 2021).

Notes

1. We imputed incomes only for single women in this period; income for married women was not reported in the registers before 1947 because they were included in their husbands' incomes. In the imputations, we employed predictive mean matching methods (PMM) to preserve the original distribution of the data when they are not normally distributed, as in the case of income (Kleinke 2017). The PMM combines standard linear regression and a nearest-neighbor imputation approach. The linear regressions give income predictions, which were applied as a distance measure to derive a set of nearest neighbors (with similar values on age and occupation) consisting of individuals with complete values. We then randomly drew a value from this set of individuals. For instance, for 1917 (with missing income), we imputed income from the closest years (previous and next) with existing income data for 1915 and 1919.
2. The Gini coefficient is derived from a Lorenz curve generated by plotting the cumulative share of income on the vertical axis, with the population ranked in ascending order by percentiles on the horizontal axis. Hence, it shows the cumulative share of all income earned by percentile. A straight 45-degree line represents total equality; that is, when a certain percentile earns exactly that share of total income, such as the bottom half of the population earning exactly half of total income (Cowell 2011).
3. The full sample includes also individuals that might never have been present in Landskrona in their life but in whose cases there may be up to second-degree of kinship with someone present in the study area before 1967.

References

Albrecht, J., A. Björklund, and S. Vroman. 2003. "Is There a Glass Ceiling in Sweden?" *Journal of Labor Economics* 21 (1): 145–177.

Alvaredo, F., A. B. Atkinson, T. Piketty, and E. Saez. 2013. "The Top 1 Percent in International and Historical Perspective." *Journal of Economic Perspectives* 27 (3): 3–20.

Anderson, L. R., P. Sheppard, and C. W. Monden. 2018. "Grandparent Effects on Educational Outcomes: A Systematic Review." *Sociological Science* 5: 114–142.

Bengtsson, T., M. Dribe, L. Quaranta, and P. Svensson. 2021. "The Scanian Economic Demographic Database: Version 7.2 (Machine-readable database)." Lund: Lund University, Centre for Economic Demography.

Björklund, A., and M. Jäntti. 1997. "Intergenerational Income Mobility in Sweden Compared to the United States." *American Economic Review* 87 (5): 1009–1018.

Bourdieu, P., and J.-C. Passeron. 1970. *La Reproduction: éléments d'une théorie du système d'enseignement*. Paris: Minuit.

Breen, R., and J. O. Jonsson. 2007. "Explaining Change in Social Fluidity: Educational Equalization and Educational Expansion in Twentieth-Century Sweden." *American Journal of Sociology* 112 (6): 1775–1810.

Chetty, R., D. Grusky, M. Hell, et al. 2017. "The Fading American Dream: Trends in Absolute Income Mobility since 1940." *Science* 356 (6336): 398–406.

Chetty, R., N. Hendren, P. Kline, et al. 2014. "Is the United States Still a Land of Opportunity? Recent Trends in Intergenerational Mobility." *American Economic Review* 104 (5): 141–147.

Corak, M. 2013. "Income Inequality, Equality of Opportunity, and Intergenerational Mobility." *Journal of Economic Perspectives* 27 (3): 79–102.

Cowell, F. 2011. *Measuring Inequality.* Oxford: Oxford University Press.

Debiasi, E., M. Dribe, and G. Brea-Martinez. 2023. "Has It Always Paid to be Rich? Income and Cause-Specific Mortality in Southern Sweden 1905–2014." *Population Studies* online: 1–21.

Dribe, M., and J. Helgertz. 2016. "The Lasting Impact of Grandfathers: Class, Occupational Status, and Earnings over Three Generations in Sweden 1815–2011." *Journal of Economic History* 76 (4): 969–1000.

Dribe, M., J. Helgertz, and B. Van de Putte. 2015. "Did Social Mobility Increase During the Industrialization Process? A Micro-Level Study of a Transforming Community in Southern Sweden 1828–1968." *Research in Social Stratification and Mobility* 41 (1): 25–39.

Domeij, D., and M. Flodén. 2010. "Inequality Trends in Sweden 1978–2004." *Review of Economic Dynamics* 13 (1): 179–208.

Edin, P. A., and K. Richardson. 2002. "Swimming with the Tide: Solidary Wage Policy and the Gender Earnings Gap." *Scandinavian Journal of Economics* 104 (1): 49–67.

Engzell, P., C. Mood, and J. O. Jonsson. 2020. "It's All About the Parents: Inequality Transmission Across Three Generations in Sweden." *Sociological Science* 7 (1): 242–267.

Erikson, R., and J. H. Goldthorpe. 1992. *The Constant Flux: A Study of Class Mobility in Industrial Societies.* Oxford: Oxford University Press.

Featherman, D. L., F. L. Jones, and R. M. Hauser. 1975. "Assumptions of Social Mobility Research in the US: The Case of Occupational Status." *Social Science Research* 4 (4): 329–360.

Fortin, N., and S. Lefebvre. 1998. "Intergenerational Income Mobility in Canada." In *Labour Markets, Social Institutions, and the Future of Canada's Children*, edited by M. Corak, 51–64. Ottawa: Statistics Canada.

Goldin, C., and L. F. Katz. 2008. *The Race Between Education and Technology.* Cambridge, MA: Harvard University Press.

Grusky, D. B., and R. M. Hauser. 1984. "Comparative Social Mobility Revisited: Models of Convergence and Divergence in 16 Countries." *American Sociological Review* 49 (1): 19–38.

Hällsten, M., and M. Kolk. 2023. "The Shadow of Peasant Past: Seven Generations of Inequality Persistence in Northern Sweden." *American Journal of Sociology* 128 (6): 1716–1760.

Heidrich, S. 2017. "Intergenerational Mobility in Sweden: A Regional Perspective." *Journal of Population Economics* 30 (4): 1241–1280.

Helgertz, J., T. Bengtsson, and M. Dribe. 2020. "Income Data in the Scanian Economic Demographic Database (SEDD)." Lund Papers in Economic Demography 2020: 6.

Helgertz, J., and M. Dribe. 2022. "Do Grandfathers Matter for Occupational and Earnings Attainment? Evidence from Swedish Register Data." *European Sociological Review* 38 (1): 54–72

Henning, M., K. Enflo, and F. N. G. Andersson. 2011. "Trends and Cycles in Regional Economic Growth: How Spatial Differences Shaped the Swedish Growth Experience from 1860–2009." *Explorations in Economic History* 48 (4): 538–555.

Humphries, J., and C. Sarasúa. 2012. "Off the Record: Reconstructing Women's Labor Force Participation in the European Past." *Feminist Economics* 18 (4): 39–67.

Johansson, M. 2006. "Inkomst och ojämlikhet i Sverige 1951–2002 [Income and Inequality in Sweden 1951–2002]." Working Paper 2006:3. Stockholm: Institute for Future Studies.

Kleinke, K. 2017. "Multiple Imputation Under Violated Distributional Assumptions: A Systematic Evaluation of the Assumed Robustness of Predictive Mean Matching." *Journal of Educational and Behavioral Statistics* 42 (4): 371–404.

Lipset, S. M., and H. Zetterberg. 1956. *A Theory of Social Mobility: Transactions of the Third World Congress of Sociology: Vol. III.* London: International Sociological Association.

Liss, E., M. Korpi, and K. Wennberg. 2019. "The American Dream Lives in Sweden: Trends in Intergenerational Absolute Income Mobility." Ratio Working Paper No. 325. Stockholm: The Ratio Institute.

Mazumder, B. 2016. "Estimating the Intergenerational Elasticity and Rank Association in the United States: Overcoming the Current Limitations of Tax Data." In *Inequality: Causes and Consequences*, edited by L. Cappellari, S. W. Polachek, and K. Tatsiramos, 83–129. Bingley: Emerald Group Publishing Limited.

Modalsli, J. 2017. "Intergenerational Mobility in Norway, 1865–2011." *Scandinavian Journal of Economics* 119 (1): 34–71.

Nielsen, F., and A. S. Alderson. 1997. "The Kuznets Curve and the Great U-Turn: Income Inequality in US Counties, 1970 to 1990." *American Sociological Review* 62 (1): 12–33.

Nybom, M., and J. Stuhler. 2016. "Heterogeneous Income Profiles and Lifecycle Bias in Intergenerational Mobility Estimation." *Journal of Human Resources* 51 (1): 239–268.

Olofsson, J. 2007. *Socialpolitik. Varför, hur och till vilken nytta?* [Social Policy: Why, How, and To What Use?]. Stockholm: SNS Förlag.

Österberg, T. 2000. "Intergenerational Income Mobility in Sweden: What Do Tax-Data Show?" *Review of Income and Wealth* 46 (4): 421–436.

Pascual, M. 2009. "Intergenerational Income Mobility: The Transmission of Socio-Economic Status in Spain." *Journal of Policy Modeling* 31 (6): 835–846.

Piketty, T. 2018. *Capital in the Twenty-First Century*. Cambridge, MA: Belknap.

Roine, J., and D. Waldenström. 2008. "The Evolution of Top Incomes in an Egalitarian Society: Sweden, 1903–2004." *Journal of Public Economics* 92 (1–2): 366–387.

Roine, J., and D. Waldenström. 2009. "Wealth Concentration Over the Path of Development: Sweden, 1873–2006." *Scandinavian Journal of Economics* 111 (1): 151–187.

SCB (Statistics Sweden). 2020. "CPI Sweden. Historical Numbers 1830–." https://www.scb.se/en/finding-statistics/statistics-by-subject-area/prices-and-consumption/consumer-price-index/consumer-price-index-cpi/pong/tables-and-graphs/consumer-price-index-cpi/cpi-historical-numbers-1830/

Schön, L. 2010. *Sweden's Road to Modernity. An Economic History.* Stockholm: SNS.

Silenstam, P. 1970. *Arbetskraftsutbudets utveckling i Sverige 1870–1965* [The Development of Labor Supply in Sweden 1870–1965]. Stockholm: Almqvist & Wiksell.

Stanfors, M. 2007. *Mellan arbete och familj. Ett dilemma för kvinnor i 1900-talets Sverige* [Between Work and Family. A Dilemma for Women in Twentieth-Century Sweden]. Stockholm: SNS.

Stanfors, M., and F. Goldscheider. 2017. "The Forest and the Trees: Industrialization, Demographic Change, and the Ongoing Gender Revolution in Sweden and the United States, 1870–2010." *Demographic Research* 36 (6): 173–226.

Treiman, D. J. 1970. "Industrialization and Social Stratification." *Sociological Inquiry* 40 (2): 207–234.
Van Leeuwen, M. H. D., and I. Maas. 2011. *HISCLASS: A Historical International Social Class Scheme*. Leuven: Leuven University Press.
Van Leeuwen, M. H. D., I. Maas, and A. Miles. 2002. *HISCO: Historical International Standard Classification of Occupations*. Leuven: Leuven University Press.

4
Migration in Times of Economic Growth and Recession

Finn Hedefalk, Patrick Svensson, and Anna Tegunimataka

Introduction

Migration is an important force for social change. Migrants respond to economic transformation, shifting norms and values, and changing familial circumstances. The decision to migrate transforms not only individual lives but also the places which migrants settle in and leave behind.

The emergence and growth of industrial cities is a prime example of how migration affects economic development and, likewise, how economic development influences migration. City populations were mobile around the turn of the twentieth century, and the growth of cities depended on in-migration. However, migration was influential beyond early urbanization and continued through the consolidation, maturity, and demise of these industrial cities. The long-term structural transformation from agriculture to industry, and later to the service sector, is an important factor behind continuous population flows. Another factor is the diverse development of cities that resulted in urban-to-urban migration and also global development that resulted in increasing international migration mostly directed toward cities.

Studies on migration and industrial cities have focused primarily on two of these phenomena, namely internal migration during early urbanization and the immigration from abroad that took place during the second half of the twentieth century. We want to add to the current state of knowledge by studying a longer period while also integrating two types of migrants, internal and external, into the structure and development of the industrial city. We study migrants' individual characteristics and the way in which flows and migrant composition may have changed in relation to its development. An extensive study of macro patterns and migrant characteristics will contribute to our overall knowledge of the role of migration and migrants in industrial cities during the twentieth century.

More specifically, this chapter studies Landskrona, Sweden, over the course of more than 100 years, focusing on the inflows and outflows of people and

Finn Hedefalk, Patrick Svensson, and Anna Tegunimataka, *Migration in Times of Economic Growth and Recession*
In: *Urban Lives*. Edited by: Martin Dribe, Therese Nilsson, and Anna Tegunimataka, Oxford University Press.
© Oxford University Press 2024. DOI: 10.1093/oso/9780197761090.003.0004

analyzing migrant heterogeneities in terms of socioeconomic status, gender, age, civil status, and origin and destination. It also studies the interrelationship between growth and recession in the industrial city and migration. We are interested in changes in migration over time, and our longitudinal data have allowed us to study the total migration, external and internal, to and from Landskrona, as well as the total population of the city.

We have structured the analysis around migration flows and migrant characteristics that are understood in relation to two overall frameworks of time: the general rise and fall of the industrial city, and the phases of transformation and rationalization of industry. The latter framework reflects five periods of major social, economic, and political change in Sweden and Landskrona.

Over the course of the twentieth century, the population of Landskrona grew and stagnated following economic expansion and recession. It increased rapidly until the 1920s, when many new industries were established, and again between 1930 and 1960 following further industrial expansion, but stagnated during the years of industrial crisis in the 1970s and 1980s. Along with these developments, Landskrona had a high inflow of international immigrants; mainly labor migrants at first, followed later by refugees.

The chapter starts with a theoretical background on migration followed by a brief overview of Sweden's overall economic development, its industrial cities, and migration. Thereafter, we use the case of Landskrona to delve deeper into the population flows and their relationship to the industrial development of the city. A third section is devoted to estimations of the migrants' characteristics over time, both in general and by origin and destination. Finally, we conclude and discuss the results in the light of the question of industrial cities and migration.

Migration and the Industrial City

Theories of Migration

Ever since the seminal work of Ernst George Ravenstein (1889), internal migration has been viewed as a function of spatial disequilibria; that people tend to move from low-income to high-income areas. Everett Lee (1966) extended Ravenstein's findings (1889) and proposed the influential *push* and *pull* framework in which migration is determined by factors at area of origin (unemployment, prices, housing opportunities), factors at destination (wages, job opportunities, rent levels), and also individual-level factors (age, gender, marital status, level of education, social class) and obstacles in the way. According to this theory, the push factors drive people out of their area of origin while the pull factors attract them to their area of destination. Lee's framework is comprehensive since it includes both macro- and micro-level factors, whereas most other theories take either a macro- or a micro-level approach. While the macro-level theories tend to focus on (macro) differences between origin and destination (unemployment, economic systems, prices) with the aim of explaining migration levels or direction of migration flow, the micro approach focuses instead on individual-level factors affecting the likelihood of migration.

An important macro-level variable is economic activity, which was already recognized by Ravenstein (1889). Growing cities and dynamic centers with access to services and opportunities tend to attract people from the surrounding countryside. The attractiveness of the urban centers may, however, depend on the level of unemployment, which is expected to increase the out-migration from an area (Salvatore 1977). That said, in countries with a strong welfare state, generous unemployment benefits may reduce the need for the unemployed to move to sustain a living.

According to neo-classical migration theory, and assuming there is access to information and free choice, individuals are expected to go where they can earn the highest wage. Likewise, the individual incentive to migrate disappears when wages are equalized between different places (Harris and Todaro 1970). Individuals who can expect higher returns to migration are, moreover, more likely to migrate (Sjaastad 1962). Thus, individuals with a higher level of education or skill level can expect higher returns to migration as they are rewarded with better jobs and better earnings, which translates into a higher likelihood of migration. Even so, in times of economic transformation when there are increasing urban job opportunities, the low-skilled move to find manual jobs and avoid unemployment in the countryside (Keung Wong et al. 2007).

Age also matters as an important selection mechanism for migration. Younger individuals with a longer life expectancy can expect greater returns to migration and are thus more likely to move. Migrants can also "self-select" on traits that are or may be unobservable (Constant and Massey 2003). These may be certain abilities and attributes that result in the higher likelihood of migration, and, even in the case of individuals who are similar in terms of age, gender, and education, there may be potential differences in unobservable characteristics affecting the decision to move (Nakosteen and Zimmer 1980).

It has been suggested that the individual cost-benefit approach needs to be expanded to include families and households as the decision-making unit. People act as a collective to maximize income and minimize risk (Massey et al. 1993). To the extent that whole families migrate, the relevant incentive is the difference in current and future expected income for the family as a whole (Mincer 1978). An alternative to the whole family migrating would be sending a family member to find urban employment, and often younger individuals and males are chosen for migration for the benefit of the family.

A more recent development in micro-level migration theory has been the focus on migrant networks. Individuals at origin and destination are linked through kinship, friendship, and a shared origin (Massey 1988). The macroeconomic conditions initially causing migration streams matter less once the migratory process expands due to the migration networks that have been formed. Certain origins and destinations are linked through these networks, and migration streams will continue regardless of the initial push and pull factors.

The individual cost-benefit approach can also be extended to more than potential earnings, instead focusing on the importance of consumption. Some individuals may prefer dense cities even if they have the same earnings potential as in the countryside. The lower transportation costs in cities not only enhance productivity for businesses but also contribute to a more enjoyable lifestyle outside of work. For instance, urban density facilitates social interactions, and this effect is particularly significant when considering the location choices of young, single individuals who tend to reside in densely populated urban areas. The concentration of people in these areas facilitates socializing and the functioning of the marriage market (Costa and Kahn 2000). Moreover, large urban markets enhance consumer welfare by providing access to goods and services that benefit from economies of scale (Glaeser et al. 2001).

Migration and Economic Development

To study population flows to and from industrial cities undergoing economic development, we need to focus on macro-level theories. Two forces on the macro level need to be discussed in relation to economic development and growth: first, the impact and strength of push and pull factors, respectively, and, second, the impact of economic activity on migration. To elaborate on this, we discuss the overall structural transformation of Sweden from agriculture to industry through a periodic development of industry and economic activity consisting of phases of transformation and rationalization (Schön 2000) to integrate this into our explanatory framework and formulate a number of expected outcomes for Landskrona.

A major pull factor for early in-migration to urban areas was the industrialization process and the factory system, which required an inflow of people from the countryside. However, during the first phase of industrialization, the agricultural population and labor force, or at least those living in rural areas (where there was a combination of agriculture and rural industrialization), also grew in absolute numbers. It was not until the 1920s that the rural population started to decline. The urban share of the population in Sweden was around 10 percent in the 1850s and increased to 25 percent in 1900, and it was not until the late 1940s that it was larger than the rural share, reaching 56 percent in 1950 (Statistics Sweden 1969, 66).

According to theory, labor migration is due to wage gaps and also employment opportunities (in industry and agriculture, respectively). A modest urban wage compensation existed throughout the late nineteenth and early twentieth centuries (Lundh and Prado 2012). Moreover, the industrial crises of the early 1920s resulted in a drastically larger wage gap since urban wages were sticky while agricultural wages were more mobile. Despite this, there was no corresponding increase in migration to the cities during this time as rural workers preferred lower wages to the risk of facing high urban unemployment. The large wage gap persisted into the 1930s, until political initiatives closed that gap between agrarian and industrial workers (Lundh and Prado 2012).

Migration from rural to urban areas was mostly connected to industrial business cycles rather than shifts in agricultural cycles. Overall, increased economic activity led to higher migration intensity (Bengtsson and Johansson 1994, 72) and industrial expansion meant relatively larger migration to the cities (Kronborg and Nilsson 1975, 56; Thomas 1941). This occurred even when agriculture experienced relatively good times. Furthermore, years of depression in agriculture did not result in migration to urban areas to the same extent (Morell 2001). For agricultural proletarians, the availability of alternative employment was an important factor in deciding to move. This means that while urban industrialization attracted workers from the countryside, their area of origin still provided an important safe haven. With industrial expansion people moved into the city, and, during a downturn, they either moved back to the rural countryside or sought their fortune in other urban settings, which meant that segments of the agricultural population functioned as a flexible labor reserve.

The first period of analysis, 1905–1929, can therefore be characterized by the growth of industry on the backs of the First and Second Industrial Revolution, requiring the in-migration of laborers both skilled and unskilled, but where growth was followed by competition from abroad resulting in rationalization and unemployment—a situation where agriculture could still offer an alternative to industrial employment for those out of work.

The phase of rationalization in the 1920s was characterized by the introduction of Taylorism, a management system that was refined in Swedish industry in the 1950s and 1960s and replaced by Fordism, a system based on assembly lines and simplified production processes, which thus integrated women and unskilled migrants from abroad in industrial production on a larger scale (Lundh 2002, 148–158). The following period, from 1950 to 1975, showed similar development to the first in terms of initial growth, building as it did on new industries established during an earlier phase which over time faced increasing competition that resulted in rationalization. This would also characterize the period after 1995

(Schön 2000). The later periods differed compared to 1905–1929 because agriculture no longer provided an alternative for the unemployed. From the 1940s, new political goals for agriculture were formulated, replacing smallholdings for large-scale efficient farms, meaning that the population engaged in agriculture fell drastically (Morell 2011). This resulted in continuous in-migration to towns and cities, driven by increased demand for labor in the cities and by structural transformation. The demand for labor resulted, moreover, in an increase in overtime and enhanced labor migration from abroad. When rationalization set in, fewer opportunities in the countryside and a similar development in other urban areas left unemployed laborers little alternative but to stay put in an urban context and search for new jobs.

Between these periods were transformation phases (i.e., times of increasing economic activity related to the establishment of new industries; Schön 2000). After the first period, the 1930s depression hit both industry and agriculture. However, a new phase of industrial growth based on electrification and motoring took place during the same decade (Schön 2000). The in-migration of workers was crucial for the industries, and—depending on structure—it was not only unskilled factory workers that were in demand but also workers equipped with the skills needed for the new industries (Isacson and Magnusson 1983, 15). A similar all-encompassing structural change took place in the 1970s.

These transformation phases required an ability to adapt to the new situation. A new set of industries became the new core, and, depending on the ability to establish them, some regions experienced a fresh inflow of people and increased growth in employment while others did not (Magnusson 1997, 437–438). Thus, for the years 1930–1949, for the period after the 1970s crisis, and for the final phase, migration patterns between the industrial cities tended to be diverse.

The strength of this transformation and rationalization also depended on the industrial structure. The early expansion of industry in urban areas was to a large extent dependent on natural resources, communications, and traditions, which meant that industrial cities and towns differed from each other in terms of branch structure. However, the use of common energy sources and the demand from other parts of society meant that certain branches existed in almost all settings. Over time there was less diversity between cities (see Chapter 2).

A sectoral change whereby industry, once dominant, was replaced by the service sector took place during the last decades of the twentieth century. To some extent this reduced vulnerability to the international market (Bengtsson and Johansson 1994, 70). At the same time, even though there was a degree of local demand for services, state and regional investment in higher education and governmental agencies also played a role in employment and local urban development.

To summarize, in- and out-migration in Landskrona depended on a number of factors, above all the city's industrial development and structure, and these factors also included the overall societal change and the structural transformation from agriculture via industry to the service sector. We expected in- and out-migration for the first decades of the twentieth century to vary with the internal growth of the city because urban wages were higher, making urban employment more attractive, while rural employment offered an alternative during periods when urban employment fell. During the first phase, 1905–1929, we expected migration to be circular—from the countryside and back again.

Net migration to and from nearby agricultural areas was low; it was long-distance migrants who accounted for the positive net migration to cities during the early part of the twentieth century (Åkerman 1975). Migration between cities also formed an important part of overall population flows. So, although the net effect of local migration on Landskrona might have been small, we expected a positive effect of long-distance migration on population, whereby migrants had certain characteristics important for the new industries (cf. Isacson and Magnusson 1983, 15).

The industrial structure of Landskrona, based initially on food industry and transport, saw the gradual rise of major industries typical of the First and Second Industrial Revolutions: textiles, mechanical workshops, shipbuilding, etc. This means that the home market-oriented food industry changed in that it became vulnerable to international competition, and the overall pattern outlined above would to a large extent be valid for Landskrona as well (in terms of the transformation and rationalization periods of industry). Periods such as the 1910s, the 1930s to 1950s, and the late 1970s to the 1980s were expected to be characterized by the emergence of new opportunities and thus by in-migration. Conversely, periods of rationalization such as the 1920s, 1960s, and 1990s should in theory have resulted in out-migration.

Bearing in mind the overall societal changes and the rapid structural change in Scanian agriculture in the environs of Landskrona, out-migration to agriculture was probably restricted from as early as the end of the 1930s onward. We therefore expected there to be few alternatives available to unskilled and low-skilled workers after World War II.

Out-migration might have persisted all the same but for other reasons, such as a simple change of residence rather than a change of employment. Technological changes after the war greatly affected urban areas, leading to a decline in their effectiveness in meeting consumer preferences. The introduction of automobiles enabled faster commutes in car-dependent suburbs. Settling in the countryside to escape the bustle of city life while still keeping one's job might have been the preferred choice, particularly for white-collar employees and workers on a higher income. First, there was the expansion in communications; improved transportation within and between cities meant that people were able to change their mode of living from a densely populated residential block near their work site to the new outer city limits situated along transport lines (Hellspong 1974, 222). Second, there was a *green wave* of people leaving the city and moving back to the countryside. Third, and finally, a number of new areas outside the cities and in neighboring municipalities or the countryside nearby were developed to provide detached or semi-detached housing for those wishing to live there and commute to work in the city. Regular "commuter towns" grew up in the areas surrounding the urban centers.

In all, the potential to live outside the city yet work in it increased from the 1960s and onward, which meant that in times of depression, a particular industry there might have seen higher levels of out-migration among the skilled and semi-skilled to other cities or the countryside. More recent decades have instead seen a resurgence and an increased attractiveness of the city, primarily evident through higher housing prices and rising incomes. Higher levels of education have fueled a greater demand for urban amenities like museums, restaurants, and concerts, and the city has become important not only for production but also consumption (Glaeser et al. 2001).

Overall, young people were expected to be more mobile than older people, and industrialization meant jobs for both men and women and in different types of industries (e.g., the shipyard and the textile factories), in administration, and in the supporting service sector. The migrants entering Landskrona were thus expected to be men and women who were younger than the native-born. This should have been true at least for the early period, in line with previous research on the late nineteenth and early twentieth centuries (e.g., Kronborg and Nilsson 1975; Vikström 2003; see also Karlsson and Lundh 2022, 127 for a later period). We expected the demand from the diverse industrial sector in Landskrona to have attracted both unskilled and skilled migrants from the surrounding local area and from other cities and rural areas in Sweden and abroad. In addition, we expected migration from abroad to follow the pattern in Sweden generally, with labor migrants entering Landskrona during the industrial expansion after World War II until restrictions put a stop to this in the early 1970s. Thereafter migration would take the form of major waves of refugees seeking asylum in Sweden.

Migration Flows to and from Landskrona

To look more closely at these general characteristics of migration, we study the case of Landskrona and follow the way in which migration streams to and from this industrial city changed during the long twentieth century, and we identify the potential links these had to industrial development. We know from previous chapters that the population growth of Landskrona was almost linear throughout the century but with two distinctive bumps: first, a rapid increase in the late 1910s followed by a drastic decline in the early 1920s, and, second, a decline in the population in the late 1970s followed by a relatively long period of stagnation until the early 2000s when the population started increasing again. Overall population increased from 16,000 to 45,000 in a little over 100 years (this includes the incorporation of several rural districts in the 1960s) (see Chapter 2).

At the turn of the twentieth century, the share of industrial workers out of all workers in Landskrona was slightly greater than 40 percent. This increased to almost 60 percent by 1920, but then the industrial crises of the early 1920s led to a drop. As of 1930, there was a new increase, and during the 1940s and '50s, the share was somewhat over 60 percent. From then on, a constant decline set in, and, by 2000, the share was down to around 35 percent. The overall development was similar to that in other Swedish industrial cities, although the share of people employed in industry during the golden age was somewhat higher in Landskrona.

We start by looking at the overall migration flows in and out of Landskrona. This consisted of both internal and external migration (i.e., from within Sweden and from abroad) and internal out-migration as well as emigration (see Figures 4.1 and 4.2). Looking at absolute numbers, we can see that there were substantial variations in people entering and leaving Landskrona over time. Second, we see that the composition of the migrants in terms of birth region changed over time. From the early twentieth century until World War II those migrating in and out of Landskrona were almost exclusively born in Sweden. A small exception here was the in-migration of Nordic and European-born migrants in the late 1910s. Right after the war in the late 1940s this changed, and even though Swedish-born migrants still predominated there was now also an inflow of Nordic and other European migrants. From the 1980s onward migrants from Asia and to some extent other parts of the world also made up a significant portion of both in- and out-migrants. We will return to these non-Swedish-born migrants below.

We turn next to the role of migration in relation to population development by looking at total migration rates (total migration divided by the mean population). The first period, 1905–1929, starts with a high overall migration rate but then experiences a downward trend (see Figure 4.3). The level of total migration of around 120 per thousand in the initial years corresponds to levels found for Scanian cities in the nineteenth century (Bengtsson 1990) and is a bit lower than in the town of Halmstad in the nearby county of Halland during the early twentieth century (Kronborg and Nilsson 1975, 55).

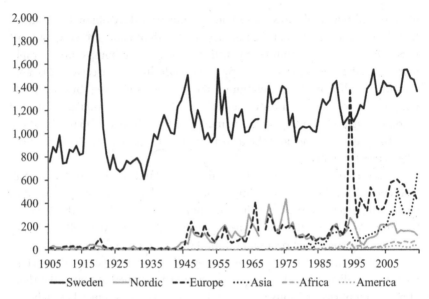

Figure 4.1 In-migration to Landskrona by birth region, 1905–2014 (absolute numbers).

Source: Scanian Economic-Demographic Database (SEDD; Bengtsson et al. 2021).

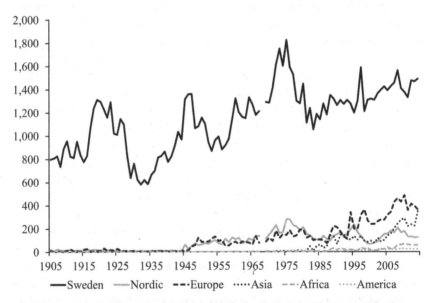

Figure 4.2 Out-migration from Landskrona by birth region, 1905–2014 (absolute numbers).

Source: Scanian Economic-Demographic Database (SEDD; Bengtsson et al. 2021).

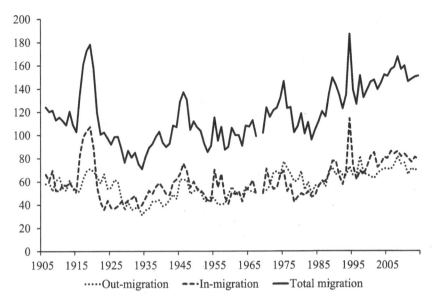

Figure 4.3 In- and out-migration, and total migration (per 1,000 population), Landskrona, 1905–2014.
Source: Scanian Economic-Demographic Database (SEDD; Bengtsson et al. 2021).

In the early urbanization phase, cities were dependent on in-migration since mortality was higher in urban areas than in the countryside (see Chapter 9). Over the nineteenth century, natural population increase in the cities became increasingly important (Bengtsson 1990). Even so, migration still had a role to play and fluctuations were significant. The percentage of population growth attributable to migration was around 11 percent for the first period (1905–1929). This figure seems low, and we return to this below. During the following periods the population continued to grow, and migration became more significant: it accounted for 58 percent of growth in the period 1930–1949 and 35 percent in 1950–1974. Overall, total migration increased during these periods from its lowest point in 1934, although it showed large fluctuations right after World War II. This pattern was interrupted in 1975, when a decline in the migration rate set in for around ten years. This was also a period of declining population numbers in Landskrona, a decline almost entirely due to declining migration. From the mid-1980s, the total migration rate increased continuously, reaching its highest levels for the whole 100-year period, and migration played an important part in total population growth once again. This surge can be attributed to both the growing influx of international migrants to Landskrona and a general revitalization of urban life.

Another way of looking at the importance of migration is to study the share of the city population born in the city (natives). In the early years of the twentieth century, around half of Landskrona's population had been born there. This was somewhat higher than in cities like Stockholm and Norrköping where the share was 41–43 percent (Godlund and Godlund 1976, 34; Puschmann et al. 2015, 330). In 1920, the share had decreased to 45 percent, reflecting the inflow during the late 1910s. Ten years later, in 1930, the share had increased again to 51 percent, indicating that the out-migration in the 1920s had included previous in-migrants. This share was at the higher end as compared to some other Swedish cities, with Göteborg (55 percent) and Norrköping (52 percent) somewhat ahead, whereas Malmö (49 percent), Helsingborg (45 percent), Stockholm (40 percent), and Linköping (37 percent) had lower shares (Godlund and Godlund 1976, 34). From then on, the share of native-born fell continuously, with a small increase in the late 1970s and '80s, resulting in around a third of all inhabitants in 2014 being born in Landskrona.

Total migration depends on in- and out-migration. Hence, an analysis of migration in terms of economic and industrial development requires us to study these aspects separately as well as jointly.

From Figure 4.3 we can see some significant variation in the short-term in- and out-migration during the early decades of the twentieth century. These are related mostly to the establishment of the shipyard in 1915 and its subsequent bankruptcy in 1922, but also to the overall economic crises of the early 1920s, which encompassed the mechanical workshops and aircraft factory as well. Several thousand migrants came to the city in the late 1910s, mostly from Sweden but also from abroad (see Figure 4.1). The shipyard required skilled laborers and actively recruited them and provided housing for them. Out-migration also increased, but with a delay, and remained high throughout the 1920s while in-migration fell drastically as a result of the crises in the early 1920s. Migration during the first period, therefore, is a good indication of the city's industrial development. As stated above, the overall effect of migration on population growth was small during this period, and this was due to in-migration being counteracted by out-migration later on.

There are differences by gender (not shown here), where men tended to move into Landskrona *before* women. This is apparent for both the period in the late 1910s and that around the 1950s, which were periods of rapid industrial growth in Landskrona where demand for male labor increased. In fact, the second period of 1930–1949 is the only one where levels of migration were higher for women than for men. Women were therefore more mobile than men during these decades. This period was characterized by an initial depression in both industry and agriculture. While industry recovered quickly, agricultural stagnation led to a transformation of that sector. The previous focus on forming smallholdings to prevent migration from the rural areas was overturned politically into policies promoting the establishment of larger farms (Morell 2011, 66). Together with difficulties for smallholders to be economically sustainable and mechanization within animal and textile production, this led to fewer opportunities for women to remain in the countryside (Flygare 2011, 80; Schön 2000, 299). While men were still wanted as workers on larger farms until the large-scale agricultural mechanization of the 1950s, women left for the cities. The changing circumstances for young female agricultural workers during this period are also recognized in political debates on the flight from the countryside (Berry 2023, 98).

From the 1930s onward, a new expansion thus gathered pace. Industries established in the 1920s were growing, and new industries were founded. Both in- and out-migration rates increased, though this was faster for the former. Besides the new shipyard, the sugar industry, and the metal industry, new textile companies started up, too, and this might also explain in part the relatively fast increase in the in-migration of women. World War II saw a fall in in-migration, but this was followed by a new peak immediately afterward, this time associated with the inflow of Nordic and European refugees.

The third period, 1950–1974, saw the continued growth of major industries in Landskrona, but it also saw rationalization and the closure of the sugar mill. In-migration increased from the mid-1950s to the early 1970s, with peaks in 1970 and 1974. Out-migration was at quite a low level but increased sharply in 1972 and the following years. The structural crises in Swedish industry hit Landskrona hard. Almost the entire textile sector closed down in the 1970s, and both the metal sector and the shipyard faced problems that resulted in job cuts and closures in the early 1980s. The new transformation period from around the mid-1970s did not give rise to new industries and new jobs in Landskrona. Instead, the crisis was prolonged until well into the 1980s. From then on, in-migration started to increase again, and the volatile decade of the 1990s was eventually followed by a positive trend in in-migration during the first decade of the 2000s, which saw out-migration increase as well, although at a slower rate, indicating the renewed attractiveness of the city.

Subtracting out-migration from in-migration gives us the net migration total (see Figure 4.4). There was in general positive net migration to Landskrona, evidence that overall migration was an important part of population growth in the city during the twentieth century. There were, however, two distinctive periods of negative net migration that coincided with the industrial crises of the 1920s and the 1970s. In addition, the years of negative net migration in the 1990s were interrupted by the massive inflow of refugees in 1994.

The flows in and out of Landskrona can thus be related to the economic development of the city. However, flows do not show who migrated in and out.

Figure 4.4 Net migration (per 1,000 population), Landskrona, 1905–2014.
Source: Scanian Economic-Demographic Database (SEDD; Bengtsson et al. 2021).

We will address one further aspect before studying migrant characteristics more closely: from where, and where to, did the migrants migrate? In- and out-migration rests on available alternatives. Following the overall development outlined above, agriculture and the countryside at large in the early period still offered alternative employment (circular migration) but less so later on. Other urban contexts might also have provided an alternative in terms of labor prospects. Moving from a rural context to a city might have been the first step in migration toward a larger city (stage migration).

Table 4.1 shows the last place of residence among in-migrants to Landskrona before they came to the city, by period. Most in-migrants came from the region of Scania (*Skåne*), predominantly from the countryside, with a fourth of them coming from within 10 kilometers. However, the cities closest to Landskrona also contributed migrants. Another important source of migration into the city was the countryside in the nearby counties and also the rest of Sweden. This bears out the fact that southwestern Scania was a positive net destination in Swedish internal migration (Kronborg and Nilsson 1975, 50; SOS 1960, table D). In-migration in the early period consisted of both rural and urban migrants and even migrants from other large Swedish cities, reflecting the diversity of demand for labor in Landskrona's industries—these were not merely unskilled former

Table 4.1 In-migration to Landskrona 1905–2014 by period and previous residence (percent).

	Urban Sweden	Rural Sweden	Urban Scania	Rural Scania	International	Total
1905–1929	9.3	23.4	20.0	43.3	3.9	100
1930–1949	10.4	26.3	21.8	35.0	6.5	100
1950–1974	11.4	28.0	17.4	29.3	14.0	100
1975–1994	7.7	18.7	15.9	41.0	16.6	100
1995–2014	8.0	13.0	18.4	37.6	22.9	100

Notes: Urban Scania consists of the cities of Malmö, Lund, and Helsingborg. Urban Sweden consists of Stockholm, Gothenburg, and the twenty largest cities during the twentieth century (except those in Urban Scania). Rural Scania and Rural Sweden are residuals of the urban categories.
Source: Scanian Economic-Demographic Database (SEDD; Bengtsson et al. 2021).

agricultural laborers. Although some relative changes took place over time, notably the declining share coming from what we call Rural Sweden, the largest change was the increasing share that came from abroad.

As for out-migration (see Table 4.2), the pattern is similar although with some differences. The share of those moving to the closest cities in Scania was higher than the in-migration from these cities, and the share of those moving abroad was significantly smaller than the inflow.

Tables 4.1–4.3 show that the net effect consists of an inflow from rural areas and an outflow to urban contexts. In the first two periods, the rural part of Scania provided most of the net, but over time this changed to include the rest of the Swedish countryside and, above all, international migration. Throughout the century more people left Landskrona for other urban contexts than the other way round. In that sense, the city functioned partly as a stage in rural to urban migration. Another interesting feature is the negative net migration to rural Scania from the 1950s to the mid-1990s. These people most probably did not return to agriculture since employment in this sector fell massively during this period. It is more likely that this migration reflected the emergence of dormitory towns and other forms of residence for the city population outside the city limits. Finally, the finding that international migration increased in significance over time brings us to the subject of immigration and emigration as separate parts of the migration flows.

Table 4.2 Out-migration from Landskrona 1905–2014 by period and destination (percent).

	Urban Sweden	Rural Sweden	Urban Scania	Rural Scania	International	Total
1905–1929	11.9	22.6	22.6	36.9	5.8	100
1930–1949	17.3	26.7	28.8	24.2	2.9	100
1950–1974	12.0	24.5	22.1	32.6	8.8	100
1975–1994	7.8	16.7	23.4	44.8	7.4	100
1995–2014	8.9	11.3	29.2	39.9	10.7	100

Notes: Urban Scania consists of the cities of Malmö, Lund, and Helsingborg. Urban Sweden consists of Stockholm, Gothenburg, and the twenty largest cities during the twentieth century (except those in Urban Scania). Rural Scania and Rural Sweden are residuals of the urban categories.
Source: Scanian Economic-Demographic Database (SEDD; Bengtsson et al. 2021).

Table 4.3 Net migration, Landskrona 1905–2014, by period and origin and destination (number of migrants).

	Rural Scania	Urban Scania	Rural Sweden	Urban Sweden	International
1905–1929	1,834	−549	314	−606	−441
1930–1949	3,359	−464	934	−892	917
1950–1974	−647	−1,323	1,644	−39	1,975
1975–1994	−1,988	−2,819	366	−148	2,884
1995–2014	766	−3,690	1,303	−28	6,156

Notes: Urban Scania consists of the cities of Malmö, Lund, and Helsingborg. Urban Sweden consists of Stockholm, Gothenburg, and the twenty largest cities during the twentieth century (except those in Urban Scania). Rural Scania and Rural Sweden are residuals of the urban categories.
Source: Scanian Economic-Demographic Database (SEDD; Bengtsson et al. 2021).

International Migration to Landskrona

One of the most important demographic developments in Sweden from World War II onward has been increasing international immigration. Landskrona has been one of the top immigrant-receiving municipalities in Sweden throughout this period, and, in 2018, about one-third of its population were either first- or second-generation immigrants, which was higher than the national average. The development and composition of Swedish migration are mirrored in the migration experience of Landskrona, which means that before World War II very few international migrants arrived in the city. By studying Figure 4.1 we see an increasing inflow of Nordic and European immigrants during the war years. Danish Jews left in the autumn of 1943 by crossing Öresund to seek refuge in Sweden. Many of them arrived in Landskrona. We see patterns of European unrest in the 1950s during which migrants who fled the Hungarian Revolution of 1956 came to Landskrona. However, those who came in the late 1950s were increasingly labor migrants, such as Yugoslavians and Finns. Growing labor demand in the post-war years increased the number of migrants entering Sweden. More than two-thirds of those coming to Landskrona during the 1950s and '60s came from other Nordic countries, with Danes being the predominant group throughout this period. Workers were also recruited from Germany, Austria, and Italy in the 1950s and from Yugoslavia, Greece, and Turkey in the 1960s. The period of labor migration to Sweden, and to Landskrona specifically, was characterized by large fluctuations in the number of immigrants entering, which can be explained by changing demand in the production industry combined with the economic performance of the sending countries. The peak in 1964–1965 (see Figure 4.1) is explained by increased immigration from southern Europe, while that in 1969–1970 mainly consists of labor migrants from Finland (Lundh and Ohlsson 1999).

Toward the end of the 1960s, the unbroken period of economic growth in Sweden came to an end, which led to decreasing demand for immigrant labor. Sweden changed its immigration policy and placed greater restrictions on labor migration, and, in the mid-1970s, most immigrants entering the country were refugees or family members of previous immigrants. Migrants from Asia started entering Landskrona in bigger numbers in the late 1970s, a share that grew further in the 1980s due to large numbers of Iranian refugees. The 1990s were dominated by European migration, explained mostly by the Balkans War, and, in the 2000s, migration consisted mainly of Europeans and Asians. The share of Nordic migrants decreased substantially from the mid-1970s, although there were periods of increased migration in the early 1990s and early 2000s. Our multivariate analysis investigates the likelihood of migrant origin groups moving to/from Landskrona from/to the surrounding countryside and neighboring larger cities.

The Migrants: Estimating Migration Flows in Landskrona

From our discussion above, we have learned that the attractiveness of the city changed over time in accordance with economic change. We are now interested in studying the characteristics of the migrants and estimating group differences, focusing particularly on the differences between social groups and individuals of different origins. We expected to see differences in characteristics regarding the likelihood of entering or leaving Landskrona in good and bad times. To estimate group differences regarding this likelihood, we applied logistic regressions and control for variables that may have differed between social groups and origin groups and that may influence the patterns seen in the tables and figures above, such as age, gender, and civil status.

We estimated group differences regarding the likelihood of (1) migrating to Landskrona and staying there for at least five years; (2) migrating out of Landskrona and staying away for at least five years; (3) migrating to Landskrona from neighboring larger cities (Malmö, Lund, and Helsingborg); (4) migrating from Landskrona to neighboring larger cities (Malmö, Lund, and Helsingborg); (5) migrating to Landskrona from the surrounding countryside within a 10-kilometer radius; and (6) migrating from Landskrona to the surrounding countryside within a 10-kilometer radius. We estimated five models, one model per time period, for every stated outcome.

To estimate differences between social classes regarding the likelihood of migration, we defined six groups based on the Historical International Social Class Scheme (HISCLASS) (see Chapter 1): higher white-collar (HISCLASS 1–2), lower white-collar (HISCLASS 3–5), skilled worker (HISCLASS 6–7), farmer (HISCLASS 8), lower-skilled worker (HISCLASS 9–10), and unskilled worker (HISCLASS 11–12). Lower-skilled serves as our reference category in all models. We also included those with missing information on occupation, which in many cases is due to unemployment. We also included region of origin, which is important since Landskrona has been a major immigrant-receiving municipality in Sweden.

As outlined, we controlled for age, defined here as age groups 16–24, 25–44, and 45–64. We excluded individuals under the age of 16 and above the age of 64. The age group 25–44 serves as the reference category in all models. Moreover, we controlled for civil status, gender, and whether the individual was born in Landskrona municipality.

It is important to emphasize that for both out-migration and in-migration we compared migrants with the population in Landskrona (our control group). This may not be optimal for analyzing in-migration, but we have no complete information about the place of origin for the in-migrants. This means that our in-migration control group was never "at risk" of migrating into Landskrona because they were already living in the city.[1]

We first analyzed in-migration to Landskrona (see Table 4.4). Starting with social class, it is evident that white-collar occupations had a higher likelihood of migrating into Landskrona compared to the reference group of lower-skilled workers in all periods. This was expected, as we know that individuals who

Table 4.4 Odds ratios of in-migration (staying at least five years). Estimates from logistic regression.

		1905–1929	1930–1949	1950–1974	1975–1994	1995–2014
Social class	Higher white-collar	1.446***	1.342***	1.537***	1.346***	1.237***
	Lower white-collar	1.210***	1.066**	1.242***	1.045	1.096***
	Skilled workers	1.097***	1.078**	1.134***	0.926**	0.985
	Lower-skilled	ref.	ref.	ref.	ref.	ref.
	Farmers	1.786***	1.513***	2.562***	2.210*	1.035
	Unskilled	0.722***	0.773***	0.779***	0.896**	0.967
	NA	2.000***	2.011***	1.244***	1.475***	1.506***
Origin	Sweden	ref.	ref.	ref.	ref.	ref.
	Nordic	0.965	1.481***	1.784***	1.043	0.903**
	Europe	1.130	1.899***	2.035***	1.711***	1.186***
	Asia	2.344	0.776	1.649**	2.189***	1.371***
	Africa			1.497	1.741***	1.214**
	N. + S. America, Oceania	0.602**	0.415***	0.666*	1.605***	1.163
Age groups	16–24	1.507***	1.480***	1.755***	1.335***	1.116***
	25–44	ref.	ref.	ref.	ref.	ref.
	45–64	0.347***	0.324***	0.437***	0.482***	0.577***
Gender	Male	ref.	ref.	ref.	ref.	ref.
	Female	1.005	0.950**	0.954**	1.010	0.994
Civil status	Married	ref.	ref.	ref.	ref.	ref.
	Single, widower/widow	1.204***	1.373***	1.128***	1.133***	0.925***
Place of birth	Landskrona	ref.	ref.	ref.	ref.	ref.
	Not Landskrona	4.376***	6.139***	4.295***	2.159***	2.277***
Observations		295,355	310,160	464,065	350,455	287,035
Individuals		32,973	33,499	49,067	41,480	41,326

Note: *p < 0.1, **p < 0.05, ***p < 0.01.
Source: Scanian Economic-Demographic Database (SEDD; Bengtsson et al. 2021).

expect higher returns on migration tend to be mobile and more likely to migrate. These patterns are not stable over time, however, and we see the strongest likelihood of both higher and lower white-collar immigration during the record years of 1950–1974, with a lower likelihood of these classes being among the migrants in the later periods. In all time periods, the unskilled were the least mobile.

Several interesting patterns are visible when looking at origin differences. First, individuals with a Nordic background were more likely to come to Landskrona in the second and third periods, which is explained by substantial Nordic labor migration to Sweden and Landskrona in these decades. In Landskrona, Danes were the predominant Nordic group. In the last two periods Nordic migration was small, as reflected in Table 4.1. Second, European migrants were most likely to come to Landskrona throughout the study period, and especially during the years of growth in 1950–1974. Third, African and Asian migrants had the highest likelihood of in-migrating in the fourth period, 1975–1994.

As expected, in terms of the highest anticipated returns to migration, the youngest age group was the most likely one to migrate into Landskrona in all time periods. This effect is strongest in the period 1950–1974, but decreases in the most recent period. During this period Landskrona had unemployment levels higher than the national average, which may partly explain the decrease in the migration of young people to Landskrona.

Finally, civil status varies in importance across periods. In the earlier periods, unmarried individuals were more likely to migrate to Landskrona. This changed over time, and, in the last period between 1995 and 2014, those who were married had a slightly higher likelihood of in-migrating. This slightly higher likelihood is not reflected in any gender patterns as we see very weak and mainly insignificant gender differences in the likelihood of migration.

Table 4.5 shows the likelihood of migration out of Landskrona without returning within the next five years. Migration can be costly both in the long run, when individuals run the risk of unemployment at their destination, and in the short run, in terms of transportation costs and other costs related to moving (Sjaastad 1962). Individuals from a higher social class are more likely to afford the costs of moving and will as a result be more mobile. For out-migration, as expected, those of a higher social class—the higher and lower white-collar workers—were more mobile than the other groups, and the likelihood of their out-migrating was even stronger except in the first period.

Patterns in origin differences appear to be similar to patterns for in-migration. In periods with a high likelihood of in-migration for particular groups, there was a high likelihood of out-migration.

For out-migration, the middle age group, 25–44, was the most likely to leave Landskrona, and this is different from in-migration, which showed the younger group was more mobile. Later, we will study migration for different age groups

Table 4.5 Odds ratios of out-migration (staying away at least five years). Estimates from logistic regression.

		1905–1929	1930–1949	1950–1974	1975–1994	1995–2014
Social class	Higher white collar	1.126**	1.801***	1.732***	1.578***	1.457***
	Lower white collar	0.923***	1.129***	1.310***	1.093***	1.260***
	Skilled workers	0.832***	0.800***	0.900***	0.869***	0.973
	Lower skilled	ref.	ref.	ref.	ref.	ref.
	Farmers	1.116	1.076	2.062***	5.895***	0.708
	Unskilled	0.529***	0.658***	0.797***	0.757***	1.005
	Missing	1.113**	1.765***	1.259***	1.170***	1.141***
Origin	Sweden	ref.	ref.	ref.	ref.	ref.
	Nordic	0.818**	1.138	1.677***	1.940***	2.295***
	Europe	0.749***	1.012	1.402***	0.929**	0.644***
	Asia	1.499	0.484	1.381	1.604***	1.137***
	Africa			2.520***	2.192***	1.478***
	N+ S America, Oceania	0.963	0.602*	1.202	0.963	1.527***
Age groups	16–24	0.946**	0.846***	0.915***	0.719***	0.772***
	25–44	ref.	ref.	ref.	ref.	ref.
	45–64	0.254***	0.212***	0.215***	0.228***	0.274***
Gender	Male	ref.	ref.	ref.	ref.	ref.
	Female	0.987	1.070***	0.884***	0.891***	0.958**
Civil status	Married	ref.	ref.	ref.	ref.	ref.
	Single, widower/widow	2.253***	2.693***	1.380***	1.163***	1.385***
Place of birth	Landskrona	ref.	ref.	ref.	ref.	ref.
	Not Landskrona	4.720***	5.113***	3.159***	2.694***	2.836***
Observations		295,355	310,160	464,065	350,455	287,035
Individuals		32,973	33,499	49,067	41,480	41,326

Notes: *p < 0.1, **p < 0.05, ***p < 0.01. For out-migration of at least five years, all individuals who returned to Landskrona, regardless of years stayed away, are again included in the risk group (the population of Landskrona).

Source: Scanian Economic-Demographic Database (SEDD; Bengtsson et al. 2021).

on the basis of their destination, which could vary. Younger individuals may have migrated to go to university or find their first job, while middle-aged individuals may instead have left Landskrona to buy a home and raise a family in one of the neighboring municipalities.

Marriage seems once again to hamper migration, as we see for out-migration, too, that married individuals were less likely to migrate than were unmarried; however, this seems to have been unrelated to gender because there are no strong gender differences in terms of out-migration.

To paint an even more nuanced picture, the following analyses illustrate the likelihood of the different groups migrating to/from another city and the surrounding countryside. When studying immigration from neighboring cities (Malmö, Lund, and Helsingborg), we once again see that individuals with white-collar occupations were more prone to migrate into Landskrona than were other groups. We also see that the likelihood of their doing so increased over time and was highest in the later periods. This mirrors the results in Table 4.4, showing that the white-collar group was the most mobile throughout the period as a result of their expected higher returns to migration than individuals of a lower social class; it also shows that individuals of a higher social class may have moved to Landskrona for the sake of finding housing.

Migrants originating from Nordic or European countries were in all periods less likely to come to Landskrona from other towns than were Swedes, an indication that international migrants came directly to Landskrona without living in one or more other towns in Sweden first. Toward the end of the period, migrants from Asia and Africa were more likely to come to Landskrona from neighboring towns.

There is an age pattern that changes at a point between our periods. In the first three periods, the younger cohorts were more likely to come to Landskrona; however, in the last two, they were less likely to do so than the reference group. In the earlier periods, it is possible that many young people moved from neighboring towns to Landskrona not only to find a job in what was an expanding industrial city but also to attend the teachers' college that existed there between 1922 and 1972. This pattern is also potentially mirrored in the gender differences we see: females were more prone to migrate in the first three periods, but not in the last two (Table 4.6).

Out-migration from Landskrona to Malmö, Lund, and Helsingborg largely follows the same patterns as in-migration. Higher mobility is observed for white-collar individuals, and for both in- and out-migration it is observed for unmarried individuals. Finally, international migrants were more likely to leave Landskrona for neighboring towns than were native Swedes in the more recent periods (Table 4.7).

Table 4.6 Odds ratios of in-migration from Malmö, Lund, Helsingborg (staying at least five years). Estimates from logistic regression.

		1905–1929	1930–1949	1950–1974	1975–1994	1995–2014
Social class	Higher white-collar	1.273**	1.949***	2.071***	2.113***	2.457***
	Lower white-collar	1.238***	1.627***	1.640***	1.237***	1.505***
	Skilled workers	1.300***	1.179**	1.022	0.762***	0.833
	Lower-skilled	ref.	ref.	ref.	ref.	ref.
	Farmers	0.772	1.242	1.564		
	Unskilled	0.567***	0.621***	0.840*	0.944	1.075
	NA	1.481***	1.623***	1.237**	1.289***	1.288***
Origin	Sweden	ref.	ref.	ref.	ref.	ref.
	Nordic	0.603**	0.557***	0.669***	0.578***	0.516***
	Europe	0.576**	0.622**	0.815**	0.741***	0.687***
	Asia			0.372	0.928	1.357***
	Africa			1.101	2.226**	0.864
	N.+ S. America, Oceania	0.773	0.445	0.597	1.286	0.952
Age groups	16–24	1.190***	1.263***	1.593***	0.760***	0.804***
	25–44	ref.	ref.	ref.	ref.	ref.
	45–64	0.345***	0.281***	0.322***	0.451***	0.576***
Gender	Male	ref.	ref.	ref.	ref.	ref.
	Female	1.176***	1.188***	1.141***	0.924	0.967
Civil status	Married	ref.	ref.	ref.	ref.	ref.
	Single, widower/widow	1.218***	1.259***	1.045	2.146***	1.697***
Place of birth	Landskrona	ref.	ref.	ref.	ref.	ref.
	Not Landskrona	2.998***	4.906***	3.734***	2.620***	3.288***
Observations		295,321	309,955	463,793	350,326	286,974
Individuals		32,965	33,460	48,999	41,467	41,322

Note: *p < 0.1, **p < 0.05, ***p < 0.01.
Source: Scanian Economic-Demographic Database (SEDD; Bengtsson et al. 2021).

Table 4.7 Odds ratios of out-migration to Malmö, Lund, Helsingborg (staying away at least five years). Estimates from logistic regression.

		1905–1929	1930–1949	1950–1974	1975–1994	1995–2014
Social class	Higher white-collar	0.737***	1.519***	2.145***	2.631***	2.297***
	Lower white-collar	0.978	1.116*	1.457***	1.484***	1.740***
	Skilled workers	0.948	0.822***	0.821***	0.776***	0.936
	Lower-skilled	ref.	ref.	ref.	ref.	ref.
	Farmers	0.957	0.318***	1.324	1.546	
	Unskilled	0.432***	0.560***	0.874**	0.821**	1.219**
	NA	0.988	1.499***	1.180***	1.319***	1.237***
Origin	Sweden	ref.	ref.	ref.	ref.	ref.
	Nordic	0.698*	0.578***	0.647***	0.773***	1.382***
	Europe	0.777	0.644***	1.275***	1.333***	0.897**
	Asia			1.517	2.853***	1.884***
	Africa			4.294***	3.155***	2.072***
	N.+S. America, Oceania	0.870	0.542	1.664	0.482*	1.906***
Age groups	16–24	0.822***	0.771***	0.969	0.810***	0.960
	25–44	ref.	ref.	ref.	ref.	ref.
	45–64	0.292***	0.272***	0.266***	0.283***	0.293***
Gender	Male	ref.	ref.	ref.	ref.	ref.
	Female	1.224***	1.180***	1.009	0.911**	0.955
Civil status	Married	ref.	ref.	ref.	ref.	ref.
	Single, widower/widow	2.223***	2.696***	1.892***	2.240***	1.691***
Place of birth	Landskrona	ref.	ref.	ref.	ref.	ref.
	Not Landskrona	3.999***	4.076***	2.290***	2.675***	2.831***
Observations		295,348	310,140	464,020	350,455	286,974
Individuals		32,971	33,494	49,054	41,480	41,322

Note: *$p < 0.1$, **$p < 0.05$, ***$p < 0.01$.
Source: Scanian Economic-Demographic Database (SEDD; Bengtsson et al. 2021).

Let us now turn to the analyses looking at in- and out-migration from/to the surrounding rural areas. Interestingly, we no longer see highest mobility among white-collar workers; instead, it is the lower-skilled who in most periods were the ones most prone to migrate. This can be linked to job opportunities that were potentially an important pull factor for migration to the city. Naturally farmers migrated to Landskrona as well. For immigration there is a strong age effect, with the youngest group having the highest likelihood of coming to Landskrona (Table 4.8) in all periods.

The likelihood of international migrants in-migrating from the surrounding rural area is comparably low. This comes as no surprise, as it was uncommon for international migrants to live in the countryside. The pattern is similar for out-migration to the surrounding rural area because there was a very low tendency among international migrants to leave Landskrona compared to Swedes.

Table 4.9 reveals that those from the highest social class were least prone to leave for the surrounding countryside, which is unexpected considering that previous analyses have shown them to be more mobile than other groups. Costs in relation to migration could also be more easily overcome by the higher social classes (Sjaastad 1962). That said, the surrounding countryside may have had fewer pull factors for the higher social classes compared to, say, the neighboring cities, as seen in Table 4.5.

Moreover, a changing age pattern is visible. For the earlier period, there was a higher likelihood of the youngest group leaving Landskrona for the surrounding countryside, while for the most recent two periods the chances were comparably low. In the earlier periods, young people could find work more easily in agriculture, attracting them to the countryside, but from the 1950s onward we no longer see this pattern.

Conclusion

The industrial city of the twentieth century rested on migration, whereby streams of people moving in and out of it illustrated and defined its changing character over time. For most periods throughout the century, the majority of its inhabitants were migrants—people not born in the city. Their origin was rural or another urban context, and they came increasingly from abroad and over greater distances. They were attracted by job opportunities and by the advantages of the buzz of city life; they were pushed out from their origins by depression and crisis. Other migrants left Landskrona, escaping the overcrowding to find peace and tranquility in the countryside, if income allowed, or taking steps to find a better job. The dynamics of migration were, and are, a vital characteristic of the industrial and post-industrial city.

Table 4.8 Odds ratios of in-migration from rural areas <10 km from Landskrona (staying at least five years). Estimates from logistic regression.

		1905–1929	1930–1949	1950–1974	1975–1994	1995–2014
Social class	Higher white-collar	0.372***	0.241***	0.350***	0.860	0.713***
	Lower white-collar	0.651***	0.521***	0.833***	0.993	0.899**
	Skilled workers	0.787***	0.907	1.038	1.090	1.210**
	Lower-skilled	ref.	ref.	ref.	ref.	ref.
	Farmers	3.799***	2.597***	4.583***	3.251**	
	Unskilled	1.174*	0.928	0.759***	1.020	0.905
	NA	2.136***	1.360**	0.789***	0.826***	0.765***
Origin	Sweden	ref.	ref.	ref.	ref.	ref.
	Nordic	0.540**	0.313***	0.795***	0.508***	0.568***
	Europe	0.043***	0.059***	0.311***	0.431***	0.196***
	Asia				0.232***	0.182***
	Africa				0.222**	0.177***
	N.+S. America, Oceania	0.188*		0.220	0.582	0.727
Age groups	16–24	2.550***	2.213***	2.464***	2.094***	1.793***
	25–44	ref.	ref.	ref.	ref.	ref.
	45–64	0.382***	0.435***	0.563***	0.577***	0.851***
Gender	Male	ref.	ref.	ref.	ref.	ref.
	Female	0.968	0.861***	1.016	1.060*	1.009
Civil status	Married	ref.	ref.	ref.	ref.	ref.
	Single, widower/widow	1.109	1.373***	0.871**	1.111**	1.023
Place of birth	Landskrona	ref.	ref.	ref.	ref.	ref.
	Not Landskrona	7.485***	10.559***	4.177***	1.559***	1.587***
Observations		295,321	309,316	463,700	350,455	286,974
Individuals		32,965	33,370	48,978	41,480	41,322

Note: *p < 0.1, **p < 0.05, ***p < 0.01.
Source: Scanian Economic-Demographic Database (SEDD; Bengtsson et al. 2021).

Table 4.9 Odds ratios of out-migration to rural areas <10 km from Landskrona (staying away at least five years). Estimates from logistic regression.

		1905–1929	1930–1949	1950–1974	1975–1994	1995–2014
Social class	Higher white-collar	0.310***	0.417***	0.882	0.816**	0.791**
	Lower white-collar	0.469***	0.691***	1.180***	0.889***	1.007
	Skilled workers	0.605***	0.642***	1.126**	1.082	1.184**
	Lower-skilled	ref.	ref.	ref.	ref.	ref.
	Farmers	2.299***	2.307**	2.923***	5.203***	0.696
	Unskilled	0.747***	0.869	0.773***	0.670***	0.827**
	NA	1.024	0.890	0.779***	0.549***	0.618***
Origin	Sweden	ref.	ref.	ref.	ref.	ref.
	Nordic	0.603*	0.366***	0.575***	0.853**	0.745***
	Europe	0.105***	0.237***	0.412***	0.438***	0.217***
	Asia			0.591	0.147***	0.285***
	Africa				0.152***	0.247***
	N.+S. America, Oceania	0.332	0.568	0.277*	0.257***	0.605**
Age groups	16–24	1.531***	1.450***	1.054	0.728***	0.586***
	25–44	ref.	ref.	ref.	ref.	ref.
	45–64	0.244***	0.263***	0.167***	0.201***	0.262***
Gender	Male	ref.	ref.	ref.	ref.	ref.
	Female	0.940	1.327***	1.005	1.066*	1.071*
Civil status	Married	ref.	ref.	ref.	ref.	ref.
	Single, widower/widow	1.400***	1.723***	0.427***	0.595***	1.164***
Place of birth	Landskrona	ref.	ref.	ref.	ref.	ref.
	Not Landskrona	6.607***	7.534***	1.836***	1.792***	1.601***
Observations		295,053	310,101	463,921	350,455	287,035
Individuals		32,933	33,476	49,021	41,480	41,326

Note: *p < 0.1, **p < 0.05, ***p < 0.01.
Source: Scanian Economic-Demographic Database (SEDD; Bengtsson et al. 2021).

The start of our study period was a time of industrial expansion and urban population growth in Landskrona and indeed in Sweden as a whole. Until the 1920s, many new industries were established in the cities which attracted workers from the surrounding countryside. This was followed by the highly volatile decade of the 1920s and the depression of the 1930s, but then came new industrial expansion based on electrification and the motor car. The volatility of this era meant that, until around 1950, migration was circular, with workers migrating back and forth between city and countryside and also between cities. The third phase, 1950–1974, was the golden age of Swedish industrial production. The urban population grew rapidly, and international migration increased. However, this period ended with the structural crisis of the early 1970s, which had far-reaching consequences for the industrial city. Traditional industrial jobs were harder to find, which in theory would have meant increasing out-migration. However, industrial cities all over Sweden were hit by this crisis, leaving few opportunities to find similar employment elsewhere. The final period, 1995–2014, is one of economic recovery but also one of changing migration patterns as a growing share of urban in-migration consisted of international migrants who came increasingly from non-Western countries.

The descriptive patterns in Landskrona's population development mirror in many ways the country's overall economic development. On the whole, there is a positive net migration to Landskrona throughout the period, although with the marked exception of two periods that coincided with the industrial crises of the 1920s and 1970s. It is important to remember that Landskrona had a large inflow of refugees in the mid-1990s, which interrupted the years of negative net migration, including those during the crisis of the 1990s.

Important results emerge in the multivariate analysis. When studying in-migration we see that, together with the higher white-collar workers, those who were lower white-collar and skilled were more likely to in-migrate compared to the lower-skilled, especially in the earlier periods. We also see that the white-collar and skilled workers came from neighboring cities rather than the surrounding countryside. Unskilled workers were, however, more likely to migrate from the surrounding countryside than the lower-skilled in the first period.

There is, moreover, a strong age effect for in-migration. Those who were younger were more mobile and prone to migrate to Landskrona, be it from a rural or an urban context. This was true for rural in-migration throughout the period but was no longer so for urban in-migration from the 1970s onward, when individuals in the middle age group became those most likely to move. In the earlier periods, interesting gender differences emerged, whereby the urban in-migration was higher among women while rural in-migration was higher among men.

Taken together, shifting types of migration, be it from other cities or the surrounding countryside (urban and rural in-migration), reflect a shifting demand for labor in the industrial city.

For out-migration, the middle age group (25–44) was more prone to move in all the periods. However, in the first two periods the youngest (16–24) were most likely to move to the surrounding countryside, which can be seen as an indication of circular migration for a group that disappeared after 1950. In terms of social class, white-collar workers were most likely to leave Landskrona, and they also tended to move to other urban areas. For rural out-migration, the lower-skilled were predominant except in one period, 1950–1974, when it was the skilled and lower white-collar workers. We can interpret this as an indication of increasing middle-class out-migration to surrounding suburbs. Civil status is also important, with married persons being more likely to leave for rural areas in this period.

Overall, we observe migration patterns that follow our overall expectations based on the economic development of Landskrona. We see patterns of circular migration in the early periods, middle-class out-migration (skilled and lower white-collar workers) to the surrounding countryside during times of economic growth, and white-collar out-migration during the economic crisis of the 1970s—although no corresponding out-migration of the unskilled workers as their options were limited during this crisis.

Note

1. For out-migration (Tables 4.5, 4.7 and 4.9), the control group (the population of Landskrona) is at risk.

Sources

Sveriges Officiella Statistik (SOS). https://www.scb.se/sv_/Hitta-statistik/Historisk-statistik/Digitaliserat---Statistik-efter-serie/Sveriges-officiella-statistik-SOS-utg-1912-/
Befolkningsstatistik 1911–2001.
Folkmängden inom administrativa områden, 1960.

References

Åkerman, S. 1975. "Internal Migration, Industrialization and Urbanisation (1895–1930): A Summary of the Västmanland Study." *Scandinavian Economic History Review* 23 (2): 149–158.

Bengtsson, T. 1990. "Migration, Wages, and Urbanization in Sweden in the Nineteenth Century." In *Urbanization in History: A Process of Dynamic Interactions*, edited by A. van der Woude, A. Hayami, and J. de Vries, 186–204. Oxford: Clarendon Press.

Bengtsson, T., M. Dribe, L. Quaranta, and P. Svensson. 2021. "The Scanian Economic Demographic Database: Version 7.2 (Machine-readable database)." Lund: Lund University, Centre for Economic Demography.

Bengtsson, T., and M. Johansson. 1994. "Internal Migration." In *Population, Economy, and Welfare in Sweden*, edited by T. Bengtsson, 65–85. Berlin: Springer.

Berry, G. 2023. *Den självstyrda periferin. Lanthushållsundervisningen och styrningen av den svenska landsbygden, 1890–1970* [The Self-Governed Periphery: Rural Domestic Education and the Governance of the Swedish Countryside, 1890–1970]. Uppsala, Sweden: Acta Universitatis Upsaliensis.

Costa, D., and M. E. Kahn. 2000. "Power Couples: Changes in the Locational Choice of the College Educated, 1940–1990." *Quarterly Journal of Economics* 115 (4): 1287–1315.

Constant, A., and D. S. Massey. 2003. "Self-Selection, Earnings, and Out-Migration: A Longitudinal Study of Immigrants to Germany." *Journal of Population Economics* 16 (4): 631–653.

Flygare, I. 2011. "Swedish Smallholdings: An Enduring Element of the Countryside." In *Agriculture and Forestry in Sweden Since 1900: Geographical and Historical Studies*, edited by H. Antonson and U. Jansson, 74–92. Stockholm: The Royal Swedish Academy of Agriculture and Forestry.

Glaeser, E., J. Kolko, and A. Saiz. 2001. "Consumer City." *Journal of Economic Geography* 1 (1): 27–50.

Godlund, S., and K. Godlund. 1976. "Norrköpings ekonomiska och sociala historia 1915–1970 [The Economic and Social History of Norrköping 1915–1970]." In *Norrköpings historia, del 6: Tiden 1914–1970* [The History of Norrköping, Part 6, 1914–1970], edited by B. Helmfrid and S. Kraft, 1–296. Stockholm: Norstedt.

Harris, J., and M. Todaro. 1970. "Migration, Unemployment and Development: A Two-Sector Analysis." *American Economic Review* 60 (1): 126–142.

Hellspong, M. 1974. "Städer [Towns]." In *Land och stad. Svenska samhällstyper och livsformer från medeltid till nutid* [Town and Country: Swedish Forms of Life and Society since the Middle Ages], edited by M. Hellspong and O. Löfgren, 179–226. Lund: LiberLäromedel.

Isacson, M., and L. Magnusson. 1983. *Vägen till fabrikerna: Industriell tradition och yrkeskunnande i Sverige under 1800-talet* [The Road to the Factories: Industrial Tradition and Occupational Skills in Sweden During the 19th Century]. Stockholm: Gidlunds.

Karlsson, T., and C. Lundh (eds.). 2022. *Liv i rörelse: Göteborgs befolkning och arbetsmarknad 1900–1950* [Life in Motion: The Population and Labor Market of Göteborg 1900–1950]. Lund: Nordic Academic Press.

Keung Wong, D. F., C. Y. Li, and H. X. Song. 2007. "Rural Migrant Workers in Urban China: Living a Marginalised Life." *International Journal of Social Welfare* 16 (1): 32–40.

Kronborg, B., and T. Nilsson. 1975. *Stadsflyttare: Industrialisering, migration och social mobilitiet med utgångspunkt från Halmstad, 1870–1910* [City Movers: Industrialization,

Migration, and Social Mobility in Halmstad, 1870–1910]. Uppsala: Almqvist & Wiksell International.

Lee, E. S. 1966. "A Theory of Migration." *Demography* 3 (1): 47–57.

Lundh, C. 2002. *Spelets regler. Institutioner och lönebildning på den svenska arbetsmarknaden 1850–2000* [The Rules of the Game: Institutions and Wage Formation on the Swedish Labor Market 1850–2000]. Stockholm: SNS förlag.

Lundh, C., and R. Ohlsson. 1999. *Från arbetskraftsimport till flyktinginvandring* [From Labor Import to Refugee Migration]. Stockholm: SNS.

Lundh, C., and S. Prado. 2012. "Markets and Politics: The Swedish Urban-Rural Wage Gap, 1865–1985." *European Review of Economic History* 19 (1): 67–87.

Magnusson, L. 1997. *Sveriges ekonomiska historia* [An Economic History of Sweden]. Stockholm: Tiden.

Massey, D. S. 1988. "Economic Development and International Migration in Comparative Perspective." *Population and Development Review* 14 (3): 383–413.

Massey, D. S., J. Arango, G. Hugo, et al. 1993. "Theories of International Migration: A Review and Appraisal." *Population and Development Review* 19 (3): 431–466.

Mincer, J. 1978. "Family Migration Decisions." *Journal of Political Economy* 86 (5): 749–773.

Morell, M. 2001. *Jordbruket i industrisamhället, 1870–1945: Det svenska jordbrukets historia, del 4* [Agriculture in Industrial Society, 1870–1945: The History of Swedish Agriculture, Part 4]. Stockholm: Natur och Kultur.

Morell, M. 2011. "Farmland: Ownership or Leasehold, Inheritance or Purchase." In *Agriculture and Forestry in Sweden Since 1900*, edited by H. Antonson and U. Jansson, 56–71. Stockholm: Royal Academy of Forestry and Agriculture.

Nakosteen, R. A., and M. Zimmer. 1980. "Migration and Income: The Question of Self-Selection." *Southern Economic Journal* 46 (3): 840–851.

Puschmann, P., N. Van den Driessche, P-O. Grönberg, et al. 2015. "From Outsiders to Insiders? Partner Choice and Marriage among Internal Migrants in Antwerp, Rotterdam & Stockholm, 1850–1930." *Historical Social Research* 40 (2): 319–358.

Ravenstein, E. G. 1889. "The Laws of Migration." *Journal of the Royal Statistical Society* 52 (2): 241–301.

Salvatore, D. 1977. "An Econometric Analysis of Internal Migration in Italy." *Journal of Regional Science* 17 (3): 395–408.

Schön, L. 2000. *En modern svensk ekonomisk historia: Tillväxt och omvandling under två sekel* [A Modern Swedish Economic History: Growth and Stagnation During Two Centuries]. Stockholm: SNS.

Sjaastad, L. A. 1962. "The Costs and Returns of Human Migration." *Journal of Political Economy* 70 (5, Part 2): 80–93.

Statistics Sweden. 1969. *Historisk statistik för Sverige, Del 1. Befolkning 1720–1967* [Historical Statistics of Sweden, Part 1. Population 1720–1967]. Stockholm: Statistiska Centralbyrån.

Thomas, D. S. 1941. *Social and Economic Aspects of Swedish Population Movements 1750–1933*. New York: Macmillan.

Vikström, L. 2003. *Gendered Routes and Courses: The Socio-Spatial Mobility of Migrants in Nineteenth-Century Sundsvall, Sweden*. PhD Dissertation, Department of Historical Studies, Umeå University.

5
Social Class Segregation in Landskrona

Gabriel Brea-Martinez, Finn Hedefalk, Therese Nilsson, and Vinicius de Souza Maia

Introduction

The spatial distribution of households among social classes has long attracted the interest of scholars from the social sciences, especially when it results in residential segregation. This means that the distribution of different groups of people, defined by factors such as class, occupation, income, and education, is uneven across neighborhoods. Individuals in areas of high residential segregation experience separate lives regardless of socioeconomic status (SES), be it high or low. This may be related to the residential choices of members of different types of households, such as those with a high income having the financial means to realize their housing and neighborhood preferences (Hulchansky 2010; Tammaru et al. 2020), whereas those with a low-income live in areas in which housing is cheap.

High levels of residential segregation raise concerns regarding social sustainability. It may diminish the status of cities and urban areas as places of opportunity with equal prospects for all regardless of SES (van Ham et al. 2021). Much research has examined the effects of socioeconomic segregation; for example, one recent strand of literature has studied the way in which residential segregation influences the individual's education and labor market outcomes. Using geocoded micro-data from the city of Landskrona, Sweden, research shows that the social class of an individual's nearest neighbors during childhood was important for both their educational achievement and adult mortality, regardless of class origin and schooling (Hedefalk and Dribe 2020; Hedefalk et al. 2023). Similarly, children who came from a randomly selected family in a US neighborhood, be it high- or low-poverty, and who were offered housing vouchers, increased their chances of college attendance and earnings in later life even though the duration of their exposure to poverty and segregation was most likely an important determinant of long-term outcomes (Chetty et al. 2016).

Another strand in the literature has examined how neighborhoods and residential segregation affect outcomes for immigrants. Neighborhood conditions in the United States increased the achievement gap between native-born and

Gabriel Brea-Martinez, Finn Hedefalk, Therese Nilsson, and Vinicius de Souza Maia, *Social Class Segregation in Landskrona* In: *Urban Lives*. Edited by: Martin Dribe, Therese Nilsson, and Anna Tegunimataka, Oxford University Press.
© Oxford University Press 2024. DOI: 10.1093/oso/9780197761090.003.0005

immigrants (Pong and Hao 2007). For Sweden, a positive effect on compulsory school grade point average (GPA) from a greater number of highly educated adults of the same ethnicity as the child in the residing neighborhood has been identified (Åslund et al. 2011; Bygren and Szulkin 2010). Taken together, although casual relationships in this kind of empirical research are generally difficult to establish (Wimark 2018), an interdisciplinary body of literature suggests that residential socioeconomic segregation can affect the life chances of the groups under study.

Despite the negative implications of residential segregation as suggested here, we have limited insight into how socioeconomic segregation have changed over time. Does the segregation we observe today mirror that in the past, or have there been major shifts in residential segregation over time? A longitudinal dimension is often lacking because of the limited access to data needed to construct the spatial distribution of socioeconomic outcomes over time. Research on European cities suggests that residential segregation between high- and low-income groups has increased in recent decades (cf. Fujita and Maloutas 2016; Musterd et al. 2017; Tammaru et al. 2020), but we have very limited insight into historical developments over long stretches of the twenty-first century—even developments covering more than ten to fifteen years in the same location.

This chapter examines how residential segregation, primarily by social class, evolved in the city of Landskrona over the twentieth century. In this regard, we address the following questions: Where did members of certain social classes reside in Landskrona? How has the residential pattern developed over time? Was there segregation in the city from the start, or did it emerge during our period of study?

Our main contribution is to examine residential segregation using geocoded information at the block level covering close to six decades. This period saw political transitions; economic crises; changes in housing policy, including measures to generate mixed-tenure forms within areas (Wimark et al. 2020); and increased migration flows to Sweden and, during certain periods, Landskrona in particular (see Chapter 4). We do not examine the determinants or effects of residential socioeconomic segregation but rather illustrate its development over time to better understand how it evolved in Landskrona and its main determinants.[1]

Put in general terms, measures of segregation map the distribution of individuals within a specific geographic area by examining how an area deviates from the expected social mix based on general demographic trends; however, other approaches are possible. Different measures of segregation have their own strengths and weaknesses (for a discussion on this see, e.g., Lloyd et al. 2014; Wilson 1987), and there is no standard way of applying them. In this chapter, we first map the concentration of several demographic and social class characteristics at the family level. Then we summarize social class segregation using the

Isolation Index, a preferred measure of segregation in spatial studies in the social sciences.

As discussed by Wimark (2018), the level of segregation, as well as the changes that affect it, relate to the geographical aggregation level to which segregation measures are applied. For practical reasons empirical research on residential socioeconomic segregation often relies on administrative divisions, but these divisions do not necessarily constitute a de facto method of assessing how residential segregation matters for the individual. In addition, when using larger geographic units, one may encounter difficulties related not only to modifiable areal units but also to the so-called uncertain geographic context problem (Fotheringham and Wong 1991; Kwan 2012). It is likely that important information on physical and social factors potentially affecting the individual's behavior is overlooked when using large geographical units for deriving neighborhood variables. This chapter uses geocoded data at the block level to produce fine-scale measures.

Theory and Previous Research

Segregation research is mainly rooted in the US experience, with studies dating back to the turn of the twentieth century and the Chicago School (Park and Burgess 1925; Logan and Bellman 2016). This research field has changed over time, and recent research can be roughly separated into two groups of theoretical frameworks: (1) constraint models and (2) residential preference models. *Constraint models*, the most common of which are based on the spatial assimilation and place stratification theories, postulate that social and structural factors primarily constrain individuals' residential decisions (Massey and Denton 1985). That said, *preference models* argue that individual preferences related to network theory and homophily lead to self-segregation (Clark 1991).

Spatial assimilation suggests that spatial inequalities are the result of socioeconomic differences between social groups that become inscribed in the urban environment (Alba and Logan 1993). Following this reasoning, segregation should correlate with the overall socioeconomic inequalities among inhabitants of different neighborhoods. If these inequalities are eliminated over time, segregation should gradually disappear as individuals who were previously disadvantaged become increasingly more likely to make integrative moves.

Support for the spatial assimilation theory has been found in both US and European studies. Research on the US context shows that socioeconomic inequality is positively correlated with segregation at the metropolitan level (Logan et al. 2004), even when controlling for other factors associated with residential segregation such as regional differences, size and growth of minority groups, and group income levels. Furthermore, studies that look at differences within groups show that higher-SES members of minority groups have a greater likelihood of moving to advantaged neighborhoods (Iceland and Wilkes 2006) whereas higher income, further education, and greater family wealth are associated with moving to neighborhoods with a higher proportion of whites and lower poverty rates for broad racial groups (Krysan and Crowder 2017). In the European context, socioeconomic segregation is associated with increasing income inequality (Tammaru et al. 2020), which is in turn linked to rising social inequality, globalization and economic restructuring, welfare regimes, and housing systems (Musterd et al. 2017).

Given the focus of spatial assimilation theory on the socioeconomic composition of neighborhood populations, some authors have raised concerns that this framework neglects other factors leading to segregation, especially that of discrimination. The *place stratification theory* posits that the most advantaged members of society wish to distance themselves from minorities. As a result, formal and informal institutions and practices are implemented to effectively prevent disadvantaged groups from making integrative moves to those areas where the more advantaged reside. Research on place stratification focuses on mechanisms whereby the charter population keeps disadvantaged groups out of desirable locations, preventing them from converting any socioeconomic resources they might have into desirable residential outcomes (Massey and Denton 1993; Roscigno et al. 2009; Ross and Turner 2005).

While several of the most obvious and institutionalized forms of discrimination are historical (e.g., the apartheid system in South Africa and the Jim Crow laws in the United States), there is also evidence of subtle or informal contemporary practices (e.g., the way discrimination affects the different stages in the search for housing and the way its effects are still felt after the search is completed; Krysan and Crowder 2017). The mortgage industry is also singled out as a major offender. Here, the historical policy of the Home Owners Loan Corporation denying housing loans to residents in black minority neighborhoods (Yinger 1995) and contemporary predatory lending and nonexclusionary discrimination (Roscigno et al. 2009; Rugh et al. 2015) stand as examples of place stratification. In the European context, segregation is often linked to the experience of non-EU migrants, who tend to live in the most deprived neighborhoods (Andersson et al. 2018). Although the European context is usually seen as less exclusionary, there is still evidence that similar practices take place in contemporary housing markets (Auspurg et al. 2019; Gouveia et al. 2020), in financial institutions (Aldén and Hammarstedt 2016; Stefan et al. 2018), and in other arenas. In the case of Sweden, research also find that ethnic discrimination exists in the Swedish rental housing market (Ahmed and Hammarstedt 2008; Ahmed et al. 2010; Bengtsson et al. 2012).

The second framework—residential preference models—suggests that residential segregation is partly driven by own-group preference for residential location (Ibraimovic and Masiero 2014; Logan et al. 2002). In other words, residents of a certain ethnicity, race, or class, for example, tend to make an actively segregating move in the direction of an own-group–dominated neighborhood. Moves of this kind may be driven by networks based on kinship and friendship ties (Massey et al. 1993) and by homophily (i.e., the preference of individuals to interact with those who share their ethnic background, culture, and/or language; Ibraimovic and Masiero 2014). Moreover, the Schelling model of segregation proposes that even small differences in preference can be compounded over time to create highly segregated neighborhoods (Clark 1991). In the United States, whites show strong preferences for these, and show low tolerance for other-race neighbors, particularly blacks. Similar results are found for other minorities in terms of own-group preference (Aradhya et al. 2016; Charles 2006; Krysan and Bader 2007).

Whereas individual preferences cannot be ruled out as a complementary explanation for segregation, the residential segregation framework has been criticized for there being little empirical correlation between stated preferences and real neighborhood composition. Some research suggests that most of the "preference" is related to white residents' rejection of integration (Farley et al. 1978), and some find that both black and white US metropolitan residents surveyed in the 1990s and 2000s expressed a preference for living in a more integrated neighborhood, but these preferences were seldom realized (Krysan and Crowder 2017). Finally, stated preferences for racial neighborhood composition can mask the "bundling" effect of previous exposure to the less attractive characteristics of minority neighborhoods, such as crime, disorder, and poverty, meaning that, in practice, it is difficult to distinguish between that attributable to preferences based on networks and homophily and the more material consequences of social disadvantage (Krysan and Crowder 2017; Sampson 2012).

Given that most segregation research deals with the United States, it can still be useful in a European context but does require an understanding of the ways in which the two contexts differ. Geographic patterns and local policies vary widely in the United States. The level of state intervention varies more between administrative units than it does in Europe, as does the overall level of state intervention in welfare in general, and segregation is lower (Andersson et al. 2018). Put in general terms, residential segregation is lower in Europe than in the United States (Musterd 2005) possibly because of the existence of more generous welfare policies and early state intervention through housing policies. Although immigrants in Europe are highly segregated, the glaring and historical racial discrimination of blacks as seen in the United States is not present in Europe to the same extent (Huttman 1991). At the same time, segregation has been increasing in recent decades following the rise in social inequality (Tammaru et al. 2020), with consequences for social cohesion (Malmberg et al. 2013).

While most research on segregation focuses on the race, ethnicity, or country of origin of disadvantaged groups, this chapter focuses on residential segregation between social classes. In contrast to contemporary contexts, there was a relatively high level of economic equality in Landskrona, whose ethnic composition remained homogeneous for most of the study period, and the few immigrants it had originated mostly from Scandinavia and Northern Europe (see Chapter 4). In such a setting, segregation is more likely to arise from distinctions in SES in a rapidly changing economic structure. Accordingly, research conducted in the United States has explained the factors determining the increase in segregation due to the proliferation of ethnic enclaves.[2] These enclaves can lead to more segregation given that they can serve as important social and cultural hubs for residents, providing a sense of belonging, access to familiar resources, and opportunities for cultural preservation and exchange (Massey and Denton 1988). Additionally, American scholars have noted increased segregation due to the presence of goods and services tailored for specific ethnic or racial groups in segregated neighborhoods (Waldfogel 2008). However, ethnic goods can also have positive aspects because they contribute to neighborhoods' social and economic vitality, which in turn bring a strong sense of community identity and cohesion (Iceland and Wilkes 2006).

Nevertheless, unlike many American cities, Landskrona in the second half of the twentieth century had a less diverse ethnic composition. In this context, one theoretical model of segregation that could explain potential increases or shifts in segregation is *Schelling's tipping model* (1971). Schelling proposed that when neighborhoods originally predominantly composed of one ethnic or social group experience an influx of individuals from different demographic, ethnic, or socioeconomic backgrounds, it can result in a relatively rapid change in the neighborhood's composition. For example, in traditionally working-class neighborhoods, the arrival of more economically advantaged individuals may lead to the displacement of less wealthy residents through a process of gentrification, although the reverse pattern could also occur.

In addition to the distinctions mentioned, this chapter explores other relevant factors. Early twentieth-century Sweden had a welfare state that was in its infancy, and the institutions capable of intervening in urban areas or the housing sector, as seen today, were still decades away. Unlike the sprawling metropolises commonly studied, Landskrona was a small and compact city. As a result, one can reasonably anticipate lower levels of segregation in Landskrona compared to contemporary cities, and the growth of industrialization may have further widened these disparities over time.

Finally, this chapter contributes to our understanding of segregation patterns in the transition from a pre-industrial to an industrial economy. For example, some scholars argue that segregation is essentially a permanent feature of urbanization throughout history, but this evidence is centered on highly segregated areas where there often exist strong institutional settings that create and maintain them (Nightingale 2016). In contrast, some point to several potential drivers of segregation that may operate in a given historical context, though these processes are far from universal and there is much variation in patterns and consequences (York et al. 2011).

Data and Measures

To illustrate the patterns of social class segregation in Landskrona from 1905 to 1967, we used detailed geographic, demographic, and occupational information from the Scanian Economic-Demographic Database (SEDD; Bengtsson et al. 2021; see Chapter 1). Regarding the geographic information, we geocoded Landskrona's total population at the block level for the period 1905–1967. In brief, we digitized blocks in the form of historical maps, harmonized the block names given in the population registers, and linked individuals to the digitized blocks where they lived. The geographic information about the blocks is recorded annually, whereas each move made by an individual and household is recorded continuously throughout the year. In addition to the geocoded data, we have historical geographic information on roads, buildings, schools, and some major industries. For all the measures we used, in cases where an individual lived in multiple blocks in the same year, we defined their block of residence in that year as the one where they lived longest.

We captured Landskrona's socioeconomic characteristics using the social class position of individuals.[3] It is a comprehensive measure of advantage when studying the individual's ability to access resources, material well-being, and status. It is also a stable measure of SES over an individual's life span, embracing economic resources and cultural attitudes and capturing likely group identity (see, e.g., Breen and Jonsson 2005; Curtis 2016; Erikson and Goldthorpe 2010). We measured social class by year based on individual and family-level occupations (commonly the father's occupation). As explained in Chapter 1 and Chapter 3, occupations are grouped according to the Historical International Social Class Scheme (HISCLASS), which we have used to define six classes: higher white-collar workers, lower white-collar workers, medium-skilled workers, lower-skilled workers, unskilled workers, and farmers. Most classes broadly reflect a status hierarchy from lowest status (unskilled workers) to highest status (higher white-collar workers).

As well as depicting segregation patterns in terms of social class, we studied spatial patterns of demography and family composition. We therefore computed for each block the average household size and age of family members, as well as the share of children and families headed by women.

We focused on two main sets of descriptive segregation measures: averages and shares at the block level and global indices capturing segregation at the town level. First, we derived the averages and shares of social class and demographic characteristics of families by block in Landskrona for the years 1920, 1940, and 1960. These three specific years represent each of the first three periods covered by this book's periodization (1905–1929, 1930–1949, 1950–1975). We separated the outcomes under study into two sets: demographic characteristics and social class. We gathered the demographic information at the family level to look at family size, age of family head, number of children, and number of families headed by women. Thereafter, we presented all these indicators averaged by block in each year for our maps, reporting the mean or shares of the different outcomes. We then produced the corresponding measures by social class, counting the different social classes the family heads belonged to by block and year.

Second, we measured segregation by computing the yearly measures of the Isolation Index for the period 1905–1967. This index is widely used in the socioeconomic segregation literature (Lloyd et al. 2015; Malmberg et al. 2013). The Isolation Index measures the probability of members of a certain social minority (e.g., higher white-collar or unskilled workers) meeting or interacting with their equals were social contact to happen at random (Massey and Denton 1988). This means that the higher its value, the more isolated a social class is, denoting more profound segregation.[4] The social structure can be divided into two groups here: the minority group (e.g., unskilled workers) and the other social classes combined as a *majority* group. The Isolation Index ranges from 0, representing no segregation, to 1, denoting the highest level of segregation.

However, the index is asymmetric and depends on the size of the group when used for more than two groups, so if we want to consider each social class separately and at the same time adjust for changes in the class structure and weight of each social class, the index requires an adjustment and will no longer total 1 (Massey and Denton 1988; Lloyd et al. 2014). Moreover, the larger social classes may bias the index, overestimating the Isolation Index.[5]

Demographic and Social Class Residential Patterns in Landskrona

This section depicts some of the most important demographic and social class patterns for families residing in the city of Landskrona during the first half of the twentieth century. The geocoded information at the block level serves as a good indicator of the main familial and social class characteristics and their spatial distribution during a period of economic and social transformation.

Demographic Residential Patterns

Figure 5.1 displays the geographic distribution by block of average family size in 1920, 1940, and 1960, respectively. In 1920, the range of mean family size for most blocks in Landskrona was between two and five household members. This range was still the modal family size in 1940 and 1960, but the overall family size decreased from just under five in most blocks in 1920 to three in 1960 (not shown in the figure). A clear pattern seen in Figure 5.1 is that the share of blocks with an average family size of more than five members decreased between 1920 and 1960, and we also see that these types of blocks, originally located in the city center, began appearing over time on Landskrona's periphery. The noted decrease in average family size by block in the city and the continuous homogenization resulting in an average family of four members coincide with two demographic developments during the first half of the twentieth century in Sweden: a general decrease in fertility, ongoing since the beginning of the century (Bengtsson and Dribe 2014), and the almost universal pattern of family nuclearization and a two-child norm.

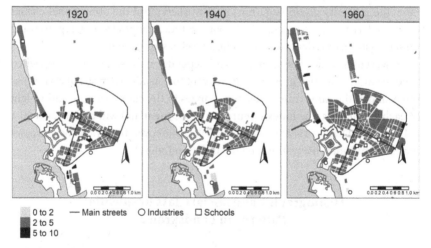

Figure 5.1 Mean family size in Landskrona by block in 1920, 1940, and 1960.
Source: Scanian Economic-Demographic Database (SEDD; Bengtsson et al. 2021).

Figure 5.2 shows the mean age of the family heads by block. We observe a transition over time from a relatively young city population in 1920, where the family heads in most blocks were younger than 40, to a more mixed composition in 1960, where they were on average aged between 40 and 50. This pattern coincides with the industrialization of the city during the same period. During the 1920s, industrial expansion was highly dependent on the shipyard attracting migratory flows from rural areas which consisted of lower-skilled and unskilled young manual laborers (see Chapter 4). Conversely, in the 1960s, Landskrona's industrial economy was much more diversified than it had been a few decades earlier, resulting in a more varied age composition (see Chapter 2).

Figure 5.3 shows the proportion of children (younger than 18) in each block in Landskrona. We can discern a natural U-shaped pattern in their presence for the three points in time under study. On the one hand, in many blocks located in the northern and western parts of the city almost 50 percent of the inhabitants were younger than 18 in 1920, further confirming that this was a relatively young city, as noted in Figure 5.2. On the other hand, the concentration of children was well below 30 percent, except in the case of a few blocks on the city's outskirts. In 1960, there was an increase once more in the number of city blocks where more than 30 percent of the inhabitants were children. Unlike at the start of our period, these blocks were more concentrated on the outskirts, as in Sandvången, which was newly built at the time. In all, families with children seem to have moved to different residential areas of Landskrona in different periods.

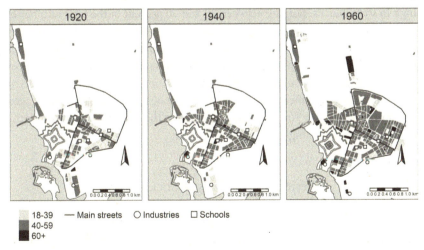

Figure 5.2 Mean age of the family head (FH) in Landskrona by block in 1920, 1940, and 1960.

Source: Scanian Economic-Demographic Database (SEDD; Bengtsson et al. 2021).

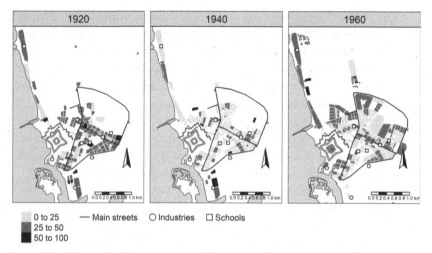

Figure 5.3 Share of children (<18 years old) in Landskrona by block in 1920, 1940, and 1960.

Source: Scanian Economic-Demographic Database (SEDD; Bengtsson et al. 2021).

Finally, we examine trends in the proportion of families headed by women across city blocks. The number and distribution of such households are traditionally linked to socioeconomic inequality, poverty, and segregation because they tended to be concentrated in the poorest neighborhoods (Massey et al. 1991). As illustrated in Figure 5.4, the share of families headed by women was high in some blocks, ranging between 30 and 50 percent of the total number of families per block in each of the three years under study. In a few blocks it even reached just below 60 percent. At the same time, the mean size of these families by block in each of the years under study was close to one, implying that most of these families were single adult women. Additionally, we note that the distribution density of the mean age of female family heads was high for those aged either older than 50 or younger than 30, denoting the presence of widows on the one hand and young single women on the other.

Residential Patterns by Social Class

Knowing the social class distribution and each class's share by block provides an indication and a general view of how segregated the city of Landskrona was at different points in time and how segregation increased over the years. We focused on the highest occupational information per year of family heads and have

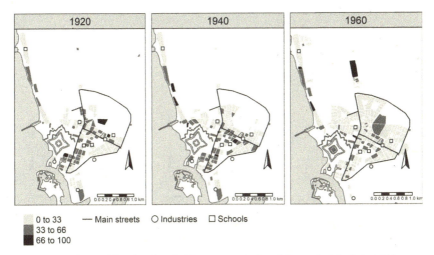

Figure 5.4 Share of families headed by women in Landskrona by block in 1920, 1940, and 1960.

Source: Scanian Economic-Demographic Database (SEDD; Bengtsson et al. 2021).

reported this for five social classes as defined above: higher and lower white-collar workers, medium and lower-skilled workers, and unskilled workers.[6]

The class structure in Landskrona was relatively stable during the period 1905–1967 for both family heads and working-age individuals (see Chapter 3). For the three years shown in Figures 5.5–5.9, about 70 percent of the family heads were distributed across three classes: lower-skilled workers (25 percent); medium-skilled workers (24–26 percent); and lower white-collar workers (22–25 percent). Among these groups, the medium-skilled workers were the most homogeneously distributed across the blocks in Landskrona from 1920 to 1960 (Figure 5.5), with a concentration of 20–40 percent in most of these. Lower white-collar family heads were initially more concentrated in the southernmost blocks in the city, but this concentration was relatively sparsely allocated in 1940 and 1960, whereby their share was in most cases below 30 percent, and in only five cases was it more than 80 percent (Figure 5.6). The location of lower-skilled workers shows a similar trend over time. While the blocks in the northwest of the city, in the traditional fishing village of Borstahusen, had a slightly higher concentration of lower-skilled workers' families (around 60–80 percent of the total share) in 1920 and 1940, the distribution of lower-skilled workers was highly homogeneous across the city by 1960 (Figure 5.7).

The remaining two social classes, both of which made a significant contribution to Landskrona's social stratification, consisted of family heads in the upper

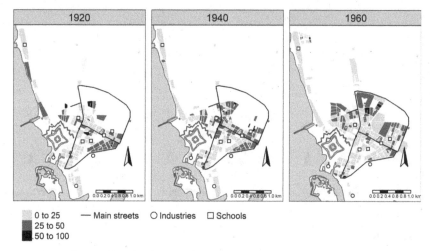

Figure 5.5 Share of families headed by a medium-skilled worker family head in Landskrona by block in 1920, 1940, and 1960.

Source: Scanian Economic-Demographic Database (SEDD; Bengtsson et al. 2021).

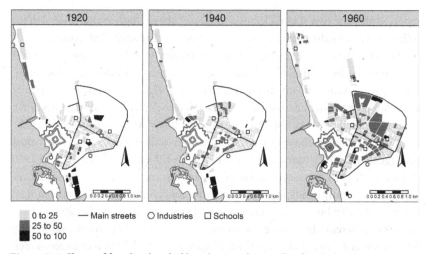

Figure 5.6 Share of families headed by a lower white-collar family head in Landskrona by block in 1920, 1940, and 1960.

Source: Scanian Economic-Demographic Database (SEDD; Bengtsson et al. 2021).

and bottom tails of the social class distribution: namely higher white-collar and unskilled workers. Family heads among unskilled workers accounted for around 15 percent of the entire occupational structure in 1920, 1940, and 1960 (Figure 5.8). In terms of their block concentration, we observe a progressive

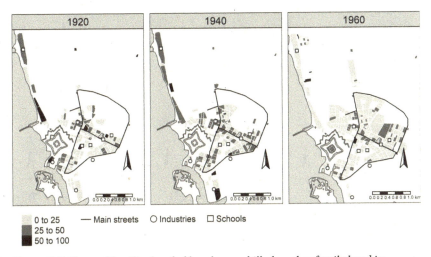

Figure 5.7 Share of families headed by a lower-skilled worker family head in Landskrona by block in 1920, 1940, and 1960.
Source: Scanian Economic-Demographic Database (SEDD; Bengtsson et al. 2021).

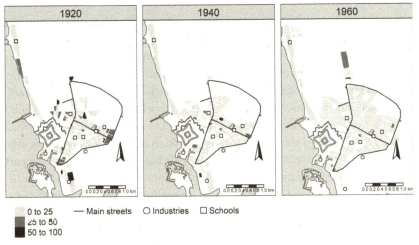

Figure 5.8 Share of families headed by an unskilled worker family head in Landskrona by block in 1920, 1940, and 1960.
Source: Scanian Economic-Demographic Database (SEDD; Bengtsson et al. 2021).

pattern of homogenization over time. In 1920, a few blocks housed between 40 and 80 percent of unskilled workers, while in 1960, almost all blocks in the city housed fewer than 20 percent. When we examine the concentration of higher white-collar workers, we see the opposite pattern (Figure 5.9). Family heads in

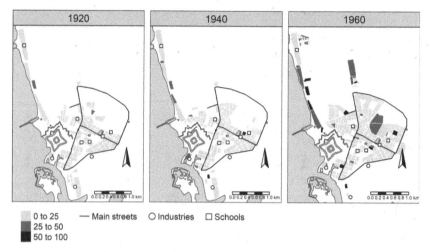

Figure 5.9 Share of families headed by a higher white-collar family head in Landskrona by block in 1920, 1940, and 1960.

Source: Scanian Economic-Demographic Database (SEDD; Bengtsson et al. 2021).

this group accounted for 6 percent of the total share of social classes in 1920 and 1940, and this increased to almost 10 percent in 1960 alongside a general increase of the white-collar groups (see Chapter 3). However, despite this increase over time, the concentration of higher white-collar family heads in 1960 was denser than could have been expected. Whereas most blocks in Landskrona in 1920 and 1940 housed fewer than 10 percent of family heads who were higher white-collar workers, the general increase in this group seems to have been mostly absorbed by just a few blocks in 1960. We see a concentration of these blocks in the northwestern suburb of Borstahusen and several newly built areas in the northern part of the city, such as Sandvången. This simple visual illustration suggests an increase in segregation in this group, which we analyze in more detail in the next section.

Social Class Segregation in Landskrona

The exploratory spatial analysis just presented suggests that, with some variation over time, socioeconomic segregation always existed in Landskrona. Below we analyze segregation for the whole city using the Isolation Index. This index suggests that the social classes we have observed would have interacted with each other had all social contact been random. In other words, it tells us how isolated a certain social class was in their block.

Figure 5.10 shows the Isolation Index. Until the beginning of the 1940s, the index was relatively low for all social classes, with levels ranging between 0.03 and 0.04 for the lower white-collar workers and lower-skilled, and between 0.04 and 0.06 for the other classes.

From the 1940s onward, we observe an important change in segregation. Whereas most social classes experienced similar levels of isolation throughout the period, the Isolation Index for higher white-collar workers increased sharply from only 0.07 or thereabouts in 1940 to almost 0.16 in 1967. Such an increase shows how Landskrona changed from having essentially no segregation in the first half of the twentieth century to having a relatively high level in the last twenty years of our period of study. It is notable that segregation existed among the very highest social classes yet remained low among the low and middle social classes throughout the period. Looking at the spatial patterns in Figure 5.5, we see that the increase in the Isolation Index as shown in Figure 5.10 is partly explained by a large share of higher white-collar workers moving to residential areas on the periphery of the city, such as the northwestern suburb of Borstahusen.

Given the trend toward increasing segregation driven by the higher white-collar class, we analyzed the possible main drivers that resulted in the isolation once again of this specific class. The share of white-collar workers increased, and this class became more diversified in the city from the 1950s

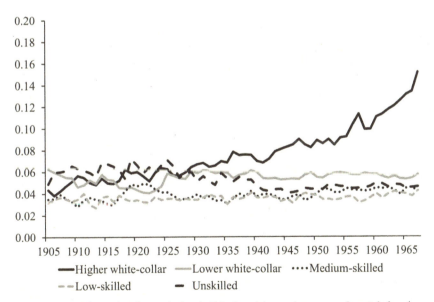

Figure 5.10 Adjusted isolation index (η^2) in Landskrona by year and social class (1905–1967).
Source: Scanian Economic-Demographic Database (SEDD; Bengtsson et al. 2021).

onward (see Chapters 2 and 3). The increasing isolation of higher white-collar workers from the 1940s onward could either have been a new phenomenon associated with younger generations of family heads who had received training or education, or it could have resulted from the movement of all higher white-collar workers regardless of age. We therefore split the data for all our family heads into two broad age groups—younger (18–34 years) and older (35–64 years)—and then calculated the Isolation Index for each social class separately by age group of family head.

Figure 5.11 displays the normalized Isolation Index for higher white-collar workers, given separately for the two age groups. We observe wide age differences between the two age groups regarding isolation; the younger age group was the driver behind the segregation described above. The isolation of the older family heads (ages 35–64) remained relatively stable with values between 0.04 and 0.06 during the whole 1940–1967 period, which is similar to all other social classes, for which the index does not differ by age group. In contrast, the isolation experienced by the young family heads (ages 18–34) increased sharply and rapidly from about 0.07 in 1945 to 0.2 in 1967.

The trend toward segregation as driven by the younger share of higher white-collar workers may be the result of two factors. First, given that the mean and median ages of the younger group of higher white-collar family heads had

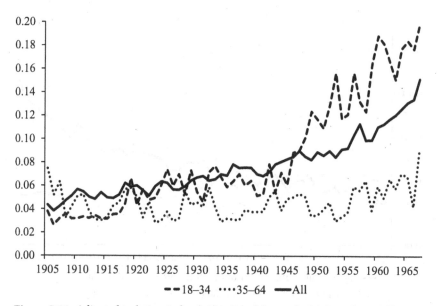

Figure 5.11 Adjusted isolation index ($\eta 2$) in Landskrona for higher white-collar workers by the age of the family head (1905–1967).
Source: Scanian Economic-Demographic Database (SEDD; Bengtsson et al. 2021).

been around 27 and 29 years since the 1950s, these individuals belonged to the first generation to benefit from the educational expansion and rapid economic growth that took place in Sweden in that period. Second, from the 1950s and especially from the 1960s onward, new residential areas consisting mainly of single and chain houses were built—areas such as Borstahusen and other smaller residential areas on the periphery of the city. Sandvången, which was built in the 1960s, did not attract the highest social classes but rather lower white-collar and higher blue-collar workers. Hence, in the 1950s and 1960s, newly established higher white-collar families, often with small children, would deliberately move into the enhanced physical and architectural living environment offered by these new areas, leading to the isolation of these classes from other social classes. In addition, these families had the necessary purchasing power to escape the housing shortage in Landskrona at the time and were thus able to acquire their homes in a restricted housing market. Although it is likely that the older higher white-collar families also had sufficient economic means to move, they may have been less motivated to move to areas further out from the city. It is notable that young lower white-collar and higher blue-collar families may have had enough purchasing power to move to the relatively cheaper newly built areas such as Sandvången (with its "multi-storey" or "apartment" buildings), but the relatively stable residential patterns of the lower-skilled workers indicate that young families of this social class did not do the same. In all, the trend in segregation in Landskrona during our period of study seems to have been driven by the interaction of supply and demand (which differed among the age groups) at the city level and perhaps also by changing factors at the macro level.

Conclusion

Landskrona changed from a relatively integrated city in the early industrial period to a more segregated urban center at the height of its industrial phase. Whereas the demographic patterns reflect only modest changes with little segregation at the block level, social class segregation did change significantly over time, albeit for the white-collar elite, young adults especially.

Landskrona experienced stable development in terms of mean number of family members and not much spatial variation over time. The number of family members was close to four for the whole city throughout the period. The mean age of family heads and their spatial variation increased over time, reflecting an influx of migrant workers and a diversification of the city's occupational structure because of industrialization. In the same vein, the proportion of children in the city decreased from 1920 to 1940 but had increased again by 1960, which suggests a demographic process of in-migration and migrant fertility driven by the inflow of young adults into the city in the 1930s who had children there over the coming decades.

For social class segregation, the period up to 1940 shows modest change, with most of the variation taking place from 1940 to 1960. The Isolation Index shows marked changes for higher white-collar workers and especially for younger families belonging to this social class. The changes indicate a higher concentration of this group in new locations on the outskirts of town, including the new residential areas of Borstahusen. This trend partially resembles the tipping model, although it is also related to newly built housing in the area. It is also particularly interesting to note that, in 1920, the higher white-collar population was evenly dispersed throughout the city, constituting an average of 10 percent in many blocks. However, over time this group became more clustered in space, and, by 1960, its members formed the majority of inhabitants in only a few blocks.

Our findings can partly be reconciled with all three theoretical frameworks previously discussed: the rise of the industrial city and the changes in its class structure also increased inequality between classes while at the same time segregation was restricted to higher white-collar workers, which is consistent with place stratification and residential choice frameworks.

Both frameworks highlight the desire of higher social classes to create distance from lower-class individuals, the former because of prejudice and discrimination, and the latter because of homophily. Taken together, the results suggest that constraint models of place stratification and spatial assimilation are likely more adequate because self-segregation was clearly restricted to higher white-collar families. We see no indication that other social classes realized own-group preferences at any time during the period of study. Although it is still possible that other groups had different preferences in terms of neighborhood social mix, they may have lacked the economic resources to realize them. Last, demographic composition alone cannot account for the observed variations in social class segregation.

Whereas the use of block-level data is an improvement compared to administrative units, which are commonly used in much of the related literature, we recognize that segregation patterns can often occur at even smaller scales (see, e.g., Logan et al. 2015). Further research would do well to consider the use of street-level or building-level measures in determining whether isolation patterns confirm the highly mixed social setting observed or whether they distinguish more fine-grained patterns of class segregation.

This chapter contributes to the literature by showing the emergent pattern of segregation during Landskrona's transition from a preindustrial setting and compact layout with socially mixed neighborhoods to a more segregated urban center undergoing the suburbanization of the upper class. It is a history consistent not only with the US literature on white flight but also with contemporary studies indicating consistently higher levels of segregation for the upper class (see, e.g., Préteceille 2016), albeit at significantly lower levels.

The levels of segregation in Landskrona may appear modest, but considering that (1) contemporary levels of socioeconomic segregation (see Fujita and Maloutas 2016 for several countries) show dissimilarity indices for occupations ranging from 0.15 to 0.4, (2) the Isolation Index is often smaller than the dissimilarity index for a similar social mix (Stearns and Logan 1986), and (3) smaller cities and metropolitan areas were often more compact and less segregated overall, an increase from 0.07 to 0.2 in the Isolation Index for higher white-collar workers represents a major shift in the neighborhood social mix in a relatively short period of time.

In conclusion, industrialization brought a change in residential patterns by social class in Landskrona that was not apparent in the early industrial phase. Limitations to external validity notwithstanding, these results suggest that contemporary patterns of segregation are related to changes in the spatial organization of the city, with greater separation between residential areas and areas of work and between the higher and lower strata of society—changes driven primarily by the former moving away from the social mix of the urban core.

Notes

1. It should be noted that it is not always straightforward to interpret developments in socioeconomic segregation over time as these fluctuate with factors such as economic fluctuations, migration, and changes in economic inequality. For example, socioeconomic segregation usually varies with economic downturns because individuals with the fewest resources are often affected more than those with greater resources, which complicates efforts to interpret developments over time, especially if the follow-up period is short. Having access to a large number of yearly observations, as in our case where we could study developments covering half a century, reduces this problem to some extent.
2. "Ethnic enclaves" refer to neighborhoods or areas where a particular ethnic or racial group is highly concentrated. These enclaves often develop due to various factors such as shared culture, language, or social networks.
3. For an overview of the relationship between spatial patterns and income in Landskrona, see Chapter 10, which looks at the relationship between income levels and inequality from the city in 1939–1967.

4. Our formal definition of the Isolation Index (II) for a specific minority social group is: II $\sum_{i=1}^{n}\left[\left(\dfrac{x_i}{X}\right)\left(\dfrac{x_i}{t_i}\right)\right]$ =, where n denotes the number of neighborhoods (blocks in this chapter), x_i stands for the population size of a specific social class in given neighborhood i, X is the sum of all individuals considered to belong to that social class in Landskrona, and t_i is the total population of a given neighborhood.
5. The index can be adjusted through a correlation ratio, which scales its value by the share of a specific social class in the total population (P). This correlation ratio is also known in the literature as η^2: $\eta^2 = \dfrac{(II-P)}{(1-P)}$
6. Although farmers and those whose occupations are missing are also present in the HISCLASS categorization, we have excluded both these groups due to their extremely low numbers in Landskrona, and their numbers are therefore not given for many of the blocks.

References

Ahmed, A. M., and M. Hammarstedt. 2008. "Discrimination in the Rental Housing Market: A Field Experiment on the Internet." *Journal of Urban Economics* 64 (2): 362–372.

Ahmed, A. M., L. Andersson, and M. Hammarstedt. 2010. "Can Discrimination in the Housing Market be Reduced by Increasing the Information About the Applicants?" *Land Economics* 86 (1): 79–90.

Alba, R. D., and J. R. Logan. 1993. "Minority Proximity to Whites in Suburbs: An Individual-Level Analysis of Segregation." *American Journal of Sociology* 98 (6): 1388–1427.

Aldén, L., and M. Hammarstedt. 2016. "Discrimination in the Credit Market? Access to Financial Capital Among Self-Employed Immigrants." *Kyklos* 69 (1): 3–31.

Andersson, E. K., T. H. Lyngstad, and B. Sleutjes. 2018. "Comparing Patterns of Segregation in North-Western Europe: A Multiscalar Approach." *European Journal of Population* 34 (2): 151–168.

Andersson, E. K., B. Malmberg, R. Costa, et al. 2018. "A Comparative Study of Segregation Patterns in Belgium, Denmark, the Netherlands and Sweden: Neighborhood Concentration and Representation of Non-European Migrants." *European Journal of Population* 34 (2): 251–275.

Aradhya, S., F. Hedefalk, J. Helgertz, and K. Scott. 2017. "Region of Origin: Settlement Decisions of Turkish and Iranian Immigrants in Sweden, 1968–2001." *Population, Space and Place* 23 (4): p. e2031.

Åslund, O., P.-A. Edin, P. Fredriksson, and H. Grönqvist. 2011. "Peers, Neighborhoods, and Immigrant Student Achievement: Evidence from a Placement Policy." *American Economic Journal: Applied Economics* 3 (2): 67–95.

Auspurg, K., A. Schneck, and T. Hinz. 2019. "Closed Doors Everywhere? A Meta-Analysis of Field Experiments on Ethnic Discrimination in Rental Housing Markets." *Journal of Ethnic and Migration Studies* 45 (1): 95–114.

Bengtsson, R., E. Iverman, and B. T. Hinnerich. 2012. "Gender and Ethnic Discrimination in the Rental Housing Market." *Applied Economics Letters* 19 (1): 1–5.

Bengtsson, T., and M. Dribe. 2014. "The Historical Fertility Transition at the Micro Level: Southern Sweden 1815–1939." *Demographic Research* 30: 493–534.

Bengtsson, T., M. Dribe, L. Quaranta, and P. Svensson. 2021. "The Scanian Economic Demographic Database: Version 7.2 (Machine-readable database)." Lund: Lund University, Centre for Economic Demography.

Breen, R., and J. O. Jonsson. 2005. "Inequality of Opportunity in Comparative Perspective: Recent Research on Educational Attainment and Social Mobility." *Annual Review of Sociology* 31 (1): 223–243.

Bygren, M., and R. Szulkin. 2010. "Ethnic Environment During Childhood and the Educational Attainment of Immigrant Children in Sweden." *Social Forces* 88 (3): 1305–1329.

Charles, C. Z. 2006. *Won't You Be My Neighbor: Race, Class, and Residence in Los Angeles*. New York: Russell Sage Foundation.

Chetty, R., N. Hendren, and L. F. Katz. 2016. "The Effects of Exposure to Better Neighborhoods on Children: New Evidence from the Moving to Opportunity Experiment." *American Economic Review* 106(4): 855–902.

Clark, W. A. V. 1991. "Residential Preferences and Neighborhood Racial Segregation: A Test of the Schelling Segregation Model." *Demography* 28 (1): 1–19.

Curtis, J. 2016. "Social Mobility and Class Identity: The Role of Economic Conditions in 33 Societies, 1999–2009." *European Sociological Review* 32 (1): 108–121.

Erikson, R., and J. H. Goldthorpe. 2010. "Has Social Mobility in Britain Decreased? Reconciling Divergent Findings on Income and Class Mobility." *British Journal of Sociology* 61 (2): 211–230.

Farley, R., H. Schuman, S. Bianchi, et al. 1978. "Chocolate City, Vanilla Suburbs: Will the Trend Toward Racially Separate Communities Continue?" *Social Science Research* 7 (4): 319–344.

Fotheringham, A. S., and D. W. S. Wong. 1991. "The Modifiable Areal Unit Problem in Multivariate Statistical Analysis." *Environment and Planning A: Economy and Space* 23 (7): 1025–1044.

Fujita, K., and T. Maloutas (eds.). 2016. *Residential Segregation in Comparative Perspective: Making Sense of Contextual Diversity*. London: Routledge.

Gouveia, F., T. Nilsson, and N. Berggren. 2020. "Religiosity and Discrimination Against Same-Sex Couples: The Case of Portugal's Rental Market." *Journal of Housing Economics* 50 (1): 101729.

Hedefalk, F., and M. Dribe. 2020. "The Social Context of Nearest Neighbors Shapes Educational Attainment Regardless of Class Origin." *Proceedings of the National Academy of Sciences* 117 (26): 14918–14925.

Hedefalk, F., I. K. van Dijk, and M. Dribe. 2023. "Childhood Neighborhoods and Cause-Specific Adult Mortality in Sweden 1939–2015." *Health & Place* 84: 103–137.

Hulchansky, D. 2010. *The Three Cities in Toronto: Income Polarization among Toronto's Neighborhoods, 1970–2005*. Toronto: University of Toronto.

Huttman, E. D., J. Saltman, and W. Blauw (eds.). 1991. *Urban Housing Segregation of Minorities in Western Europe and the United States*. Durham: Duke University Press.

Ibraimovic, T., and L. Masiero. 2014. "Do Birds of a Feather Flock Together? The Impact of Ethnic Segregation Preferences on Neighborhood Choice." *Urban Studies* 51 (4): 693–711.

Iceland, J., and R. Wilkes. 2006. "Does Socioeconomic Status Matter? Race, Class, and Residential Segregation." *Social Problems* 53 (2): 248–273.

Krysan, M., and M. Bader. 2007. "Perceiving the Metropolis: Seeing the City Through a Prism of Race." *Social Forces* 86 (2): 699–733.

Krysan, M., and K. Crowder. 2017. *Cycle of Segregation: Social Processes and Residential Stratification*. New York: Russell Sage Foundation.

Kwan, M. 2012. "The Uncertain Geographic Context Problem." *Annals of the Association of American Geographers* 102 (5): 958–996.

Lloyd, C. D., I. G. Shuttleworth, and D. W. S. Wong (eds.). 2015. *Social-Spatial Segregation: Concepts, Processes and Outcomes*. Bristol: Policy Press.

Logan, J. R., and B. Bellman. 2016. "Before The Philadelphia Negro: Residential Segregation in a Nineteenth-Century Northern City." *Social Science History* 40 (4): 683–706.

Logan, J. R., B. J. Stults, and R. Farley. 2004. "Segregation of Minorities in the Metropolis: Two Decades of Change." *Demography* 41 (1): 1–22.

Logan, J. R., W. Zhang, and R. D. Alba. 2002. "Immigrant Enclaves and Ethnic Communities in New York and Los Angeles." *American Sociological Review* 67 (2): 299–322.

Logan, J. R., W. Zhang, and M. D. Chunyu. 2015. "Emergent Ghettos: Black Neighborhoods in New York and Chicago, 1880–1940." *American Journal of Sociology* 120 (4): 1055–1094.

Malmberg, B., E. Andersson, and J. Östh. 2013. "Segregation and Urban Unrest in Sweden." *Urban Geography* 34 (7): 1031–1046.

Massey, D. S., J. Arango, G. Hugo, et al. 1993. "Theories of International Migration: A Review and Appraisal." *Population and Development Review* 19 (3): 431–466.

Massey, D. S., and N. A. Denton. 1985. "Spatial Assimilation as a Socioeconomic Outcome." *American Sociological Review* 50 (1): 94–106.

Massey, D. S., and N. A. Denton. 1988. "The Dimensions of Residential Segregation." *Social Forces* 67 (2): 281–315.

Massey, D. S., and N. A. Denton. 1993. *American Apartheid: Segregation and the Making of the Underclass*. Cambridge: Harvard University Press.

Massey, D. S., A. B. Gross, and M. L. Eggers. 1991. "Segregation, the Concentration of Poverty, and the Life Chances of Individuals." *Social Science Research* 20 (4): 397–420.

Musterd, S. 2005. "Social and Ethnic Segregation in Europe: Levels, Causes, and Effects." *Journal of Urban Affairs* 27 (3): 331–348.

Musterd, S., S. Marcinczak, M. van Ham, and T. Tammaru. 2017. "Socioeconomic Segregation in European Capital Cities. Increasing Separation Between Poor and Rich." *Urban Geography* 38 (7): 1062–1083.

Nightingale, C. H. 2016. *Segregation: A Global History of Divided Cities*. Chicago: University of Chicago Press.

Park, R. E., and E. W. Burgess. 1925. *The City*. Heritage of Sociology Series. Chicago: University of Chicago Press.

Préteceille, E. 2016. "Segregation, social mix and public policies in Paris." In *Residential Segregation in Comparative Perspective*, edited by Kuniko Fujita and Thomas Maloutas, 153–176. London: Routledge.

Pong, S. L., and L. Hao. 2007. "Neighborhood and School Factors in the School Performance of Immigrants' Children." *International Migration Review* 41 (1): 206–241.

Roscigno, V. J., D. L. Karafin, and G. Tester. 2009. "The Complexities and Processes of Racial Housing Discrimination." *Social Problems* 56 (1): 49–69.

Ross, S. L., and M. A. Turner. 2005. "Housing Discrimination in Metropolitan America: Explaining Changes Between 1989 and 2000." *Social Problems* 52 (2): 152–180.

Rugh, J. S., L. Albright, and D. S. Massey. 2015. "Race, Space, and Cumulative Disadvantage: A Case Study of the Subprime Lending Collapse." *Social Problems* 62 (2): 186–218.

Sampson, R. J. 2012. *Great American City: Chicago and the Enduring Neighborhood Effect*. Chicago: University of Chicago Press.

Schelling, T. C. 1971. "Dynamic Models of Segregation." *Journal of Mathematical Sociology* 1 (2): 143–186.

Stearns, L. B., and J. R. Logan. 1986. "Measuring Trends in Segregation: Three Dimensions, Three Measures." *Urban Affairs Quarterly* 22 (1): 124–150.

Stefan, M., F. Holzmeister, A. Müllauer, and M. Kirchler. 2018. "Ethnical Discrimination in Europe: Field Evidence from the Finance Industry." *PLOS ONE* 13 (1): e0191959.

Tammaru, T., S. Marcinczak, R. Aunap, et al. 2020. "Relationship Between Income Inequality and Residential Segregation of Socioeconomic Groups." *Regional Studies* 54 (4): 450–461.

Van Ham, M., T. Tammaru, R. Ubarevičienė, and H. Janssen. 2021. *Urban Socioeconomic Segregation and Income Inequality: A Global Perspective*. Springer.

Waldfogel, J. 2008. "The Median Voter and the Median Consumer: Local Private Goods and Population Composition." *Journal of Urban Economics* 63 (2): 567–582.

Wilson, W. J. 1987. *The Truly Disadvantaged: The Inner City, the Underclass, and Public Policy*. Chicago: University of Chicago Press.

Wimark, T. 2018. "Boendesegregation i Sverige—en översikt av det aktuella forskningsläget [Residential Segregation in Sweden—A Survey of Recent Research]." *Bostad 2030 Rapport 5*, 1–44. Stockholm: Bostad 2030.

Wimark, T., E. K. Andersson, and B. Malmberg. 2020. "Tenure Type Landscapes and Housing Market Change: A Geographical Perspective on Neo-Liberalization in Sweden." *Housing Studies* 35 (2): 214–237.

Yinger, J. 1995. *Closed Doors, Opportunities Lost: The Continuing Costs of Housing Discrimination*. New York: Russell Sage Foundation.

York, A. M., M. E. Smith, B. W. Stanley, et al. 2011. "Ethnic and Class Clustering Through the Ages: A Transdisciplinary Approach to Urban Neighborhood Social Patterns." *Urban Studies* 48 (11): 2399–2415.

6
The Gender Revolution
Marriage, Fertility, and Divorce in the Industrial City

Luciana Quaranta and Maria Stanfors

Introduction

While the story of the Industrial Revolution is often told, its relationship to the activities of men and women and to the family is a less common subject. Economic historians agree that the Industrial Revolution is one of the most important events in history, but their primary focus is on its effects on production and its contribution to economic growth and increasing living standards among Western nations (e.g., Ashton 1970; Crafts 1985; Lindert and Williamson 1983). Yet, in addition to raising living standards, industrialization had far-reaching effects because it transformed the family from a unit of production into a unit of consumption. This had consequences for social relations between individuals within families that went beyond their economic activities and resulted in the fertility transition, which, together with an increase in women's opportunities to engage in paid work outside of the home, revolutionized women's roles. This change occurred gradually and unevenly across social classes. Thus, the Industrial Revolution not only drove economic transformation, radically changing men's productive lives as they moved out of agriculture and into industry and establishing the "separate spheres,"[1] but also contributed to a longer life span and, in the end, to a smaller family unit that changed both women's reproductive (Davis 1945; Demeny 1968; Notestein 1945; Thompson 1929) and productive lives (Oppenheimer 1970; Stanfors and Goldscheider 2017).

However, it was not understood at first that these demographic changes were connected to changing gender roles. It was, for example, simply assumed that reduced fertility would change women's domestic activities as housewives and mothers in that they would no longer be caring for a large brood but could make sure that their children enjoyed a different life by having fewer of them (Becker and Lewis 1974). Therefore, it was unexpected that married women chose to use their time to add paid employment to their role set, and it caused much concern when family change advanced in the 1970s through delaying life course transitions like marriage and parenthood that required a high level of commitment and, at the same time, created greater union instability. These trends, commonly known as features of the *second demographic transition* (SDT), meant reduced fertility, and reduced marital stability (i.e., increased divorce rates), as well as a substantial increase in both nonmarital cohabitation and nonmarital childbearing. These trends are often linked with the rise in women's economic independence, notably through increasing female labor force participation (Cherlin 1996; Lesthaeghe 1983, 2010; van de Kaa 1987).

In an international context, Sweden and its Nordic neighbors are frequently referred to as forerunners regarding gender equality and family change and have therefore gained much attention in research on these topics. There is ample evidence of the trends and their determinants after 1970, yet most studies have focused on shorter periods, especially those exploring the role of micro-level determinants. While Sweden and the other Nordic countries represented early examples of the SDT and the trend towards increasing family complexity, these trends seemed to have leveled off around the turn of this century (e.g., Dribe and Stanfors 2010; Esping-Andersen and Billari 2015; Ohlsson-Wijk 2011; Thomson 2014). This indicates that change regarding gender and family relations is continuous and ongoing rather than set according to a certain scheme with a general equilibrium or final endpoint toward which all societies are converging. Recent theoretical arguments have linked the comparatively high fertility of the Nordics and trends indicating reversals in marriage and stabilization in divorce to the extant gender regime, notably the second stage of an ongoing gender revolution (Goldscheider et al. 2015).

According to the gender revolution perspective, the link between industrialization and female employment and family change is important because the separation of work and home is a precondition for both the separate spheres and the rise in female independence—the occurrence of which cracked open the separate spheres' construction of the family and signified the first half of the gender revolution (Stanfors and Goldscheider 2017).

In this chapter, we add a gender framework to the story of industrialization and family change, studied at the local level of Landskrona and surrounding parishes. We describe trends in family demographic behavior against the backdrop of economic structural change and welfare state expansion, important not least when it comes to gender relations and women's economic independence. We document trends, first regarding family formation (i.e., marriage and fertility) and second regarding union dissolution through death or divorce. We focus on gender and socioeconomic status (SES) as determinants of family demographic processes and use SES as a proxy for economic independence. By doing so, we show that taking a long temporal perspective reveals dramatic changes regarding gender and family over the past century and how they relate to each other. We document change in gender and family over time, ranging from the time when men moved into industry while women focused on family care to the current situation where gender roles are less rigid, both men and women are economically independent primarily through employment, and family arrangements are more voluntary and at the individual's discretion than ever before. We contribute to the literature on family change by applying a long-term perspective when most other studies focus on shorter periods. By analyzing both men and women, we believe we capture change over time that partly reflects the gender revolution at the micro-level.

Background

The notion that a strict gender division of labor in the family and in the market produces interdependence and organic solidarity was first presented by Emile Durkheim in 1893. It was further developed during the 1950s and 1960s by social theorists such as Talcott Parsons (1959) and William Goode (1963) who, in taking their structural-functionalist approach, assumed that traditional sex-role differentiation was key to family stability. The importance of sex-specific roles for the stability (i.e., economic efficiency) of the family was also stressed by the economist Gary Becker. According to Becker (as summarized in 1981), women's growing earning power not only reduced the appeal that marriage held for men and women (because the division of labor became less beneficial for both sexes) but also increased the value of mothers' time and the relative cost of having children, thereby reducing the demand to have them.

The implications of women's increased economic independence relate to Becker's theory of marriage (1973, 1974), which treats marriage as a rational choice and one only taken if it will increase the utility for both individuals compared to their remaining in their single state. According to Becker, the gains to marriage primarily arise from mutual dependence between the spouses and specialization whereby each partner assigns themselves certain functions within the household. Men are assumed to be more productive in market work that is paid while women are assumed to be more productive in non–market activities, such as housework and childcare, and thus the model predicts a gender-based division of labor. According to Becker, the benefits of marriage are highest for both spouses when each specializes in either market or home production and produces different goods and services that are traded within the household. Hence, specialization and trade at the household level stabilize marriage (Becker 1973, 1974, 1985), but if this configuration is challenged, for example through increased work opportunities and improved wages for women, the gains to marriage will decrease[2] Consequently, marriage becomes less desirable to enter or stay in. Thus, women's increased economic independence may explain postponed family formation (i.e., marriage and childbearing), smaller family size, and the retreat from marriage (i.e., increased cohabitation or single living), as well as the increased incidence of divorce.

A positive association between married women's labor force participation and family demographic change is generally supported by historical trends, but evidence for this association at the individual level is more ambiguous, limited primarily to modern periods, and varies quite distinctly across geographical contexts reflecting different policy regimes. There is currently a vast research literature on family demographic change in the past and present, but it rarely captures the full period of industrialization and modernization and is rarely able to study it in depth as we aim to do here.

William Goode (1963) emphasized the importance of a long-term perspective when studying family change. According to Goode, industrialization and urbanization affected all societies. Traditional family systems were changing due to these forces, though at different rates. He suggested that industrialization and its associated modernization would see family structures converge toward an end point at which the nuclear family unit of a couple and their children typical of the 1950s and 1960s dominated. This prediction was evidently wrong, partly because Goode did not take account of the ongoing increase in married women's labor force participation at the time of writing—and thus he also overlooked the way industrialization affected the family partly through changing gender relations.[3]

The development of similar family behavior across industrializing contexts was, according to Goode, linked to socioeconomic and cultural change, notably ideological and value changes among increasingly large segments of the population. He argued that it was important to distinguish ideal family patterns from real family behavior and values, and for this it was necessary to differentiate the behavior of the upper class from that of most of the rest of society. This argument is an important part of his socioeconomic growth theory (1963), which may explain transitions as diverse as those from high to low fertility and from low to high divorce. Irrespective of demographic outcome, an element of diffusion is implicit in this reasoning. It is equally valid regarding the adoption of cohabitation, contraception, or divorce that may be seen as cultural innovations in societies where these phenomena are rare due to legal, economic, and normative barriers. Usually those with high SES (i.e., the educated and financially comfortable upper classes) are early adopters, partly because they can marshal enough resources to overcome extant barriers. Thus, according to Goode's socioeconomic growth theory, there should be a negative relationship between SES and fertility and a positive relationship between SES and divorce in the early industrialization period, one characterized by high fertility and low divorce rates. As different barriers to fertility control and divorce, for example, are overcome through changes in legislation and social norms, improved living standards, and economic independence among women, the adoption of this innovation should extend across the population. Until now, there have been few empirical tests of Goode's hypothesis across extended time periods, but we intend to fill this gap regarding marriage, fertility, and (to some extent) divorce.

At the end of the historical decline in mortality and fertility, new family demographic phenomena spread throughout the Western world. Sweden was a precursor regarding the systematic postponement of marriage and parenthood, below-replacement fertility, the rise in nonmarital cohabitation, and parenthood outside marriage. Sweden was also at the vanguard of rising female labor force participation. The concept of the *second demographic transition* (SDT) became influential in capturing these trends. It greatly impacted research on family and fertility and was developed into a widely applied theoretical framework. On the one hand, in line with Goode's conjectures, the SDT stresses the importance of ideational change in bringing about certain new demographic behaviors observable at the macro level.[4] On the other hand, the SDT perspective at the micro level has emphasized individualization, subjective evaluation, and the prioritization of higher-order needs (such as self-fulfillment through leisure or high levels of consumption) that influence family behaviors. This is obviously connected to the macro-level idea of the SDT, whereby in certain countries a larger share of the population holding progressive values regarding family life corresponds to a greater prevalence of such behaviors. The connection between values and behaviors may, however, be indirect and vary across contexts.

The SDT has also been criticized regarding determinants and consequences and how general these are (Cliquet 1992; Coleman 2004; van de Kaa 2004). One of the strongest reactions to the theoretical argument of the SDT came from Frances Goldscheider and co-authors (2015), who launched an alternative explanation of family demographic trends: that of the gender revolution. They argue that the trends normally linked with SDT correspond to the first stage of the gender revolution (i.e., when women venture into the public sphere and engage in education and paid work, family building is postponed and pressure put on the family), but these may be reversed as the gender revolution enters its second stage (i.e., when men become more engaged in the family through childcare and housework, union formation and fertility may increase and so will union stability). The crux is that the same countries paved the way in both the SDT and the gender revolution analyses.

In this study, we explore the above-mentioned theoretical perspectives by applying them to data from Landskrona and its surrounding parishes—data that provide an example of the often-cited Swedish exceptionalism when it comes to being at the forefront of family demographic behaviors and gender equality.

Data and Methods

We use data from the Scanian Economic-Demographic Database (SEDD; Bengtsson et al. 2021)[5] and the linked modern population registers from Statistics Sweden to study marriage, fertility, and divorce in Landskrona and five surrounding rural parishes. The analyses focus on identifying patterns of change over a long period (1905–2015) and across four subperiods (1905–1949, 1950–1974, 1975–1994 and 1995–2015), often distinguishing between rural and urban areas and providing results by SES. We cover both men and women in our analyses of marriage. In the case of fertility, we only analyzed women, while for divorce we consider married couples.

Sample sizes and populations at risk differ according to which demographic event we studied. For marriage, the sample consists of all unmarried individuals aged 18–49. In the case of fertility, we studied women aged 18–49. When studying first births, we only included childless women, while the sample is more inclusive and thus larger when studying higher-parity childbearing. Cox proportional hazards models were used to estimate the impact of the individual's SES and other factors on men's and women's likelihood of experiencing a first marriage or on women's likelihood of having a first or higher-order birth. The time variable is age in the models for first marriage and first birth, and time since last birth in the models for higher-order births. The models were estimated for an unrestricted sample of all individuals residing in the study area at any time between ages eighteen and forty-nine. We also estimated models using a restricted sample which only included individuals observed in the SEDD from age eighteen. This sample gives us more accurate measures of marital status and birth parity but is smaller, and therefore we only refer to these results in the text. Overall, the results from this smaller sample are robust and do not affect the conclusions drawn from the unrestricted sample.

When studying union dissolution, the population at risk covered married individuals. We only studied men and women in their first marriage because union dissolution works differently in higher-order marriages. We used a multinomial logistic regression (controlling for wife's age at marriage and duration of marriage) to estimate the competing risks of death and divorce versus remaining married.

When applicable, separate models were estimated by gender, study period, and—when analyzing family formation—also area of residence. In some cases, it was not possible to make the distinction between Landskrona and the rural parishes due to small numbers.[6] Because divorce, for example, was a rare phenomenon particularly before 1970 and most divorces were filed among the population living in Landskrona, we did not distinguish between the city and rural parishes by using separate models when studying this outcome. Instead, we estimated one model with a control for place of residence.

As in the other chapters of this book, SES is measured by social class, which in turn is based on occupation as registered in the vital events registers, the population registers, the poll-tax registers, and the income and taxation registers. Information on social class is time varying, and the coding and classification is described in Chapter 3. Social class is categorized into seven groups, according to the Historical International Social Class Scheme (HISCLASS): higher white-collar workers (HISCLASS 1–2), lower white-collar workers (HISCLASS 3–5), medium-skilled workers (HISCLASS 6–7), farmers (HISCLASS 8), lower-skilled workers (HISCLASS 9–10), unskilled workers (HISCLASS 11–12), and NA when there is no occupational notation or when it cannot be coded into the Historical International Standard Classification of Occupations (HISCO). This group is both heterogeneous and selected. Farmers are also a heterogeneous group, as explained in Chapter 3. They are difficult to fit into the class scheme at any time. In the analyses of the present chapter, farmers are only considered in the rural areas. We did so because they were rural-based, mostly small-scale farmers. In the Cox models used to study the likelihood of marrying or giving birth, the higher and lower white-collar workers are grouped together to allow for statistical inference.

For the historical SEDD (1905–1967), occupations were considered valid for up to 10 years after their date of declaration in the sources. When we studied marriage, we based social class on the individual's own occupation. Because the study of fertility focuses on women, whose gainful employment for the first half of the study period varied over the life course depending on marital status, we considered individual social class for unmarried women and the husband's social class for married women.

Because the scope of this chapter is complex and multifaceted, we do not go into detail here regarding methods and modeling but have instead provided detailed information in each figure and table and have elaborated in the text where relevant.[7]

Family Formation

Marriage is a fundamental institution in most societies, with implications for economic and social development. For example, the historical marriage pattern in Western Europe has been given a major role in explaining the demographic and economic development of early modern Europe (De Moor and Van Zanden 2010; Hajnal 1965; Wrigley and Schofield 1981). High age at first marriage and many who never married were factors related to the required formation of an independent household upon marriage (Hajnal 1983). This reduced fertility and kept population growth on a par with available resources (Malthus 1803 [1992]; Wrigley and Schofield 1981).

Over time, marriage has changed in meaning, prevalence, and duration. One way of putting it is that marriage has changed from being institutional to companionate. Institutional marriage is what we observe historically, with clear rules and partner roles and an emphasis on male authority and conformity to social norms. Such norms were upheld by the local community and supported by the church and the law, but changed with modernization that coincided with industrialization, urbanization, and declining mortality. For example, Edward Shorter (1975) argued that, during this modernization process which started in the late eighteenth century, marriage became increasingly determined by sentimental reasons, with greater emphasis on romantic love. This had implications for partner selection (e.g., when it comes to age and SES) and family dynamics. Friendship, happiness, mutual interests, and sexual intimacy became the goals of marriage and family life instead of, as before, the linkage of lineages, consolidation of property, and other materialistic factors.[8] At the same time, the family was based on a sharp division of labor along the lines of separate spheres. This nonetheless marks a major transformation compared to the past, when marriage and family life were mainly an arena for childbearing and securing family property.

Indeed, companionate marriage can be viewed as the first step toward the individualization of marriage, which took its final form in the period after the 1960s, with emphasis on self-development, more flexible division of roles between partners, and communication about problems, which is distinctive for that captured within the frameworks of the SDT and the gender revolution (Cherlin 2004; Cohen 2018; Goldscheider et al., 2015; Lesthaeghe 1983). Though there are more forms of marriage today, and alternatives to marriage are socially acceptable, marriage remains important to many in Sweden. Why a large segment of the population still marry may be explained by its symbolic importance, which is still considerable (Ohlsson-Wijk 2011); by some legal aspects making it easier to deal with potential family issues; and perhaps by the fact that it ensures trust in the other partner and their commitment to stay.

In this chapter, we have studied the changing structure of the family in terms of marriage and fertility during the twentieth century. The information here refers to heterosexual couples because there are insufficient data and research to incorporate same-sex couples (and other arrangements) into a historical analysis. Moreover, the data did not allow us to document the growing practice of cohabitation since the early 1970s or see how this correlates with change in marriage patterns and probabilities; neither do we have data enabling us to cover the quality of relationships within the family.

Marriage

We start by presenting a descriptive set of figures and tables to illustrate the changing nature and frequency of marriage in Landskrona and the rural parishes. We present all results separately by gender and in many cases by gender and social class. We then present multivariate regression results based on Cox proportional hazards models that were used to study the impact of social class and place of residence on the likelihood of marrying. These results are also presented by gender.

Figure 6.1 panels A and B show the distributions of civil status among men and women by age and illustrate graphically how these changed over time in Landskrona. They show the percentage of person years[9] by civil status for each age group and by gender and period. Figure 6.1 panels C and D show the same for the five rural parishes. The distributions of civil status reflect profound demographic change in line with the standard narrative of industrialization and modernization.

Figure 6.1 confirms that the proportion of married in the population of Landskrona was large and increasing until the mid-1970s (see Chapter 2, Figure 2.16). Marriage was by far the most common civil status until 1994, whereafter other statuses (unmarried, divorced, or widowed) became more common and together challenged the primacy of marriage. Nevertheless, marriage is still an important way of organizing family life. The "unmarried" group has changed most over time. It was always the most common state among young people, typically those in education or informal training and searching for a partner. A considerable group of urban individuals, particularly women, never married in the first half of the twentieth century. Over the course of the century, however, it became less common to remain unmarried. In the 1950s and 1960s (as shown later in Figure 6.4), age at marriage declined as marriage became highly normative. At the end of the period (1995–2015), the large share of unmarried reflected the spread of unmarried cohabitation at younger adult ages though it does not really indicate an increase in single living at older ages. It was uncommon to be divorced in the early twentieth century yet more common to be widowed. Widowhood could occur when still at a young age, though less commonly, and was primarily a common civil state among the population older than sixty-five. Due to gender differences in mortality and the tendency for husbands to be older than their wives, widowhood was more common among women than men throughout the period of our study. The panels in Figure 6.1 mirror the increase in divorce over time in parallel with declining mortality. While in 1905–1949 the majority of those living in a post-marital state were widowed, this had changed by 1995–2015, when the majority were divorced. We will follow-up on these developments in the section on the death-to-divorce transition below.

GENDER REVOLUTION 179

A. Landskrona (men in upper panels, women in lower panels)

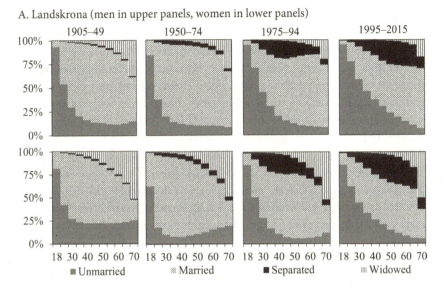

B. Five parishes (men in upper panels, women in lower panels)

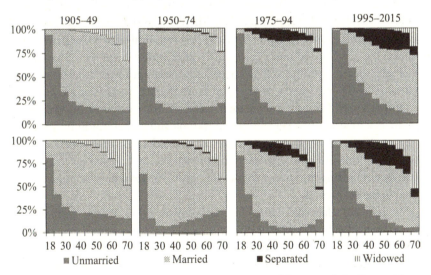

Figure 6.1 Civil status among men and women in Landskrona and the five parishes, 1905–2015.
The category age 70 includes all individuals aged 70 and older.
Source: Own calculations based on the Scanian Economic-Demographic Database (SEDD).

Figure 6.1 panels C and D show essentially the same patterns for the five parishes. There are, however, notable disparities reflecting urban–rural differences in the adoption of divorce (less common in the rural parishes) and the fact that urban centers have generally been more attractive places of residence for the unmarried. Urban centers have always offered more efficient labor and marriage markets, not to mention urban amenities in terms of shopping, services, entertainment, and public transportation. These amenities may be particularly important for those singles who are older.

Figure 6.2 shows crude marriage rates (CMRs) and their yearly trends in 1905–2015. Figure 6.3 shows CMRs by social class and place of residence. We then moved on to age at first marriage to see its development in terms of general trends for men and women (Figure 6.4). We also delved deeper into marriage patterns by means of Cox proportional hazards models (results displayed in Table 6.1).

Figure 6.2 illustrates an increasing propensity to marry during the 1940s and 1950s. It also closes the gap in Figure 2.15 in Chapter 2, which lacked city-level data for 1965–2000. There was clearly a decline in the propensity to marry after 1970 in Landskrona, which supports the view that what we often call the baby boom coincided with a marriage boom. There are level differences between the CMR in Landskrona and that in the rural parishes until circa 1970 (particularly during the marriage boom in 1940–1960), after which the propensity to marry is similar regarding both levels and patterns of variation across the areas studied. Of note, while first marriages made up more than 85 percent of all marriages contracted until 1975, their share then decreased with an increasing prevalence of divorce to around 70 percent in Landskrona and 75 percent in the parishes. That said, remarriage increased between 1975 and 1994, after which its share stabilized. This increase was more comprehensive in Landskrona than in the parishes, reflecting the faster adoption of new marriage mores in urban centers than in the countryside.

There were class differences in the propensity to marry, primarily in Landskrona that had long had a different social class composition than the rural parishes. The graphs in Figure 6.3 panel A show that the marriage boom was most marked among the working classes, and because these groups were the largest, they also impacted the marriage developments the most. There was a convergence in propensity to marry across social classes after 1980. The CMRs in the rural parishes display less variation between and within social classes and are at lower levels than the CMRs in Landskrona.

The marriage boom, which was particularly strong in Landskrona, is reflected in the declining average age at first marriage for both men and women (Figure 6.4). In many ways, the period 1940–1970, particularly the 1950s and 1960s, stands out in terms of family demographic behavior. There was a strong family norm, with early, almost universal marriage and a sharp household

A. Landskrona

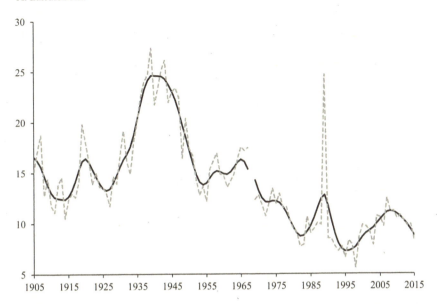

B. Five parishes

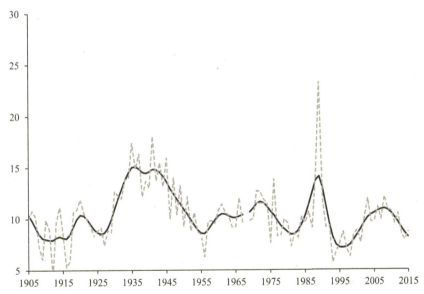

Figure 6.2 Crude marriage rates in Landskrona and the five parishes, 1905–2015. Crude marriage rates (CMRs) were calculated as the number of marriages (i.e., first marriages and remarriages) divided by the total number of person years from the perspective of women in the study area. CMRs were detrended using the Hodrick Prescott filter with a filtering factor of 6.25. Solid lines represent trends in CMR and dashed lines represent the actual values. The year 1968 was excluded because we lack full information on population at risk in this year, in which the historical SEDD data are connected to the modern register data.
Source: Own calculations based on the Scanian Economic-Demographic Database (SEDD).

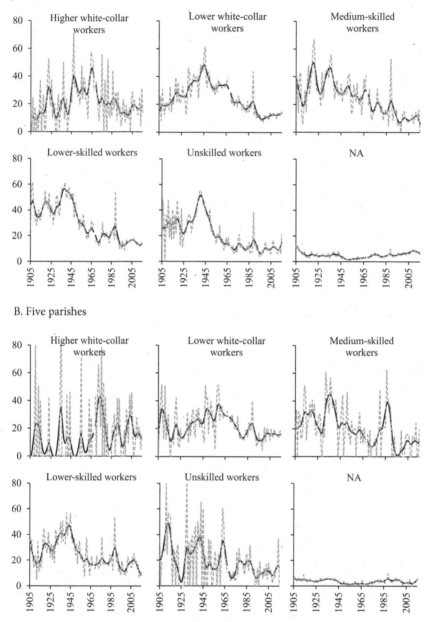

Figure 6.3 Crude marriage rates by social class in Landskrona and the five parishes, 1905–2015.

Crude marriage rates (CMRs) were calculated as the number of marriages (i.e., first marriages and remarriages) divided by the total number of person years from the perspective of women in the study area. CMRs were detrended using the Hodrick Prescott filter with a filtering factor of 6.25. Solid lines represent trends in CMR and dashed lines represent the actual values. Annual CMR for farmers not shown due to too few events in the parishes. The year 1968 was excluded because we lack full information on population at risk in this year, in which the historical SEDD data are connected to the modern register data.

Source: Own calculations based on the Scanian Economic-Demographic Database (SEDD).

A. Landskrona

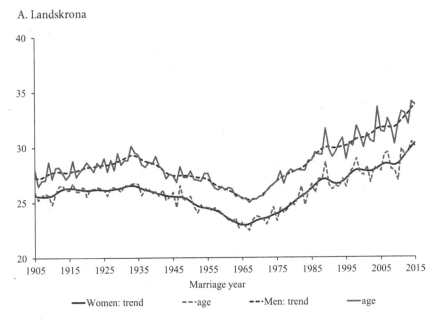

B. Five parishes

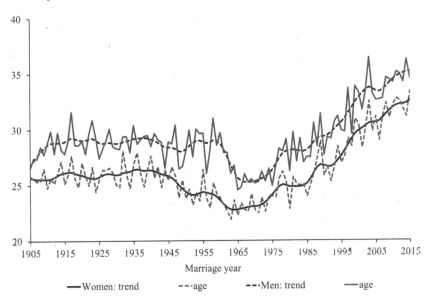

Figure 6.4 Average age at first marriage by gender in Landskrona and the five parishes, 1905–2015.

Source: Own calculations based on the Scanian Economic-Demographic Database (SEDD).

division of labor. Economic conditions enabled young people from all classes to start a family earlier than usual, and they upheld the traditional division of labor. Of note, there is a discernible gender difference between Landskrona and the five rural parishes in the trend for age at first marriage in that it is much more similar for women across areas than it is for men. For men, the trend until 1960 is more stable and somewhat higher at around twenty-eight years. There is a sharp rise in age at marriage in the early 1970s for both men and women and in Landskrona as well as in the parishes, indicating postponement of marriage along with a change in dating behavior and the emergence of pre-marital cohabitation, at least in some segments of the population.[10]

Turning to the multivariate results concerning class differences in first marriage, we looked at who were the early adopters of changing marriage patterns by adding an interaction between class and age.[11] Table 6.1 displays results separately for women (panel A) and men (panel B) and by period. For women, we can see the difference between the white-collar group and the others, with the former being less likely to marry and, as regards timing, marrying later than others. This association is indicative throughout the study period but is most significant in 1905–1949 and 1995–2015. During the early period, the postponement of marriage is also evident for those older than twenty-five in Landskrona. Marrying later reflects preferences among those with educational and career opportunities, for whom family formation is costly and temporarily incompatible due to high opportunity costs, which is the cost of giving up one opportunity to take another one (i.e., the next best alternative that must be given up comes with a cost). A shift occurred around 1950, indicating that female white-collar workers were an integral part of the marriage boom. However, the results for 1995–2015 should rather be seen in light of the change in marriage as an institution, the general postponement of marriage, and the fact that many of those marrying (both men and women) had established themselves in the labor market and found a partner. Moreover, we should not forget that earnings potential is an asset in the context of marriage and, given the increasing compatibility between work and family formation, this has become important for women as well as for men.

For men, we can also see that white-collar workers were less likely to marry and, as regards timing, married later than lower-skilled workers. This association is indicative throughout the study period but only significant in 1905–1949. There is, however, not as clear a difference between this group and the others, as was the case for women. Rather, it is medium-skilled and white-collar workers who for most of this period stand out among the others as being more likely to marry. The significant and positive coefficients for white-collar and medium-skilled workers (particularly those aged 25 and older) reflect the fact that this group was attractive as breadwinners, did not suffer from incompatibility issues,

Table 6.1 Cox proportional hazard estimates of first marriage in ages 18–49 in Landskrona and the five parishes, 1905-2015.
A. Women

	1905–1949		1950–1974		1975–1994		1995–2015	
	Parishes	Landskrona	All	Parishes	Landskrona	All	Parishes	Landskrona	All	Parishes	Landskrona	All
Individual social class												
White-collar: age 20–24	0.64***	0.74***	0.72***	0.89	0.94	0.93*	0.84	0.92	0.90	0.77	0.56***	0.59***
White-collar: age 25+	0.84	0.78***	0.79***	1.25	1.11	1.13*	1.21	1.11	1.13*	1.46***	1.28***	1.35***
Medium-skilled: age 20–24	0.95	1.09	1.06	1.09	0.86*	0.88	1.58	0.98	1.04	2.67**	0.35**	0.60
Medium-skilled: age 25+	1.46**	1.13*	1.19***	1.50	0.86	0.93	0.53	0.67**	0.66***	0.68	1.00	0.91
Farmers: age 20–24	1.99*		2.12**	1.32		1.12	1.34		1.32			
Farmers: age 25+	0.21		0.19									
Lower skilled (ref.)	1.00	1.00	1.00	1.00	1.00	1.00	1.00	1.00	1.00	1.00	1.00	1.00
Unskilled: age 20–24	0.97	1.29***	1.26***	1.07	1.11	1.11	1.15	1.20	1.19	0.81	0.78	0.76*
Unskilled: age 25+	0.85	1.07	1.06	1.55	0.95	1.02	0.84	0.61***	0.67***	0.90	0.84	0.87
NA: age 20–24	0.97	1.04	1.03	0.51***	0.49***	0.49***	0.66***	0.93	0.87**	0.99	1.08	1.11
NA: age 25+	1.13	1.06	1.07	0.94	0.69**	0.72**	1.05	0.78***	0.84**	1.00	1.11	1.06
Area												
Landskrona (ref.)	1.00		1.00	1.00		1.00	1.00		1.00	1.00		1.00
Five parishes			0.69***			0.82***			1.18***			1.05
Number of individuals	6,543	17,916	24,269	2,309	8,869	11,054	3,669	9,610	12,896	5,765	15,040	20,176
Number of marriages	1,408	6,943	8,351	709	3,882	4,591	690	2,063	2,753	740	2,012	2,752

(*continued*)

Table 6.1 Continued

B. Men

	1905–1949			1950–1974			1975–1994			1995–2015		
	Parishes	Landskrona	All	Parishes	Landskrona	All	Parishes	Landskrona	All	Parishes	Landskrona	All
Individual social class												
White-collar: age 20–24	0.39***	0.61***	0.58***	0.98	0.93	0.93	0.85	0.87	0.85	0.66	0.88	0.87
White-collar: age 25+	0.95	1.03	1.02	1.51**	1.77***	1.72***	1.51***	1.21***	1.28***	1.38***	1.23***	1.28***
Medium-skilled: age 20–24	0.90	1.10*	1.07	1.23	1.24***	1.23***	0.54***	1.19	1.01	1.84	0.78	0.93
Medium-skilled: age 25+	1.36***	1.17***	1.19***	1.26*	1.28***	1.27***	1.40***	1.18**	1.24***	0.98	0.96	0.97
Farmers: age 20–24	0.45***		0.52**	1.04		1.10	1.90		2.18			
Farmers: age 25+	1.21*		1.16	1.17		1.29	1.01		0.91			
Lower skilled (ref.)	1.00	1.00	1.00	1.00	1.00	1.00	1.00	1.00	1.00	1.00	1.00	1.00
Unskilled: age 20–24	0.53***	0.76***	0.71***	0.56**	0.79**	0.73***	1.18	0.98	1.02	2.00	1.29	1.36
Unskilled: age 25+	0.68***	0.58***	0.60***	0.61**	0.75***	0.72***	0.87	1.14	1.10	0.92	0.89	0.90
NA: age 20–24	0.30***	0.33***	0.33***	0.24**	0.36***	0.34***	0.43***	0.59***	0.54***	1.25	1.01	1.08
NA: age 25+	0.33***	0.33***	0.33***	0.16**	0.46***	0.42***	0.69**	0.42***	0.47***	0.89	0.95	0.93
Area												
Landskrona (ref.)	1.00	1.00	1.00	1.00	1.00	1.00	1.00	1.00	1.00	1.00	1.00	1.00
Five parishes			0.64***			0.78***			1.21***			1.13***
Number of individuals	6,646	18,114	24,557	3,079	12,274	15,187	4,153	11,905	15,631	6,268	17,052	22,673
Number of marriages	1,358	6,762	8,120	766	4,332	5,098	712	2,061	2,773	768	1,963	2,731

Note: *p < .10, **p < .05, ***p < .01.
Source: Own calculations based on the Scanian Economic-Demographic Database (SEDD).

and thus had a higher propensity to marry. For men, this is true more generally, not just a feature peculiar to the marriage boom during the 1950s and 1960s. Another difference to note in comparison to women is that, for a long time, men with fewer resources were less likely to marry and, as a group, they were more likely to marry later. Until 1974, the importance of social class was more significant for men's marriage behavior, but it became less so with the comprehensive change in family demographic behavior from the 1970s onward. At the end of the study period, class mattered little for men. If anything, in 1995–2015, economic resources are correlated with marriage irrespective of gender, which is line with previous research (Dribe and Stanfors 2010).

Table 6.1 shows that both men and women in the five parishes were less likely to marry or married later than individuals in Landskrona in 1905–1974. After 1975, however, individuals in the five rural parishes were more likely to marry and married earlier as a group compared to individuals in Landskrona. The results consider differences in the socioeconomic composition across the areas and should be seen as an indication of the changing nature of marriage after 1975 (i.e., not as normative as before occurring later in life and being confirmative after a spell of cohabitation) and as a reflection of the fact that the five parishes were no longer countryside but suburbia, thus attracting individuals who were starting a family.

Fertility

For a long time, marriage and fertility were closely related. The separation of marriage and fertility became an integral part of the changing family formation patterns emerging in the 1970s and becoming established around 1990. The increasing prevalence of cohabitation in the form of both transitory and more long-term relationships was followed by an increase in out-of-wedlock childbearing. Unlike in the past, most out-of-wedlock births in more recent times were not associated with single deserted mothers but rather took place in unions where the parents cohabited but were not married. Marriage became a way for many to seal a deal that already included a common home and children.

In this section, we add fertility to the history of changing family formation patterns over the course of the twentieth century. We start by presenting a descriptive set of figures and tables to illustrate fertility variation over time in Landskrona and the rural parishes. We present all results in terms of women giving birth. Results by social class are based on the woman's own occupation if she was unmarried and on her husband's occupation if she was married. We do this with one important distinction in mind: while being unmarried and having a child in the early part of the period was related to economic hardship and stigma among single mothers, this was not so much the case at the end of the study period, when more than half of all births and 75 percent of all first births took place in partnership configurations other than marriage. We also present multivariate regression results based on Cox proportional hazards models that were used to study the impact of class and place of residence on the likelihood of having a first or higher-parity birth, with age considered the time variable in the former models and time since last birth in the latter.

The simplest measure of fertility is the number of live births in a given time period. However, this is of little use because it is heavily influenced by the size of population experiencing the event and by the number of women of childbearing age. Naturally, the larger the population, the more births, and therefore rates that measure the number of events in relation to population size were used in demographic analysis. To indicate the level of fertility over time, the period total fertility rate (TFR) is commonly used. This indicator is based on a hypothetical cohort or groups of cohorts of women aged 15–49. The TFR is computed as the sum of age-specific fertility rates. It thus indicates the average number of children born to the hypothetical cohort of women 15–49, where, throughout their reproductive period, they had children according to unchanged age-specific fertility rates.

A distinction is frequently made between TFR and the total marital fertility rate. The TFR is used here. In Sweden, the illegitimacy rate has been increasing ever since 1751 to the present day except for the war years and the 1940s. This rate was stable at around 10 percent during the early part of the fertility transition in 1876–1900, after which out-of-wedlock births increased to 15 percent in 1911–1935. In the post-war period, out-of-wedlock fertility has risen considerably, and today more than every second child is born outside marriage. This has to do with the fact that cohabitation and marriage-like consensual unions have gradually become more common. It has been estimated that during the 1990s less than 10 percent of all births took place outside of marriage and consensual unions, which takes us back to the same level of illegitimacy as in earlier days.

Figure 6.5 shows the TFR and its trends. It illustrates that fertility declined during the first decades of the twentieth century, and notably so in the 1920s and early 1930s, when, at some point, even though the precise timing is difficult to determine, fertility decline turned into cyclical variation. The development of fertility in Sweden is interesting since the TFR has changed considerably over time by international comparison. We can identify both a secular decline as well as cyclical variation in Figure 6.5. The rural parishes lagged behind Landskrona in terms of the fertility transition, then ended up at higher levels when the long-term fertility trend turned into wave-like movements and variations. Landskrona nevertheless saw quite high fertility compared to other cities until 1950 but has since then been at a more average level. It is, however, also clear that the development of the TFR from the 1930s onward did not proceed evenly and continuously since there were periods of decline as well as increase and periods when fertility was fairly stable.

After an all-time low in the mid-1930s, the TFR increased and culminated in the 1940s baby boom, which was also a marriage boom, as noted above. After 1945, the TFR remained at quite a high level throughout the 1950s and 1960s. Looking at both urban Landskrona and the five rural parishes, it becomes evident that the baby boom of the 1960s, which was less extensive than that of the 1940s, probably resulted from the combination of increased fertility in urban centers and persistently higher fertility levels in rural areas. Figure 6.5 shows that fertility varied more in Landskrona, and thus falling fertility rates in the late 1960s and 1970s and 1990s, as well as increasing rates from 1983 to 1990 and after the bust in the late 1990s, are more discernible here than in the rural parishes. We thus fill the gap in Figure 2.14 in Chapter 2 that lacked short-term variations (which are typically lost when one looks only at the census years). This distinction helps us understand patterns of urban–rural differences that seem to have been more important than county-level regional variation (Stanfors 2003, Chapter 2).

Figure 6.6 shows the TFR by social class and place of residence. There were class differences in the TFR, primarily pertaining to medium-skilled and unskilled workers who lagged in the fertility transition (though the initial rates should be interpreted with caution). Class differences in fertility were similar across the areas studied, though the composition of workers differed according to area, with industrial workers dominating in Landskrona and farmers and farm workers dominating in the five parishes.

Fertility decline was associated with a certain increase in age at first birth in Landskrona and a decrease in age at first birth in the five parishes, as can be seen in Figure 6.7. While the decrease in age at first birth was sharper in Landskrona than in the parishes, the rural areas featured a sharper increase in age at first birth from 1990 onward. Of note, the period of a stable and young age at first birth was marked by a lower level in Landskrona than in the five parishes, but it lasted longer (until 1990) in the latter. Again, this contributes to our understanding of urban–rural differences in fertility patterns that are often masked by more aggregate measures of decreasing fertility rates among those younger than 30 and increasing fertility among those older than 30. In Landskrona, we can also look at age at first birth by social class. Here, the increase in age at first birth in the early decades of the twentieth century was driven by white-collar women for the reasons mentioned above as important determinants of later marriage. White-collar women have a consistently higher age at entry into parenthood across the study period, and this group features the sharpest increase in age at first birth from the mid-1960s onward. Unskilled workers and those without occupation persistently feature the lowest age at first birth.

A. Landskrona

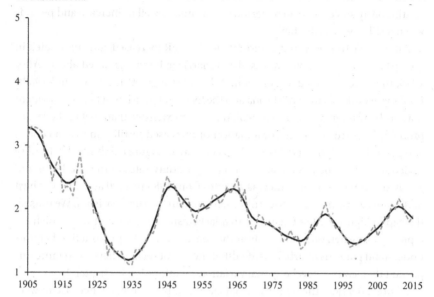

B. Five parishes

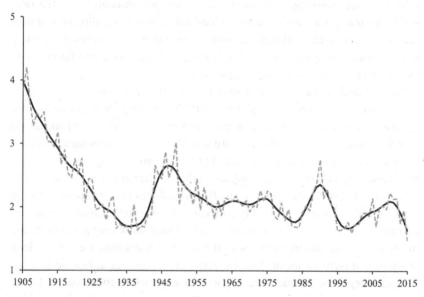

Figure 6.5 Total fertility rates in Landskrona and the five parishes, 1905–2015. Solid lines represent trends in total fertility rates (TFR) and dashed lines represent the actual values.

Source: Own calculations based on the Scanian Economic-Demographic Database (SEDD).

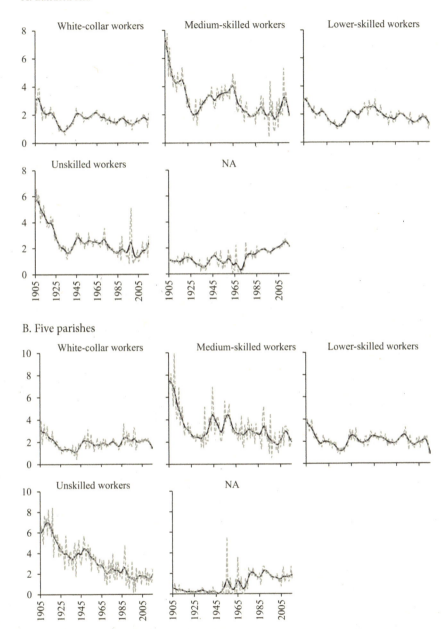

Figure 6.6 Total fertility rates by social class in Landskrona and the five parishes, 1905–2015.
Solid lines represent trends in total fertility rates and dashed lines represent the actual values. Of note, annual TFR for farmers is not shown due to too few events in the parishes.
Source: Own calculations based on the Scanian Economic-Demographic Database (SEDD).

A. Landskrona

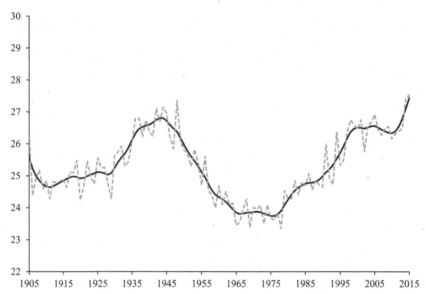

B. Five parishes

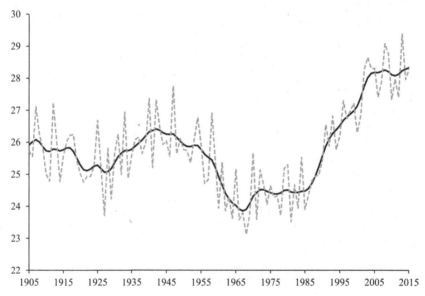

Figure 6.7 Average age at first birth among women aged 18–49 in Landskrona and the five parishes, 1905–2015.
Solid lines represent trends in average age at birth and dashed lines represent the actual values.

Source: Own calculations based on the Scanian Economic-Demographic Database (SEDD).

Previous research has shown that the timing of fertility at different parities has changed over time. Figure 6.8 documents increasing average birth intervals during the last phase of the fertility transition (1905–1930). The interval between first and second births is consistently shorter than other intervals, and there is also less variation in the first interval. The interval between second and third births and higher-parity birth intervals are longer and display more variation, which is in line with it being less common to make the transition from second to third birth and even less common to transition to higher-order births. These transitions typically occur at times when the TFR is on the rise.

Cox proportional hazard models were used to study the impact of social class on the likelihood of giving birth, whereby first, second, and higher-order births were looked at separately. Age was considered the time variable in the models for first births. The models for second and higher-order births considered birth interval the time variable and truncated intervals eight years on from previous birth. In both types of models, interactions with time (either age or birth interval) were included because of violations of the proportional hazards assumptions. As before, we can interpret the results in terms of propensity to give birth and timing of birth. Separate models were estimated by area of residence and study period. For Landskrona, two separate models were estimated for the likelihood of experiencing second and higher-order births, but this distinction was not possible to make for the rural parishes due to small numbers.

Turning to the multivariate results concerning class differences in entry into motherhood (first births), we looked at who were the early adopters of changing fertility patterns by adding an interaction between class and age. From Table 6.2 we can see that the white-collar group was less likely to have a first birth and were thus older on average when they became first-time mothers compared to lower-skilled workers. At ages older than 25 the white-collar group was no different from the reference category, except after 1995, when the likelihood of first birth was higher among white-collar women residing in the rural (then suburban) areas. Those without an occupation (either in their own right as single mothers or through their husband) were consistently less likely to have a first birth (though this group is indeed select). Another select group is that of farmers. Over the course of the twentieth century, they were more likely to have a first birth and on average entered parenthood earlier than the reference category. We added a control for marital status to the model to net out differences between out-of-wedlock transitions and transitions within marriage. Net of social class, unmarried women were less likely to have a first birth and on average entered motherhood later than those who were married. There is surprising stability in patterns regarding first births across areas and across time.

Table 6.3 documents birth intervals for women in Landskrona, and Table 6.4 does the same for those in the five parishes. From these tables we can establish

A. Landskrona

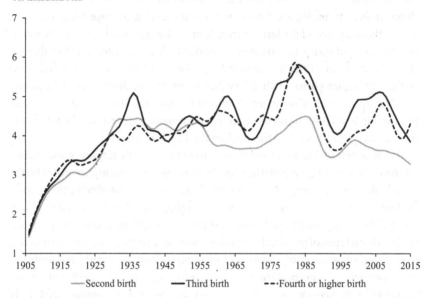

B. Five parishes

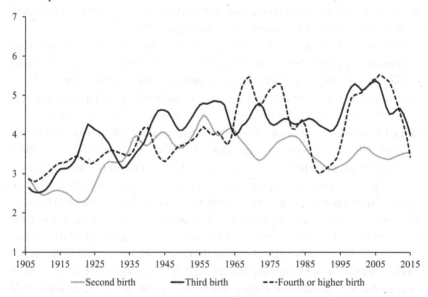

Figure 6.8 Average birth intervals in years (trends) by parity among women aged 18–49 in Landskrona and the five parishes, 1905–2015.
Source: Own calculations based on the Scanian Economic-Demographic Database (SEDD).

that early on (in 1905–1949) white-collar workers stood out from the others by having birth intervals that were shorter between first and second births yet longer at higher parities, which is commonly found for present-day populations. After 1950, however, this pattern disappeared for 45 years. Those without an occupation were more likely to have shorter birth intervals than lower-skilled workers after 1975. That said, in Landskrona across time there is surprisingly little variation by social class. Again, net of class, unmarried women were less likely to have a second or higher-order birth than those who were married. For the five parishes, we needed to collapse all birth intervals from first to second and higher-order due to small numbers. In the parishes across time, there is even less variation by social class than in Landskrona. We identified shorter birth intervals among farmers and those without an occupation in line with that we had already noted. We also see that unmarried women were less likely to have a second or higher-order birth than those who were married, net of class.

Union Dissolution

Sweden is often seen as a frontrunner in family demography, particularly regarding the trends that emerged in the 1970s (Lesthaeghe 2010). Though it featured high divorce rates together with other SDT trends in the early 1970s, it was not an early adopter of high divorce rates compared to other industrialized countries. For a long time, the rise in divorce in Sweden paralleled developments (albeit at different levels) in the United States, United Kingdom, Netherlands, and France (Phillips 1988).

Divorce law reform was a prerequisite for the increase in divorce across the Western world (Stone 1990), and Sweden was one of the first countries to introduce *bilateral no-fault divorce* in 1915 (Sandström and Garðarsdóttir 2018).[12] This meant that spouses could apply for divorce if they agreed on the "irretrievable breakdown" of their marriage. Fault-based reasons, such as adultery, allowed one of the spouses to apply for divorce unilaterally, but this soon became uncommon because already in the 1930s, most divorces were "no fault" (Sandström 2011). The 1915 divorce law was an integral part of a broader social reform movement aimed at reshaping family relationships and promoting welfare which also resulted in the Marriage Code of 1920. The way it regulated the legal relationship between spouses was progressive by contemporary standards. It underscored equality between spouses, although it is important to recognize that the understanding of this concept differed much from present-day interpretations (Melby et al. 2006, Chapters 1 and 6).[13] There were also concerns about divorce in early twentieth-century Sweden and elsewhere that were related to its moral and social implications. In many ways, such concerns were confounded by worries about

Table 6.2 Cox proportional hazard estimates of first birth among women in ages 18–49 in Landskrona and the five parishes, 1905–2015.

	1905–1949		1950–1974		1975–1994		1995–2015	
	Parishes	Landskrona	Parishes	Landskrona	Parishes	Landskrona	Parishes	Landskrona
Social class								
White-collar: age 18–24	0.59***	0.60***	0.75**	0.77***	0.82*	0.66***	0.50***	0.68***
White-collar: age 25+	0.96	0.95	1.07	1.08	1.06	0.92	1.30***	0.96
Medium-skilled: age 18–24	1.23*	0.86***	0.86	1.07	1.30	1.06	0.83	0.89
Medium-skilled: age 25+	1.12	0.91*	0.97	0.80***	0.85	0.91	1.03	1.15
Farmers: age 18–24	1.00		0.94		0.99			
Farmers: age 25+	1.52***		1.49*		1.63		9.56***	
Lower-skilled (ref.)	1.00	1.00	1.00	1.00	1.00	1.00	1.00	1.00
Unskilled: age 18–24	1.15	1.07	1.05	1.02	1.44**	1.22**	1.21	0.85
Unskilled: age 25+	1.19	0.95	0.95	0.77**	1.09	0.85	0.74	0.90
NA: age 18–24	0.38***	0.60***	0.44**	0.29***	0.78**	0.74***	0.60***	1.01
NA: age 25+	0.23***	0.79**	0.57	0.87	1.00	0.81**	0.75**	0.85**
Marital status								
Married (ref.)	1.00	1.00	1.00	1.00	1.00	1.00	1.00	1.00
Other: age 18–24	0.03***	0.05***	0.05**	0.08***	0.13***	0.17***	0.11***	0.12***
Other: age 25+	0.04***	0.06***	0.04**	0.10***	0.29***	0.24***	0.29***	0.23***
Number of women	7,450	19,353	3,141	11,649	3,476	9,096	5,013	13,170
Number of births	1,545	5,775	884	4,177	902	2,703	990	3,052

Note: *p < .10, **p < .05, ***p < .01.
Source: Own calculations based on the Scanian Economic-Demographic Database (SEDD).

Table 6.3 Cox proportional hazard estimates of second and higher order births among women in ages 18–49 in Landskrona, 1905–2015.

	1905–1949		1950–1974		1975–1994		1995–2015	
	Birth 2	Birth 3+	Birth 2	Birth 3+	Birth 2	Birth 3+	Birth 2	Birth 3+
Social class								
White-collar: interval 0–2 years	1.19**	0.83***	0.95	0.75***	0.94	0.86	1.36***	0.92
White-collar: interval 3–8 years	1.23**	0.81**	1.12	0.85	0.99	0.83	1.21**	0.84
Medium-skilled: interval 0–2 years	0.99	0.94	0.93	0.93	0.81**	0.92	1.12	1.27
Medium-skilled: interval 3–8 years	0.94	0.99	1.01	0.92	0.95	1.06	1.07	1.01
Lower-skilled (ref.)	1.00	1.00	1.00	1.00	1.00	1.00	1.00	1.00
Unskilled: interval 0–2 years	1.17*	1.19***	1.18	1.21	0.82	1.39	1.39**	1.44*
Unskilled: interval 3–8 years	1.07	1.01	0.91	1.1	0.92	1.09	0.83	0.85
NA: interval 0–2 years	1.11	1.22*	1.54	1.14	1.31**	1.67***	1.53***	1.87***
NA: interval 3–8 years	1.11	0.90	0.95	0.61	0.93	1.48***	0.94	1.59***
Marital status								
Married (ref.)	1.00	1.00	1.00	1.00	1.00	1.00	1.00	1.00
Other	0.45***	0.83***	0.40***	0.90	0.47***	0.84**	0.58***	0.84***
Number of women	5,951	5,046	5,680	5,288	4,324	4,403	4,554	4,862
Number of births	2,477	4,020	2,249	1,373	1,793	831	1,882	1,153

Note: *p < .10, **p < .05, ***p < .01.
Source: Own calculations based on the Scanian Economic-Demographic Database (SEDD).

Table 6.4 Cox proportional hazard estimates of second and higher order births among women in ages 18–49 in the five parishes, 1905–2015.

	1905–1949	1950–1974	1975–1994	1995–2015
	Birth 2+	Birth 2+	Birth 2+	Birth 2+
Social class				
White-collar: interval 0–2 years	0.88	0.80	0.93	1.24**
White-collar: interval 3–8 years	0.88	1.13	1.03	1.09
Medium-skilled: interval 0–2 years	0.97	0.97	0.87	1.15
Medium-skilled: interval 3–8 years	1.05	1.01	0.98	0.91
Farmers: interval 0–2 years	1.44***	1.85***	1.31	1.15
Farmers: interval 3–8 years	1.04	1.38*	1.00	1.00
Lower-skilled (ref.)	1.00	1.00	1.00	0.93
Unskilled: interval 0–2 years	1.29***	1.65***	0.90	0.93
Unskilled: interval 3–8 years	1.18	1.34*	0.94	1.00
NA: interval 0–2 years	1.06	0.98	0.96	1.32**
NA: interval 3–8 years	0.95	2.20	0.87	0.94
Marital status				
Married (ref.)	1.00	1.00	1.00	1.00
Other	0.52***	0.49***	0.87**	0.99
Number of women	3,190	2,258	2,807	3,266
Number of births	2,527	830	1,274	1,292

Note: *p < .10, **p < .05, ***p < .01.
Source: Own calculations based on the Scanian Economic-Demographic Database (SEDD).

industrialization, urbanization, and modernization more generally and how these processes of fundamental change might affect family dynamics (Phillips 1988, Chapter 12). The rise in divorce from low to high levels over the course of the twentieth century may be described as the "divorce transition." Though it was not theorized as part of the demographic transition, it is inherently related to the developments described within this framework.

Divorce law in Sweden was further liberalized in 1974, when *unilateral no-fault* divorce (still in place) was enacted, and the mandatory one-year separation period was removed. Spouses with a common child under the age of 16 were (and still are) required to wait 6 months and confirm their intention to divorce before that can be legally granted.[14]

In the context of our study, we have reason to believe that both socioeconomic growth, which extended the opportunity to divorce beyond the upper classes to the general population, and women's economic independence mattered for divorce because married women became more able to overcome the economic barriers in their way. Access to own income, either directly through employment (rare among married women) or indirectly through work experience (common), improved women's opportunities for opting out of a dysfunctional marriage. Over time, the increasing acceptance of married women in paid work, as well as that of divorce, eased the normative consequences of leaving an unhappy marriage, which made divorce more "affordable" (Goode 1963, 1993; Phillips 1991). Nevertheless, because women were the primary caregivers for children and other dependents, they found themselves, in the event of divorce, in the dual role of being both the primary breadwinner and caregiver.

The Death-to-Divorce Transition

During the twentieth century, life for many changed in several ways. Improved living conditions extended the life span, and average marriage duration increased despite the increasing prevalence of divorce. These transitions occurred simultaneously and changed the family life cycle (Phillips 1988; Stone 1990, 140). More generally, what was once normative in family life generally became subject to free choice. Fertility declined and concentrated childbearing and childrearing to a shorter period in women's lives. Companionate marriage, which had emerged with industrialization, was gradually transformed into just one of many possible forms of partnership. Before the twentieth century, marriage typically ended with the death of one partner, but this changed over the course of the century until divorce became a common endpoint of marriage.

In this chapter, we have studied the divorce transition in Landskrona and surrounding parishes from the perspective of the long-term transformation in the way most marriages ended. We have examined the death-to-divorce transition, which has not been studied for Sweden before.[15] There is surprisingly little research on this shift despite it being an interesting aspect of the divorce transition. We believe that the approach applied here is useful because it links developments during the first and second demographic transition yet requires longitudinal data and a long-term perspective. The context of our study allowed us to document rural–urban differences in the way marriages ended over the course of time.

We studied first marriages (for both spouses) contracted in 1905–2015. We estimated the relative risk of marriage ending through divorce or death (of either spouse) by means of multinomial logistic regression.[16] We used this model because we did not consider the outcomes as being ordered compared to remaining married, though they differ to the extent that divorce is a choice, unlike that of death. Because the outcome events differ in nature, and given the age at which they generally occurred, we followed individuals for up to 40 years after their entry into marriage. We did not want to confuse general patterns in the transformation of union dissolution with those of change in age-specific mortality and divorce, and we therefore focused on the death-to-divorce transition within the 40-year period and explored shorter intervals for reasons of robustness. We could not separate by area due to small numbers and divorce being a rare event, but instead controlled for place of residence in the multivariate models. For ease of interpretation, estimates are reported in their exponential form (i.e., as the relative risk ratios of divorce or death of either partner).

Table 6.5 displays average age at first marriage and duration of marriage for men and women by period. From this table we see that age at marriage was on average higher for men than women. The age difference is in line with that commonly observed for both historical and present-day populations. Up to the mid-1990s, those who divorced, irrespective of sex, were younger when they married for the first time. In the following decades, those who divorced were older at marriage. In contrast, until the mid-1990s, there is little age difference between those who remained married and those who were widowed. In the decades that followed, those widowed were younger when they married for the first time. These aggregate patterns likely reflect compositional differences in the groups who divorced and had a higher risk of being widowed.

When it comes to duration of marriage, it is evident that for those who divorced it was much shorter than for other groups, though there is a stable average of about 10 years across the periods studied, while marriage duration for the other groups increased steadily (with survival) over time.

Figure 6.9 shows the relative risk ratios of a marriage ending in divorce or the death of either spouse (widowhood) within 40 years of marriage. The reference category is those remaining married. This figure shows us trends converging over time and then diverging. Until the 1950s, the relative risk of widowhood (i.e., the marriage ending through the death of a spouse) was higher than the relative risk of divorce. Although the differences are small compared to 1950–1959, when there was a convergence in divorce risks, married partners in the first half of the twentieth century experienced a significantly higher risk of widowhood than divorce. Already in the 1960s it was more common for a marriage to end in divorce than the death of a partner. We see that the trends diverge immediately after converging, mainly because of the increased risk of divorce. From the 1970s on, it has become far more common for a marriage to end through divorce than through the death of either partner. These results show that divorce was already becoming an important feature of the marital cycle as divorce risks increased and mortality declined. The results suggest that, over the course of the twentieth century, spouses experienced fundamental changes in what they could expect from marriage in terms of duration and stability, with implications for exit strategies. This is rarely considered as part of either of the demographic transition frameworks but is an important feature of the divorce transition.

Table 6.5 Average age at first marriage and duration of marriage for married, divorced, and widowed women and men in Landskrona and the five parishes, 1905–2015.

	1905–1949	1950–1974	1975–1994	1995–2015
A. Women				
Married: age at marriage	25.5	24.8	24.3	25.3
Married: marriage duration	13.1	19.1	25.1	26.9
Divorced: age at marriage	24.3	22.9	23.4	26.5
Divorced: marriage duration	11.1	9.7	10.9	10.2
Widowed: age at marriage	25.8	25.1	24.5	23.9
Widowed: marriage duration	19.9	23.4	36.4	46.8
B. Men				
Married: age at marriage	27.8	27.6	27.0	27.8
Married: marriage duration	11.8	19.7	28.5	28.6
Divorced: age at marriage	26.9	25.6	26.2	29.3
Divorced: marriage duration	10.1	9.6	10.7	10.3
Widowed: age at marriage	28.2	27.7	26.9	26.1
Widowed: marriage duration	21.4	25.7	35.4	46.2

Source: Own calculations based on the Scanian Economic-Demographic Database (SEDD).

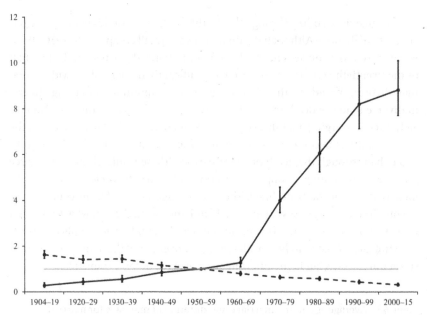

Figure 6.9 Relative risk ratios of divorce and widowhood among women and men in their first marriages in Landskrona and the five parishes, 1905–2015. Estimates restricted to union dissolution within 40 years after marriage.
Source: Bergvall, M. (forthcoming).

For reasons of robustness and to consider whether the results change by restricting the window of observation after marriage, we repeated the analysis observing individuals only 10 years after marriage instead of 40 (which allows for greater mortality). As can be seen in Figure 6.10, there is a highly similar pattern regarding convergence and divergence over time, similar significance, and surprisingly stable levels of relative risk ratios (albeit higher in the case of 10 years compared to 40 years).

We delved deeper into this matter by estimating multinomial logistic regressions of the divorce or death of either spouse as competing outcomes versus remaining married. We did this by observing individuals for 10–40 years after marriage. Table 6.6 displays the results that clearly show an increasing trend in the relative risk for divorce over time. This is consistent irrespective of how long after marriage we observed the individuals. Net of this trend, we also see that those who lived in Landskrona were more likely to divorce. Mirroring the results for divorce, the relative risks of widowhood decreased over time (consistently so, irrespective of how long we observed the individuals after marriage). Net of this trend, we see that those who

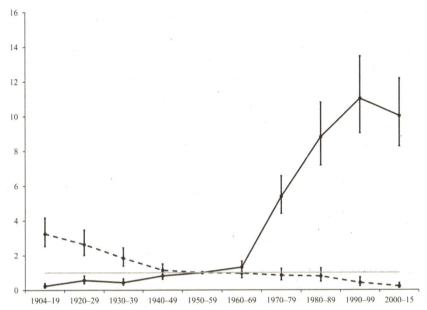

Figure 6.10 Relative risk ratios of divorce and widowhood among women and men in their first marriages in Landskrona and five parishes, 1905–2015.
Estimates restricted to union dissolution within 10 years after marriage.
Source: Bergvall, M. (forthcoming).

lived in Landskrona were more likely to exit marriage through widowhood than those who remained married. This reflects the higher divorce rates in Landskrona.

We documented the divorce transition in parallel with mortality decline and the changing risks of marriage ending through the death of one spouse. At the onset of the twentieth century, the latter was an obvious risk, as early as at a young age, but it was already declining. Divorce, on the other hand, presented itself as a possibility more in theory than practice through a legal reform in 1915. Divorce risks increased slowly yet steadily. Divorce rates increased sharply in the 1940s, took off in the 1960s, and rocketed after the introduction of unilateral no-fault divorce in 1974. The study area was no different than the region of Scania, which was slightly more progressive than the national average yet closely followed the same trend. After 1960, the risk of widowhood saw a steady decline. The results show that as divorce became more common, marriages in general lasted longer and were less likely to end in widowhood. Given the fact that marriage had become less normative and more voluntary, and divorce was readily available to all, this was very much a free choice, which indicates that the concept of marriage

Table 6.6 Results from multinomial logistic regressions: the relative risk of divorce and death (of either spouse) compared to remaining married among first marriages in Landskrona and the five parishes, 1905–2015. Estimates restricted to union dissolution within 40, 25, and 10 years.

	40 years	25 years	10 years
A. Divorce			
Period			
1905–1949	0.09***	0.08***	0.06***
1950–1974	0.24***	0.21***	0.18***
1975–1994 (ref.)	1.00	1.00	1.00
1995–2014	1.43***	1.39***	1.21***
Area			
Landskrona	1.84***	1.93***	2.22***
Five parishes (ref.)	1.00	1.00	1.00
B. Death			
Period			
1905–1949	2.49***	3.10***	2.99***
1950–1974	1.50***	1.71***	1.43***
1975–1994 (ref.)	1.00	1.00	1.00
1995–2014	0.60***	0.58***	0.36***
Area			
Landskrona	1.29***	1.42***	1.64***
Five parishes (ref.)	1.00	1.00	1.00
Number of person years	482,580	340,439	154,704

Notes: Models control for wife's age at marriage and duration of marriage (in years).
*p < .10, **p < .05, ***p < .01.
Source: Own calculations based on the Scanian Economic-Demographic Database (SEDD).

and the conditions for marriage in Sweden had changed rapidly during the first half of the twentieth century.

The data did not allow us to explore the death-to-divorce transition by social class. In a related study, also based on SEDD data, Bergvall and Stanfors (2022) explored SES as a micro-level determinant of divorce during the first part of the divorce transition in 1905–1967, exploring husband's SES as an indicator of household SES, testing Goode's theory of socio-economic growth. Wife's SES was also explored as a determinant of divorce, testing the *economic independence* hypothesis under the assumption that women with a recorded occupation and labor market experience were more likely to divorce than other women. The results primarily relate to Landskrona, where most divorces occurred, and suggest that greater equality along class and gender lines changed the returns to marriage and enabled more individuals to divorce during the first phase of the divorce transition. Thus, divorce risks increased, though divorce was still a rare event. Even in a low-divorce context, women's economic independence was positively related to divorce, and this relationship became stronger over time. As for household SES, a negative gradient in divorce risks emerged as divorce spread to the broader layers of the population. These findings support that the primary explanations for divorce in modern contexts, including that of women's economic independence, are also valid for historical divorce.[17]

Conclusion

We motivated the theme of this chapter against the backdrop of industrialization and how it impacted living standards and the lives of men and women through their paid activities and through family life. We added a gender framework to the ongoing story of industrialization and family change and described more than century-long trends in family demographic behavior. Though we did not elaborate on economic structural change and welfare state expansion, which were crucial for developments in gender relations and women's economic independence, it is obvious that trends regarding family formation (i.e., marriage and fertility) as well as union dissolution through death or divorce developed in parallel with economic and institutional change.

At the onset of our study period, industrialization was under way in Sweden, and the country's welfare state was nonexistent. Only a small percentage of married women were considered gainfully employed, though about 50 percent of never-married women were employed, primarily in agriculture and domestic service. In 1970, the year that marks a great shift in most of the demographic trends we have explored, more than half of all married women were in the labor force (where those with older children were even more likely to participate in the labor force), with less importance now attached to employing them on the basis of their civil status (Stanfors 2003, chapter 4). Most working women were in sales, administration, services, and the manufacturing industry. The most important employer was the government in the sense that (at both national and local levels) it provided women with work opportunities and services in terms of childcare, schooling, and eldercare that enabled them to leave the domestic sphere and enter the public sphere. This marks the definite decline of the separate spheres approach to the activities of men and women in Sweden and had important implications for family demographic trends because of fundamental changes in the relationship between family and work. Women's economic contributions became visible and meaningful, and their options outside of the home increased and put family formation on a more voluntary footing and made union dissolution possible through divorce rather than widowhood. In hindsight, by taking a long enough historical perspective it becomes evident that the male breadwinner/female homemaker family, which was at its peak around 1950, was in fact on the decline by the time it was, in theory, considered normal and even necessary. Few realized that the transitional decades of the mid-twentieth century were an extraordinary period which would have implications for decades to come. Had comparisons been made then with the past, it would have been obvious that a situation where both men and women were involved in productive activities could be compatible with family life and even beneficial for family demographic development.

The developments regarding women's economic independence and family change in Sweden and its neighboring Nordic countries after 1970 are well-known, not least when studied in the SDT framework. However, the dynamics between work and family and its (in)compatibilities need to be considered in a historical context. For example, during the early decades of the twentieth century, working conditions were generally bad, hours were long, and wages low. From an economic perspective it was rational for men to take these jobs, leaving the domestic responsibilities to their wives who, given they had children at home and because of their relatively high productivity in domestic work, found that the value of their time spent at home was greater than that in the labor market. Economists would label this a big income effect (exceeding by far the substitution effect), given that women's potential earnings were too low to outsource their domestic activities. Outsourcing was only an option for high-SES women who did not work because of norms, institutions such as the marriage bar, and the general incompatibility between education and a career (Goldin 2021).

Institutions, opportunities, and incompatibility issues came to change over the decades between 1930 and 1960. Fertility decline had come to an end, and, at the same time, life expectancy had increased. Most individuals, including women, could expect to spend more time at work. For women, more time spent on activities other than childcare and housework extended their time horizon, making it meaningful to undergo training both before starting and during their career (Goldin 2006, 2021). With economic growth and welfare state expansion there was an increased demand for office workers, teachers, and nurses—jobs that were attractive to return to once children were older or had flown the nest. These were important preconditions for an increase in married women's employment and for family change. These developments were seen most clearly in Sweden and its Nordic neighbors in the 1960s and 1970s. The processes of change that had evolved at an earlier stage became more important, many times over in fact. During this period there was a strong expansion in the job market, particularly in the public sector.

From 1970 to 1990, the average woman attained a higher level of education than before, and families had become small and dispensable. With better jobs and higher wages, women were able to pay for childcare, which meant a dramatic increase in female labor force participation among married (or cohabiting) mothers. This increase was particularly strong in Sweden, where the woman's predicament of choosing between work and family was eased by female-friendly jobs, primarily in the public sector, and the launch of government-sponsored family-friendly policies. In this context, the significance of the income effect diminished and the substitution effect became more important, as the correlation between husband's earnings and his wife's employment weakened, while the connection between a woman's own potential earnings and employment strengthened. Government initiatives which affected both the demand and the supply side made education, career, and family more compatible for all women. As a result, gender differences decreased because market forces were supported by policy initiatives (see Stanfors 2003, chapter 4 for more detail), including separate taxation (1971), which increased the incentives for married women to work and encouraged policy initiatives such as paid parental leave (1974) and daycare expansion (1980s).

Economic independence on the part of women saw a marked improvement in the 1970s and 1980s. Despite the fears of social theorists in the 1960s, the family unit remained strong. The trends we have documented for Landskrona and its surrounding parishes show that the family may have changed in nature and meaning, becoming more voluntary and flexible, but it was not on the decline. At the end of the study period (1995–2015), it seems there was a reversal in the associations expected between social class and women's economic independence and family demographic outcomes. One way of understanding this is to interpret family demographic change by seeing (heterosexual) marriage as a gendered institution and noting that the expectations of men and women as husbands and wives have changed over time. Women are more likely to have careers and work full-time to the same degree as men, who are also expected to be engaged parents. This perspective conjectures that family demographic events (such as marriage, fertility, and divorce) are determined by work and money in a symbolic way (rather than through their economic implications) and by whether spouses conform to the gendered expectations of what it means to be a good husband or wife. Risman (2011, 19–20) argues that each society's gender structure "shape[s] the social roles women and men are expected to follow, what 'doing' gender means in any given interactional encounter, and how marriage is understood and defined." What "doing gender" means is therefore context-specific and changes over time.

In the context of our study, wives' employment was non-normative at the onset of our study period, after which it increased from 10 percent to more than 50 percent between 1945 and 1970. In 1990, married (or cohabiting) women's labor force participation had surpassed that of women as a whole (87 vs. 82 percent), and the labor force participation of mothers (of children 0–16) was even higher (90 percent), which clearly manifests the dual-earner norm and indicates that the foundations of marriage had changed, likely with implications for gendered expectations regarding spouses' paid work and engagement in family care. This is one way of understanding family change as part of what is nothing less than a gender revolution from the vantage point of Landskrona and its five surrounding parishes.

Notes

1. The notion of "separate spheres" dominated ideas regarding gender and the roles of men and women in many countries from the late eighteenth century throughout the nineteenth century. As such, it also determined notions of "proper" behavior. In brief, a woman's place was in the private sphere, which included family life and the home, whereas a man's place was in the public sphere, which included politics, the church, and other nonfamily institutions. With industrialization, work became increasingly separate from the home, thus making the public–private distinction more salient for gender roles in the family.
2. Becker (1981) also argues that transfers from the government to women and children, associated with the expansion of the welfare state, help women achieve economic independence.
3. Twenty years later after this work was published, Goode (1982) recognized many of the implications of the rise in married women's labor force participation.
4. This view has been subject to debate, not least regarding the persistence of differences between the patterns of family demographic behavior in the vanguard countries (including Sweden) in northwestern Europe and southern and eastern European societies and regarding whether family behavior will converge to a common standard.
5. The dataset for analysis was constructed using programs developed by Quaranta (2015, 2016).
6. Small numbers were also a problem in other respects (see notes to figures and tables when applicable).
7. For more information on data and methods, see information in Chapter 1.

8. A similar view of the fundamental change in marriage as an institution that occurred around the time of industrialization had been put forward by Ernest Burgess and Harvey Locke in 1945.
9. "Person years" is a concept that measures the total sum of years that each individual in the study population has been under observation. The concept is commonly used when exploring longitudinal data.
10. This is in line with the increasing share of unmarried individuals shown in Figure 6.1.
11. We tested this interaction to capture timing differences without violating hazards proportionality.
12. This law was similar to the divorce laws introduced in the other Nordic countries in the early decades of the twentieth century. It also resembled the laws introduced in most other Western countries in the mid-1970s.
13. These reforms established a new legal framework that recognized men and women as equal partners within a marriage, challenging the notion of women being subordinate to men. With the conceptual shift towards seeing marriage as a union of two equals, there was a need for revising the opportunity to exit marriage through divorce.
14. The 1974 divorce law removed spousal support (alimony) after divorce.
15. Pinsof (2002) introduces the death-to-divorce shift from an applied psychological and family therapeutic perspective.
16. This section is based on joint work in progress between Maria Stanfors and Martin Bergvall. We also tried Cox regression with competing risks, but this approach did not work well due to violations to proportionality.
17. Similar results have been found for Northern Sweden in the case of the 1880–1954 marriage cohorts in Västerbotten (Sandström and Stanfors 2023).

References

Ashton, T. 1970. *The Industrial Revolution, 1760–1830*. London: Oxford University Press.
Becker G. S. 1973. "A Theory of Marriage: Part I." *Journal of Political Economy* 81 (4): 813–846.
Becker, G. S. 1974. "A Theory of Marriage: Part II." *Journal of Political Economy* 82 (1): 11–26.
Becker, G. S. 1981. *A Treatise on the Family*. Cambridge: Harvard University Press.
Becker, G. S. 1985. "Human Capital, Effort, and the Sexual Division of Labor." *Journal of Labor Economics* 3 (1): 33–58.
Becker, G., and G. Lewis. 1974. "Interaction Between Quantity and Quality of Children. In *Economics of the Family: Marriage, Children, and Human Capital*, edited by T. Schultz, 81–90. Cambridge: National Bureau of Economic Research.
Bengtsson, T., M. Dribe, L., Quaranta, and P. Svensson. 2021. "The Scanian Economic Demographic Database. Version 7.2 (machine-readable database)." Lund: Lund University, Centre for Economic Demography.
Bergvall, M. (forthcoming). *Untying the Knot: Studies of the Swedish Divorce Transition, 1900–2020*. PhD Dissertation, Department of Economic History, Lund University.

Bergvall, M., and M. Stanfors. 2022. "Documenting the Determinants of the Divorce Transition. Micro-Level Evidence from Sweden 1905–1967." Lund Papers in Economic Demography 2022: 3.

Burgess, E. W., and H. J. Locke. 1945. *The Family: From Institution to Companionship*. New York: American Book.

Cherlin, A. 1996. *Public and Private Families: An Introduction*. New York: McGraw-Hill.

Cherlin, A. 2004. "The Deinstitutionalization of American Marriage." *Journal of Marriage and Family* 66 (4): 848–861.

Cliquet, R. 1992. "The Second Demographic Transition: Fact or Fiction? Council of Europe Population Studies 23. Strasbourg: Council of Europe.

Cohen, P. N. 2018. *The Family: Diversity, Inequality, and Social Change*. New York: W. W. Norton.

Coleman, D. 2004. "Why We Don't Have to Believe Without Doubting in the 'Second Demographic Transition': Some Agnostic Comments." *Vienna Yearbook of Population Research* 2: 11–24.

Crafts, N. 1985. *British Economic Growth During the Industrial Revolution*. New York: Oxford University Press.

Davis, K. 1945. "The World Demographic Transition." *The Annals of the American Academy of Political and Social Science* 237 (1): 1–11.

Demeny, P. 1968. "Early Fertility Decline in Austria-Hungary: A Lesson in Demographic Transition." *Daedalus* 97 (2): 502–522.

De Moor, T., and J. L. van Zanden. 2010. "Girl Power: The European Marriage Pattern and Labour Markets in the North Sea Region in the Late Medieval and Early Modern Period." *Economic History Review* 63 (1): 1–33.

Dribe, M., and M. Stanfors. 2010. "Family Life in Power Couples: Continued Childbearing and Union Stability among the Educational Elite in Sweden, 1991–2005." *Demographic Research* 23 (30): 847–878.

Esping-Andersen, G., and F. C. Billari. 2015. "Re-Theorizing Family Demographics." *Population and Development Review* 41 (1): 1–31.

Goldin, C. 2006. "The Quiet Revolution that Transformed Women's Employment, Education, and Family." *American Economic Review* 96 (1): 1–21.

Goldin, C. 2021. *Career and Family: Women's Century-Long Journey Toward Equity*. Princeton: Princeton University Press.

Goldscheider, F., E. Bernhardt, and T. Lappegård. 2015. "The Gender Revolution: A Framework for Understanding Changing Family and Demographic Behavior." *Population and Development Review* 41 (2): 207–239.

Goode, W. 1963. *World Revolution and Family Patterns*. New York: Free Press.

Goode, W. 1982. "Why Men Resist. In *Rethinking the Family: Some Feminist Questions*, edited by B. Thorne and M. Yalom, 131–150. New York: Longman.

Goode, W. 1993. *World Changes in Divorce Patterns*. New Haven: Yale University Press.

Hajnal, J. 1965. "European Marriage Patterns in Perspective." In *Population in History. Essays in Historical Demography*, edited by D. V. Glass and D. E. C. Eversley, 101–143. London: Edward Arnold.

Hajnal, J. 1983. "Two Kinds of Pre-Industrial Household Formation System." In *Family Forms in Historic Europe*, edited by R. Wall, J. Robin, and P. Laslett, 65–104. Cambridge: Cambridge University Press.

Lesthaeghe, R. 1983. "A Century of Demographic and Cultural Change in Western Europe: An Exploration of Underlying Dimensions." *Population and Development Review* 9 (3): 411–435.

Lesthaeghe, R. 2010. "The Unfolding Story of the Second Demographic Transition." *Population and Development Review* 36 (2): 211–251.

Lindert, P., and J. Williamson. 1983. "English Workers' Living Standards during the Industrial Revolution: A New Look." *Economic History Review* 36 (1): 1–25.

Malthus, T. R. 1803 [1992]. *An Essay on the Principle of Population*. Cambridge: Cambridge University Press.

Melby, K., A. Pylkkänen, B. Rosenbeck, and C. Carlsson Wetterberg. 2006. *Inte ett ord om kärlek: Äktenskap och politik i Norden ca 1850-1930*. [Not a Word About Love: Marriage and Politics in the Nordic Countries, ca 1850-1930]. Göteborg: Makadam förlag.

Notestein, F. 1945. "Population: The Long View." In *Food for the World*, edited by T. Schultz, 36–57. Chicago: Chicago University Press.

Ohlsson-Wijk, S. 2011. "Sweden's Marriage Revival: An Analysis of the New-Millennium Switch from Long-Term Decline to Increasing Popularity." *Population Studies* 65 (2): 183–200.

Oppenheimer, V. 1970. *The Female Labor Force in the United States: Demographic and Economic Factors Governing its Growth and Changing Composition*. Population Monograph Series, No. 5. Berkeley, CA: University of California.

Parsons, T. 1959. "The Social Structure of the Family." In *The Family: Its Function and Destiny. (Revised Edition)*, edited by R. Anshen, 241–274. New York: Harper and Row Publishers.

Phillips, R. 1988. *Putting Asunder: A History of Divorce in Western Society*. Cambridge: Cambridge University Press.

Phillips, R. 1991. *Untying the Knot: A Short History of Divorce*. Cambridge: Cambridge University Press.

Pinsof, W. M. 2002. "The Death of 'Till Death Us Do Part': The Transformation of Pair-Bonding in the 20th Century." *Family Process* 41 (2): 135–157.

Quaranta, L. 2015. "Using the Intermediate Data Structure (IDS) to Construct Files for Statistical Analysis." *Historical Life Course Studies* 2: 86–107.

Quaranta, L. 2016. "STATA Programs for Using the Intermediate Data Structure (IDS) to Construct Files for Statistical Analysis." *Historical Life Course Studies* 3: 1–19.

Risman, B. J. 2011. "Gender as Structure or Trump Card?" *Journal of Family Theory & Review* 3 (1): 18–22.

Sandström, G. 2011. "Socio-Economic Determinants of Divorce in Early Twentieth-Century Sweden." *The History of the Family* 16 (3): 292–307.

Sandström, G., and Ó. Garðarsdóttir. 2018. Long-Term Perspectives on Divorce in the Nordic Countries: Introduction." *Scandinavian Journal of History* 43 (1): 1–17.

Sandström, G., and M. Stanfors. 2023. "Socio-economic Status and the Rise of Divorce in Sweden: The Case of the 1880-1954 Marriage Cohorts in Västerbotten." *Population Studies* 77 (3): 417–135.

Shorter, E. 1975. *The Making of the Modern Family*. New York: Basic Books.

Stanfors, M. 2003. *Education, Labor Force Participation and Changing Fertility Patterns: A Study of Women and Socioeconomic Change in Twentieth Century Sweden*. Stockholm: Almqvist and Wiksell International.

Stanfors, M., and F. Goldscheider. 2017. "The Forest and the Trees: Industrialization, Demographic Change, and the Ongoing Gender Revolution in Sweden and the United States, 1870–2010." *Demographic Research* 36 (1): 173–216.

Stone, L. 1990. *Road to Divorce: England 1530–1987*. Oxford: Oxford University Press.

Thompson, W. 1929. "Population." *American Journal of Sociology* 34 (6): 959–975.

Thomson, E. 2014. "Family Complexity in Europe." *Annals of the AAPS* 654 (1): 245–258.

Van de Kaa, D. 1987. "Europe's Second Demographic Transition." *Population Bulletin* 42 (1): 1–59.

Van de Kaa, D. 2004. "Is the Second Demographic Transition a Useful Research Concept? Questions and Answers." *Vienna Yearbook of Population Research* 2: 4–10.

Wrigley, E. A., and R. S. Schofield. 1981. *The Population History of England 1541–1871: A Reconstruction*. London: Edward Arnold.

7
A Healthy Marriage?
Marital Status and Adult Mortality

Ingrid K. van Dijk and Martin Dribe

Introduction

Married people tend to have better health and live longer than the single and the widowed. When they do fall ill, they are more likely to recover and to do so more quickly, as when suffering from cancer (Aizer et al. 2013). Health differences by marital status are not limited to physical health but extend to mental health (see Coombs 1991; Rendall et al. 2011). Such differences in health and mortality by marital status are found in many contemporary societies (Valkonen et al. 2004) and are not exclusively a modern phenomenon; they have also existed in societies in the past, including Sweden (Grundy and Tomassini 2010; Mineau et al. 2002; Willner 1999). At the same time, health and survival differ markedly by both gender and socioeconomic status (SES), and trends in these differentials have not been stable over time (Bengtsson et al. 2020; Willner 1999, 2005). The long-term change in the mortality differentials by marital status and its interaction with gender and social class have not been systematically addressed in the literature. Exploring mortality differentials along these social dimensions over time could generate important insights into the mechanisms that lead to the marriage premium in health and survival. In this chapter, we explore these interactions by looking at the city of Landskrona, Sweden, and the five rural parishes in its hinterland.

The development of marital status differences in mortality is related to societal transformation and changing marriage patterns, especially the increased frequency of divorce and the postponement of widowhood to a later age. In Landskrona as elsewhere in Sweden, the share of married increased and then declined, while life expectancy has increased strongly during the twentieth century. We follow individuals grouped by marital status over the long term and address marital status differences in mortality and different patterns across time, by gender, and by social class. We do not address causal mechanisms but describe changes in average mortality across time. During the second half of the twentieth century socioeconomic differences in mortality became larger (see Chapter 9). We find that marital differences in mortality predate socioeconomic differences in mortality. Initially mortality differences by marital status were smaller among women than men, but with convergence between men and women over time.

Why is marriage beneficial for survival and health? Part of the explanation could be the increased likelihood of healthy individuals to marry. Individuals are selected on health into marriage and are also selected on health to remain married (Goldman et al. 1995; Lillard and Panis 1996). Next to selection effects, there is also evidence for causal protection effects associated with marriage and partnership for both men and women (Requena and Reher 2021) that tend to link marriage, or other kinds of stable relationships, with improved health and also link bereavement and divorce with negative health outcomes. Marriage may provide spouses with social support, care, financial support, and protection against economic shocks through the pooling of resources and may promote healthy behaviors (see Bowling 1987; House et al. 1988). In times of hardship, spouses can provide practical and emotional support to each other. After disease diagnosis and during recovery, people provide their partners with practical and social support (Datta et al. 2009). Social support is provided not only by partners themselves but also potentially through the partner's social and family network (Murphy et al. 2007).

Furthermore, marriage promotes healthy living. Single living, especially for men, is often associated with an adverse lifestyle in the form of, say, smoking, alcohol consumption, and sedentary behavior. Such associations, however, depend on context and there are counter examples where more adverse lifestyle was more common among the married. Among men born in the early twentieth century who were interviewed in Göteborg in 1970, the never-married were less likely to have ever smoked than the married (Mellström et al. 1982). This was at a time when smoking was common at social gatherings. For divorced men in Norway, the health penalty seems to increase with time since separation (Berntsen and Kravdal 2012), suggesting that the mortality penalty for this group may be associated with lifestyle effects that accumulate over time. Similarly, the benefits of marriage accumulate with time since length of marriage is positively associated with the gap in life span between married and unmarried individuals (Murphy et al. 2007).

Over and above the protective effects of a long marriage, bereavement is strongly related to increased mortality among widows and widowers, at least in the short run. Bereavement and divorce are related to poorer mental health and a higher likelihood of suicide (Bowling 1987; Williams and Umberson 2004) and increased all-cause mortality. Effects are especially pronounced immediately after the loss of a partner but remain detectable for a long time after the partner's death, and they are especially strong for young people. That is, divorce and widowhood appear to affect the survival of individuals who are in their twenties and thirties in particular, in comparison to married individuals of the same age (Hu and Goldman 1990). With age these negative effects persist but diminish (Tatangelo et al. 2017).

Some of the mechanisms linking marital status and health build on the assumption that spouses are in a happy marriage. For unhappily married couples, the positive effects of marriage are likely smaller or even absent altogether. Indeed, previous studies have found that unhappy marriages are associated with lower self-reported health and a higher mortality rate (Lawrence et al. 2019). In most cases, it is impossible to empirically distinguish happy from unhappy marriages, but these survey results suggest that some of the protective effects of marriage on health manifest themselves through the partners' emotional well-being and closeness.

The magnitude of the effects of marital status on health and survival is likely to depend on institutional and cultural differences across time and place. Previous research on rural Scania (Skåne) shows that widowhood had a stronger effect on mortality in the nineteenth century than it has today (Nystedt 2002). Important causes of contemporary social differences in mortality include lifestyle and health-related behavior. Given the decline in mortality from infectious diseases during the nineteenth and early twentieth centuries, the concurrent increase in mortality related to lifestyle diseases, and the differences between the married and the single in lifestyle and behavior, it is likely that mortality differences by marital status returned with renewed strength over the course of the twentieth century.

Furthermore, mortality differences by marital status might have been larger at times and in areas where a small proportion of the population never married (Hu and Goldman 1990; Livi-Bacci 1985), possibly because the groups of never-married were more likely to have been negatively selected on both health and SES. By the middle of the twentieth century the proportion of never-married had declined in most Western European societies, and marriage was taking place at a younger age. Toward the turn of the twenty-first century, the share of never-married and age at marriage increased once more (e.g., Lesthaeghe 2010). In Sweden, marriage rates declined until the late 1980s and have since then started to increase again. This pattern of decline followed by an increase in marriage rates, with a turning point in the early 1990s among cohorts born after 1970, is also reflected in the variations in age at marriage and the proportion ever marrying (Ohlsson-Wijk 2011). Around this period, a smaller proportion of the population remained unmarried so that differentiation by health into marriage or singlehood may have increased. Furthermore, some studies have indicated a widening mortality gap by marital status over time in contemporary developed societies (e.g., Hu and Goldman 1990; Jaffe et al. 2007; Martikainen et al. 2005; Murphy et al. 2007; Valkonen et al. 2004).

Data and Methods

We used the Scanian Economic-Demographic Database (SEDD) for the period 1905–1967 and national official register data after 1967 (Bengtsson et al. 2021; see Chapter 1). Both the SEDD and the national registers include information about marital status. This is divided into single/unmarried, married and those in a registered partnership (for same-sex couples between 1995 and 2009), and widows and widowers and individuals surviving their partner. We excluded same-sex marriages (from 2009) and registered partnerships (1995–2009), but these constitute only a tiny proportion of all unions (0.14 percent of the exposure time in the period 1995–2015). The divorced are included separately as of 1975. Sweden introduced a no-fault divorce law as early as in 1915, and the divorce rate increased for much of the twentieth century from very low levels, rising rapidly in the early 1970s and peaking in 1974 when the divorce law was further liberalized (Sandström 2012; Sandström and Stanfors 2020; Stanfors et al. 2020; see also Andersson 1995).

Marriage in Sweden historically followed the Western European marriage pattern (Hajnal 1965), in which lifelong singlehood was common and mean age at marriage quite high (e.g., Lundh 2013). In the nineteenth and early twentieth centuries, most unmarried women lived together with relatives or in a household where they worked as servants. Over time, increasing numbers of single men and women began living alone, which gave rise to the singlehood patterns of living and working that we know today (e.g., Sandström and Karlsson 2019). In the nineteenth and early twentieth centuries, widows and widowers who did not remarry were likely to move in with relatives as boarders or as servants to supplement labor in the household (Dribe et al. 2007). Widowhood during working age became increasingly rare over the twentieth century as mortality rates declined across the life course, including a decline in maternal mortality. Today widowhood is most common among elderly women due to the spousal age gap and the longer life expectancy of women and is very rare among young people. Unmarried individuals today are much more likely to have been divorced or never married than widowed.

Alongside marital status we included social class (Historical International Social Class Scheme [HISCLASS]) in our analyses based on information about occupation (Van Leeuwen and Maas 2011; see Chapter 1). We used an aggregated version of the class scheme: white-collar workers (nonmanual, HISCLASS 1–5), blue-collar workers (manual, HISCLASS 6–7, 9–12), and farmers and fishermen (HISCLASS 8). Observations of those without a recorded occupation were included as "missing." For individuals aged 60 and older, we used the highest social class recorded between ages 50 and 60.

Historically, occupational information for women has generally not been registered or is incomplete. We therefore used the highest social class (time-varying) observed for a couple. We performed a robustness check using an individual social-class measurement (see Appendix, Table A7.3). For unmarried men and women we used individual occupation. For single men, 11 percent of the observations lack occupational information; for single women, the corresponding number is 17 percent. Overall, information on social class was missing for about 7 percent of the women and about 5 percent of the men.

The empirical analyses are based on survival analysis, which allowed us to follow individuals from age 30 up to age 80. Hence, only individuals who survived to age 30 are included in the sample. Individuals were followed until death, out-migration, or the year 2015. The dataset is organized into observation periods, which are sequences of the life course during which the covariates included are constant. When an individual changed status, such as from married to widowed, there is a new period that reflects this change. In this way, all covariates are time-varying except gender, year of birth, and migrant status (native-born or foreign-born). We used Kaplan-Meier estimates of survivor functions and Cox proportional hazards models to analyze the association between marital status and mortality. We looked at patterns for men and women separately and also by period to assess how the associations changed over time. Moreover, we looked at how the changes over time in the association between marital status and mortality differed by social class. Results are presented as hazard ratios, where the mortality for the group in question is compared to the reference category.

Year of birth was included to adjust for secular (cohort) changes in mortality. We further adjusted for migration status to distinguish between native-born and foreign-born. Table 7.1 reports the descriptive statistics of the covariates by gender and period. It indicates the same changes over time in marital status and class structure that were discussed above (see also Chapter 3 for a more detailed analysis of the changes in the class structure and Chapter 9 for an analysis of the development of class differentials in adult mortality over time). The table also shows the dominance of observations from Landskrona in the analytical sample and the increasing proportion of foreign-born over the twentieth century and especially after 1950.

Union Formation and Union Dissolution

We start by looking at the distribution of marital status over time, as displayed in Figure 7.1. The proportion of married individuals aged 30–79 stayed fairly constant at around 60 percent between the beginning of the nineteenth century

Table 7.1 Descriptive statistics, men and women aged 30–79, by person-year, Landskrona and the five parishes.

	Men					Women				
	1905–1929	1930–1949	1950–1975	1976–1994	1995–2015	1905–1929	1930–1949	1950–1975	1976–1994	1995–2015
Marital status										
Single	20.64	18.32	14.59	17.20	25.62	25.38	22.54	14.02	10.99	17.61
Married	72.42	75.41	80.51	68.70	55.42	60.72	64.73	72.56	62.09	53.83
Widowed	6.36	5.75	4.47	3.55	2.33	13.17	11.95	12.53	13.65	8.61
Widowed, first year	0.58	0.53	0.43	0.36	0.24	0.73	0.78	0.89	0.97	0.62
Divorced	-	-	-	10.19	16.38	-	-	-	12.30	19.33
Social class										
White-collar	22.17	25.49	34.41	45.70	49.35	23.78	32.25	43.07	48.16	52.28
Blue-collar	63.62	67.16	58.04	46.41	41.48	57.27	59.41	48.28	43.37	39.40
Farmer	7.69	5.43	3.04	2.54	0.80	5.97	4.40	2.80	2.37	0.82
NA	6.53	1.92	4.51	5.35	8.37	12.98	3.94	5.85	6.09	7.50
Urban area	70.48	74.32	79.28	81.66	78.63	72.39	76.39	80.20	82.38	78.81
Mean year of birth	1874	1896	1916	1935	1956	1873	1894	1913	1933	1954
Foreign migrant	3.43	3.11	7.01	6.97	12.66	2.71	2.56	4.42	4.65	8.76
Deaths	1,769	1,781	3,142	3,833	2,942	1,775	1,745	2,439	2,432	2,068
Mean age at death	60.80	63.40	65.82	68.04	67.95	62.53	65.14	67.89	69.68	69.11
N individuals	12,928	14,286	21,779	25,157	30,834	13,706	14,717	20,438	24,133	29,495
Person-years	118,601	132,325	230,432	263,072	314,135	133,456	143,287	237,748	274,195	317,325

Note: Distributions are shown as percentages of total number of person years.
Source: Own calculations based on SEDD (Bengtsson et al. 2021).

and the 1930s, followed by a sharp increase which peaked around 1970 and then declined. The trend in the proportion of single adults was the opposite of that in the proportion of married, while the share of widows and widowers remained fairly stable over the whole period. The proportion of divorcees increased from low levels in 1975 to about 20 percent of the population who had divorced and not remarried by 2015. There was a steady increase in nonmarital cohabitation from at least as early as the 1960s, but it is most likely this started well before then (e.g., Bracher and Santow 1998; Hoem and Rennermalm 1985). In the period after 1970, long-term cohabitation became more common, too, including among couples with children (e.g., Kiernan 2004). In our analysis we included nonmarital cohabitation among the single, widowed, and divorced, depending on previous changes in marital status. Cohabiting couples with common children can be traced in the data from 1990, and, in a sensitivity analysis, we exclude them from our analyses (see Appendix, Table A7.4). Since cohabiting individuals with children are usually relatively young, only one death is observed in this group.

Figure 7.2 shows the marriage and divorce rates in the area compared to Sweden as a whole. The local series has been smoothed using a three-year moving average. The trends and longer-term cycles for the local and national levels are similar to each other, and most of the short-term fluctuations are quite similar as well. Marriage rates increased somewhat until the 1930s, but then turned sharply upward and peaked during the post-World War II baby boom of the 1940s. It is well-known that the baby boom was to a large extent a marriage boom (see, e.g., Van Bavel and Reher 2013). Thereafter the rates declined again to levels similar to those in the early 1900s. From the 1960s on, marriage rates declined until the early 1990s, after which they began to increase. The peak in 1989 relates to changes in the conditions for receiving a widow's pension (Hoem 1991; Ohlsson-Wijk 2011) and was more visible in the local data—and similar to the nationwide data—before the smoothing.

Divorce rates in the study area increased only gradually until the late 1960s, when they turned sharply upward and peaked in 1974, which is similar to the national trend (e.g., Sandström 2012). This trend was associated with both macro-economic conditions and changes relating to women's independence and family support (Stanfors et al. 2020). The rise in divorce started among the higher SES groups, but already in the mid-1930s the socioeconomic differences reversed, and divorce became more common in the lower socioeconomic groups. This change also contributed to the increasing trend in divorce rates as it spread to broader segments of society (Sandström 2012; Sandström and Stanfors 2020; see also Hoem 1997).

We next look in more detail at patterns of bereavement and widowhood. Figure 7.3 shows the proportions of widowed men and women per person-year

A. Men

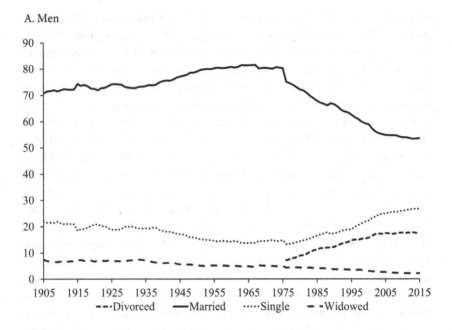

B. Women

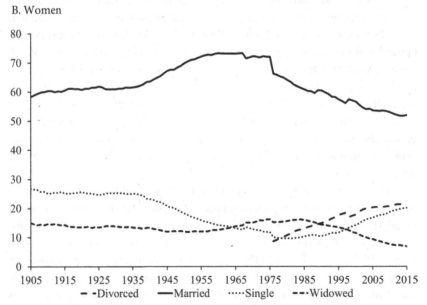

Figure 7.1 Marital status in Landskrona and the five parishes, ages 30–79. Proportions calculated by person-years of exposure.

Source: Own calculations based on the Scanian Economic-Demographic Database (SEDD; Bengtsson et al. 2021).

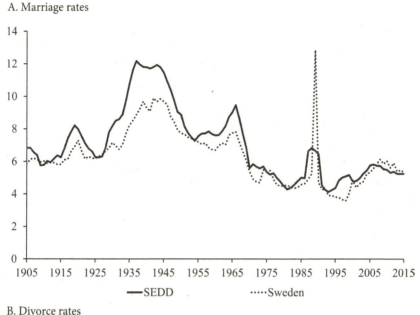
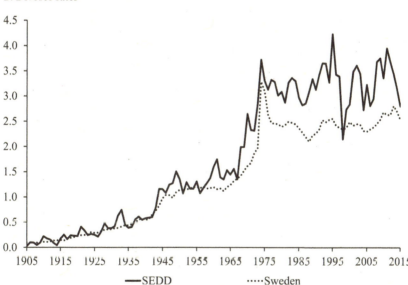

Figure 7.2 Marriage and divorce rates in Sweden and Landskrona and the five parishes.
Marriage and divorce rates are per 1,000 population.
Source: Source: Own calculations based on the Scanian Economic-Demographic Database (SEDD; Bengtsson et al. 2021); Statistics Sweden (2020).

of exposure in the area of study. In the early twentieth century, about 0.5 percent of married individuals experienced bereavement in any one year. For women this share increased from the 1950s to around 1990, after which it declined. For men, the bereavement rate declined throughout the twentieth century, whereby the rates diverged between men and women. This divergence reflects the long-term development of life expectancy by gender. These life expectancy differences increased in the post-World War II period until the mid-1970s and then converged as women's life expectancy became longer than men's (e.g., Statistics Sweden 1999). As is clear from Figure 7.3, the risk of bereavement increases with age, and, on average, the age of the married population increases, too, as indeed it did in our case between 1950 and 1990, implying that the proportion of the population who lost a spouse also increased. Since 1990, mortality among the elderly has declined significantly while at the same time there has been an increase in the proportion of younger couples among the married in the study area. Together these trends have led to a decline in the risk of losing one's spouse.

Marital Status and Adult Mortality

We now turn to an analysis of the relationship between marital status and mortality and begin by looking at survival functions without adjusting for any variables. Figure 7.4 displays the curves for men (panel C) and women (panel D) in the period 1975–2015. The solid lines represent the proportion of the population who were currently married, and the broken lines show estimates for those who were single, widowed, or divorced. In this period, the currently married had lower mortality than all other groups. This pattern appears from about age 50, while differences under this age are minor, following that mortality in younger years is very low. It is also notable that there is a clear ordering whereby the mortality rate was highest among those who were single, and for the widowed and divorced it lay somewhere between the rates for the single and the married. Figure 7.4 also displays the curves for men (panel A) and women (panel B) in the period 1905–1974. The divorces were so few in this period that they are not included in the figure. Again, there is a clear ordering where the currently married had lower mortality than all other groups, with larger differences for men than for women, similar to the period 1975–2015.

Table 7.2 reports hazard ratios of mortality by marital status among those age 30–79 for Landskrona and the five parishes together (Panel A) and for Landskrona only (Panel B). Results are largely similar for the town and its rural hinterland and for the town on its own, although the magnitude appears to be somewhat larger among men in the period 1930–1974. All models adjust for social class, migrant status, and birth year. The reference group contains

A HEALTHY MARRIAGE? 223

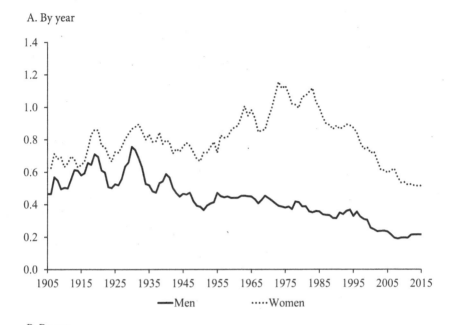

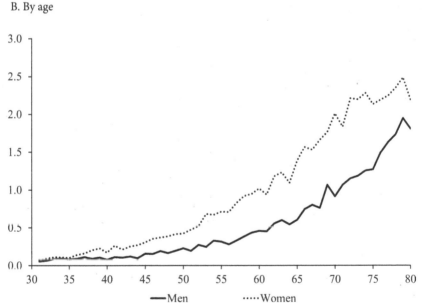

Figure 7.3 Proportion of women and men newly bereaved (bereaved in the past year) in Landskrona and the five parishes.

Source: Own calculations based on the Scanian Economic-Demographic Database (SEDD; Bengtsson et al. 2021).

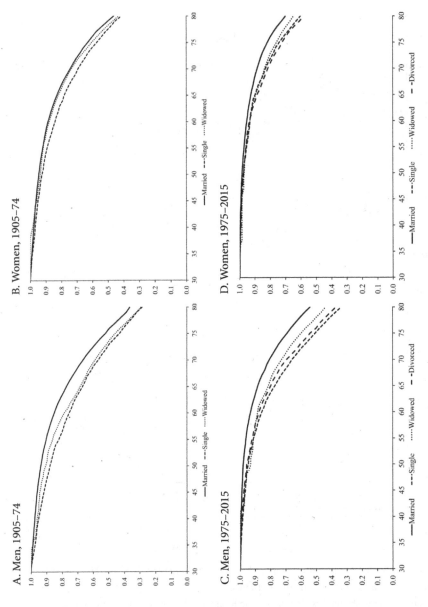

Figure 7.4 Kaplan-Meier survivor functions by gender and period.
Source: Own calculations based on the Scanian Economic-Demographic Database (SEDD; Bengtsson et al. 2021).

Table 7.2 Marital status and mortality (hazard ratios) by gender and period, age 30–79.

A. Landskrona and the five parishes

	1905–1929	1930–1949	1950–1974	1975–1994	1995–2015
Men					
Single	1	1	1	1	1
Married	0.730***	0.853**	0.709***	0.644***	0.485***
Widowed	0.834**	0.935	0.868**	0.753***	0.634***
Divorced	-	-	-	1.127*	0.861*
N individuals	12,928	14,286	21,779	25,157	30,834
Deaths	1,769	1,781	3,142	3,833	2,942
Person years	118,601	132,325	230,432	263,072	314,135
Women					
Single	1	1	1	1	1
Married	0.911	0.913	0.900*	0.933	0.549***
Widowed	0.945	0.964	0.975	0.966	0.663***
Divorced	-	-	-	1.310***	0.936
N individuals	13,706	14,717	20,438	24,133	29,495
Deaths	1,775	1,745	2,439	2,432	2,068
Person years	133,456	143,287	237,748	274,195	317,326

B. Landskrona

	1905–1929	1930–1949	1950–1974	1975–1994	1995–2015
Men					
Married	1	1	1	1	1
Single	1.389***	1.387***	1.535***	1.633***	2.105***
Widowed	1.158*	1.031	1.189***	1.213***	1.348***
Divorced	-	-	-	1.762***	1.819***
N individuals	8,638	10,350	17,173	20,193	24,690
Deaths	1,282	1,372	2,563	3,160	2,411
Person years	83,594	98,348	182,683	214,814	252,534
Women					
Married	1	1	1	1	1
Single	1.125	1.043	1.110*	1.126	1.820***

(*continued*)

Table 7.2 Continued

	1905–1929	1930–1949	1950–1974	1975–1994	1995–2015
Widowed	1.056	1.084	1.059	1.059	1.198***
Divorced	-	-	-	1.437***	1.701***
N individuals	9,354	10,904	16,246	19,387	23,417
Deaths	1,277	1,336	1,982	2,015	1,663
Person years	96,606	109,456	190,684	225,895	254,680

Notes: ***p < 0.01, **p < 0.05, *p < 0.1. All models control for social class (white-collar, blue-collar, farmers, and missing), migrant status, and birth year. Same model as in Table 7.2 but with married as reference category.
Source: Own calculations based on SEDD (Bengtsson et al. 2021).

individuals who were single (never married). In comparison to single men, married and widowed men had lower mortality. For example, in the period 1905–1929, married men in Landskrona and the five parishes had a hazard ratio of mortality of 0.730 relative to that of unmarried men, and widowed men had a hazard ratio of 0.834. Over time, mortality differentials by marital status grew, especially when comparing the single and married, but also when comparing the single and widowed. Divorced men had a strong mortality disadvantage as well, of the same order of magnitude as single men (the hazard ratio was 1.127 in the period 1975–1994 and 0.861 in the period 1995–2015). These differences are marginally statistically significant (p = 0.10). Divorced men in the last two periods had much higher mortality than married men, and also mortality among widowed men was higher than for married men in all periods, although the difference is not statistically significant for the period 1930–1949 (see Appendix, Table A7.1, which presents the results with the married as the reference category). The magnitudes of the differences are larger for the divorced than for the widowed.

For women, the development over time closely resembles that for men, with larger differentials by marital status in the final period (1995–2015). However, differences by marital status are noticeably smaller further back in time. In the period 1905–1974, there are no statistically significant differences in mortality by marital status except for married women in the period 1950–1974. Divorced women were forerunners in the change toward mortality divergence by marital status. In the period 1975–1994, their mortality rate was significantly higher than that for single, widowed, and married women. The difference with married women grew over time (Appendix, Table A7.1). In the period 1995–2015, married and widowed women all had considerably lower mortality than single women. In the most recent decades, divorced and single women have had comparable, not statistically significantly different, mortality. For widows, mortality was higher than for currently married women only in the last period (see Appendix, Table A7.1).

Overall, there appears to have been an increase in the marriage premium in survival over the twentieth century. This development is especially notable in more recent decades. Moreover, the marriage premium is increasingly converging between men and women since a single-person penalty for women seems to have been largely absent in the early twentieth century.

In the final period (1995-2015), the hazard of mortality among married men was more than halved in comparison to that among single men, while the corresponding figure for women saw a reduction by almost half. A similar widening of the mortality differential can also be seen for widowed and divorced men and women. Apart from the increase in these differences, the mortality patterns by marital status were fairly stable over time, with the currently married having the lowest mortality, followed by the widowed and the unmarried. The divorced had the highest mortality in the period 1975-1994, among both men and women. In the period 1990-2015, there was a sharp increase in the differences between the married and unmarried and the married and widowed, so that, despite an increase in the survival difference between the married and the divorced, single men and women now had the highest mortality. This is remarkable given the fact that an increasing number of cohabiting couples, who are likely to share some of the benefits of stable partnership, are included among the single individuals over time.

Table 7.3 shows differences by timing of bereavement, using the currently married as the reference category. For men, bereavement had an immediate effect on mortality in the period 1905-1974. More than a year after losing their partner, mortality was still higher than among the currently married but lower than in the first year of widowhood and lower than among never-married men (this difference is also statistically significant, as shown in Appendix, Table A7.2). In the period 1975-2015, men widowed for less than a year no longer had a statistically significant mortality disadvantage in comparison to married men, whereas men widowed for a longer time still had higher mortality than the married. The patterns for women are highly similar to those for men. There is an immediate effect of bereavement in the first period but not in the second, while there is a long-term effect in both periods. Overall, magnitudes are somewhat lower for widows than for widowers.

Table 7.4 presents analyses by social class and shows that the protective effect for currently married men was largely consistent across classes, with decreased mortality for the married and widowed compared to the single. For women, the widening of the mortality differentials by marital status seems to have occurred

Table 7.3 Timing of widowhood and mortality (hazard ratios) by gender and period, age 30–79. Landskrona and the five parishes.

	1905–1974	1975–2015
Men		
Married	1	1
Single	1.324***	1.743***
Widowed >1 year	1.167***	1.275***
Widowed <1 year	1.372***	1.054
Divorced	-	1.756***
N individuals	34,926	42,366
Deaths	6,692	6,775
Person years	481,359	577,208
Women		
Married	1	1
Single	1.134***	1.345***
Widowed >1 year	1.083*	1.160***
Widowed <1 year	1.212**	0.952
Divorced	-	1.573***
N individuals	33,784	39,619
Deaths	5,959	4,500
Person years	514,493	591,521

Notes: ***$p < 0.01$, **$p < 0.05$, *$p < 0.1$. All models control for social class, urban residence, migrant status, and birth year.
Source: Own calculations based on SEDD (Bengtsson et al. 2021).

earlier among blue-collar workers. Already in the period before 1975, married women from this class had lower mortality than did the currently single and widowed, a pattern which we do not observe among white-collar women. Widows from farming backgrounds had significantly lower mortality in the early period, but the number of these cases is low.

Table 7.5 displays the results from separate models by age group for the periods 1905–1974 and 1975–2015. Overall, mortality differences between the married and the single were larger for young men than for young women in the first period, while the patterns are more similar between men and women in the final period. The lower mortality rate for the married relative to the unmarried is visible among both old and young men and women across periods. There was not much of a change over time in the widowhood penalty for men, irrespective of age. For women, the association between widowhood and

Table 7.4 Marital status and mortality (hazard ratios) by social class gender and period, age 30–79. Landskrona and the five parishes.

	Men		Women	
	1905–1974	1975–2015	1905–1974	1975–2015
White-collar				
Single	1	1	1	1
Married	0.672***	0.528***	0.911	0.726***
Widowed	0.815**	0.636***	0.933	0.804**
Divorced	-	0.999	-	1.182
N individuals	12,570	20,986	13,455	21,167
Deaths	1,639	2,572	1,516	1,710
Person years	139,313	275,264	180,325	297,969
Blue-collar				
Single	1	1	1	1
Married	0.715***	0.591***	0.876***	0.750***
Widowed	0.793***	0.718***	1.027	0.834**
Divorced	-	0.987	-	1.108
N individuals	21,646	21,530	18,509	19,070
Deaths	3,869	3,530	3,112	2,252
Person years	298,060	252,388	276,363	243,928
Farmer				
Single	1	1	1	1
Married	0.925	0.559***	0.641	0.528
Widowed	1.135	0.504**	0.522**	0.627
Divorced	-	0.904	-	1.044
N individuals	1,732	654	1,515	640
Deaths	324	146	264	112
Person years	23,305	9,201	20,921	9,126

Notes: ***p < 0.01, **p < 0.05, *p < 0.1. All models control for migrant status and birth year.
Source: Own calculations based on SEDD (Bengtsson et al. 2021).

mortality was only statistically significant for older women in the period from 1975. Older widows had lower mortality than single women of the same age. Previous to that, older widows had higher mortality, similar to single women. The survival premium of older married women becomes larger between the two periods.

Table 7.5 Marital status and mortality (hazard ratios) by gender, age, and period. Landskrona and the five parishes.

	Men		Women	
	1905–1974	1975–2015	1905–1974	1975–2015
30–59 years				
Single	1	1	1	1
Married	0.574***	0.454***	0.829***	0.750**
Widowed	0.769**	0.518***	0.765**	0.821
Divorced	-	0.859**	-	1.003
N individuals	32,274	35,556	30,556	31,915
Deaths	2,154	1,309	1,617	736
Person years	363,359	387,597	370,470	372,402
60–79 years				
Single	1	1	1	1
Married	0.908**	0.603***	0.950**	0.771***
Widowed	1.016	0.737***	1.002	0.875**
Divorced	-	1.074	-	1.286***
N individuals	11,916	18,175	13,513	19,333
Deaths	4,538	5,466	4,342	3,764
Person years	114,285	183,950	139,906	213,288

Notes: ***p < 0.01, **p < 0.05, *p < 0.1. All models control for social class, urban residence, migrant status, and birth year.
Source: Own calculations based on SEDD (Bengtsson et al. 2021).

In the younger age group, married women had a survival advantage in comparison to the single in the period 1975–2015, and the divorced do not differ significantly from the single. The hazard ratio for the widowed also indicates an advantage but is not statistically significant. In the period before 1975, both the married and widowed young women had lower mortality than single women.

Finally, we conducted two robustness checks. First, we analyzed class-specific marriage premiums in survival using individual social class instead of family social class and found no significant changes in our results (see Appendix, Table A7.3). Second, we excluded from the singles category people who cohabited and had common children. Furthermore, we excluded from the analysis those who had remarried, so that the married category only included first marriages. In both cases, results remain the same (see Appendix, Table A7.4).

Explaining Gender Differences

We are not the first to report considerable gender differences in the association between marital status and mortality. The literature generally identifies stronger health protective effects of marriage for men than for women (e.g., Stroebe et al. 1996). In nineteenth-century Sweden, never-married men and widowers had considerably higher mortality than the married, while for women marital status did not matter so much for longevity, with the exception of younger widows. Married women of reproductive age even had higher mortality than the never-married women and higher mortality than married men as well, due to maternal mortality (Willner 1999). Around the turn of the twentieth century the mortality differentials by marital status had declined somewhat. The marital status differentials were quite similar across regions in Sweden, with the exception of relatively higher mortality for married women in the northernmost part of the country. Hence, at the beginning of our study in 1905, marital status differentials for men had declined somewhat but were still clearly visible, while the differentials for women were much smaller and, in some cases, completely absent (Willner 1999).

There are several reasons why the protective effects of marriage may be stronger for men than for women. Women often have stronger nonmarital networks than men (Bowling 1987; Murphy et al. 2007). For men, the stress experienced after the loss of a partner may be stronger, and their social support networks tend to be weaker than women's. Women may therefore be less dependent on social support from their spouse and his social and family network. At least historically, adverse health behaviors such as smoking and excessive alcohol consumption were much more prevalent among men, and it is possible that the mortality difference between married and unmarried men was in part related to a more orderly life among the married than among the never-married or the widowed or divorced (Willner 1999). However, as already mentioned, there are some indications that never-married men born in the early twentieth century were less likely to have ever smoked (Mellström et al. 1982).

We find higher mortality for newly bereaved men than for newly bereaved women. Previous literature has reported that it appears to take men longer than women to recover after bereavement (Bowling 1987). Occasionally, the loss of a spouse results in suicide, as was studied as far back as in 1897 in a classic study by Émile Durkheim (e.g., Coombs 1991; see also Mellström et al. 1982 for Sweden). The risk of suicide after partner loss declines more slowly among men, and men suffer more from the loss of their spouse (Erlangsen 2004). Moreover, after a divorce women appear to recover faster than men, and they retain their survival premium for a longer time after union dissolution (Brockmann and Klein

2004). The loss of men's "homemaker, housekeeper and friend" (Bowling 1987, 121) may imply that changes in their lives after such loss may be stronger than those for women. Elderly men may be ill-prepared to take on domestic chores, and the feeling of helplessness as well as the potential physical effects of not taking adequate care of themselves and their household may as a result negatively affect their survival in both the short run and the long run. Younger cohorts, in contrast, may on average divide household and caretaking chores rather more equally so that effects for both men and women are mitigated.

At the same time, the relationship between gender and survival after bereavement may also stem from the higher average age of men when they lose their partner, as women tend to live longer than men. In addition, bereavement is more common among men with lower SES due to the earlier age in general at death and the larger variation in age at death than among higher SES groups (Martikainen et al. 2005). In lower SES groups, men are also more likely to have an excess risk of early death, regardless of the survival of their spouse. However, in our analyses, we controlled for SES, and in our Cox proportional hazard models, age was the duration variable whereby estimated differences by marital status were assumed to be proportional to age. Hence, age and social class are unlikely to explain our findings regarding gender differences.

Explaining Changes over Time

Our findings showed increasing mortality differentials by marital status from the 1950s onward. This was the case for both men and women and both younger and older age groups regardless of social class. Before 1950, there was not much change in the relationship between marital status and mortality, and, while there was a clear mortality penalty for single and widowed men, we do not see a penalty for women. A similar widening of marital status differentials over time and a convergence between men and women have been observed in other Western countries as well (Berntsen 2011; Murphy et al. 2007; Martikainen et al. 2005; Valkonen et al. 2004).

The period after 1950 was characterized by rapid economic and social change, with an increase in the standard of living in terms of both real earnings and consumption and housing. This economic expansion was especially pronounced in the period up to the mid-1970s, but there was still considerable economic growth and a rise in living standards during the 1980s and from the mid-1990s and onward as well (see, e.g., Schön 2010). The economic development of Landskrona followed the general pattern in Sweden, but the industrial cycles were more pronounced and the industrial crisis of the 1970s and early 1980s hit the city especially hard (see Chapter 2). The period after 1950 also saw the tremendous expansion of the welfare state, with improvements in almost all areas of life from poverty eradication to schooling, childcare, healthcare, pensions, and income compensation related to sickness, unemployment, and parenthood. There were also periods of economic crisis and cutbacks in welfare, but, overall, these were quite brief (Schön 2010; Stanfors 2007).

During the second half of the twentieth century, dramatic changes also took place in family patterns in Sweden as a result of the increase in divorce and nonmarital cohabitation together with widely fluctuating fertility (see Stanfors 2007). Married women in particular entered the labor market in large numbers, initially during the years when they did not have small children, but then increasingly during those years as well. This led to an almost complete transition from a male breadwinner model to a dual-earner model (Goldscheider et al. 2015; Olah and Bernhardt 2008; Stanfors 2014; Stanfors and Goldscheider 2017).

The period after 1950 has been characterized by a rise in life expectancy for both men and women and, in more recent times, by a convergence between genders (Statistics Sweden 1999). In the mid-twentieth century, infectious diseases were no longer major causes of death and were replaced by cardiovascular disease and cancer as the leading causes of death among adults. Since the mid-twentieth century mortality has been concentrated among those who are older, cardiovascular diseases have declined in relative importance, and cancer and old age-related diseases (e.g., dementia) have become relatively more important in terms of causes of death, even though cardiovascular and respiratory diseases are still important (see, e.g., Socialstyrelsen 2021; Willner 2005).

It is remarkable that, during a period of societal change so profound that it has led to vastly improved living conditions for the population in general, mortality differentials by marital status became increasingly important for both men and women. The protective effect of being married has become stronger while the institution of marriage itself seems to have lost at least some of its former importance. It is difficult to see any clear connection between the social and economic development, in Sweden generally or in Landskrona specifically, and the increased importance of marital status for mortality. The significant transformation of the family and the labor market for women created greater independence for women in relation to their husbands, yet clearly this has not diminished the role of marriage in their survival. Quite the contrary, this greater independence coincided with a convergence of the marital status differentials in mortality between men and women. The difference in mortality between the divorced and the married also increased when divorce became more common and more accepted.

There could be several reasons for the increased importance of marital status for health and survival over time. One is simply that as mortality among those of working age and in early retirement has declined, stress, loneliness, and grief connected to singlehood, divorce, and widowhood may have become more important as risk factors for lifestyle and behaviors related to suicide, accidents, and heart failure. These causes of death have become relatively more important over time because baseline mortality is so low. Another possible reason for the large role of marital status is the increasing importance of dementia as a cause of death among the elderly and a correlation between widowhood and the onset of dementia or the rate of progression of the disease (see Martikainen et al. 2005). Moreover, most families today are dependent on two incomes, which may have contributed to increased financial stress among the divorced and may also have had health consequences (see, e.g., Berntsen 2011). A further explanation could be a change in the selection into different types of marital status, whereby those who are not in such good health and perhaps those with a particularly unhealthy lifestyle are more likely to be single and divorced. There is not much evidence for this in our analysis. We see a trend toward greater mortality differentials by marital status during both periods of decline and increase in marriage (cf. Martikainen et al. 2005; Murphy et al. 2007; Valkonen et al. 2004).

Valkonen et al. (2004) hypothesize that urbanization, increased geographic and social mobility, and smaller families as well as attitudinal change in Western countries have made social support from relatives and neighbors less accessible—support that was previously of crucial importance to well-being, especially for single women. Among elderly widows in particular these societal changes could help explain the convergence between men and women in terms of the protective effect of marriage. The living arrangements of the elderly and especially their proximity to kin could be a crucial factor, even though the evidence of a secular increase in loneliness among the elderly seems quite weak (Dahlberg et al. 2018; Dykstra 2009).

Overall, differences in lifestyle are more important for mortality today than in the past and are probably related to the widening of class differences in adult mortality that has taken place since the 1970s (Bengtsson et al. 2020; see also Chapter 9). Having a partner is associated with a more regular lifestyle and fewer unhealthy behaviors, and it can also promote health monitoring (Coombs 1991; Willner 1999). Even though this factor has mainly been highlighted as important for men, the convergence of lifestyles between men and women (e.g., regarding smoking and alcohol consumption) may have resulted in partners being of crucial importance for women's health as well (Coombs 1991).

Finally, access to social support and networks has been stressed as being important for good health and longevity (Bowling 1987; Coombs 1991; House et al. 1988). For men it has long been emphasized that living as a single person is associated with less support and less extensive networks and that divorce and widowhood in particular are detrimental as they both imply the loss of existing support and networks. In addition, being single on a long-term basis might erode social networks and limit access to emotional support, especially during those stages in life when married people are focused on raising their families. Those who are married are also reported to be happier than those who are single, divorced, or widowed, and they experience less stress (Coombs 1991). It is possible that this difference in the degree of happiness has increased in recent decades or has become more consequential for health and mortality.

Conclusion

This chapter shows that marital status has had a fairly consistent association with mortality over the entire twentieth century, especially for men but increasingly so for women, too. Married men have a survival premium today, and the same was true in the past. For them, marriage has been associated with lower mortality throughout the twentieth century and into the twenty-first century, while widowhood in particular has been associated with higher mortality. The widowhood penalty is highest shortly after bereavement but does persist in the long run, too. Over time, mortality differentials by marital status have increased for men, especially since 1950. It is remarkable that there is such stability in the survival advantage of married men despite the massive social, economic, and demographic changes during this period.

The patterns for women are somewhat different than for men. Mortality differentials by marital status are smaller for them and absent for much of the twentieth century. It is only between 1990 and 2015 that divorced, single, and widowed women had higher mortality than the currently married. The overall relationship between widowhood and mortality also appears to be much weaker for women than for men. Over time, it appears that there has been convergence of the patterns of mortality by marital status for men and women. Our findings suggest that the divergence in mortality by marital status for women started among blue-collar workers and was initially largely absent among the white-collar group. For men, there were no consistent differences in the association between marital status and mortality by social class. Overall, marital status had quite a similar effect on white-collar and blue-collar men alike, and there were no major changes over time in the patterns by SES.

The main conclusion of this chapter is that marital status is important for longevity. It has been so for the entire twentieth century for men and increasingly so for women. These findings are in line with the international literature on the relationship between marital status and survival. A growing survival advantage for the married and a widening of differences among single, widowed, and divorced women compared to married women has been found in a range of developed countries including Canada, England, Wales, and France (Valkonen et al. 2002), and the survival advantage is commonly larger for men than for women. In Norway, in the period 1970–2007, as in Sweden, excess mortality was higher among single men but has increased more strongly among single women (Berntsen 2011).

The widening of the marital status differentials that took place after 1950 is particularly interesting given the fundamental societal improvements seen in Sweden generally and in Landskrona. It is difficult to pinpoint the exact reasons for this widening, but it could be related to a decline in baseline mortality, the change in selection into single living, the increased importance of lifestyle differences between the married and the single, and possibly the greater emotional and stress effects of singlehood. Comparing the findings of this chapter with those of Chapter 9 on social class differences, it is interesting to see that these differentials seemed to widen in the period after 1950, and even more so in the period from the 1970s on. It suggests that the more advantaged groups in society have been able to benefit more in terms of health than have the less advantaged as mortality has declined and living standards increased. The precise causes behind this development are not yet fully understood.

Appendix

Table A7.1 Marital status and mortality (hazard ratios) by gender and period, age 30–79. Landskrona and the five parishes. Married as the reference category.

A. Landskrona and the five parishes

	1905–1929	1930–1949	1950–1974	1975–1994	1995–2015
Men					
Married	1	1	1	1	1
Single	1.370***	1.173**	1.411***	1.554***	2.063***
Widowed	1.142*	1.097	1.225***	1.169***	1.307***
Divorced	-	-	-	1.751***	1.776***
N individuals	12,928	14,286	21,779	25,157	30,834
Deaths	1,769	1,781	3,142	3,833	2,942
Person years	118,601	132,325	230,432	263,072	314,135
Women					
Married	1	1	1	1	1
Single	1.097	1.096	1.111*	1.072	1.822***
Widowed	1.037	1.056	1.083	1.036	1.207***
Divorced	-	-	-	1.405***	1.706***
N individuals	13,706	14,717	20,438	24,133	29,495
Deaths	1,775	1,745	2,439	2,432	2,068
Person years	133,456	143,287	237,748	274,195	317,326

Table A7.1 Continued

B. Landskrona

	1905–1929	1930–1949	1950–1974	1975–1994	1995–2015
Men					
Single	1	1	1	1	1
Married	0.720***	0.721***	0.652***	0.612	0.475***
Widowed	0.834*	0.743***	0.774***	0.743	0.641***
Divorced	-	-	-	1.078	0.864**
N individuals	8,638	10,350	17,173	20,193	24,690
Deaths	1,282	1,372	2,563	3,160	2,411
Person years	83,594	98,348	182,683	214,814	252,534
Women					
Single	1	1	1	1	1
Married	0.889*	0.959	0.901*	0.888	0.549***
Widowed	0.939	1.040	0.954	0.941	0.658***
Divorced	-	-	-	1.277*	0.935
N individuals	9,354	10,904	16,246	19,387	23,417
Deaths	1,277	1,336	1,982	2,015	1,663
Person years	96,606	109,456	190,684	225,895	254,680

Notes: ***$p < 0.01$, **$p < 0.05$, *$p < 0.1$. All models control for social class, migrant status, and birth year.
Source: Own calculations based on SEDD (Bengtsson et al. 2021).

Table A7.2 Timing of widowhood and mortality (hazard ratios) by gender and period, age 30–79. Landskrona and the five parishes. Single as the reference category.

	1905–1974	1975–2015
Men		
Single	1	1
Married	0.755***	0.574***
Widowed >1 year	0.881***	0.731***
Widowed <1 year	1.036	0.605***
Divorced	-	1.007
N individuals	34,926	42,366
Deaths	6,692	6,775
Person years	481,359	577,208

(continued)

Table A7.2 Continued

	1905–1974	1975–2015
Women		
Single	1	1
Married	0.882**	0.744***
Widowed >1 year	0.956	0.863***
Widowed <1 year	1.069	0.708***
Divorced	-	1.170***
N individuals	33,784	39,619
Deaths	5,959	4,500
Person years	514,493	591,521

Notes: ***p < 0.01, **p < 0.05, *p < 0.1. All models control for social class (white-collar, blue-collar, farmers, and missing), urban residence, migrant status, and birth year. Same model as in table 7.2 but with single as reference category.
Source: Own calculations based on SEDD (Bengtsson et al. 2021).

Table A7.3 Individual social class, marital status, and mortality (hazard ratios) by gender and period, age 30–79. Landskrona and the five parishes.

	Men		Women	
	1905–1974	1975–2015	1905–1974	1975–2015
White collar				
Single	1	1	1	1
Married	0.686***	0.527***	0.905	0.711***
Widowed	0.828*	0.652***	0.960	0.798**
Divorced	-	0.964	-	1.139
N individuals	11,769	17,600	7,101	16,865
Deaths	1,627	2,219	659	1,263
Person years	134,143	224,185	91,839	238,462
Blue collar				
Single	1	1	1	1
Married	0.709***	0.552***	0.828***	0.675***
Widowed	0.785***	0.679***	0.920	0.793***
Divorced	-	0.997	-	1.111
N individuals	21,963	22,757	12,958	19,588
Deaths	3,862	3,832	1,951	2,307
Person years	302,023	296,595	212,327	275,027

Table A7.3 Continued

	Men		Women	
	1905–1974	1975–2015	1905–1974	1975–2015
Farmer				
Single	1	1	1	1
Married	1.038	0.512	0.837	0.315**
Widowed	1.268	0.522	0.346*	0.454
Divorced	-	0.935	-	1.337
N individuals	1,747	728	102	295
Deaths	319	151	264	112
Person years	23,248	11,239	20,921	9,126

Notes: ***p < 0.01, **p < 0.05, *p < 0.1. All models control for migrant status and birth year. Social class measured by individual occupation.
Source: Own calculations based on SEDD (Bengtsson et al. 2021).

Table A7.4 Marital status, timing of widowhood mortality (hazard ratios) by gender, age 30–79. Landskrona and the five parishes. Cohabitors (after 1990) excluded from the single group. 1975–2015.

	Men	Women
Single	1	1
Married	0.604***	0.766***
Widowed >1 year	0.735***	0.854***
Widowed <1 year	0.626***	0.710***
Divorced	0.970	1.123*
N individuals	41,093	39,619
Deaths	6,771	4,499
Person years	536,193	553,859

Notes: ***p < 0.01, **p < 0.05, *p < 0.1. All models control for social class (white collar, blue collar, farmers, and missing), urban residence, migrant status, and birth year.
Source: Own calculations based on SEDD (Bengtsson et al. 2021).

References

Aizer, A. A., M.-H. Chen, E. P. McCarthy, et al. 2013. "Marital Status and Survival in Patients with Cancer." *Journal of Clinical Oncology* 31 (31): 3869–3876.

Andersson, G. 1995. "Divorce-Risk Trends in Sweden 1971–1993." *European Journal of Population,* 11 (4): 293–311.

Bengtsson, T., M. Dribe, and J. Helgertz. 2020. "When Did the Health Gradient Emerge? Social Class and Adult Mortality in Southern Sweden, 1813–2015." *Demography* 57 (3): 953–977.

Bengtsson, T., M. Dribe, L. Quaranta, and P. Svensson. 2021. "The Scanian Economic Demographic Database, Version 7.2 (Machine-readable database)." Lund: Lund University, Centre for Economic Demography.

Berntsen, K. N. 2011. "Trends in Total and Cause-Specific Mortality by Marital Status Among Elderly Norwegian Men and Women." *BMC Public Health* 11: 537.

Berntsen, K. N., and Ø. Kravdal. 2012. "The Relationship Between Mortality and Time since Divorce, Widowhood or Remarriage in Norway." *Social Science & Medicine* 75 (12): 2267–2274.

Bowling, A. 1987. "Mortality after Bereavement: A Review of the Literature on Survival Periods and Factors Affecting Survival." *Social Science & Medicine* 24 (2): 117–124.

Bracher, M., and G. Santow. 1998. "Economic Independence and Union Formation in Sweden." *Population Studies* 52 (3): 275–294.

Brockmann, H., and T. Klein. 2004. "Love and Death in Germany: The Marital Biography and Its Effect on Mortality." *Journal of Marriage and Family* 66 (3): 567–581.

Coombs, R. H. 1991. "Marital Status and Personal Well-Being: A Literature Review." *Family Relations* 40 (1): 97–102.

Dahlberg, L., N. Agahi, and C. Lennartsson. 2018. "Lonelier than Ever? Loneliness of Older People Over Two Decades." *Archives of Gerontology and Geriatrics* 75 (1): 96–103.

Datta, G. D., B. A. Neville, I. Kawachi, et al. 2009. "Marital Status and Survival Following Bladder Cancer." *Journal of Epidemiology & Community Health* 63 (10): 807–813.

Dribe, M., C. Lundh, and P. Nystedt. 2007. "Widowhood Strategies in Preindustrial Society." *Journal of Interdisciplinary History* 38 (2): 207–232.

Dykstra, P. A. 2009. "Older Adult Loneliness: Myths and Realities." *European Journal of Ageing* 6 (2): 91–100.

Erlangsen, A. 2004. "Loss of Partner and Suicide Risks Among Oldest Old: A Population-Based Register Study." *Age and Ageing* 33 (4): 378–383.

Goldman, N., S. Korenman, and R. Weinstein. 1995. "Marital Status and Health Among the Elderly." *Social Science & Medicine* 40 (12): 1717–1730.

Goldscheider, F., E. Bernhardt, and T. Lappegård. 2015. "The Gender Revolution: A Theoretical Framework for Understanding Changing Family and Demographic Behavior." *Population and Development Review* 41 (2): 207–239.

Grundy, E. M., and C. Tomassini. 2010. "Marital History, Health and Mortality Among Older Men and Women in England and Wales." *BMC Public Health* 10 (1): 554.

Hajnal, J. 1965. "European Marriage Patterns in Perspective." In *Population in History. Essays in Historical Demography*, edited by D. V. Glass, and D. E. C. Eversley, 101–143. London: Edward Arnold.

Hoem, J. 1991. "To Marry, Just in Case . . .: The Swedish Widow's-Pension Reform and the Peak in Marriages in December 1989." *Acta Sociologica* 34 (2): 127–135.

Hoem, J. 1997. "Educational Gradients in Divorce Risks in Sweden in Recent Decades." *Population Studies* 51 (1): 19–27.
Hoem, J. M., and B. Rennermalm. 1985. "Modern Family Initiation in Sweden: Experience of Women Born Between 1936 and 1960." *European Journal of Population* 1 (1): 81–112.
House, J. S., K. R. Landis, and D. Umberson. 1988. "Social Relationships and Health." *Science* 241 (4865): 540–545.
Hu, Y., and N. Goldman. 1990. "Mortality Differentials by Marital Status: An International Comparison." *Demography* 27 (2): 233–250.
Jaffe, D. H., O. Manor, Z. Eisenbach, and Y. D. Neumark. 2007. "The Protective Effect of Marriage on Mortality in a Dynamic Society." *Annals of Epidemiology* 17 (7): 540–547.
Kiernan, K. 2004. "Unmarried Cohabitation and Parenthood in Britain and Europe." *Law & Policy* 26 (1): 33–55.
Lawrence, E. M., R. G. Rogers, A. Zajacova, and T. Wadsworth. 2019. "Marital Happiness, Marital Status, Health, and Longevity." *Journal of Happiness Studies* 20 (5): 1539–1561.
Lesthaeghe, R. 2010. "The Unfolding Story of the Second Demographic Transition." *Population and Development Review* 36 (2): 211–251.
Lillard, L. A., and C. W. A. Panis. 1996. "Marital Status and Mortality: The Role of Health." *Demography* 33 (3): 313–327.
Livi-Bacci, M. 1985. "Selectivity of Marriage and Mortality: Notes for Future Research." In *Population and Biology*, edited by N. Keyfitz, 99–108. Liège: Ordina Editions.
Lundh, C. 2013. "The Geography of Marriage. Regional Variations in Age at First Marriage in Sweden, 1870–1900." *Scandinavian Journal of History* 38 (3): 318–343.
Martikainen, P., T. Martelin, E. Nihtilä, et al. 2005. "Differences in Mortality by Marital Status in Finland from 1976 to 2000: Analyses of Changes in Marital-Status Distributions, Socio-Demographic and Household Composition, and Cause of Death." *Population Studies* 59 (1): 99–115.
Mellström, D., Å. Nilsson, A. Odén, et al. 1982. "Mortality Among the Widowed in Sweden." *Scandinavian Journal of Social Medicine* 10 (1): 33–41.
Mineau, G. P., K. R. Smith, and L. L. Bean. 2002. "Historical Trends of Survival Among Widows and Widowers." *Social Science & Medicine* 54 (2): 245–254.
Murphy, M., E. Grundy, and S. Kalogirou. 2007. "The Increase in Marital Status Differences in Mortality up to the Oldest Age in Seven European Countries, 1990–99." *Population Studies* 61 (3): 287–298.
Nystedt, P. 2002. "Widowhood-Related Mortality in Scania, Sweden During the 19th Century." *History of the Family* 7 (3): 451–478.
Olah, L. S., and E. M. Bernhardt. 2008. "Sweden: Combining Childbearing and Gender Equality." *Demographic Research* 19 (28): 1105–1144.
Ohlsson-Wijk, S. 2011. "Sweden's Marriage Revival: An Analysis of the New-Millennium Switch from Long-Term Decline to Increasing Popularity." *Population Studies* 65 (2): 183–200.
Rendall, M. S., M. M. Weden, M. M. Favreault, and H. Waldron. 2011. "The Protective Effect of Marriage for Survival: A Review and Update." *Demography* 48 (2): 481–506.
Requena, M., and D. Reher. 2021. "Partnership and Mortality in Mid and Late Life: Protection or Selection?" *Social Science & Medicine* 279: 113971.
Sandström, G. 2012. *Ready, Willing and Able. The Divorce Transition in Sweden 1915–1974*. PhD dissertation, Department of History, Umeå University.

Sandström, G., and L. Karlsson. 2019. "The Educational Gradient of Living Alone: A Comparison Among Working-Age Population in Europe." *Demographic Research* 40 (55): 1645–1670.

Sandström, G., and M. Stanfors. 2020. "Growing More Equal and Growing Apart? Socioeconomic Status and the Rise of Divorce in Sweden." Lund Papers in Economic Demography 2020: 4.

Schön, L. 2010. *Sweden's Road to Modernity: An Economic History*. Stockholm: SNS.

Socialstyrelsen. 2021. *Statistik om dödsorsaker år 2020. Sveriges Officiella Statistik, Hälso- och sjukvård*. [Cause of Death Statistics 2020. Sweden's Official Statistics, Health Care] Stockholm: Socialstyrelsen.

Stanfors, M. 2007. *Mellan arbete och familj. Ett dilemma för kvinnor i 1900-talets Sverige* [Between Work and Family. A Dilemma for Women in Twentieth-Century Sweden]. Stockholm: SNS.

Stanfors, M. 2014. "Women in a Changing Economy: The Misleading Tale of Participation Rates in a Historical Perspective." *History of the Family* 19 (4): 513–536.

Stanfors, M., and F. Goldscheider. 2017. "The Forest and the Trees: Industrialization, Demographic Change, and the Ongoing Gender Revolution in Sweden and the United States, 1870–2010." *Demographic Research* 36 (6): 173–226.

Stanfors, M., F. N. G. Andersson, and G. Sandström. 2020. "A Century of Divorce: Long-Term Socioeconomic Restructuring and the Divorce Rate in Sweden 1915–2010." *Lund Papers in Economic Demography* 2020:2.

Statistics Sweden. 1999. "Befolkningsutvecklingen under 250 år. Historisk statistik för Sverige [The Population Development During 250 Years. Historical Statistics of Sweden]." *Demografiska rapporter* 1999:2. Stockholm: Statistics Sweden.

Stroebe, W., M. Stroebe, G. Abakoumkin, and H. Schut. 1996. "The Role of Loneliness and Social Support in Adjustment to Loss: A Test of Attachment Versus Stress Theory." *Journal of Personality and Social Psychology* 70 (6): 1241–1249.

Tatangelo, G., M. McCabe, S. Campbell, and C. Szoeke. 2017. "Gender, Marital Status and Longevity." *Maturitas* 100: 64–69.

Valkonen, T., P. Martikainen, and J. Blomgren. 2004. "Increasing Excess Mortality Among Non-Married Elderly People in Developed Countries." *Demographic Research* SC2 (12): 305–330.

Van Bavel, J., and D. S. Reher. 2013. "The Baby Boom and Its Causes: What We Know and What We Need to Know." *Population and Development Review* 39 (2): 257–288.

Van Leeuwen, M. H. D., and I. Maas. 2011. *HISCLASS: A Historical International Social Class Scheme*. Leuven: Leuven University Press.

Williams, K., and D. Umberson. 2004. "Marital Status, Marital Transitions, and Health: A Gendered Life Course Perspective." *Journal of Health and Social Behavior* 45 (1): 81–98.

Willner, S. 1999. *Det svaga könet? Kön och vuxendödlighet i 1800-talets Sverige* [The Weak Sex: Gender and Adult Mortality in 19th Century Sweden]. PhD dissertation, University of Linköping, Tema hälsa och samhälle.

Willner, S. 2005. "Hälso- och samhällsutveckling i Sverige 1750–2000 [Health and Society in Sweden 1750–2000]." In *Svenska folkets hälsa i historiskt perspektiv* [The Health of the Swedish People in Historical Perspective], edited by J. Sundin, C. Hogstedt, J. Lindberg, and H. Moberg, 35–80. Stockholm: Statens folkhälsoinstitut.

8
Maternal and Infant Health
Understanding the Role of Institutions and Medical Innovations[*]

Ingrid K. van Dijk, Volha Lazuka, and Luciana Quaranta

Introduction

In 1905, in Landskrona, Sweden, and its rural hinterland, 34 infants out of a total of 547 newborns did not survive to their first birthday, and for 1 in 180 births the mother died shortly after giving birth. Such rates of maternal and infant mortality are high from the perspective of today's developed world but would be considered low in other countries at the time. These relatively favorable rates were reached in the absence of modern medical technology, including antibiotics. In the period from 1860 to the 1890s, a dramatic fall in maternal mortality took place in Sweden, accompanied by a fall in mortality among newborns (Woods 2009). During this period midwifery in Northwest Europe took on professional status, and antiseptic techniques such as handwashing and the use of clean sheets and boiled aprons were discovered and implemented (Løkke 2012; Woods 2009). The general standard of living rose, so that pregnant women and infants were better nourished and lived in better conditions than previously.

The fall in maternal and newborn mortality occurred in a period in which general mortality decline in the population accelerated and life expectancy increased across the board. General improvements in the standard of living, medical breakthroughs, infrastructural improvements including the provision of clean water, and many other factors may have contributed to the improvements in life expectancy. While it remains debated which factors were the main causes of this large transition in health in the population, the role of medical knowledge and technology has been suggested to outweigh any influences of income (Cutler et al. 2006). In this chapter, we explore whether and to what extent medicine and improvements in hospital and care facilities contributed to the mortality reduction among mothers and infants. Dramatic improvements in maternal and infant health continued through the twentieth century. These changes happened against a backdrop of the increasing medicalization of birth, although this development was less pronounced in Sweden than in other countries

Ingrid K. van Dijk, Volha Lazuka, and Luciana Quaranta, *Maternal and Infant Health* In: *Urban Lives*. Edited by: Martin Dribe, Therese Nilsson, and Anna Tegunimataka, Oxford University Press. © Oxford University Press 2024. DOI: 10.1093/oso/9780197761090.003.0008

(Larsson 2022). Before 1930, most women in labor were assisted by midwives, with delivery taking place at home. Thereafter, births took place increasingly in maternity wards in nursing homes and in hospitals (Lazuka 2023). Medical interventions in childbirth became more feasible with time, as infection could be treated with the use of antibiotics from the 1930s onward. Similarly, the arrival of antibiotics made bacterial infections among infants less deadly (Cronberg 1997). Generally, medical breakthroughs, health policies, changes in institutional care arrangements for pregnant women and young infants, and a continuous rise in living standards probably contributed to the continued improvement in maternal and infant health.

The modernization of healthcare reached the cities and towns first. In Landskrona, a maternity ward was opened at the nursing home (*sjukhem*) in 1912, and another was opened at the city hospital in 1935. At the end of the 1930s, a home visiting program for mothers and their newborns was introduced. In the rural hinterland of Landskrona, change came more slowly, but midwives attending home births were now receiving increasingly better training in modern methods and standards of hygiene. Home births gradually became less common, and hospital births the standard. Antenatal and postnatal care programs providing antenatal care and postnatal health check-ups became routine for pregnant women and mothers. These changes in midwifery and antenatal and postnatal care programs were implemented early in Sweden in comparison to other countries.

Class differences in post-neonatal and child mortality—higher mortality among unskilled compared to higher social classes—emerged in Scania (*Skåne*) during the second half of the nineteenth century and persisted well into the 1960s (Dribe and Karlsson 2022; see Chapter 9). Neonatal mortality, commonly assumed to be related to complications from pregnancy and childbirth rather than to socioeconomic factors, did not show a similar class distinction. Although in this chapter we do not study socioeconomic differences in maternal and infant mortality, the institutional context suggests that interventions in medicine and institutional care should have reduced socioeconomic differences in mortality. In Landskrona, new water and sewerage systems and investments in public health benefitted the whole population of the town (see Chapter 9). In addition, several interventions to improve maternal and infant health in the first half of the twentieth century were specifically targeted toward lower socioeconomic status women and their families and, through the mid-twentieth century, became universal (Sundin and Willner 2007). The universal provision of public health was a characteristic of health policies in Sweden and other Scandinavian countries (Wüst 2022).

In this chapter, we used the Scanian Economic-Demographic Database (SEDD; Bengtsson et al. 2021) to analyze the development of maternal and infant health in five rural parishes and the town of Landskrona over the past 110 years. First, we address the overall development of maternal, perinatal (health during the second half of gestation, at birth, and during the first week of life), and infant health using a range of indicators, such as maternal mortality, neonatal mortality, and stillbirth rates. We also describe how institutional and medical changes reached the town of Landskrona and the surrounding rural areas. Second, we relate the development of maternal and infant health in the area to the institutions and medical innovations available, such as the expansion of hospital facilities, the availability of antibiotics, and the opening of maternity wards and neonatal intensive care units. We also estimate the magnitude of the impact of these changes on mother and infant health using time series analysis. While we cannot fully distinguish which interventions were the most beneficial to maternal and child health and survival following the rapid medical and social changes that occurred in the same period, magnitude estimates will provide insights regarding which developments contributed to the health and survival of mothers and infants in this period.

Background

Maternal and Infant Health

In Scania, infant mortality had already declined substantially during the nineteenth century, ranging from about 250 per 1,000 in the 1810s to around 90 per 1,000 in the 1890s in the rural areas covered by SEDD (Quaranta 2013). This decline continued during the twentieth century, falling from 62 to 6 per 1,000 in 1905 and 1999, respectively, in the rural and urban areas covered, which suggests that the improvement in infant health was at least in part due to the lower impact of infectious disease over time. As a result of the epidemiological transition, there was a change in the disease environment from infectious to chronic diseases. Twenty-six percent of all deaths of children younger than 10 in the study area were caused by infectious disease in 1905–1949, with this share declining to 2 percent in 1950–1974. No children younger than 10 died from an infectious disease in the years that followed.[1] It is also likely that general improvements in living standards and public health contributed to the fall in mortality rates (Woods 2009). Infants and their mothers were in better health thanks to the rising standard of living. Knowledge about the causes of disease and mortality increased, and, by the end of the twentieth century, the germ theory of disease had become accepted. Previously, infectious disease had been commonly attributed to "miasma"—unhealthy air—but now bacterial and viral causes of food- and waterborne diseases were being discovered and appropriate preventive measures put in place. Sewage systems were developed, starting in the cities where problems related to contaminated water sources were largest, and clean drinking water became a priority (Helgertz and Önnerfors 2019).

In healthcare, from the 1860s onwards, antiseptic methods were developed, contributing to the strong decline in maternal mortality caused by puerperal fever (childbirth infection), late fetal death, and infant death (Løkke 2012; Woods 2009). Before sulfa drugs (1938) and penicillin (1947) were widely available, childbirth infection often resulted in the death of the mother, fetus, or newborn infant, or of both mother and offspring. Neonatal deaths in the first 28 days after birth are generally considered to be the most likely result of conditions during pregnancy and childbirth (Woods 2009), whereas deaths in later infancy are considered to be affected more strongly by environmental exposure and social factors. Social factors in infant mortality are proximate determinants of infant death; that is to say, factors that contribute to the likelihood of death but are not a direct cause of it (Mosley and Chen 1984). One example is the level of resources and wealth of the child's family, which may affect infant mortality in terms of the quality of housing and nourishment, but which are not direct causes of death. Developments in post-neonatal deaths thus point toward improvements in the general standard of living and change in the disease environment, as well as a role for interventions targeted at improving care for older infants.

Childbirth and Midwifery

At the end of the nineteenth century, when Sweden was experiencing an economic boom, extensive reforms were made in the institutional framework of public healthcare and midwifery. These reforms were part of the wider developments in Europe related to the rise of the hygienist movement, increasing concern about the health conditions of the poor in the growing cities, and concern about public health more generally (Sundin and Willner 2007). The availability of doctors in the population increased, and medical knowledge became more widely available. Medical care became increasingly institutionalized, and national and regional boards of health were set up. In the period 1890–1920, all communities throughout Sweden eventually received access to public healthcare (Lazuka et al. 2016). Regional health services in the towns usually had a medical officer, hospital doctor, regimental medical officer, and a provincial doctor and midwives. Popular movements played an important role in the spread of information about hygiene and gave rise to further movements for the improvement of welfare (Sundin and Willner 2007). Thanks to these movements, collective health insurance schemes were set up in the early twentieth century.

Later, public services increasingly replaced philanthropic institutions (Sundin and Willner 2007).

The training of midwives was, from an international perspective, already well developed in Sweden as of the eighteenth century (Loudon 1992). Midwifery has a long tradition in Sweden, and training in midwifery had been institutionalized relatively early on. From its beginnings in 1819, the formal training period had been 6 months, and midwives could receive 3 months of additional training in how to use obstetrical instruments (Högberg 2004). Receiving training was possible in Stockholm and Lund, and, from 1856, in Göteborg. The period of obligatory training had doubled by the 1880s.

Maternal mortality rates had fallen over most of the nineteenth century but stagnated about halfway through the century before continuing their fall in the period 1860–1890. A potential contributing factor to the stagnation was the generally low standard of living that persisted in the nineteenth century, resulting in poor health among pregnant women. The stagnation may also have been attributable to the *increased* availability of doctors and midwives (Woods 2009). In the absence of antiseptic techniques, higher rates of medicalization and surgical intervention could be detrimental to the survival of mother and child (Woods 2009) since infections following medical intervention were hard to treat (e.g., Leavitt 1986). Once antiseptic procedures were discovered and were being implemented, maternal and infant mortality declined further.

The professionalization of midwifery and the increase in the number of births assisted by a properly trained midwife had a beneficial effect on maternal and infant survival. In the period 1830–1894, a doubling of the number of trained midwives in Sweden, from 1,000 in 1830 to 2,600 in 1894, reduced maternal mortality by 20–40 percent (Lorentzon and Pettersson-Lidbom 2021). The increases in the number of trained midwives had a greater impact on the reduction of maternal mortality in the late nineteenth century, when training for midwives was better (Lorentzon and Pettersson-Lidbom 2021). Although midwives in Sweden were well qualified from an international perspective already in the 1880s (Loudon 1992), training was still poor by modern standards, and there was wide variation between traditional birth attendants and midwives trained in modern methods. In the early nineteenth century, some midwives still used long-established, nonscientific methods in their work, especially in rural areas. Traditional birth attendants used methods during childbirth that could be harmful to the mother and reduce the chances of survival of her infant, including procedures to hasten the delivery such as pressing on the abdomen and the improper and medically unnecessary use of drugs, instruments, and surgical procedures. In addition, home births sometimes took place in crowded or insufficiently hygienic conditions.

Around the turn of the twentieth century, public policy made midwifery services more widely available and also gave midwives access to improved and more advanced training, which included both theory and practice in bacteriology, thus enhancing their professional status and competence. Although childbirth now more commonly occurred in hospital facilities, midwives continued to have a central role in home deliveries until the 1930s. At the time, they were considered among the most highly trained and efficient in the world (Loudon 1992). Midwives with better-quality training who attended home births could, unlike traditional midwives, greatly improve the chances of maternal and neonatal survival with the use of antiseptics and preventive procedures (Lazuka 2018; Løkke 2012; Woods 2009).

Childbirth in Maternity Wards

Box 8.1 summarizes the various reforms and medical innovations related to maternal and child health in Sweden from 1900 to the present day. From the 1920s to the 1950s, an increasing number of childbirths transitioned from a system of midwife-assisted home deliveries to that of delivery in a maternity ward, where midwives were still the main care providers for women during the birth. The transition to institutionalized births occurred earlier in urban areas than in rural settings. There were different categories of institutions, including the maternity hospital (*barnbördshuset*) and nursing home (*sjukhem*) (Vallgårda 1996). The conditions surrounding childbirth, including the presence and level of training of birth attendants (doctors or midwives), the level of hygiene during delivery, and instruments and health monitoring after birth varied considerably. Additionally, the hospital staff were given training in how to treat preterm babies, including constant care, the use of prototype incubators, and providing advice to mothers on feeding small babies (Gröne 1949). As of 1919, properly trained district nurses working for the municipality in rural regions were subsidized by the state and worked under the supervision of a provincial doctor. This replaced an earlier system which had offered less than satisfactory employment conditions and limited training for nurses. District nurses now gave young mothers advice on providing care and on hygiene and breastfeeding (Sundin and Willner 2007).

Prior to the 1930s, those admitted to a hospital to give birth were predominantly low SES women and complicated cases. In the period 1930–1946, a nationwide maternity ward reform made hospital childbirth available for both complicated and straightforward cases and also for women from all social classes (Lazuka 2023). During this time the state began subsidizing the hospital stay of women giving birth there and providing a childbirth allowance. By 1950, almost

Box 8.1 Reforms and medical innovations related to maternal and child health in Sweden, 1900–Present

1900–1920	Increasing availability of properly trained and professional midwives
1920–1950	Rise of institutionalized childbirth in maternity wards
1930–1946	Maternity ward reform leading to a rapid increase in hospital births
1931–1933	Trial of program for preventive care for mothers and infants
1938–1945	Preventive health program offered at child healthcare centers (*barnavårdscentral*; BVC) rolled out nationwide
1939	Wide availability of sulfa medication to treat pneumonia
1947	Wide availability of penicillin
1960s	Ultrasound became available
1970s	Neonatal intensive care units introduced
1973	Neonatal care expanded and improved with the use of ventilators
1990s	Increasing attention given to preconception care (e.g., folic acid supplementation)

all births took place in hospital. The shift from home births to hospital births further reduced infant mortality, especially those deaths related to pregnancy and childbirth (stillbirth and neonatal deaths). The nationwide reform saw a decrease of 20 infant deaths per 1,000 live births—60 percent in relative terms (Lazuka 2023). Hospital births benefited the survival of infants because of the round-the-clock care provided by highly qualified staff with modern medical training. Compared with home births, there was a reduced risk of infection in hospital, and, for preterm newborns, special medical care was available. Long-term effects were also found for school grades, educational attainment, and adult mortality (Fischer et al. 2021; Lazuka 2023). Possibly the change from home to hospital births reduced childhood morbidity, thus resulting in improved grades and other outcomes along the life course.

The opening of a maternity hospital in the 1910s in Sundsvall (a town in northern Sweden) was associated with a significant reduction in both neonatal and post-neonatal mortality thanks to the proper childbirth care provided especially for complicated births and for poor and unmarried mothers. At the same time, in the early days of the increase in hospital births, conditions were sometimes crowded and there was a lack of space and privacy as much larger numbers of women needed care than before the reforms (Wisselgren, 2005).

Interventions and changes in more recent decades appear to have had a more modest effect on maternal and infant health outcomes. Studies looking at changes in healthcare provision for women have included indicators of maternal health such as the length of postpartum stay in hospital, maternal trauma, and contact with a general practitioner in the years after childbirth. Additional healthcare resources in the form of extra and specialist care for mothers were found to have had no effect on maternal health for uncomplicated cases but were beneficial for high-risk births (Advic et al. 2018; Almond and Doyle 2011; Kronborg et al. 2016).

Medical Innovations

Further reductions in infant mortality as of the 1960s have been attributed to the inception of neonatal intensive care units. Incubators, invented in France at the end of the nineteenth century, were found to reduce mortality among prematurely born children in the 1960s and became the standard in Swedish hospitals by the 1970s. The first neonatal intensive care units in Sweden were set up in the 1960s, at Karolinska University Hospital in Stockholm and at the Children's Hospital (*Barnsjukhuset*) in Göteborg. Neonatal intensive care units with ventilators adapted for prematurely born infants (the so-called Gregory box) were first set up in Sweden in 1973 (Lagercrantz 2015). Intensive care units accounted for about one-fifth of the decline in infant mortality in the United States between 1983 and 1998 (Cutler et al. 2012). For births after the mid-1960s, infants of very low birth weight who were put on a lung respirator experienced substantially lower mortality during the first year of life (Bharadwaj et al. 2013). High-quality hospital facilities and staff could and still did make a difference in a developed setting in the 2000s and were shown to have a substantial positive effect on early neonatal survival and health (Daysal et al. 2015; Miller 2006).

Medical breakthroughs at the start of the twentieth century contributed to the increased survival rate of infants, especially through the treatment of disease for mother and child. The arrival of antibiotics had been preceded by the use of sulfonamide (sulfa) drugs in the late 1930s. These early antibacterials were effective against pneumonia and scarlet fever. In the late 1940s, penicillin, which was effective against all bacterial infectious diseases, became widely available and led to a strong decline in infant deaths from this cause. It is likely that infant mortality in the post-neonatal period was particularly strongly affected by the introduction of the new medication. Treatment with sulfa drugs led to a 7–32 percent decline in pneumonia mortality and a 52–65 percent decline in scarlet fever mortality between 1937 and 1943 in the United States (Jayachandran et al. 2010)—these diseases being the leading causes of infant mortality at the time. The effects of sulfonamides when they were introduced in Sweden in 1939 were found to be similar in magnitude (Lazuka 2020). A sudden sharp decline in post-neonatal mortality (before the first birthday and after the first 28 days of life) occurred around the time that penicillin became available.

Penicillin also greatly reduced the risk of life-saving surgical procedures for pregnant women, making it possible to conduct more invasive interventions (Løkke 2012). Prior to the antibiotic era such procedures posed a great risk to the mother's life. For example, in 1920s Sweden, 1 in 10 cesarian procedures ended in maternal death (Rehn and Boström 2011). When antibiotics became available in the 1930s, an infection after childbirth could be treated. After the introduction of antibiotics an increase of 100 hospital births per 100,000 births was associated with 80–129 fewer maternal deaths in the United States (Thomasson and Treber 2008). A similar, sizable decline in maternal mortality has been found due to the introduction of sulfa drugs, amounting to a 24–36 percent reduction in maternal mortality (Jayachandran et al. 2010).

Preventive Care Programs

A further innovation in the provision of healthcare resources consisted of conducting home visits and doctor's check-ups for infants. Such check-ups initially took place under the auspices of organizations with the original aim of providing those women unable to breastfeed with milk and solid food for their newborns and older infants (*Mjölkdroppen*). These services were first implemented in 1901, in Stockholm, for disadvantaged women and were similar to *Gouttes de Lait* in France and milk depots in the United Kingdom (Meckel 1998). The programs provided women without means not only with milk but also with advice on care and nutrition for infants. They are therefore one of the earliest examples of preventive care programs (Meckel 1998). Women could enroll if they provided evidence from a medical doctor or the church that they had no means themselves (Stenhammar and Ohrlander 2001). Home visit programs for the broader population were developed in Scandinavia in the 1920s and 1930s. Previous studies establish that targeted infant health programs improved infant health (Wüst 2022).

The home visit program initiated in Denmark in 1937 seems to have led to a decline of around 5–8 infant deaths per 1,000 live births (a 1 percent mortality reduction in relative terms), especially deaths from diarrheal diseases (Wüst 2012). The main cause of these diseases was spoiled or inappropriate food, and exclusive breastfeeding could protect infants from this. The home visits may thus have been successful because the visiting nurse promoted breastfeeding and proper infant nutrition. In the context of Norway, access to infant health centers increased completed years of schooling by 0.15 years and earnings by 2 percent, and such effect was driven by better nutrition within the first year of life (Bütikofer et al. 2019). In Sweden, a similar program of house visits also encompassed mandatory doctor's check-ups at health centers for infants. The trial program in the period 1931–1933 led to a 2 percentage point decrease (24 percent reduction) in infant mortality in the trial areas, primarily due to a reduction in infant deaths related to preterm birth, low birth weight, and congenital malformation (Bhalotra et al. 2017). The nationwide rollout of the infant care program in the period 1938–1945 was associated with a decline in post-neonatal deaths from pneumonia (Knutsson 2018). Early detection of disease, improved nutrition, and improved access to antibiotics were therefore the likely reasons of the program's effectiveness in reducing post-neonatal deaths among infants.

One of the unique features of the program in Sweden was its attention to antenatal care in the form of general advice and detecting signs of retarded growth in fetuses (Bhalotra et al. 2017). However, no effects on infant mortality and mother survival have been found regarding the prenatal care features of the program (e.g., Bhalotra et al. 2017; Lazuka 2023). It is likely that these features were not, in fact, specific to the program itself but were a continuation of recognized forms of care for pregnant women in Sweden that existed prior to the program's implementation. As such, it is likely that the introduction of antenatal care practices was gradual and that we therefore see no sharp decrease in complications at birth around the time these programs were formalized. Antenatal care took place at health centers and was not part of the home visiting part of the program, which could be another explanation for the small effects on survival.

In other countries, antenatal care programs became more common only in the 1980s, about four decades later than in Sweden. The bulk of the literature on the effects of antenatal care has focused on recent, highly specialized care interventions. Overall, it provides evidence of beneficial effects on the health of mothers and infants. For instance, targeted antenatal care for at-risk mothers positively affects their newborn's survival. A randomized controlled trial in a public system of obstetric and pediatric care in the United States was found to lead to improvements in birth weight and infant survival (Olds et al. 2007). The efficiency of these improvements depends on the professional qualifications of the home visitor and points to his or her intervention as the decisive mechanism. In the case of the United States, as of the 1980s, access to health insurance, which is associated with the extended access of low-income families to prenatal care and other healthcare resources, has been found to ensure an increase in birth weight and gestational age at birth and a decrease in the number of hospitalizations related to infant health after birth (e.g., Aizer et al. 2007). In addition, for pregnancies considered low-risk but where the mothers were on a low income, perinatal medical treatment decreased early neonatal mortality (the first 7 days after birth) by 4 deaths per 1,000 live births in the Netherlands in the 2000s (Daysal et al. 2019). They argue that the presence of a physician reduced the likelihood of adverse events such as fetal distress or an emergency cesarean section.

The mother's health is known to affect her pregnancy outcomes. Mothers in poor health are more likely to have a miscarriage, especially if the unborn is a boy. Male fetuses in utero are more sensitive to the condition of the mother. Women who reproduce in disadvantageous conditions tend to have more girls than boys (i.e., there is a lower sex ratio of boys to girls at birth; Almond and Edlund 2007; Andersson and Bergstrom 1998; Bruckner et al. 2010; Nonaka et al. 1999; Norberg 2004). The natural sex ratio at conception leans toward a higher ratio (more boys), but at every stage of development relatively more male fetuses than female ones are lost, possibly because they are more vulnerable to disease, genetic mutations, and environmental conditions (Lindahl-Jacobsen et al. 2013). Although earlier literature addressed the relationship between maternal condition and sex ratio at birth, sex ratios at birth have rarely been used as an indication of maternal health and prenatal healthcare.

The Modernization of Childbirth in Scania

The development of maternity care in Landskrona and its rural hinterland resembles the development in Sweden as a whole. Until the early 1910s, almost all births took place at home. The midwives were usually paid by the municipality. Most graduate midwives found employment in the cities, which meant there was a shortage of qualified midwives in the countryside. Between 1880 and 1911, one-third of all births in the countryside were assisted by licensed midwives employed by the municipality, while traditional medical practitioners attended the other births (Lazuka 2018).

Births in institutional settings rose steadily in the times that followed. From 1912 onward, a woman could give birth in Landskrona in a maternity ward (*barnbördsavdelning*) at the nursing home *(sjukhem)* which was run by the City of Landskrona. In 1930, the city's maternity hospital *(stadens barnbördshus)* replaced the nursing home's maternity ward (Landskrona Stads Hälsovårdsnämnd 1929). It was annexed to the county hospital *(länslasarett)* and located in the old epidemic hospital. Conditions for delivery improved because the new facility was more isolated and the wards more spacious than previously. There was also a separate delivery room suitable for surgery (Jönsson 1997).

Box 8.2 summarizes institutional developments in Landskrona in relation to infant and maternal health. Figure 8.1 shows, for the years 1912–1947, the percentage of births that took place in Landskrona at the nursing home/city maternity hospital (*sjukhem/stadens barnbördshus*) and other hospitals and also the percentage of births in hospitals in the rural parishes. The percentage of births in Landskrona that took place at the nursing home or the city maternity hospital increased from about 50 percent in 1912 to about 75 percent in 1934. Although the opening of the maternity wards was part of a program directed at poor and unmarried women, our data show that women of all socioeconomic groups delivered their babies at these institutions. In fact, between 1912 and 1934, in 43 percent of these cases the children were born into families of higher- and medium-skilled workers.

As part of a state policy, a separate maternity ward was opened at the county hospital in 1935. In that year, women could give birth either in the city hospital or in the newly opened maternity ward at the county hospital, and, in 1936, the old maternity ward at the nursing home was closed. The maternity ward at the county hospital was in a makeshift condition since nothing of this kind had been foreseen when the hospital was built. The temporary ward was too small and sometimes had up to seventeen or eighteen women in one room (Jönsson 1997). The conditions there were not ideal for childbirth either since it was not isolated from other wards in the hospital. When it opened in 1935, it had four beds and one delivery room, thought to suffice for both normal and complicated childbirths. Given the demand, it was enlarged to twelve beds the following year (Landskrona Länslasarett 1936). Nevertheless, the ward faced problems of overcrowding. Contributing to the pressure on it were the high birth rates in the city and the fact that women stayed there for an average of 10 days after giving birth. As can be seen in Figure 8.1, panel A, as early as 1936 onward, almost all births in Landskrona took place in the county hospital

In 1945, a newly built children's hospital was opened in a separate building next to the county hospital. This had an open ward, and, in addition, it had space to accommodate twelve lying-in patients and four isolation rooms (Jönsson 1997; Landskrona Stads Hälsovårdsnämnd 1945; Landskrona Stads Hälsovårdsnämnd 1946). The temporary maternity ward that had already opened at the county hospital was transferred to the ground floor of the children's hospital in April 1945 and made more permanent. This newly opened maternity ward not only was more spacious (with twenty-six beds for women, three delivery rooms, and a separate operating theater), but also offered a more hygienic environment since it was isolated from the hospital's main building. The fact that the ward was so closely situated to the children's hospital was also desirable from a medical point of view. It provided more complete and closely linked care, not only during delivery but also during the periods preceding and following birth. The

> **Box 8.2 Institutional developments in Landskrona related to maternal and child health**
>
> 1912 Opening of the nursing home's maternity ward *(sjukhemmets barnbördsavdelning)*
> 1930 Opening of the city maternity hospital *(stadens barnbördshus)*, annex to the nursing home *(sjukhem)*
> 1931 Children's healthcare center *(barnavårdcentral;* BVC) opened by the charity foundation *Barnavärn* (Children's Protection)
> 1935 Separate maternity unit at the county hospital *(länslasarett)* opened
> 1936 The city maternity hospital *(stadens barnbördshus)* closed
> 1938 Antenatal healthcare center *(mödravårdscentral;* MVC) opened at the county hospital on a voluntary basis
> 1944 The antenatal healthcare center (MVC) taken over by the county authority, and an expansion of services
> 1945 New children's hospital opened in a separate building at the county hospital, and this included an antenatal healthcare center (MVC) and a children's healthcare center (BVC)
> 1972 The maternity ward *(barnbördsavdelning)* in the county hospital closed; postnatal care department remained open
> 1981 The postnatal care ward closed; all types of care moved to the Helsingborg hospital

newly opened children's hospital also housed an antenatal healthcare center *(mödravårdscentral;* MVC) and a children's healthcare center *(barnavårdscentral;* BVC). The collaboration between the specialist wards sought to ensure better planning for childcare needs in society, reduce child mortality, and promote family health. The connectedness between the wards also improved the survival chances of infants with problems, such as those born prematurely. In 1945, the standard care fees at the hospital were 11 SEK per day for a single room and 7.50 SEK per day for a shared room. For reference, this is around the mean daily labor income for men in Landskrona in the same year (cf. Chapter 3).

The modernization of care regarding childbirth took place in towns and cities earlier than in the countryside, and the institutionalization of births was swiftest in urban areas. But with the opening of maternity hospitals in towns and cities, women who gave birth in the rural areas gradually came under institutionalized care as well. As can be seen in Figure 8.1 panel B, the percentage of children who came from Landskrona's five rural hinterland parishes and were born in hospital rose from about 9 percent in 1912 to about 47 percent in 1926, 60 percent

A. Landskrona

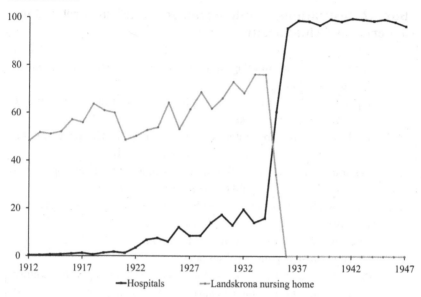

B. Five parishes

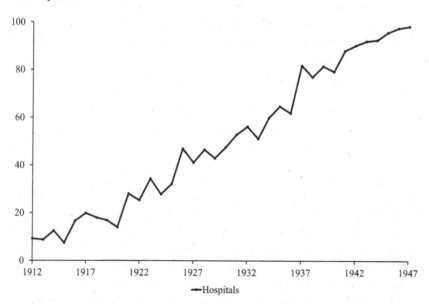

Figure 8.1 Percentage of births in maternity wards by area, 1912–1947.
Source: Own calculations based on the Scanian Economic-Demographic Database (SEDD; Bengtsson et al. 2021).

in 1936, and 98 percent in 1947. Women from the rural areas near Landskrona gave birth primarily in the hospitals of Lund, Landskrona, or Helsingborg. In 1972, the maternity ward (*barnbördsavdelning*) at the Landskrona hospital closed, although a postnatal care department remained open there for another decade before closing in 1981. From then on, hospital births for women residing in Landskrona took place at the Helsingborg hospital about 30 kilometers from Landskrona (Jönsson 1997).

The Introduction of Antenatal and Postnatal Care Programs in Landskrona

Developments in antenatal and postnatal care in Landskrona and the five rural parishes broadly reflected changes in Sweden as a whole, but the new institutions and medical innovations, aimed at women across the board, were made available earlier in the towns than in the countryside.

The first interventions directed at infants in Landskrona were initiated by the charity foundation Barnavärn (Children's Protection). Barnavärn was founded in 1907, and it ran a home for up to twenty children aged 0–2 who could not receive parental care. These children stayed in the home for a period of time and were generally returned to their families thereafter. Mothers visited their children at home and breastfeeding was encouraged. Barnavärn also educated girls in childcare.

In 1927, Barnavärn set up the *Mjölkdroppe* service in Landskrona with the help of local government funds in order to donate milk and a number of solid foods for infants from poor families (Jönsson 1997; Landskrona City Archive; Landskrona Stads Hälsovårdsnämnd 1927). The fee charged for this service depended on parental income, and most children received it for free. Health records were kept during such visits, including information on the weight of the child, the type of food given, and any illness. In connection with setting up *Mjölkdroppe*, Barnavärn also opened a child healthcare center (BVC) in the same building in 1931. The center soon became very popular, and Barnavärn had to borrow an additional room in another location in the city. A nurse and a doctor were employed at the center to receive mothers with small children, and nurses also conducted home visits. In addition to seeing infants to carry out health check-ups, the nurses gave advice on their care. Most children were registered on these programs before the age of 6 months, and they received care under it until the age of 1. The fee charged was either zero, 2.50, or 5 SEK per quarter, depending on the parents' financial situation.

In 1938, antenatal care was provided at the antenatal healthcare center (MVC) at the county hospital and was run by the hospital's midwives and doctors on a voluntary basis (Landskrona Länslasarett 1941). From that year on, midwives were obliged to conduct urine tests on women to check for protein (a sign of preeclampsia, which can be a life-threatening condition for mother and child) and sugar (a sign of pregnancy diabetes). Doctor's check-ups were also conducted at the MVC. In 1944, the county MVC was put on a more formal footing and received compensation from the county authority (Landskrona Länslasarett 1944). When the children's hospital opened in 1945, it also housed an MVC and a BVC. The BVC at Barnavärn was therefore closed at this time.

Generally speaking, healthcare was readily available for women of all economic classes, unlike the healthcare provided elsewhere in Europe around the same period. Financial contributions for admittance to hospital were tied specifically to the level of income and wealth of the patient's household. Medication, including antibiotics when they became available, was relatively cheap and often covered by health insurance or the state.

Quantifying Developments in Maternal and Infant Health and Survival

In this section, we use a series of graphs to show the developments over time regarding a range of health outcomes for mothers and infants. In the next section, we use time series analysis to address the probable reasons for the improvement in maternal and infant health. The care given to mothers before, around the time of, and after childbirth is likely to affect both their health and the survival of their infants. Our aim is not to establish robust causal relationships, which cannot be shown with time series analysis. Instead, we aim to illustrate the developments over time in infant and maternal health and understand the possible contributions to such developments from medical progress and institutional change in childbirth and infant care.

Our study focuses on the town of Landskrona and five rural parishes. These areas are not statistically representative for Sweden as a whole, but, in the period 1905–2010, life expectancy in these Scanian parishes did reflect that in the rest of Sweden (Quaranta 2013). Cohort life expectancy at birth for Sweden as a whole and for the five rural parishes and the town of Landskrona developed in a similar way (Debiasi 2020; Lazuka 2017). This indicates that the area might well serve as a testing ground for studying developments in Sweden as a whole.

We start with the indicators of maternal health, in particular the maternal mortality ratio (MMR) and crude death rate (CDR) among women of reproductive age, and indicators of perinatal health, in particular stillbirth rate and sex ratio at birth. Stillbirths and sex ratio at birth are a good reflection of conditions experienced during gestation and birth. Figure 8.2 shows the MMR) and female

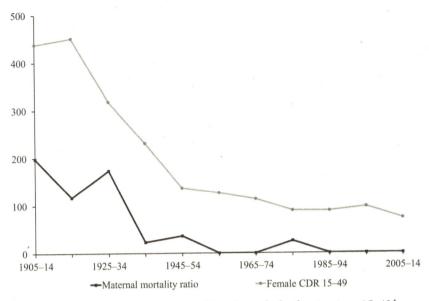

Figure 8.2 Maternal mortality ratio and female crude death rates at age 15–49 by decade in the study area.
Source: Own calculations based on the Scanian Economic-Demographic Database (SEDD; Bengtsson et al. 2021).

CDR at age 15–49 (CDR_{15-49}) by decade for the entire study area (Landskrona and the five rural parishes). The MMR was calculated as the number of deaths of women within 42 days of the delivery of a live birth per 100,000 live births per year.[2] As can be seen in the figure, maternal mortality was already low at the beginning of the period as a result of the wide availability of trained midwives as early as in the nineteenth century (Lorentzon and Pettersson-Lidbom 2021) and of the widespread use of antiseptics from 1880 onward (Lazuka 2018; Løkke 2012). Large drops in the MMR are seen from the period 1935–1944, after which it stays at low levels. In fact, starting from these two decades zero deaths in the 42 days following birth were observed in most cases, and only one or two deaths in others. Drops in female CDR_{15-50} are also seen around the same time. The decline in maternal mortality and its virtual disappearance illustrate further improvements in the care practices around childbirth that were available to women, including its institutionalization and the availability of medical drugs to treat infections as well as the decline in fertility in the area over time.

Figure 8.3 shows stillbirth rates for Landskrona and the five rural parishes. Information on stillbirths is available only for 1905–1967. We measured stillbirth rates as the number of stillbirths per 1,000 singleton births per year. Fetal deaths during pregnancy without a known (still)birth were not included in the

A. Landskrona

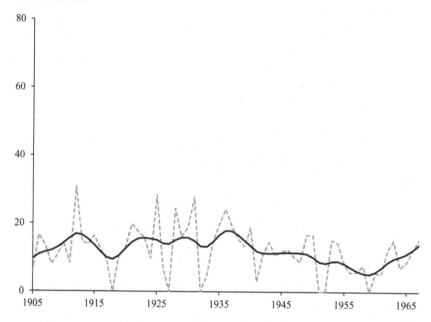

B. Five parishes

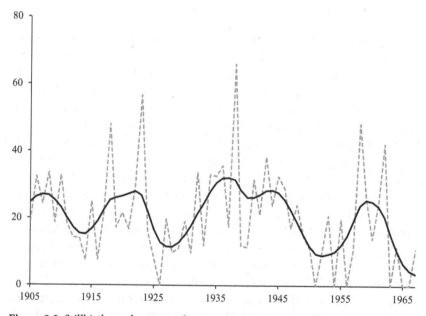

Figure 8.3 Stillbirth rate by year and area, 1905–1967.
Dashed lines are yearly rates and solid lines are trends.

Source: Own calculations based on the Scanian Economic-Demographic Database (SEDD; Bengtsson et al. 2021).

calculations since they were not available in the data. The series of stillbirths and other indicators shown were detrended[3] to remove short-term variation related to specific events happening in a certain year, such as epidemic disease outbreaks, and both the yearly rates (dashed lines) and the trends (solid lines) are included in the figures. As can be seen from Figure 8.3, the number of stillbirths was already low at the beginning of the period of study, and the trend in stillbirth rates declined very moderately over time. The five rural parishes show higher stillbirth rates and larger year-to-year fluctuations than Landskrona, which probably relates to the smaller number of births.

We also calculated the yearly sex ratio at birth, measured as the number of live male births divided by the number of live female births and multiplied by 100. As can be seen in Figure 8.4, there were large fluctuations over time for the parishes, but a much more stable ratio is identified for the town of Landskrona. The changes may well be related to the much lower number of births in the parishes, which may in turn be related to temporary sex imbalances in a small group. Interestingly, we observe a very slow increase in the sex ratio over time in Landskrona. However, the variation over time is not large.

Since infant mortality rates are indicators of infant health, we calculated these as well as the rates of early neonatal (deaths in the first week of life: days 0–7), late neonatal (deaths in the second, third and fourth week of life: days 8–28), and post-neonatal (deaths between the end of the fourth week and the day before the first birthday: days 29–365) mortality. All mortality rates were calculated by dividing the number of deaths by the number of live births in a given year multiplied by 1,000, and these were also later detrended.

Figure 8.5 shows for the entire SEDD area the development in total infant mortality as well as the rates of post-neonatal, late neonatal, and early neonatal mortality. Over the whole period 1905–2015, infant mortality declined dramatically in Landskrona and the five rural parishes. From a rate of about 80 per 1,000 in the early 1900s, it declined to about 25 per 1,000 in 1950 and to 5 per 1,000 toward the end of the research period. From the 1990s onward, the rates of infant mortality have been very low for all years. In the middle of the twentieth century (in the 1940s), post-neonatal mortality decreased sharply within a few years. In the same period, a much more gradual decline in early neonatal mortality (birth to day 7) is observed. The decline in late neonatal mortality (day 8 to day 28) had already begun earlier, in the 1910s. From the 1950s, late neonatal and post-neonatal mortality rates were quite low. Initially, early neonatal mortality, late neonatal mortality, and post-neonatal mortality constituted about 30 percent, 20 percent, and 50 percent, respectively, of total infant mortality. The share of infant deaths taking place in the early neonatal period increased over time to around 50 percent in the 1930s and 70 percent in the 1950s.

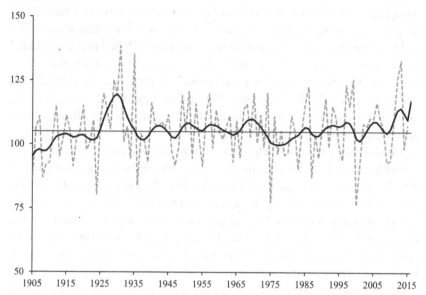

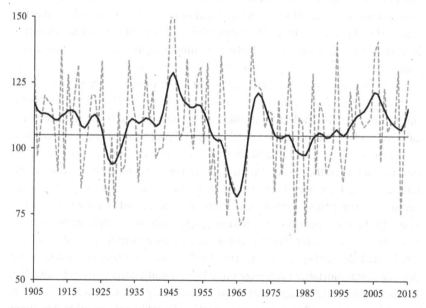

Figure 8.4 Sex ratio at birth by year and area, 1905–2015.
Dashed lines are yearly rates and solid thick lines are trends. The thin lines represent 105, the current normal sex ratio at birth.

Source: Own calculations based on the Scanian Economic-Demographic Database (SEDD; Bengtsson et al. 2021).

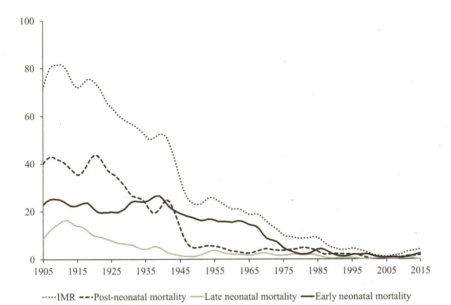

Figure 8.5 Infant, post-neonatal, late neonatal, and early neonatal mortality rates in the study area by year, 1905–2015.
Trends are shown.
Source: Own calculations based on the Scanian Economic-Demographic Database (SEDD; Bengtsson et al. 2021).

Taken together, these developments suggest a transition away from a hazardous first year for infants, where infant deaths were primarily related to infectious diseases, to infant deaths becoming predominantly driven by congenital malformations or other birth defects. These developments are also suggestive of a possible relationship between the decline in early deaths concurrent with the increase in the share of births taking place in hospital and the availability of sulfa and antibiotics to treat infectious diseases. Table 8.1 shows the number and percentage of infant deaths by cause across the entire study area and by period. The table provides evidence of a strong decline in the share of infant deaths caused by infectious disease coupled with substantial increases in the proportion of infant deaths caused by congenital or perinatal problems. In fact, the share of infant deaths from infectious disease declined from 20 percent in 1905–1949 to only one death in the years that followed, while the share of infant deaths caused by congenital or perinatal problems increased from 35 percent in 1905–1949 to 50 percent in 1950–1974, 62 percent in 1975–1994, and 73 percent in 1995–2015. As the table shows, in terms of absolute numbers, large declines in infant deaths related to congenital or perinatal problems are also observed across time.

Table 8.1 Share of infant deaths by cause in Landskrona and the five parishes by period, 1905–2015.

Period	Infectious diseases	Congenital or perinatal problems	Other known cause	Unknown cause	All causes
1905–1949	249 (20.4%)	425 (34.8%)	471 (38.5%)	77 (6.3%)	1,222 (100%)
1950–1974	1 (0.5%)	101 (50.3%)	71 (35.3)	28 (13.9%)	201 (100%)
1975–1994	0 (0%)	32 (61.5%)	20 (38.5%)	0 (0%)	52 (100%)
1995–2015	0 (0%)	19 (73.1%)	7 (26.9%)	0 (0%)	26 (100%)
1905–2015	250 (16.7%)	577 (38.4%)	569 (37.9%)	105 (7.0%)	1,501 (100%)

Note: Calculations based on the main cause of death.
Source: Own calculations based on the Scanian Economic-Demographic Database (SEDD; Bengtsson et al. 2021).

MATERNAL AND INFANT HEALTH 265

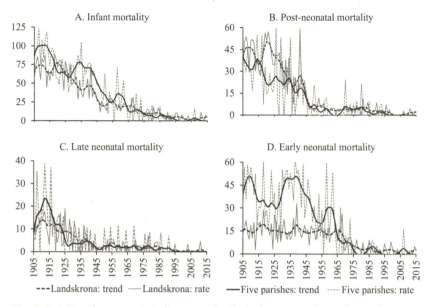

Figure 8.6 Developments in infant mortality by infant age in the study area by year, 1905–2015.
Source: Own calculations based on the Scanian Economic-Demographic Database (SEDD; Bengtsson et al. 2021).

Important differences existed between Landskrona and the five rural parishes in terms of total infant mortality and its different components (Figure 8.6). Infant mortality was lower in the town than in the parishes as early as in 1905 (Panel A). It is possible that the ready access to hospitals and maternity wards and modern-day medical care for infants in the town played a role in this. After a steep decline in infant mortality rates, the rates in the parishes and city became much more aligned in the late 1950s and 1960s. The rural–urban convergence in mortality patterns was mostly driven by a decline in the early neonatal mortality rate in the five parishes (Panel D). Whereas early neonatal mortality was already low in Landskrona at the start of the period (early twentieth century) and remained relatively stable up to the 1960s, it was over 40 per 1,000 in the parishes initially and declined to about half that number in the 1960s. Early neonatal mortality is commonly assumed to be related to pregnancy and childbearing (Woods 2009).

Mortality in the late neonatal period (Panel C) was also higher initially in the five parishes than in Landskrona, after which rates declined and leveled off between the two areas as early as in the late 1930s. As for mortality in the post-neonatal period (Panel B), rates were initially higher in Landskrona than in the parishes, while in both areas a steep decline was observed until the 1950s, and very low rates are seen in the years that followed.

Intervention Analysis

As we have seen, maternal and infant health and survival improved exactly in parallel with medical progress and institutional change in childbirth and infant care throughout the twentieth century. Changes for the better included a range of factors, such as the introduction of antibiotics, vital for both mothers and newborns, broader access to maternity wards, the opening of infant healthcare centers, and the introduction of neonatal intensive care units. What remains unclear is which factors contributed to the decline in infant and maternal mortality and to what magnitude (e.g., Loudon 1992). Even if one can see where a dramatic change in health development coincided with a specific intervention, it is easy to mistake the magnitude of the effect because different kinds of development in healthcare strongly correlate over time. Moreover, the effect of an intervention usually has a lasting effect.

To assess the possible role of public health and medical interventions, we conducted an intervention analysis. We considered as outcomes indicators of perinatal and infant health: offspring sex ratio at birth, stillbirth rate, neonatal and post-neonatal mortality, and infant mortality in total. We did not include maternal mortality due to the small numbers. Intervention analysis is a time series regression technique that links together interventions and outcomes whereby interventions are considered to be "exogenous" (i.e., not affected by the outcome). To give one illustration, the arrival of sulfa antibiotics in Sweden in 1939 was a sudden event not related to the level of infant or pneumonia mortality itself (Lazuka 2019). Intervention analysis allows us to obtain the magnitudes of the intervention effects that account for correlation over time and are suited as a formal test of change in the mean of a time series (Enders 2014).

Intervention analysis, like any time-series technique, is limited in the extent it provides causal estimates. At the same time our intervention estimates are unlikely to be driven by trends as they are accounted for explicitly in the models or by socioeconomic differences in access to interventions, due to their universal character. Giving birth in a modern hospital since 1931 was free for women of any socioeconomic class, and, before that time, no hospital fee was taken from the poorest or unmarried women (Lazuka 2023). Similarly, infants received access to sulfa antibiotics in a maternity ward or infant care clinic, which very quickly attracted universal coverage (Knutsson 2018; Lazuka 2020). Turning to modern interventions, intensive neonatal care units were organically introduced into existing childbirth hospital facilities for the general public for no extra fee. Our intervention effects therefore cannot be explained by socioeconomic differences in access to the facilities (Wüst 2022). Instead, for the first decades of the twentieth century, we may somewhat underestimate the intervention effects because of greater inclusion of poorer women who were more likely to give birth in a hospital setting (Vallgårda 1996).

The detailed description of the evolution of changes in care of mothers and infants in the previous section helped us define how to measure the progress of intervention and create so-called intervention dummies. These dummies are equal to zero in years before a medical or healthcare intervention became available; they equal one in value when in full force, and they equal intermediate values between zero and one for the years before being universally implemented (see Figure 8.7).

Medical change reached the city earlier than it did the rural areas, and the development of mortality differed between Landskrona and rural parishes. Therefore, we ran the intervention analysis separately for these two areas. The expansion of access to maternity wards for delivery was gradual and specific to each locality, and we measured this using the share of inpatient live births. For Landskrona such a share included deliveries that took place in the nursing home's maternity ward (*sjukhemmets barnbördsavdelning*; 1912–1929), in the city's maternity hospital (*stadens barnbördshus*; 1930–1935), and in the city hospital's maternity ward (from 1935), as well as in hospitals in other cities. We also included the share of infants attending the infant healthcare center (BVC) in Landskrona.

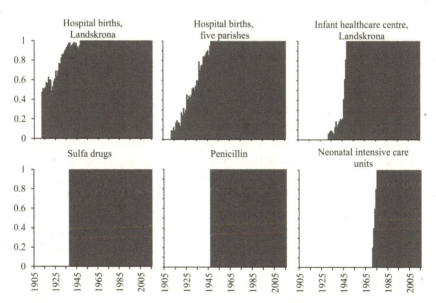

Figure 8.7 Medical and healthcare interventions included in the analyses (shares of affected children).

Source: Own calculations based on the Scanian Economic-Demographic Database (SEDD; Bengtsson et al. 2021).

The impact of sulfa (1938) and penicillin drugs (1947) was much more sudden and universal from the first year of their availability, and we have therefore used the same periodization for Landskrona and the five rural parishes. As for the neonatal intensive care units, we do not know their availability exactly in the study area and have therefore assumed they were rolled out starting from 1971 over the course of 5 years and across all areas.

To obtain magnitudes of intervention effects that are free from serial correlation (unaccounted serial correlation distorts the intervention effect), we defined the underlying time series model based on unit-root tests for each of the outcomes. Such tests enable the determination of the nature of a trend in a series, if any, and the number of lags in the outcomes that should be included in the model. The results of three different tests are shown in the Appendix. The tests are coherent in their conclusions, in that all series for both areas include a deterministic trend except for sex ratio at birth, which has no trend. The tests also suggest the inclusion of not more than three lags in the outcome to account for serial correlation. Therefore, our final model adds not only an intervention dummy but also another trend (excluded for stillbirth rate and early neonatal mortality in the maternity ward model and for sex ratio at birth in all models) and three lags of the outcome.

Results of the Intervention Analysis

Table 8.2 presents the results for the impact of expanded access to maternity wards and neonatal intensive care units on indicators of perinatal health. An inspection of the trends in the previous section shows little sign of significant improvement in these indicators in the first part of the twentieth century, when births in maternity wards became more common. Nevertheless, our results show that access to maternity wards reduced early neonatal mortality by 6 and 11 deaths per 1,000 births in Landskrona and the rural parishes, respectively. Moreover, the stillbirth rate also declined due to the introduction of modern hospital facilities, from 1935. This reduction was even greater in rural parishes, 65 deaths per 1,000 births, which suffered from relatively higher stillbirth mortality. Smaller effects in Landskrona should be related to relatively lower rates of early neonatal and stillbirth mortality. Moreover, Landskrona's hospital might have suffered from overcrowded conditions, given the rapid increase in the number of deliveries taking place there (Vallgårda 1996).

Table 8.2 also includes the results for the impact of neonatal intensive care units on stillbirths and early neonatal mortality. We have seen that the decline in the stillbirth rate and early neonatal mortality was gradual and took place mostly in the second half of the twentieth century. In line with these developments, we

Table 8.2 Intervention effects of the expansion of maternity wards and neonatal intensive care units (NICUs) as interventions, Landskrona and the five parishes, 1905–2015.

	Landskrona				Five parishes		
	Stillbirths 1905–1935	Stillbirths 1936–1967	Early neonatal mortality 1905–2015	Early neonatal mortality 1905–2015	Stillbirths 1905–1935	Stillbirths 1936–1967	Early neonatal mortality 1905–2015	Early neonatal mortality 1905–2015
Maternity wards	3.775	−50.998	−6.164**		−5.345	−65.475**	−10.787**	
	(4.904)	(42.284)	(2.653)		(12.086)	(24.616)	(4.919)	
NICU				−13.746***				−4.630
				(2.683)				(5.255)
Observations	30	32	108	108	30	32	108	108

Notes: Standard errors in parentheses. ***p < 0.01, **p < 0.05, *p < 0.1.
Source: Own calculations based on the Scanian Economic-Demographic Database (SEDD; Bengtsson et al. 2021).

find a strong negative association between neonatal intensive care units and early neonatal mortality that is equal to a reduction of 13.8 deaths for Landskrona, which is highly statistically significant, and 4.6 deaths per 1,000 births for rural parishes. It is not surprising that the results are weaker for rural parishes than for the city. Residence near a hospital with a neonatal intensive care unit has been shown to determine the survival perspectives of newborns (Daysal et al. 2015).

We also present in Table 8.3 the results for the expanded access to infant healthcare in Landskrona. The outcomes analyzed include not only infant health but also the sex ratio at birth and stillbirth rate, which can be considered indicators of perinatal and maternal health. Doctors at the infant healthcare center performed check-ups on the pregnant women in addition to those on the infants (Knutsson 2018). As was seen in Figure 8.5, post-neonatal mortality plummeted in the 1930s and the 1940s, and the share of infant deaths taking place at this infant age dropped by a factor of two.

The results in Table 8.3 show that expanded access to care at the BVC reduced the stillbirth rate by 9.3 deaths per 1,000 births. The post-neonatal death rate declined due to this intervention by 12.5 per 1,000. The overall impact of the introduction of the infant healthcare center—on the infant mortality rate—is a reduction of 13.9 deaths per 1,000 births. Both estimates are statistically significant at a 5 percent level, although we did not find statistically significant effects of the BVC on neonatal mortality. Data on access to infant healthcare services in the five rural parishes are not available; however, we expect this access was much lower, as borne out by the aggregate information on the participation rates in infant healthcare centers when compared between rural and urban areas. Given this, the fairly similar declines in post-neonatal mortality that we observed when comparing rural and urban parishes could be related not to the BVC intervention but to another common intervention, such as the introduction of vital medicines (cf. Lazuka 2023).

Our final set of results is related to the impact of innovative medications, such as the introduction of sulfa antibiotics and penicillin. Table 8.4 presents the results of this analysis on different indicators of maternal and infant health for both areas. Because it is based on the results in each of the areas, the sudden introduction of sulfa antibiotics in 1939, which was effective against puerperal sepsis and pneumonia, exercises a strong negative association on late neonatal and post-neonatal mortality. The drug-induced reduction in post-neonatal mortality is 12.9 and 8.5 deaths per 1,000 births in the rural parishes and the city, respectively. In relation to the introduction of penicillin in 1947, we have found an indication that it reduced the stillbirth rate by 5.8 and 12.6 deaths per 1,000 in Landskrona and the five parishes, respectively. Similar to the impact of the sulfa antibiotics, penicillin was strongly negatively associated with post-neonatal mortality. As a result of the beneficial influences of either the introduction of sulfa drugs or that of penicillin, the infant mortality rate declined by at least 8.5 deaths per 1,000 in each area.

Table 8.3 Intervention effects of the opening of the infant healthcare center, Landskrona, 1905–2015.

	Sex ratio at birth	Stillbirth, 1905–1967	Early neonatal mortality	Late neonatal mortality	Post–neonatal mortality	Infant mortality
BVC	0.909	−9.343**	3.482	−1.983	−12.516**	−13.915**
	(2.480)	(4.592)	(2.355)	(1.583)	(4.938)	(6.043)
Observations	108	60	108	108	108	108

Notes: Standard errors in parentheses. ***p < 0.01, **p < 0.05, *p < 0.1.
BVC, children's healthcare center (*barnavårdscentral*).
Source: Own calculations based on the Scanian Economic-Demographic Database (SEDD; Bengtsson et al. 2021).

Table 8.4 Intervention effects of the introduction of antibiotics, Landskrona and the five parishes, 1905–2015.

	Sex ratio at birth	Stillbirth, 1905–1967	Early neonatal mortality	Late neonatal mortality	Post-neonatal mortality	Infant mortality
Landskrona						
Sulfa drugs	0.653	−5.722	5.666***	−4.284***	−8.466**	−10.212**
	(2.488)	(3.496)	(2.128)	(1.385)	(3.623)	(4.389)
Penicillin	0.603	−5.814*	1.802	−0.908	−7.354*	−9.092*
	(2.343)	(3.467)	(2.031)	(1.350)	(3.846)	(4.865)
Five parishes						
Sulfa drugs	−0.021	−6.391	−2.332	−2.195	−12.911***	−8.564
	(4.000)	(7.329)	(4.347)	(2.209)	(4.596)	(5.348)
Penicillin	−2.883	−12.615*	−8.616*	−0.426	−14.797***	−19.500***
	(3.758)	(6.798)	(4.626)	(2.239)	(4.715)	(6.466)
Observations	108	60	108	108	108	108

Notes: Models with sulfa drugs and penicillin are estimated separately. Standard errors in parentheses. ***$p < 0.01$, **$p < 0.05$, *$p < 0.1$.
Source: Own calculations based on the Scanian Economic-Demographic Database (SEDD; Bengtsson et al. 2021).

Conclusion

The twentieth century was a period of massive change in the care of pregnant women and infants (Løkke 2012; Woods 2009). Childbirth became increasingly medicalized and took place in maternity wards instead of at home under the care of a midwife. Attention was increasingly focused on the antenatal health of mothers and the postnatal follow-up of both mother and child (Sundin and Willner 2007). Sulfa and penicillin reduced infectious disease deaths among mothers and children and made further medical breakthroughs possible; surgical interventions in previously fatal complications during pregnancy and childbirth were much safer than before (Woods 2009). By the end of the twentieth century, infant deaths had become extremely uncommon and maternal deaths almost unheard of. This chapter has explored the development of maternal and infant healthcare and the connection to maternal and infant survival in the city of Landskrona and its rural hinterland between 1905 and 2015.

Maternal mortality was already low at the beginning of the study period, probably a result of the wide availability of trained midwives in Sweden by the turn of the twentieth century (Lazuka 2018; Woods 2009), and it declined further in the early decades of that century. Stillbirth rates were also low at the beginning of the study period, and a moderate decline followed. Perinatal and infant health improved significantly. The infant mortality rate declined from about 80 per 1,000 in 1905 to about 5 per 1,000 in 2015. Late neonatal mortality declined first, followed by post-neonatal mortality and last by early neonatal mortality. There was a decline especially in the share of infant deaths caused by infectious disease that reflected the overall decline in the share of deaths due to infectious disease during the epidemiological transition. The remaining infant deaths—often due to congenital and perinatal problems—also declined in absolute numbers. Infant mortality, especially in the early neonatal period, declined earlier in the town of Landskrona than in its rural hinterland. Mortality rates converged between Landskrona and the five rural parishes later.

We conducted a macro-level intervention analysis based on detailed demographic data combined with information about the timing of institutional change in care arrangements in Landskrona and the surrounding rural parishes to address the question of which public health and medical interventions contributed to reductions in infant and perinatal mortality. Maternal mortality was such a rare event across the period of study, given that it was largely related to improvements in the training of midwives and availability of antiseptic techniques, that the same type of analysis could not be done for changes in maternal health. Our analysis shows that the reduction in young-age deaths can be attributed to most institutional changes in medicine and healthcare that we studied. The availability of maternity wards for delivery was associated with a reduction in 6 and 11 early neonatal deaths per 1,000 births in Landskrona and the five parishes, respectively. The introduction of modern hospital facilities also substantially reduced stillbirth mortality. The institutionalization of childbirth likely benefited newborns through reduced exposure to infection and through advances for complicated surgery or low birthweight babies (see, e.g., Lazuka 2018, 2023). The introduction of the infant care center in Landskrona was related to a reduction in the stillbirth rate and early neonatal and late neonatal mortality rates, as well as to the overall infant mortality rate, which was reduced by 13.9 deaths per 1,000 live-born children. Care at infant care centers focused on prevention and treatment from infection and better nutrition for all babies but also followed-up with the check-ups of preterm babies in the referral from hospitals (Bhalotra et al. 2017; Knutsson 2018; Lazuka 2023). We also find that new medications—sulfonamide and penicillin—led to a reduction of 18 deaths per 1,000 live-born children. Toward the end of the twentieth century, neonatal intensive care units reduced early neonatal mortality by 13.7 deaths per 1,000 live-born children in town.

A natural question is how interventions in hospital facilities and medicine relate to developments in socioeconomic differences in infant mortality. In the twentieth century, socioeconomic differences in infant mortality increased in Landskrona and the five rural parishes (Dribe and Karlsson 2022). Neonatal mortality did not show a social gradient in mortality, but social differences in post-neonatal mortality—a period of life that is more susceptible to behavioral factors—increased. While our examination did not focus on socioeconomic differences, we argue that medical and care interventions should have led to the decrease in socioeconomic differences in young-age mortality. Childbirth in the hospital was free for poorer families and unmarried women in the beginning, and fully subsidized for every woman from the 1930s, creating no significant differences in the treatment effects between women of different classes (Lazuka 2023). Other interventions, such as the introduction of infant care centers, were free to all, or, as with sulfa drugs and penicillin, were very cheap and access was almost universal (Knutsson 2018; Lazuka 2020). The large magnitudes of the effects that we find align well with the observation that universal interventions achieve great results for infant well-being, but do not necessarily eliminate inequality (Mackenbach 2012).

Except for the introduction of intensive care units, which occurred later than other reforms, many changes in institutional and medical care around childbirth occurred simultaneously. For example, the institutionalization of childbirth, the inception of infant health centers, and the introduction of antibiotics all occurred in the same period. The strongest effects on infant survival are found for expanded access to innovations in medical care and inception of infant health centers. The expansion of childbirth hospital facilities benefited especially the survival of newborns. Both city dwellers and those living in the countryside profited from the modernization of midwifery, access to maternity wards, and medical progress.

Appendix

Table A.8.1 Results for the unit root tests for the demographic outcomes, Landskrona and the five parishes.

	Augmented Dickey–Fuller test	Phillips–Perron test	Elliott, Rothenberg, and Stock test	Conclusion
Sex ratio at birth: Landskrona	−7.51 < −2.88	−11.36 < −2.88	−3.31 < −1.94	Stationary
Five parishes	−7.02 < −2.88	−9.31 < −2.88	−4.51 < −1.94	Stationary
Stillbirth rate: Landskrona	−5.92 < −3.45	−7.02 < −3.48	−4.95 < −3.03	Trend stationary
Five parishes	−4.62 < −3.45	−7.12 < −3.48	−4.65 < −3.03	Trend stationary
Early neonatal mortality: Landskrona	−5.99 < −3.43	−10.54 < −3.45	−4.83 < −2.93	Trend stationary
Five parishes	−5.04 < −3.43	−8.21 < −3.45	−4.20 < −2.93	Trend stationary
Late neonatal mortality: Landskrona	−6.49 < −3.43	−8.51 < −3.45	−6.53 < −2.93	Trend stationary
Five parishes	−5.89 < −3.43	−8.84 < −3.45	−5.28 < −2.93	Trend stationary
Post neonatal mortality: Landskrona	−3.06 < −3.43	−8.51 < −3.45	−3.05 < −2.93	Trend stationary
Five parishes	−6.57 < −3.43	−10.01 < −3.45	−5.45 < −2.93	Trend stationary
IMR: Landskrona	−3.85 < −3.43	−7.04 < −3.45	−3.47 < −2.93	Trend stationary
Five parishes	−4.96 < −3.43	−6.98 < −3.45	−4.76 < −2.93	Trend stationary

Note: The first value indicates the test statistic, and the second is a critical value at a 5 percent significance level. The underlying equation included a linear trend. The number of lags was chosen by Akaike Information Criterion.

IMR, infant mortality rate.

Source: Own calculations based on the Scanian Economic-Demographic Database (SEDD; Bengtsson et al. 2021).

Notes

* The authors are grateful for funding received from the research programme "Landskrona Population Study," funded by the Swedish Foundation for Humanities and Social Sciences (Riksbankens Jubileumsfond), and from the research project "How welfare shapes our future" (FORTE, dnr 201700866).
1. In 1905-1949 the five most common causes of infectious mortality for children younger than 10, based on International Classification of Disease (ICD10) codes and in order of prevalence, were A09 Infectious gastroenteritis and colitis, unspecified; A17 Tuberculosis of nervous system; A37 Whooping cough; A36 Diphtheria; and B05 Measles.
2. The WHO definition of MMR also includes among maternal deaths that occurred during pregnancy, something we cannot account for due to lack of data.
3. We detrended all series using a Hodrick Prescott filter with a filtering factor of 6.25.

Sources

Landskrona City Archive. *Barnavärn.*
Landskrona Länslasarett. 1936. *Årsberättelse.*
Landskrona Länslasarett. 1941. *Årsberättelse.*
Landskrona Länslasarett. 1944. *Årsberättelse.*
Landskrona Stads Hälsovårdsnämnd. 1927. *Landskrona Stads Hälsovårdsnämnds Årsberättelse.*
Landskrona Stads Hälsovårdsnämnd. 1929. *Landskrona Stads Hälsovårdsnämnds Årsberättelse.*
Landskrona Stads Hälsovårdsnämnd. 1945. *Landskrona Stads Hälsovårdsnämnds Årsberättelse.*
Landskrona Stads Hälsovårdsnämnd. 1946. *Landskrona Stads Hälsovårdsnämnds Årsberättelse.*

References

Advic, D., P. Lundborg, and J. Vikström. 2018. "Mergers and Birth Outcomes: Evidence from Maternity Ward Closures." IZA Discussion Paper No. 11772.
Aizer, A., J. Currie, and E. Moretti. 2007. "Does Managed Care Hurt Health? Evidence from Medicaid Mothers." *Review of Economics and Statistics* 89 (3): 385-399.
Almond, D., and J. J. Doyle. 2011. "After Midnight: A Regression Discontinuity Design in Length of Postpartum Hospital Stays." *American Economic Journal: Economic Policy* 3 (3): 1-34.
Almond, D., and L. Edlund. 2007. "Trivers-Willard at Birth and One Year: Evidence from US Natality Data 1983-2001." *Proceedings of The Royal Society. Biological Sciences* 274 (1624): 2491-2496.
Andersson, R., and S. Bergstrom. 1998. "Is Maternal Malnutrition Associated with a Low Sex Ratio at Birth?" *Human Biology* 70 (6): 1101-1106.

Bengtsson, T., M. Dribe, L. Quaranta, and P. Svensson. 2021. "The Scanian Economic Demographic Database, Version 7.2 (Machine-readable database)." Lund: Lund University, Centre for Economic Demography.

Bhalotra, S., M. Karlsson, and T. Nilsson. 2017. "Infant Health and Longevity: Evidence from A Historical Intervention in Sweden." *Journal of the European Economic Association* 15 (5): 1101–1157.

Bharadwaj, P., K. V. Løken, and C. Neilson. 2013. "Early Life Health Interventions and Academic Achievement." *American Economic Review* 103 (5): 1862–1891.

Bruckner, T. A., R. Catalano, and J. Ahern. 2010. "Male Fetal Loss in the US Following the Terrorist Attacks of September 11, 2001." *BMC Public Health* 10 (1): 1–6.

Bütikofer, A., K. V. Løken, and K. G. Salvanes. 2019. "Infant Health Care and Long-Term Outcomes." *The Review of Economics and Statistics* 101(2): 341–354

Cronberg, S. 1997. *Infektioner. Sjukdomsbild, miljö, behandling* [Infections: Disease Pattern, Environment, Treatment]. Stockholm: Liber.

Cutler, D., A. Deaton, and A. Lleras-Muney. 2006. "The Determinants of Mortality." *Journal of Economic Perspectives* 20 (3): 97–120.

Cutler, D. M., E. Meara, and S. Richards-Shubik. 2012. "Induced Innovation and Social Inequality: Evidence from Infant Medical Care." *Journal of Human Resources* 47 (2): 456–492.

Daysal, N. M., M. Trandafir, and R. van Ewijk. 2015. "Saving Lives at Birth: The Impact of Home Births on Infant Outcomes." *American Economic Journal: Applied Economics* 7 (3): 28–50.

Daysal, N. M., M. Trandafir, and R. van Ewijk. 2019. "Low-Risk Isn't No-Risk: Perinatal Treatments and the Health of Low-Income Newborns." *Journal of Health Economics* 64 (1): 55–67.

Debiasi, E. 2020. *The Historical Origins of the Mortality Gradient: Socioeconomic Inequalities in Adult Mortality Over Two Centuries in Sweden*. PhD dissertation, Lund University, Department of Economic History. Lund: Media-Tryck.

Dribe, M., and O. Karlsson. 2022. "Inequality in Early Life: Social-Class Differences in Childhood Mortality in Southern Sweden, 1815–1967." *Economic History Review* 75 (2): 475–502.

Enders, W. 2014. *Applied Econometric Time Series*. 4th ed. Wiley.

Fischer, M., M. Karlsson, and N. Prodromidis. 2021. "The Long-Term Effects of Hospital Deliveries." IZA Working Paper. DP No. 14562.

Gröne, O. 1949. "Hur den första lasarettläkartjänsten vid en barnbördsavdelning kom till [How the First Hospital Doctor Position at a Maternity Ward Was Established]." *Svenska Läkartidningen*: 1487–1493.

Helgertz, J., and M. Önnerfors. 2019. "Public Water and Sewerage Investments and the Urban Mortality Decline in Sweden 1875–1930." *The History of the Family* 24 (2): 307–338.

Högberg, U. 2004. "The Decline in Maternal Mortality in Sweden: The Role of Community Midwifery." *American Journal of Public Health* 94 (8): 1312–1320.

Jayachandran, S., A. Lleras-Muney, and K. V. Smith. 2010. "Modern Medicine and the Twentieth Century Decline in Mortality: Evidence on the Impact of Sulfa Drugs." *American Economic Journal: Applied Economics* 2 (2): 118–146.

Jönsson, Å. 1997. *Historien om en stad. Del 3: Landskrona 1900–1997* [The History of a Town. Part 3. Landskrona 1900–1997]. Landskrona kommun.

Knutsson, D. 2018. *Public Health Programmes, Healthcare and Child Health.* PhD dissertation, Stockholm University, Department of Economics.

Kronborg, H., H. H. Sievertsen, and M. Wüst. 2016. "Care Around Birth, Infant and Mother Health and Maternal Health Investments: Evidence from a Nurse Strike." *Social Science & Medicine* 150 (1): 201–211.

Lagercrantz, H. 2015. "Neonatologins historia: ett svenskt perspektiv [The History of Neonatalogy: A Swedish Perspective]." In *Neonatologi*, edited by H. Lagercrantz, L. Hellström-Westas, and M. Norman, 17–18. Lund: Studentlitteratur.

Larsson, M. 2022. *Kläda blodig skjorta: Svenskt barnafödande under 150 år* [Wear a Bloody Shirt: Swedish Childbirth during 150 Years]. Stockholm: Natur & Kultur.

Lazuka, V. 2017. *Defeating Disease: Lasting Effects of Public Health and Medical Breakthroughs Between 1880 and 1945 on Health and Income in Sweden.* PhD dissertation, Lund University, Department of Economic History. Lund: Media-Tryck.

Lazuka, V. 2018. "The Long-Term Health Benefits of Receiving Treatment from Qualified Midwives at Birth." *Journal of Development Economics* 133 (1): 415–433.

Lazuka, V. 2019. "Early-Life Assets in Oldest-Old Age: Evidence from Primary Care Reform in Early Twentieth Century Sweden." *Demography* 56 (2): 679–706.

Lazuka, V. 2020. "Infant Health and Later-Life Labor Market Outcomes Evidence from the Introduction of Sulfa Antibiotics in Sweden." *Journal of Human Resources* 55 (2): 660–698.

Lazuka, V. 2023. "It's a Long Walk: Lasting Effects of Maternity Ward Openings on Labour Market Performance." *Review of Economics and Statistics*, 105 (6): 1411–1425.

Lazuka, V., L. Quaranta, and T. Bengtsson. 2016. "Fighting Infectious Disease: Evidence from Sweden 1870–1940." *Population and Development Review* 42 (1): 27–52.

Leavitt, J. W. 1986. *Brought to Bed.* New York: Oxford University Press.

Lindahl-Jacobsen, R., H. A. Hanson, A. Oksuzyan, et al. 2013. "The Male–Female Health-Survival Paradox and Sex Differences in Cohort Life Expectancy in Utah, Denmark, and Sweden 1850–1910." *Annals of Epidemiology* 23 (4): 161–166.

Løkke, A. 2012. "The Antibiotic Transformation of Danish Obstetrics: The Hidden Links Between the Decline in Perinatal Mortality and Maternal Mortality in the Mid-Twentieth Century." *Annales de démographie historique* 123 (1): 205–224.

Lorentzon, L., and P. Pettersson-Lidbom. 2021. "Midwives and Maternal Mortality: Evidence from a Midwifery Policy Experiment in 19th-century Sweden." *Journal of the European Economic Association* 19 (4): 2052–2084.

Loudon, I. 1992. *Death in Childbirth: An International Study of Maternal Care and Maternal Mortality 1800–1950.* Oxford: Clarendon Press.

Mackenbach, J. P. 2012. "The Persistence of Health Inequalities in Modern Welfare States: The Explanation of a Paradox." *Social Science & Medicine* 75 (4): 761–769.

Meckel, R. 1998. *Save the Babies: American Public Health Reform and the Prevention of Infant Mortality, 1850–1929.* Ann Arbor: University of Michigan Press.

Miller, A. R. 2006. "The Impact of Midwifery-Promoting Public Policies on Medical Interventions and Health Outcomes." *Advances in Economic Analysis & Policy* 6 (1): 1–36.

Mosley, W. H., and L. C. Chen. 1984. "An Analytical Framework for the Study of Child Survival in Developing Countries." *Population and Development Review* 10 (Suppl.): 25–45.

Nonaka, K., B. Desjardins, H. Charbonneau, et al. 1999. "Human Sex Ratio at Birth and Mother's Birth Season: Multivariate Analysis." *Human Biology* 71 (5): 875–884.

Norberg, K. 2004. "Partnership Status and the Human Sex Ratio at Birth." *Proceedings of the Royal Society of London. Series B: Biological Sciences* 271 (1555): 2403–2410.

Olds, D. L. et al. 2007. "Effects of Nurse Home Visiting on Maternal and Child Functioning: Age-9 Follow-up of a Randomized Trial." *Pediatrics* 120 (4): e832–e845.

Quaranta, L. 2013. *Scarred for Life. How Conditions in Early Life Affect Socioeconomic Status, Reproduction and Mortality in Southern Sweden, 1813–1968*. PhD dissertation, Lund University, Department of Economic History. Lund: Media-Tryck.

Rehn, M., and D. Boström. 2011. *300 år i livets tjänst* [300 Years in the Service of Life]. Stockholm: Svenska barnmorskeförbundet.

Stenhammar, A. M., and K. Ohrlander. 2001. *Mjölkdroppen: filantropi, förmynderi eller samhällsansvar* [Drops of Milk: Philanthropy, Guardianship, or Societal Responsibility]? Stockholm: Carlsson.

Sundin, J., and S. Willner. 2007. *Social Change and Health in Sweden: 250 Years of Politics and Practice*. Solna: National Institute of Public Health.

Thomasson, M. A., and J. Treber. 2008. "From Home to Hospital: The Evolution of Childbirth in the United States, 1928–1940." *Explorations in Economic History* 45 (1): 76–99.

Vallgårda, S. 1996. "Hospitalization of Deliveries: The Change of Place of Birth in Denmark and Sweden from the Late Nineteenth Century to 1970." *Medical History* 40 (2): 173–196.

Wisselgren, M. J. 2005. *Att föda barn — från privat till offentlig angelägenhet: Förlossningsvårdens institutionalisering i Sundsvall 1900–1930* [To Give Birth—From Private to Public: The Institutionalization of Maternity Care in Sundsvall 1900–1930]. PhD dissertation, Umeå University, Department of Historical Studies.

Woods, R. 2009. *Death Before Birth: Fetal Health and Mortality in Historical Perspective*. Oxford: Oxford University Press.

Wüst, M. 2012. "Early Interventions and Infant Health: Evidence from the Danish Home Visiting Program." *Labour Economics* 19 (4): 484–495.

Wüst, M. 2022. "Universal Early-Life Health Policies in the Nordic Countries." *Journal of Economic Perspectives* 36 (2): 175–198.

9
The Late Emergence of the Socioeconomic Gradient in Adult Mortality

An Urban Phenomenon?

Tommy Bengtsson, Martin Dribe, and Jonas Helgertz

Introduction

Despite the long-term decline in mortality across all ages, socioeconomic differences in adult health have been growing in recent decades in developed countries. Regardless of whether socioeconomic status (SES) is measured by education, income, or social class, higher-status individuals on average live longer and in better health than those of lower status. The differences are substantial; in Sweden, for example, the gap in remaining life expectancy at age 30 between highly and lowly educated is more than 5 years (Statistics Sweden 2016, table 1). However, it is not only the lowest-status individuals who experience a health disadvantage relative to high-status individuals. Instead, there is an almost linear negative association between SES and health. This *health gradient* has received much attention in epidemiology and the social sciences, with most evidence pointing to a widening of the relative mortality differentials in recent decades (e.g., Mackenbach 2019).

It has been argued that the socioeconomic gradient in mortality is not a new phenomenon but one that has always existed (e.g., Deaton 2016; Elo 2009; Marmot 2004). According to the *fundamental causes theory*, SES is a key determinant of health and mortality at all times and places even if the causal mechanisms may vary across contexts (Clouston et al. 2016; Link and Phelan 1995, 1996; Phelan et al. 2010). Recent research has, however, refuted the historical consistency of the adult mortality gradient, with evidence for Sweden indicating that it only emerged in the second half of the twentieth century (Bengtsson and Dribe 2011; Bengtsson et al. 2020; Debiasi and Dribe 2020; Debiasi et al. 2023). Studies on Providence, Rhode Island in 1865 (Chapin 1924) and Paris in the 1860s (Blum et al. 1990) found higher mortality rates among non-taxpayers and lower-status individuals than among more well-off groups. Other studies on nineteenth-century Netherlands (Van Poppel et al. 2009; Schellekens and Van Poppel 2016) and Britain (Woods 2000; Woods et al. 2004) found adult mortality differences between certain classes or occupations, but no consistent survival advantage for individuals belonging to a higher social class. Indeed, for Britain, several studies have suggested that class differences in mortality only emerged after the 1930s (Pamuk 1985; Smith and Lynch 2004). For the United States, only modest mortality differences by educational attainment were observed for cohorts born during the end of the 1800s and early 1900s (Masters et al. 2012). Some studies also found a mortality advantage for higher-status women, but not for higher-status men, around the turn of the twentieth century in Sweden (Dribe and Eriksson 2023) and Estonia (Jaadla et al. 2017). In some cases, higher-status men even had higher mortality than lower-status men, possibly due to adverse lifestyles or different exposures to diseases (Dribe and Eriksson 2023; Razzel and Spence 2006).

There are several factors contributing to the contemporary health and mortality gradient. Lifestyle factors, such as tobacco smoking, alcohol consumption, and diet—nowadays strongly related to social class—have direct effects on both the prevalence and the outcome of many diseases (see Bengtsson et al. 2020; Probst et al. 2022). Smoking especially has a strong impact on mortality in both lung cancer and cardiovascular diseases and shortens life expectancy by several years (Darden et al. 2018; Doll et al. 2004).

During the first half of the twentieth century smoking was less prevalent in Sweden than in the other Nordic countries, the United States, and Britain. This was especially the case for cigarette smoking, which grew rapidly only from the 1940s onward. Instead, there was widespread use of snuff (*snus*)—a wet tobacco product that was placed under the lip—and pipe tobacco (Nordlund 2005). Nonetheless, by the end of the 1940s, about half of all Swedish men, but less than a tenth of all women, were daily smokers. During the post-World War II period smoking increased among women, while it started to decline among men from the late 1960s, resulting in about a third of both men and women being daily smokers in the mid-1970s. Since then, smoking has been declining, but at the same time a strong socioeconomic gradient has appeared (Nordlund 2005).

In addition to the direct effects on mortality, lifestyles can also have indirect effects through how they influence the success of medical treatment as well as the likelihood of seeking early medical care (Mills et al. 2011). While one could expect the latter to be the case in societies lacking universal provision of healthcare at a low cost (Adler and Stewart 2010), it appears to be a universal phenomenon in contemporary contexts (Van Doorslaer et al. 2000), where, in particular, groups with lower levels of education underutilize healthcare services (Steingrímsdóttir et al. 2012; Smith 1999).

In contemporary contexts, the lack of control of one's work situation, often associated with low-skilled jobs, leads to stress. This has been argued to contribute to the health gradient through susceptibility to infection and morbidity in cardiovascular diseases (Kivimäki and Kawachi 2015; for an overview, see Marmot 2004). Some research has questioned part of the empirical evidence for this mechanism from the so-called Whitehall studies (see, e.g., Marmot 2004) and argued it may be a result of selection of certain individuals into certain jobs and better chances of promotion for healthier individuals (Case and Paxson 2011).

Differences in living and working environments by SES could also produce a health gradient if certain socioeconomic groups systematically are more exposed to toxic substances or pollution. Air pollution is associated with mortality even at low pollution levels (Strak et al. 2021). In addition, the negative health effects of air pollution are larger for smokers because the functioning of their respiratory system is already compromised (Wong et al. 2007). Hence, smoking is potentially more harmful in urban areas with higher levels of pollution.

The high mortality in urban environments relative to rural areas in historical contexts— often referred to as the "urban penalty"—is frequently attributed to the inability of growing cities to make the necessary investments in sanitary services and the provision of clean water (see Harris and Helgertz 2019). To take Landskrona as an example, the town made investments in its water and sewerage infrastructure as early as from 1869 onward. While the sanitary aspects of the services provided were initially questionable due to rather rudimentary technology, the infrastructure expanded rapidly, with at least 90 percent of dwellings being connected to both services by 1909 (Sveriges kommunaltekniska förening 1909; see also Chapter 2). The national health statute of 1874 may also have been important for public health in Landskrona. It stipulated the formation of local health councils to serve towns, in addition to promoting the establishment of epidemic hospitals (one was set up in Landskrona in 1893) and the mandatory inspection of pork (1881) and milk (1894) sold to the public.

Independent of these health infrastructure investments, the increasing population density in the urban areas, along with crowded housing, created conditions for the transmission of infectious diseases, which were a significant cause of death at the beginning of the twentieth century. The spread of infectious diseases was also facilitated by urban areas being migratory hubs characterized by greater population turnover and crowding (Reher 2001). The ability of the upper social classes to protect themselves from exposure to infectious disease may therefore have been lower in urban than rural areas.

It is also known that conditions in early life, such as poor nutrition and exposure to disease during the fetal stage and infancy, affect organ development and increase the risk of disease in adulthood (e.g., Barker 1998; Bengtsson and Lindström 2003; Elo and Preston 1992; Finch and Crimmins 2004). This could in turn affect socioeconomic attainment and thus potentially explain part of the observed association between SES and health in adulthood (e.g., Bengtsson and Broström 2009; Chandra and Vogl 2010; Cutler et al. 2012).

Finally, it has been argued that the direction of causality between SES and health may be reversed, meaning that poor health in adulthood results in socioeconomic disadvantage rather than the other way around (e.g., Cutler et al. 2012; Smith 1999, 2004). Still, several empirical studies using quasi-experimental designs have identified a causal effect of SES on health and mortality (e.g., Lindahl 2005; Lleras-Muney 2005; Lundborg et al. 2016).

We have previously shown that the mortality gradient for adults emerged after the mid-twentieth century in southern Sweden (Bengtsson and Dribe 2011; Bengtsson et al. 2020; Debiasi 2020) despite the rapid improvements in medical care and welfare provisions that took place in that period. This chapter takes the analysis one step further by examining whether the emergence of the class gradient in adult mortality differed between urban and rural areas. We start by summarizing our previous research on the emergence of the social gradient in mortality, then extend the analysis by examining urban–rural differences in adult and old age mortality between 1905 and 2015.

Socioeconomic and Urban–Rural Differences in Mortality

Together with different collaborators, we have previously examined the emergence of the socioeconomic mortality gradient in the study area by gender, age, and cause of death. These studies are based on the same data as those used in this chapter, albeit with some variation in time periods, and have generated results that are robust to whether SES is measured by social class or income.

When examining adult mortality between 1815 and 2015, including data for Landskrona from 1922, we found that a social class gradient in adult mortality emerged quite recently. For individuals aged 30–59 we observed a gradient only after 1950 for women and after 1970 for men, and even later for individuals aged 60–89 (Bengtsson et al. 2020; see also Bengtsson and Dribe 2011 for an earlier study based on the five rural and semi-urban parishes, using a similar class scheme). The patterns are also similar for income differentials in adult mortality (Debiasi et al. 2023).

The socioeconomic gradient emerges at roughly the same time for all groups of causes of death (Debiasi and Dribe 2020; Debiasi et al. 2023). Before the emergence of the gradient, men from the higher classes experience higher mortality from circulatory diseases, consistent with a greater prevalence of certain lifestyles, such as smoking and alcohol consumption which are known to be strongly associated with these causes of death among the higher classes. For women, a somewhat earlier gradient appears in infectious disease mortality, but its precise explanations are unknown.

The socioeconomic gradient emerged much earlier for children than for adults. It was present for post-neonatal infant mortality already in the second half of the nineteenth century (Dribe and Karlsson 2022), almost a century before social differences in adult mortality emerged. This means that the emergence of class differences in childhood mortality took place in the middle of the epidemiological transition, after infant and child mortality began to decline, when highly virulent infectious diseases such as smallpox, measles, and whooping cough were replaced as the leading causes of death by less virulent infections both airborne (e.g., tuberculosis and pneumonia) and food- and waterborne (e.g., typhoid and diarrhea) (Clouston et al. 2016; Omran 1971). Morbidity and mortality from several of these less virulent infectious diseases were dependent on the level of nutrition as well as on crowding and access to uncontaminated food and water (see, e.g., Kunitz 1983; Rotberg and Rabb 1985). Thus, our argument is not that the link between factors such as early-life conditions, nutrition, or exposure to disease and health was weaker in the past but that the role of social class in determining these exposures was either less pronounced or even reversed, thereby explaining the general absence of a class gradient in adult mortality.

In the past, the difficulty in protecting oneself from disease in urban areas led to higher mortality than in rural areas, in Sweden and elsewhere (Condran and Crimmins 1980; Feigenbaum et al. 2020; Helgertz and Önnerfors 2019; Hubbard 2000; Kearns 1988; Reher 2001). This pattern changed during the second half of the nineteenth century when urban and rural mortality started to converge, first among children, then among women, and later among men (Statistics Sweden 1920, table 43; Statistics Sweden 1950, table 57).

Taken together, the socioeconomic gradient in adult mortality emerged in the second half of the twentieth century regardless of whether SES is measured by social class or income. Thus, there is no support for a universal association between SES and health, as has been argued in previous research (e.g., Deaton 2016; Elo 2009; Link and Phelan 1995, 1996; Marmot 2004). While our findings are based on Landskrona and the five parishes, they are almost identical to results for Sweden as a whole after 1970, when there are nationwide data available to make comparisons (Torssander and Eriksson 2010; Hederos et al. 2018). Moreover, the patterns identified in our research are similar to those for Sweden as a whole in a study of class differences in life span after age 40 for cohorts born 1841–1920 (Dribe and Eriksson 2023).

While many factors affecting mortality are context-specific, such as access to clean water, pollution, and the spread of diseases, little attention has been given to differences between urban and rural environments as regards the socioeconomic gradient in mortality. Although Landskrona, due to its size, differed in urban character from larger cities studied in previous research (e.g., Alsan and Goldin 2019; Kesztenbaum and Rosenthal 2017; Molitoris 2015; Önnerfors 2021), it also shared many similarities. Population growth was initially driven by in-migration from nearby rural areas and later by immigration from abroad, like most other Swedish towns at the time (see Chapter 2). In fact, most towns in Sweden were very small from an international perspective. Still, they were characterized by distinctly higher population density and mortality than rural areas well into the twentieth century (Statistics Sweden 1920, table 43; Statistics Sweden 1950, table 57).

Data and Variables

We examine the determinants of mortality in a sample of men and women aged 30–89 years, residing in Landskrona or the five parishes at any time between 1905 and 2015 (Bengtsson et al. 2021). Individuals are followed from age 30 or time of in-migration until time of out-migration, becoming 90 years of age, or death. Consequently, individuals dying or permanently out-migrating before the age of 30 are not included in the study sample. Landskrona is completely urban, consisting of the population of the town parish. Kävlinge is located at a railroad crossing and was home to several industries including textile, leather, and sugar-making, but it was also a considerable farming community (see Chapter 1). Despite its semi-urban character, we define Kävlinge as rural to keep the urban area as homogeneous as possible. The other parishes are overwhelmingly rural throughout the study period.

The key variables in the analysis are place of residence and social class. Using information about occupation, we measure social class at both the individual and family levels, but in the main analysis we use family social class, defined as the highest social class observed among spouses (married individuals) at any given point in time (see Chapter 1 for a more detailed discussion on the measurement of social class and Chapter 3 for an analysis of changes in the class structure over the entire study period). For those older than 60, we define social class as the highest social class observed in the age interval 50–60 years. The motivation for this is that occupation is often not observed over age 60, and we therefore assume that the highest observed social class in the age interval 50–60 is a reasonable approximation of the individual's class position for the remainder of their life. Missing own occupation is an issue for women in particular due to their shorter and frequently interrupted labor market career.

Since there are only a few observations in some classes in the smaller rural parishes, we use an abbreviated class scheme where we merge the higher status white-collar and lower status white-collar workers into one class and the lower-skilled and unskilled workers into another. This gives us the following four classes: white-collar workers, skilled workers, low/unskilled workers, and farmers. We also include individuals with missing occupation as a separate category in the analysis.

The distributions of the variables included in the analysis are shown in the Appendix (Table A9.1) separately by gender, period, and area. Apart from the variables already presented, we include marital status, foreign born, and birthyear. Throughout the study period, between 70 and 80 percent of the population lived in Landskrona. Regardless of whether social class is measured at the individual or family level, there is a dramatic increase in the share of white-collar workers over time at the expense of low/unskilled workers and farmers. The data also reveal an increasing union instability and prevalence of alternative family forms through a greater proportion of never married and previously married men and women (see Chapter 6).

Apart from the decline in the proportion of farmers in the rural area, a rather similar social class structure emerges over time in Landskrona and the five parishes (see also Chapter 3). The proportion of individuals with missing occupational information is considerably higher in Landskrona than in the rural area, especially in the last period, reflecting a lower employment rate in the city than in the countryside. Among women, the proportion married is lower in the urban area in all periods, and this is also the case among men after the mid-1970s. There is a sharp divergence in the proportion of foreign-born starting as early as in the 1950–1974 period, particularly in Landskrona. In the final period, more than 20 percent of the population in Landskrona are foreign born, an even higher share than at the national level, while the corresponding proportion in the rural area is just over 10 percent.

Absolute Mortality Differentials

We begin our analysis by examining absolute differences in mortality by social class for ages 30–89 years. Figure 9.1 shows age-standardized death rates for Landskrona and the five parishes separately. Age-standardized rates allow for a comparison between groups with different age structures. Due to small numbers of observations in some groups, we base the standardization on 10-year age groups using the total population in the study area as the standard population. This means that we use the age-specific mortality rates (in the 10-year age groups between age 30 and 89) to calculate a summary measure based on the age structure of the total population. Hence, the age-standardized mortality rates in different social classes and areas tell us the mortality rate for individuals aged 30–89 that they would have experienced had they all had the age structure of the total population of the study area.

Figure 9.1 shows that a considerable mortality decline took place over the twentieth century, with mortality rates in some cases reduced by as much as 70–80 percent between the first and last periods.

There is no clear mortality gradient by social class for men in the first period (1905–1929). In Landskrona, white-collar workers have the highest mortality and skilled workers the lowest, with that for the low/unskilled in between. Also, in the rural area, there are only small class differences, with white-collar workers having the lowest mortality and low/unskilled workers the highest. In the mid-twentieth century, there is no class gradient for men in either Landskrona or the rural area. In the final period, 1995–2015, there is, however, a clear mortality gradient in the urban area but not in the rural. In Landskrona, white-collar workers now have the lowest mortality and the blue-collar working class, regardless of skills, the highest.

Turning to women, we find no strong class gradient in mortality in either Landskrona or the five parishes at the beginning of the twentieth century. In the urban area, mortality is highest for low/unskilled workers and lowest for skilled and white-collar workers, who have similar levels. In the rural area, mortality is highest for skilled workers and lowest for low/unskilled workers with mortality for white-collar workers in between. A clearer gradient is established for women in the period 1950–1974 in both rural and urban areas, although mortality differences are quite small. Then, in the final period, 1995–2015, there are minor differences within the working class, but white-collar workers have lower mortality in both rural and urban areas.

There is a clear urban penalty in terms of higher mortality in the urban area than in the rural for men in the early twentieth century. This is especially pronounced for the white-collar workers but is also present in the blue-collar working class. Over the twentieth century, there is a complete convergence in urban and rural mortality for white-collar and skilled workers, but not for the low/unskilled for whom an urban–rural difference persisted in the final period as well as throughout the time period of our study. For women, there is an urban penalty in the first half of the twentieth century, but the differences are generally smaller than for men. In the final period, there is an almost complete convergence in mortality between urban and rural areas for all social classes.

SOCIOECONOMIC GRADIENT IN ADULT MORTALITY 289

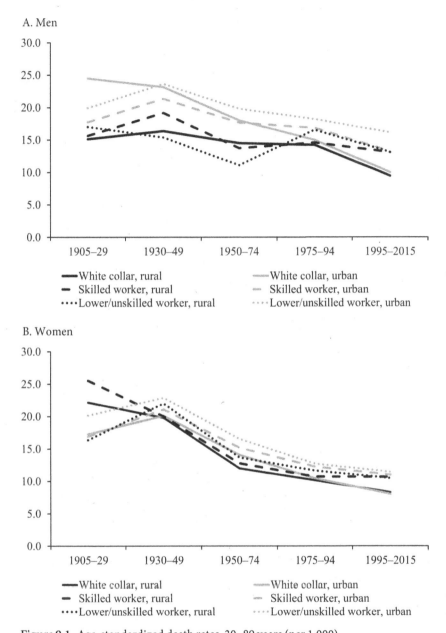

Figure 9.1 Age-standardized death rates, 30–89 years (per 1,000). Age-standardized death rates based on 10-year age groups.
Source: Bengtsson et al. (2021) and Statistics Sweden, see text and Chapter 1.

Relative Mortality Differentials

While absolute mortality differentials are informative when assessing mortality inequalities, a more common approach in demography and epidemiology is to look at relative differences (i.e., how much higher in relative terms mortality is in one group compared to another, rather than how much higher it is in absolute terms). When analyzing relative mortality differentials, however, it is important to remember that considerable relative differences may correspond to very small differences in the actual risk of dying. For example, if the mortality in one group is 50 percent higher than in another group, this is a large relative difference, but in absolute terms it could be equivalent to a difference in mortality rates between 2 and 3 per 1,000.

We analyze relative mortality differences using event-history analysis, more specifically a Cox proportional hazards model, with estimates presented as hazard ratios. The Cox model effectively deals with both left truncation (individuals moving into the study population after age 30) and right censoring (individuals exiting the study population for reasons other than death) and allows for adjustment of the influence of other variables potentially confounding the relationship between social class and mortality. Table 9.1 displays hazard ratios for the entire study sample, aged 30–89 years, separately by gender and period.

The results for men confirm the absence of mortality differences by social class before 1950. In addition to all estimates being statistically insignificant, their magnitudes are small, with hazard ratios close to one. A gradient similar to the one we have today does not emerge until 1975–1994. More specifically, white-collar workers have the lowest mortality, followed in turn by skilled and low/unskilled workers. In the final period, farmers have a hazard ratio between those for low/unskilled and white-collar workers, but it should be emphasized that this group constitutes less than 1 percent of the population in this period. The pattern is quite similar for women, with a gradient emerging as of the period 1950–1974. Already in the period 1930–1949, white-collar and skilled workers have lower mortality than low/unskilled workers, but mortality for skilled workers is lower than for white-collar workers. The patterns are quite similar when measuring class based on individual occupation rather than on the highest class position in the family, but class differences in mortality are generally somewhat larger when using individual class position (see Appendix Table A9.2).

Table 9.1 also shows differences between the different parishes, where we are primarily interested in the urban–rural differences. In the first period, mortality among men is highest in Landskrona, but the hazard ratio for Kävlinge is almost as high. Among the rural parishes, residents in Hög (adjacent to Kävlinge) have

Table 9.1 Hazard ratios of mortality, age 30–89, Landskrona and the five parishes.

A. Men

	1905–1929	1930–1949	1950–1974	1975–1994	1995–2015
Social class					
White-collar workers	1.096	1.014	1.014	0.902**	0.767***
Skilled workers	0.951	0.941	0.965	0.967	0.897**
Low/unskilled workers	ref	ref	ref	ref	ref
Farmers	1.081	1.083	0.977	0.808**	0.864
NA	1.028	0.944	1.415***	1.980**	1.551***
Parish					
Hög	0.528***	0.908	0.655**	0.615**	0.793
Kävlinge	0.930	0.721***	0.680***	0.895**	0.939
Halmstad	0.768	0.601***	0.531***	0.926	0.902
Sireköpinge	0.824	0.658***	0.658***	0.744**	0.758**
Kågeröd	0.724***	0.735***	0.666***	0.849**	0.871*
Landskrona	ref	ref	ref	ref	ref

B. Women

	1905–1929	1930–1949	1950–1974	1975–1994	1995–2015
Social class					
White-collar workers	0.911	0.873**	0.879***	0.845***	0.835***
Skilled workers	0.858*	0.868**	0.924	0.957	1.101
Low/unskilled workers	ref	ref	ref	ref	ref
Farmers	0.995	0.820	0.989	1.136	0.811
NA	1.557***	1.196***	1.028	1.167***	1.267***
Parish					
Hög	1.149	0.642*	0.739	0.714	1.144
Kävlinge	0.958	0.878*	0.822***	0.898**	0.988
Halmstad	0.717*	1.116	0.663*	1.110	0.531
Sireköpinge	0.856	1.042	0.797*	0.635***	0.860
Kågeröd	1.001	1.025	0.890	0.932	0.943
Landskrona	ref	ref	ref	ref	ref

Notes: ***p < 0.01, **p < 0.05, *p < 0.1. Number of deaths and time at risk are presented in Table A9.1. Models control for birth year, foreign born, and marital status.
Source: Bengtsson et al. (2021) and Statistics Sweden, see text and Chapter 1.

the lowest mortality, while the other parishes have mortality levels between those for Hög and Landskrona. For later periods the pattern is similar, with a decline in the urban–rural differences in the final two periods after 1975. For women, there are no distinct urban–rural mortality differences in any of the periods, but in the earlier ones they show a lower level of mortality in some of the rural parishes. In the final period, there are no significant differences between any of the parishes.

We next turn to analyze the mortality differences by social class in the rural and urban areas separately. Table 9.2 shows estimates for the two subsamples. For men, there is a clear mortality gradient in the urban area in the final period, while in the rural area white-collar workers have lower mortality than blue-collar, but there is no difference by skill level among the working class. Among women, from the 1950–1974 period, white-collar workers have lower mortality than blue-collar, even though the difference is not statistically significant in the rural sample. From around that same time period, men and women without a registered occupation have the highest mortality in both rural and urban areas.

Looking at earlier periods, it seems clear that the gradient for men first emerges in the urban area as of the period 1975–1994. For women, none of the estimates is statistically significant in the rural sample, but they do indicate that a weak gradient is established as of the period 1950–1974.

Finally, we look at mortality patterns for men and women by age group. Table 9.3 shows hazard ratios for the full sample for two different age groups separately: 30–59 years (working age) and 60–89 years (elderly). For women especially, the class gradient emerges earlier for the younger age group than for the older. Already in the period 1930–1949, skilled and white-collar workers have significantly lower mortality than low/unskilled workers. In general, class differences are also larger in the working-age group for both men and women.

Turning to the urban–rural differences, the patterns are quite similar between the age groups. Men in Landskrona experienced higher mortality than those in the rural parishes for much of the twentieth century in both age groups. Differences are often somewhat larger in the working-age group than among the elderly. Also in the final period, most of the rural parishes show lower mortality for men than does Landskrona, even though most estimates are not statistically significant. For women, few of the estimates are statistically significant, and it is difficult to see any clear pattern of difference in the urban penalty by age group.

Table 9.2 Hazard ratios of mortality by social class, ages 30–89, by urbanity.

A. Men

	1905–1929	1930–1949	1950–1974	1975–1994	1995–2015
Rural (Five parishes)					
White-collar workers	1.068	1.105	1.261**	0.928	0.847**
Skilled workers	0.836	1.189	1.176	0.927	1.035
Low/unskilled workers	ref	ref	ref	ref	ref
Farmers	1.027	1.158	1.155	0.791*	0.884
NA	1.526	1.860*	1.656**	1.175	1.721***
Urban (Landskrona)					
White-collar workers	1.037	0.962	0.955	0.857**	0.736***
Skilled workers	0.987	0.911	0.959	1.036	0.885**
Low/unskilled workers	ref	ref	ref	ref	ref
Farmers	NA	NA	NA	NA	NA
NA	0.992	0.859	1.440***	2.419***	1.545***

B. Women

	1905–1929	1930–1949	1950–1974	1975–1994	1995–2015
Rural (Five parishes)					
White-collar workers	0.873	1.003	0.870	0.844	0.895
Skilled workers	0.833	0.979	0.964	0.847	1.176
Low/unskilled workers	ref	ref	ref	ref	ref
Farmers	0.855	0.837	0.957	1.070	0.664**
NA	0.987	1.090	1.146	1.023	1.359***
Urban (Landskrona)					
White-collar workers	1.103	0.798	0.819**	0.760***	0.621***
Skilled workers	0.878	0.851	0.923	0.980	1.075
Low/unskilled workers	ref	ref	ref	ref	ref
Farmers	NA	NA	NA	NA	NA
NA	1.923***	1.264***	1.023	1.210***	1.246***

Notes: ***p < 0.01, **p < 0.05, *p < 0.1. Number of deaths and time at risk are presented in Table A9.1. Models control for birth year, foreign born, and marital status.
Source: Bengtsson et al. (2021) and Statistics Sweden, see text and Chapter 1.

Table 9.3 Hazard ratios of mortality by social class and age group. Landskrona and the five parishes.

A. Men

	1905–1929	1930–1949	1950–1974	1975–1994	1995–2015
30–59 years					
Social class					
White-collar workers	1.098	1.045	0.915	0.739**	0.535***
Skilled workers	0.992	0.866	0.934	0.690**	0.731*
Low/unskilled workers	ref	ref	ref	ref	ref
Farmers	1.027	0.884	1.037	0.708	NA
NA	1.207	2.200**	3.609***	4.218***	2.268***
Parish					
Hög	0.629	0.707	0.447	0.384	1.445
Kävlinge	0.947	0.606***	0.587***	0.774*	0.878
Halmstad	0.646	0.632	0.498	0.964	0.771
Sireköpinge	0.742	0.514**	0.677	0.425**	0.771
Kågeröd	0.667**	0.804	0.572***	0.844	0.983
Landskrona	ref	ref	ref	ref	ref
60–89 years					
Social class					
White-collar workers	1.084	0.999	1.063	0.923*	0.787***
Skilled workers	0.901	0.975	0.978	0.994	0.910*
Low/unskilled workers	ref	ref	ref	ref	ref
Farmers	1.145	1.133	0.946	0.783**	0.881
NA	1.049	0.845	1.025	1.220**	1.269***
Parish					
Hög	0.462**	0.964	0.749	0.704	0.684
Kävlinge	0.918	0.766***	0.719***	0.964	0.955
Halmstad	0.912	0.599**	0.549**	0.953	0.926
Sireköpinge	0.900	0.701***	0.670***	0.826	0.773*
Kågeröd	0.784	0.715***	0.711***	0.877*	0.866*
Landskrona	ref	ref	ref	ref	ref

B. Women

	1905–1929	1930–1949	1950–1974	1975–1994	1995–2015
30–59 years					
Social class					
White-collar workers	0.878	0.755**	0.762**	0.700**	0.493***
Skilled workers	0.850	0.667***	0.818	0.985	0.736
Low/unskilled workers	ref	ref	ref	ref	ref
Farmers	1.190	0.799	0.757	0.999	NA
NA	2.437***	1.626***	2.388***	3.460***	2.838***
Parish					
Hög	0.711	0.367*	0.647	0.928	1.323
Kävlinge	0.813	0.955	0.832	1.054	1.074
Halmstad	0.586*	0.602	0.563	3.200**	0.857
Sireköpinge	0.643**	1.300	0.659	0.934	0.691
Kågeröd	0.753	0.913	1.099	0.937	1.001
Landskrona	ref	ref	ref	ref	ref
60–89 years					
Social class					
White-collar workers	0.977	0.943	0.923	0.873***	0.867***
Skilled workers	0.857	0.991	0.950	0.956	1.122*
Low/unskilled workers	ref	ref	ref	ref	ref
Farmers	0.861	0.841	1.035	1.117	0.814
NA	1.137	1.174**	0.972	1.067	1.155***
Parish					
Hög	1.584*	0.731	0.760	0.711	1.146
Kävlinge	1.122	0.834**	0.821***	0.905*	0.991
Halmstad	0.824	1.282	0.683	0.961	0.477
Sireköpinge	1.012	0.966	0.817	0.616***	0.897
Kågeröd	1.219	1.036	0.865	0.954	0.952
Landskrona	ref	ref	ref	ref	ref

Notes: ***p < 0.01, **p < 0.05, *p < 0.1. Models control for birth year, foreign-born, and marital status. Number of deaths and time at risk are presented in Table A9.1.
Source: Bengtsson et al. (2021) and Statistics Sweden, see text and Chapter 1.

Conclusion

This chapter examines whether social-class differences in adult mortality emerged at the same time in the urban as in rural parts of the study area. We found in our previous research that the adult mortality gradient in the study area emerged in the mid-twentieth century; it was slightly earlier for women than men and slightly later for the elderly than the working-age adults, regardless of whether SES was measured by social class or income. While our findings are limited to Landskrona and the five parishes, they are almost identical to findings for Sweden as a whole for the period after 1970, when we can make this comparison (see, e.g., Hederos et al. 2018; Torssander and Erikson 2010). Likewise, they are very similar to what has been found in Sweden as a whole for cohorts born 1880–1920 (Dribe and Eriksson 2023). This means that our findings have relevance not only for the southern part of Sweden but for other parts of the country as well.

The late emergence of the mortality gradient does not support that SES is of universal importance for health, as has often been argued—or at least implied—in previous research. The emergence of the gradient is consistent with the timing of socioeconomic differences in lifestyles, including smoking behavior, which is getting a successively stronger socioeconomic gradient after 1970 (Nordlund 2005). Moreover, it is consistent with changes in working conditions affecting work-related stress, as has been underlined as an explanation of the health gradient. Stress has indeed increased and is today the most common reason for sick leave in Sweden (Folkhälsomyndigheten 2022). Even though conditions in early life are known to affect adult health, it is unlikely that the class gradient in infant mortality that emerged in the second half of the nineteenth century could help explain the emergence of the adult mortality gradient in the period after 1970.

A new result presented in this chapter is that the social class gradient in mortality was more pronounced in urban than in rural areas. The fact that adult mortality rates among white-collar and skilled workers of both genders were similar in Landskrona and the five parishes in the final period but different for low/unskilled workers is consistent with findings for contemporary Finland and Denmark, showing a very small and stable adult life span variability for high- and medium-status groups but high and increasing variability among the lower-status groups regardless of whether measured by education, social class, or income (Brönnum-Hansen 2017; Van Raalte et al. 2018). The reasons for the weaker mortality gradient in the rural area we can only speculate about. It could be connected to different lifestyles in the rural and urban working classes or possibly factors related to working conditions and work environment.

We also found that the urban mortality penalty lasted considerably longer than has been found at the aggregate level in Sweden (Statistics Sweden 1969). In fact, there is still higher mortality in the urban area for lower-skilled and unskilled male workers. However, the explanations for the higher urban mortality most likely changed over time. In the early twentieth century, poorer public hygiene in the city was probably a crucial factor, together with crowded housing and the spread of infectious diseases. In the late twentieth and early twenty-first century, on the other hand, a greater prevalence of work-related stress and urban–rural differences in lifestyles may have become increasingly important. It seems more unlikely that the higher urban mortality was due to access to healthcare, although we cannot rule out that there were some differences in its utilization between Landskrona and the countryside.

Appendix

Table A9.1 Relative frequencies of the variables included in the analysis (percent).

A. 30–89 years, Landskrona and the five parishes

	Men					Women				
	1905–1929	1930–1949	1950–1974	1975–1994	1995–2015	1905–1929	1930–1949	1950–1974	1975–1994	1995–2015
Social class (%)										
White-collar workers	25.0	28.9	40.1	46.3	44.8	21.4	28.0	39.6	45.8	45.9
Skilled workers	23.7	25.7	23.6	18.1	11.5	18.7	20.9	19.3	13.5	7.2
Low/unskilled workers	42.0	39.5	31.9	25.7	26.1	38.6	35.8	31.5	28.0	29.4
Farmers	7.2	5.0	2.7	1.7	0.7	5.3	3.5	2.0	1.1	0.6
NA	2.1	0.9	1.7	8.2	17.0	16.0	11.8	7.6	11.5	16.9
Individual class (%)										
White-collar workers	22.9	24.7	31.5	36.9	36.8	8.9	15.1	24.3	33.6	37.7
Skilled workers	23.1	25.2	25.7	20.7	13.3	5.4	8.5	7.7	6.9	4.0
Low/unskilled workers	43.2	43.5	37.7	30.5	28.9	23.2	36.0	41.3	36.7	35.6
Farmers	7.3	5.2	2.9	1.9	0.8	0.5	0.3	0.2	0.6	0.5
NA	3.5	1.4	2.2	9.9	20.3	62.1	40.1	26.5	22.2	22.1
Marital status (%)										
Never married	20.1	17.3	12.8	16.6	25.1	23.7	20.9	12.4	10.4	16.0
Married	73.8	74.5	78.2	66.1	53.4	64.0	64.2	69.3	56.3	47.5

Previously married	6.2	8.1	9.0	17.3	21.5	12.4	15.0	18.3	33.3	36.5
Foreign born (%)										
No	97.1	97.1	92.7	86.3	76.6	97.4	97.1	93.8	88.0	77.2
Yes	2.9	2.9	7.3	13.7	23.4	2.6	2.9	6.2	12.0	22.8
Parish (%)										
Hög	1.9	1.4	0.8	0.9	0.8	2.0	1.4	0.7	0.6	0.6
Kävlinge	10.3	10.5	10.9	14.6	17.6	10.7	10.9	10.8	13.7	17.1
Halmstad	2.8	1.8	0.9	0.6	0.5	2.9	1.5	0.7	0.4	0.4
Sireköpinge	5.3	3.7	2.4	2.1	2.1	5.6	3.7	2.2	1.7	1.6
Kågeröd	7.6	6.9	5.4	5.7	5.4	7.5	6.1	4.8	4.9	4.7
Landskrona	72.0	75.6	79.6	76.1	73.6	71.4	76.5	80.8	78.8	75.7
Birth year (mean)	1872.9	1891.3	1911.1	1930.4	1950.9	1871.4	1890.3	1909.4	1927.5	1948.0
Time at risk (years)	112,985	137,272	236,096	205,827	248,081	119,378	147,519	249,158	222,045	257,832
Deaths	1,328	2,121	3,569	4,242	4,295	1,274	2,211	3,140	3,395	3,821

(continued)

Table A9.1 Continued

B. Rural, 30–89 years

	Men					Women				
	1905–1929	1930–1949	1950–1974	1975–1994	1995–2015	1905–1929	1930–1949	1950–1974	1975–1994	1995–2015
Social class (%)										
White-collar workers	17.8	19.5	28.9	42.7	49.9	15.7	19.6	28.6	42.4	50.4
Skilled workers	15.7	18.5	18.2	14.6	10.8	15.5	17.8	17.4	11.3	6.2
Low/unskilled workers	41.9	41.8	38.8	30.3	28.2	40.7	37.3	35.1	30.3	30.9
Farmers	22.7	18.8	12.3	6.4	2.2	16.9	14.1	9.7	4.7	2.2
NA	1.9	1.4	1.8	6.0	8.9	11.2	11.3	9.2	11.3	10.2
Individual class (%)										
White-collar workers	16.8	17.8	22.8	32.5	39.7	5.7	8.9	15.5	30.1	41.2
Skilled workers	15.2	17.3	18.5	17.1	13.2	6.3	8.4	7.5	4.4	2.7
Low/unskilled workers	42.9	44.0	43.5	35.4	32.7	25.6	28.6	36.6	39.1	39.0
Farmers	23.2	19.4	13.1	7.1	2.4	1.6	1.1	0.8	2.5	1.9
NA	2.0	1.5	2.2	8.0	12.1	60.9	53.1	39.5	23.8	15.2
Marital status (%)										
Never married	19.5	22.2	17.4	16.8	24.7	20.5	21.9	14.3	10.0	16.1
Married	75.2	71.0	76.1	69.1	56.5	70.0	66.4	72.9	64.1	52.0
Previously married	5.3	6.9	6.5	14.1	18.8	9.5	11.7	12.8	25.9	31.9
Foreign born (%)										
No	96.9	96.6	95.5	91.4	88.9	97.6	96.8	96.1	92.2	88.4
Yes	3.1	3.4	4.5	8.6	11.1	2.4	3.2	3.9	7.8	11.6
Birth year (mean)	1871.3	1889.4	1909.1	1931.8	1951.6	1870.9	1888.8	1907.6	1929.4	1949.3
Time at risk	31613	33436	48048	49159	65446	34163	34612	47853	47184	62757
Deaths	337	480	627	869	1,013	337	519	591	620	836

C. Urban, 30–89 years

	Men					Women				
	1905–1929	1930–1949	1950–1974	1975–1994	1995–2015	1905–1929	1930–1949	1950–1974	1975–1994	1995–2015
Social class (%)										
White-collar workers	27.9	31.9	43.0	47.5	43.0	23.8	30.6	42.2	46.8	44.5
Skilled workers	26.9	28.0	25.0	19.2	11.7	19.9	21.9	19.8	14.1	7.5
Low/unskilled workers	42.0	38.8	30.1	24.2	25.3	37.8	35.3	30.7	27.4	28.9
Farmers	1.1	0.5	0.3	0.2	0.2	0.6	0.3	0.2	0.1	0.1
NA	2.1	0.8	1.7	8.8	19.9	17.9	11.9	7.3	11.6	19.0
Individual class (%)										
White-collar workers	25.3	27.0	33.8	38.3	35.8	10.2	17.0	26.4	34.5	36.6
Skilled workers	26.2	27.7	27.5	21.9	13.3	5.0	8.6	7.8	7.6	4.4
Low/unskilled workers	43.4	43.4	36.2	29.0	27.5	22.3	38.3	42.4	36.0	34.5
Farmers	1.1	0.6	0.3	0.3	0.2	0.0	0.0	0.1	0.1	0.1
NA	4.0	1.3	2.2	10.5	23.2	62.5	36.1	23.4	21.8	24.4
Marital status (%)										
Never married	20.3	15.8	11.6	16.5	25.2	24.9	20.6	11.9	10.5	16.0
Married	73.2	75.7	78.8	65.1	52.2	61.6	63.5	68.5	54.2	46.1
Previously married	6.5	8.6	9.6	18.3	22.5	13.5	16.0	19.6	35.3	37.9
Foreign born (%)										
No	97.2	97.3	92.0	84.6	72.1	97.4	97.2	93.2	86.8	73.6
Yes	2.8	2.7	8.0	15.4	27.9	2.6	2.8	6.8	13.2	26.4
Birth year (mean)	1873.5	1892.0	1911.6	1930.0	1950.7	1871.6	1890.7	1909.9	1927.0	1947.6
Time at risk	81373	103837	188048	156668	182635	85215	112907	201305	174861	195074
Deaths	991	1,641	2,942	3,373	3,282	937	1,692	2,549	2,775	2,985

Source: Bengtsson et al. (2021) and Statistics Sweden, see text and Chapter 1.

Table A9.2 Hazard ratios of mortality, age 30–89. Individual social class. Landskrona and the five parishes.

	Men					Women				
	1905–1929	1930–1949	1950–1974	1975–1994	1995–2015	1905–1929	1930–1949	1950–1974	1975–1994	1995–2015
Higher white-collar	1.127*	1.061	1.012	0.927*	0.807***	0.968	0.844**	0.847***	0.846***	0.840***
Skilled workers	0.971	0.967	0.941	0.993	0.933	0.826	0.820**	0.989	1.049	1.146**
Unskilled	ref	ref	ref	ref	ref	ref	ref	ref	ref	ref
Farmers	1.073	1.118	0.978	0.849	0.857	0.799	0.705	0.882	0.713	0.793
NA	0.868	0.924	1.566***	2.147***	1.682***	1.100	0.985	1.082*	1.242***	1.339***

Notes: ***p < 0.01, **p < 0.05, *p < 0.1. Models control for birth year, foreign-born, marital status, and parish of residence. Number of deaths and time at risk are presented in Table A9.1.

Source: Bengtsson et al. (2021) and Statistics Sweden, see text and Chapter 1.

References

Adler, N. E., and J. Stewart. 2010. "Health Disparities Across the Lifespan: Meaning, Methods, and Mechanisms." *Annals of the New York Academy of Sciences* 1186 (1): 5–23.

Alsan, M., and C. Goldin. 2019. "Watersheds in Child Mortality: The Role of Effective Water and Sewerage Infrastructure, 1880–1920." *Journal of Political Economy* 172 (2): 586–638.

Barker, D. J. P. 1998. *Mothers, Babies, and Health in Later Life*. London: Churchill Livingstone.

Bengtsson, T., and G. Broström. 2009. "Do Conditions in Early Life Affect Old-Age Mortality Directly and Indirectly? Evidence from 19th-Century Rural Sweden." *Social Science & Medicine* 68 (9): 1583–1590.

Bengtsson, T., and M. Dribe. 2011. "The Late Emergence of Socioeconomic Mortality Differentials: A Micro-Level Study of Adult Mortality in Southern Sweden 1815–1968." *Explorations in Economic History* 48 (3): 389–400.

Bengtsson, T., M. Dribe, and J. Helgertz. 2020. "When Did the Health Gradient Emerge? Social Class and Adult Mortality in Southern Sweden, 1813–2015." *Demography* 57 (3): 953–977.

Bengtsson, T., M. Dribe, L. Quaranta, and P. Svensson 2021. "The Scanian Economic Demographic Database. Version 7.2 (Machine-readable database)." Lund: Lund University, Centre for Economic Demography,

Bengtsson, T., and M. Lindström. 2003. "Airborne Infectious Diseases During Infancy and Mortality in Later Life in Southern Sweden, 1766–1894." *International Journal of Epidemiology* 32 (2): 286–294.

Blum, A., J. Houdaille, and M. Lamouche. 1990. "Mortality Differentials in France During the Late 18th and Early 19th Centuries." *Population an English Selection* 2 (1): 163–185.

Brønnum-Hansen H. 2017. "Socially Disparate Trends in Lifespan Variation: A Trend Study on Income and Mortality Based on Nationwide Danish Register Data." *BMJ Open* 7: e014489.

Case, A., and C. Paxson. 2011. "The Long Reach of Childhood Health and Circumstance: Evidence from the Whitehall II Study." *Economic Journal* 121 (554): F183–F204.

Chandra, A., and T. S. Vogl. 2010. "Rising Up with Shoe Leather? A Comment on *Fair Society, Healthy Lives* (the Marmot Review)." *Social Science & Medicine* 71 (7): 1227–1230.

Chapin, C. V. 1924. "Deaths Among Taxpayers and Non-Taxpayers Income Tax, Providence, 1865." *American Journal of Public Health* 14 (8): 647–651.

Clouston, S. A., M. S. Rubin, J. C. Phelan, and B. G. Link. 2016. "A Social History of Disease: Contextualizing the Rise and Fall of Social Inequalities in Cause-Specific Mortality." *Demography* 53 (5): 1631–1656.

Condran, G. A., and E. Crimmins. 1980. "Mortality Differentials Between Rural and Urban Areas of States in the Northeastern United States 1890–1900." *Journal of Historical Geography* 6 (2): 179–202.

Cutler, D. M., A. Lleras-Muney, and T. Vogl. 2012. "Socioeconomic Status and Health: Dimensions and Mechanisms." In *The Oxford Handbook of Health Economics* edited by M. Gleid and P. C. Smith, 124–163. Oxford: Oxford University Press.

Darden, M., D. B. Gilleskie, and K. Strumpf. 2018. "Smoking and Mortality: New Evidence from a Long Panel." *International Economic Review* 59 (3): 1571–1619

Deaton, A. 2016. "On Death and Money: History, Facts, and Expectations." *Journal of American Medical Association* 315 (6): 1703–1705.

Debiasi, E. 2020. *The Historical Origins of the Mortality Gradient: Socioeconomic Inequalities in Adult Mortality over Two Centuries in Sweden*. PhD dissertation, Lund University, Department of Economic History. Lund: Media-Tryck.

Debiasi, E., and M. Dribe. 2020. "SES Inequalities in Cause-Specific Adult Mortality: A Study of the Long-Term Trends Using Longitudinal Individual Data for Sweden (1813–2014)." *European Journal of Epidemiology* 35 (11): 1043–1056.

Debiasi, E., M. Dribe, and G. Brea-Martinez. 2023. "Has It Always Paid to be Rich? Income and Cause-Specific Mortality in Southern Sweden 1905–2014." *Population Studies* online: 1–21.

Doll, R., R. Peto, J. Boreham, and I. Sutherland. 2004. "Mortality in Relation to Smoking: 50 Years' Observations on Male British Doctors." *British Medical Journal* 328 (1519): 1–9.

Dribe, M., and B. Eriksson. 2023. "Socioeconomic Status and Adult Lifespan 1881–2020: New Estimates from Swedish Death Registers and Full-Count Census Data." *Lund Papers in Economic Demography* 2023:3.

Dribe, M., and O. Karlsson. 2022. "Inequality in Early Life: Social Class Differences in Childhood Mortality in Southern Sweden, 1815–1967." *Economic History Review* 75 (2): 475–502.

Elo, I. T. 2009. "Social Class Differentials in Health and Mortality: Patterns and Explanations in Comparative Perspective." *Annual Review of Sociology* 35 (1): 553–572.

Elo, I. T., and S. H. Preston. 1992. "Effects of Early-Life Conditions on Adult Mortality: A Review." *Population Index* 58 (2): 186–212.

Feigenbaum, J., L. Hoehn-Velasco, and E. Wrigley-Field. 2020. "Did the Urban Mortality Penalty Disappear? Revisiting the Early Twentieth-Century's Urban-Rural Mortality Convergence." *MPC Working Paper* 2020-2009.

Finch, C. E., and E. M. Crimmins. 2004. "Inflammatory Exposure and Historical Changes in Human Life-Spans." *Science* 305 (5691): 1736–1739.

Folkhälsomyndigheten [The Public Health Agency of Sweden]. 2022. "Folkhälsans utveckling. Årsrapport 2022 [The Development of Public Health. Annual Report 2022]." Stockholm: Folkhälsomyndigheten.

Harris, B., and J. Helgertz. 2019. "Urban Sanitation and the Decline of Mortality." *History of the Family* 24 (2): 207–226.

Hederos, K., M. Jäntti, L. Lindahl, and J. Torssander. 2018. "Trends in Life Expectancy by Income and the Role of Specific Causes of Death." *Economica* 85 (339): 606–625.

Helgertz, J., and M. Önnerfors. 2019. "Public Water and Sewerage Investments and the Urban Mortality Decline in Sweden 1875–1930." *History of the Family* 24 (2): 307–338.

Hubbard, W. H. 2000. "The Urban Penalty: Towns and Mortality in Nineteenth Century Norway." *Continuity and Change* 15 (2): 331–350.

Jaadla, H., A. Puur, and K. Rahu. 2017. "Socioeconomic and Cultural Differentials in Mortality in a Late 19th Century Urban Setting: A Linked Records Study from Tartu, Estonia, 1897–1900." *Demographic Research* 36 (1): 1–40

Kearns, G. 1988. "The Urban Penalty and the Population History of England." In *Society, Health and Population During the Demographic Transition*, edited by A. Brändström and L.-G. Tedebrand, 213–235. Stockholm: Almqvist & Wiksell International.

Kesztenbaum, L., and J. L. Rosenthal. 2017. "Sewers' Diffusion and the Decline of Mortality: The Case of Paris, 1880–1914." *Journal of Urban Economics* 98 (Suppl C): 174–186.

Kivimäki, M., and I. Kawachi. 2015. "Work Stress as a Risk Factor for Cardiovascular Disease." *Current Cardiology Reports* 17 (74): 1–9.

Kunitz, S. J. 1983. "Speculations on the European Mortality Decline." *Economic History Review* 36 (3): 349–364.

Lindahl, M. 2005. "Estimating the Effect of Income on Health and Mortality Using Lottery Prizes as an Exogenous Source of Variation in Income." *Journal of Human Resources* 40 (1): 144–168.

Link, B. G., and J. C. Phelan. 1995. "Social Conditions as Fundamental Causes of Disease." *Journal of Health and Social Behavior* extra issue: 80–94.

Link, B. G., and J. C. Phelan. 1996. "Understanding Sociodemographic Differences in Health: The Role of Fundamental Social Causes." *American Journal of Public Health* 86 (4): 471–473.

Lleras-Muney, A. 2005. "The Relationship Between Education and Adult Mortality in the United States." *Review of Economic Studies* 72 (1): 189–221.

Lundborg, P., C. H. Lyttkens, and P. Nystedt. 2016. "The Effect of Schooling on Mortality: New Evidence from 50,000 Swedish Twins." *Demography* 53 (4): 1135–1168.

Mackenbach, J. P. 2019. *Health Inequalities: Persistence and Change in European Welfare States*. Oxford: Oxford University Press.

Marmot, M. 2004. *The Status Syndrome: How Social Status Affects our Health and Longevity*. London: Bloomsbury Press.

Masters, R. K., R. A. Hummer, and D. A. Powers. 2012. "Educational Differences in U.S. Adult Mortality: A Cohort Perspective." *American Sociological Review* 77 (4): 548–572.

Mills, E., O. Eyawo, I. Lockhart, et al. 2011. "Smoking Cessation Reduces Postoperative Complications: A Systematic Review and Meta-Analysis." *American Journal of Medicine* 124 (2): 144–154.

Molitoris, J. 2015. *Life and Death in the City: Demography and Living Standards during Stockholm's Industrialization*. PhD dissertation, Lund University, Department of Economic History. Lund: Media-Tryck.

Nordlund, A. 2005. "Tobaksrökning och hälsa i Sverige under 1900-talet [Tobacco Smoking and Health in Sweden During the 20th Century]." In *Svenska folkets hälsa i ett historiskt perspektiv* [Swedish People's Health from a Historical Perspective], edited by J. Sundin, C. Hogstedt, J. Lindberg, and H. Moberg, 304–361. Stockholm, Sweden: Statens folkhälsoinstitut.

Omran, A. 1971. "The Epidemiological Transition: A Theory of the Epidemiology of Population Change." *The Milbank Quarterly* 83 (4): 731–757.

Önnerfors, M. 2021. *Water for the Many. Health, Neighbourhood Change and Equality of Access during the Expansion of Swedish Urban Water Networks*. PhD dissertation, Lund University, Department of Economic History. Lund: Media-Tryck.

Pamuk, E. R. 1985. "Social Class Inequality in Mortality from 1921 to 1972 in England and Wales." *Population Studies* 39 (1): 17–31.

Phelan, J. C., B. G. Link, and P. Tehranifar. 2010. "Social Conditions as Fundamental Causes of Health Inequalities: Theory, Evidence, and Policy Implications." *Journal of Health and Social Behavior* 51 (Suppl.): S28–S40.

Probst, C., M. Könen, J. Rehm, and N. Sudharsanan. 2022. "Alcohol-Attributable Deaths Help Drive Growing Socioeconomic Inequalities in US Life Expectancy, 2000–18." *Health Affairs* 41 (8): 1160–1168.

Razzell, P., and C. Spence. 2006. "The Hazards of Wealth: Adult Mortality in Pre-Twentieth-Century England." *Social History of Medicine* 19 (3): 381–405.

Reher, D. 2001. "In Search of the 'Urban Penalty': Exploring Urban and Rural Patterns in Spain During the Demographic Transition." *International Journal of Population Geography* 7 (2): 105–127.

Rotberg, R. I., and T. K. Rabb. 1985. *Hunger and History: The Impact of Changing Food Production and Consumption Patterns on Society.* Cambridge: Cambridge University Press.

Schellekens, J., and F. Van Poppel. 2016. "Early-Life Conditions and Adult Mortality Decline in Dutch Cohorts Born 1812–1921." *Population Studies* 70 (3): 327–343.

Smith, G. D., and J. Lynch. 2004. "Life Course Approaches to Socioeconomic Differentials in Health." In *A Life Course Approach to Chronic Disease Epidemiology*, edited by D. Kuh and Y. Ben-Shlomo, 77–115. Oxford: Oxford University Press.

Smith, J. P. 1999. "Healthy Bodies and Thick Wallets: The Dual Relation Between Health and Economic Status." *Journal of Economic Perspectives* 13 (2): 145–166.

Smith, J. P. 2004. "Unraveling the SES-Health Connection." *Population and Development Review* 30 (Suppl.): 108–132.

Statistics Sweden. 1920. *Statistisk årsbok för Sverige 1920.* [Statistical Yearbook for Sweden 1920]. Stockholm: Statistics Sweden.

Statistics Sweden. 1950. *Statistisk årsbok för Sverige 1950.* [Statistical Yearbook for Sweden 1950]. Stockholm: Statistics Sweden.

Statistics Sweden. 1969. *Historisk statistik för Sverige. Del 1. Befolkning. 1720–1967* [Historical Statistics for Sweden. Part 1. Population. 1720–1967]. Stockholm: Statistics Sweden.

Statistics Sweden. 2016. *Livslängd och dödlighet i olika sociala grupper. Demografiska rapporter 2.* [Life Expectancy and Mortality for Different Social Groups. Demographic Reports]. Stockholm: Statistics Sweden.

Steingrímsdóttir, Ó. A., Ø. Næss, J. O. Moe, et al. 2012. "Trends in Life Expectancy by Education in Norway 1961–2009." *European Journal of Epidemiology* 27 (3): 163–171.

Strak, M., G. Weinmayr, S. Rodopoulou, et al. 2021. "Long Term Exposure to Low Level Air Pollution and Mortality in Eight European Cohorts Within the ELAPSE Project: Pooled Analysis." *British Medical Journal* 374 (1904), 1–11.

Sveriges kommunaltekniska förening. 1909. "Årlig publikation 1909 [Annual Publication 1909]." Technical report. Stockholm.

Torssander, J., and R. Erikson. 2010. "Stratification and Mortality: A Comparison of Education, Class, Status, and Income." *European Sociological Review* 26 (4): 465–474.

Van Doorslaer, E., A. Wagstaff, H. Van der Burg, et al. 2000. "Equity in the Delivery of Health Care in Europe and the US." *Journal of Health Economics* 19 (5): 553–583.

Van Poppel, F., R. Jennissen, and K. Mandemakers. 2009. "Time Trends in Social Class Mortality Differentials in the Netherlands, 1820–1920: An Assessment Based on Indirect Estimation Techniques." *Social Science History* 33 (2): 119–153.

Van Raalte, A., I. Sasson, and P. Martikainen. 2018. "The Case for Monitoring Life-Span Inequality. Focus on Variation in Age at Death, Not Just Average Age." *Science* 362 (6418): 1002–1004.

Wong, C.-M., C.-Q. Ou, N.-W. Lee et al. 2007. "Short-Term Effects of Particulate Air Pollution Among Male Smokers and Never-Smokers." *Epidemiology* 18 (5): 593–598.

Woods, R. 2000. *The Demography of Victorian England and Wales.* Cambridge: Cambridge University Press.

Woods, B., P. Boyle, S. Curtis, et al. 2004. "The Origins of Social Class Mortality Differentials." In *The Geography of Health Inequalities in the Developed World*, edited by P. Boyle, S. Curtis, T. Gatrell, E. G. Graham, and E. Moore, 37–52. Hants, UK: Ashgate.

10
Income, Inequality, and Geography
Disparities in Age at Death

Gabriel Brea-Martinez, Finn Hedefalk, and Therese Nilsson

Introduction

Throughout the world there is a clear health and mortality gradient by education, social class, and income (Chetty et al. 2016; Hederos et al. 2018; Kondo et al. 2014). It is debated to what extent such a gradient has always existed (see Bengtsson and Dribe 2011; Bengtsson et al. 2020; Chapter 9), but it is well established that socioeconomic health differences have widened in many countries over the past decades (Mackenbach 2019) and thus become a key topic for epidemiologists, sociologists, demographers, and economists.

The idea that income and socioeconomic status are important for people's health and well-being seems reasonable. Having more resources can directly or indirectly allow for different lifestyles and behaviors compared to when resources are scarce, which can in turn have health consequences. At the same time, research shows that the pattern of socioeconomic health disparities is very different when evaluated across countries and societies. Specifically, the slope of the gradient is much steeper in some contexts than others (Beckfield et al. 2013; Vågerö and Lundberg 1989). It was particularly notable early on that the health gradient was more evident in societies that were less equal in economic terms (Bergh 2021; Wilkinson 2001; Wilkinson and Pickett 2009). This pattern gave rise to the so-called *income inequality hypothesis* (IIH) which states that income inequality affects health over and above own socioeconomic status and that income inequality in society is harmful to the health of every individual regardless of whether they are at the top or bottom of the income distribution.[1]

Independent of underlying mechanisms, the idea that income inequality is detrimental for individual health is clearly suggestive. If income differences within society matter for our well-being, progressive and pro-poor transfers could be a way of improving general health both because such economic resources directly can facilitate and improve access to, for example, high-quality healthcare, proper nutrition, and education, but also that such transactions would per se reduce economic inequality. Research in several academic fields

Gabriel Brea-Martinez, Finn Hedefalk, and Therese Nilsson, *Income, Inequality, and Geography* In: *Urban Lives*.
Edited by: Martin Dribe, Therese Nilsson, and Anna Tegunimataka, Oxford University Press.
© Oxford University Press 2024. DOI: 10.1093/oso/9780197761090.003.0010

has studied the relationship between income inequality and health using a plethora of health outcomes and has also asked whether inequality can make us ill. Most studies use population data from which one cannot disentangle the individual impacts of own absolute income, relative income, and income inequality on health outcomes (see Pickett and Wilkinson 2015; Tibber et al. 2021 for reviews).[2] More recent contributions to the literature therefore generally use individual-level data. A recent extensive summary of the state of this research concludes that the evidence is mixed, with a considerable amount of variation across studies (Bergh et al. 2016) present. Many studies using individual-level data find no support for the IIH, although there are several empirical studies suggesting that inequality significantly harms or, in contrast, even improves individual health (Du et al. 2019; Gerdtham and Johannesson 2004; Grönqvist et al. 2012; Jen et al. 2009; Karlsson et al 2010; Zagorski et al. 2014).

One clear pattern in the literature is the assumption about an instant connection between income inequality and health. Studies generally consider a contemporary correlation, assessing income inequality and health outcomes at around the same point in time. A few studies explore the lagged effects of income inequality, suggesting that the association between health and exposure to inequality over a period of up to 15 years is stronger than the association between health and current inequality (Blakely et al. 2000; Kondo et al. 2014; Zheng 2012). However, these cannot follow individuals over time in the sense of successfully identifying the individual's long-term exposure to inequality. Moreover, the health consequences of income inequality may not manifest themselves until after some time, and the long-term effects of income inequality on individual health may be stronger in some periods or life stages than in others. Hence, inequality is either measured with errors or not necessarily measured at stages that really matter for health and which could explain the mixed evidence regarding the IIH. To improve the accuracy and precision of these measurements, we need information about individuals' residence and income over time.

A second pattern in the literature shows that most studies use measures based on income inequality that are aggregated at coarse geographical levels, such as at country, state, or region. Some studies highlight the role of the geographical level (and which level of aggregation regarding inequality that is relevant in evaluating health effects) by examining the relationship between inequality and health in US metropolitan areas and counties, respectively. For example, no relationship between income inequality across metropolitan areas and self-assessed health (Blakely et al. 2002), whereas research focusing on state and county inequality and various self-reported health measures (including insurance status, influenza vaccination, and self-assessed health) found some evidence in line with the IIH (Chen and Crawford 2012). Few studies have focused on the role of local or micro-level inequality in health and longevity. An exception is one study on the role of inequality in self-reported health in the urban capital area of Stockholm which finds some support for the idea that high and very high inequality are detrimental to individual well-being (Rostila et al. 2012).

Local (neighborhood) income inequality may be a relevant aggregation level when studying the implications for individual health (the underlying potential mechanisms are described in detail in this chapter under "Data, Analytical Strategy, and Methods"). In addition, there are advantages in measuring exposure to inequality over a longer period and having the exact information on the individual's residence. The scarcity of appropriate data is the main reason that exposure to income disparities over time and the role of local inequality in health in later life are areas that have been neglected in the literature. To investigate such effects, we need to know an individual's migration history to measure properly their long-term exposure to income inequality together with later-life information on health or mortality, which requires detailed individual residential histories. It also requires geocoded information and adequate income data from historical times.

This chapter brings light to the relationship between income, income inequality, and health in Landskrona, Sweden. We first examine how neighborhood inequality developed over time and study if long-term exposure to local income inequality had an impact on adult mortality. We use detailed geocoded data and evaluate changes and persistence in spatial inequality for the period 1939–1967. This spatial analysis complements the analyses in Chapter 3 on the general trend in income inequality and social mobility in Landskrona across the twentieth century.

Second, we discuss the theoretical relationship between income inequality and mortality and present three interconnected hypotheses. In addition to the IIH, we discuss another two hypotheses. The first is the *absolute income hypothesis* (AIH), which says income is important for how long people live, but the health benefits from higher income lessen over higher levels of income. The second is the *relative income hypothesis* (RIH), which suggests that their economic position may influence a person's health and life span compared to others around them. This means that if someone compares their income to others and feels worse off, it could negatively affect their health.

Finally, we use the information derived in the spatial analysis together with our individual-level data to assess these three hypotheses. The results section summarizes the findings from the empirical analysis, which addresses the question of temporality and locality using the information on characteristics regarding income and income inequality in the neighborhood and age at death. That is, we test the hypothesis that long-term exposure to local inequality can affect adult health and mortality.

We use rich individual-level longitudinal information on income and demographic outcomes, including death, for individuals residing in the town of Landskrona geocoded at the address level (Hedefalk and Dribe 2020). This information provides a unique opportunity to examine the development of spatial inequality and test the relationship between local inequality and mortality. In addition, Landskrona is an interesting case for our purposes. First, the setting allows us to study the development in local inequality and its role in health during a period when income inequality first decreased, then stagnated, and then increased again in less than 30 years. While the underlying processes determining income inequality are generally known to be very stable and change little over time, the Gini coefficient for working-age individuals in Landskrona decreased from 0.44 to 0.25 and then increased again to 0.28 between 1935 and 1965 (see Chapter 3). Second, the socioeconomic mortality gradient in Sweden today has mostly appeared in the post-World War II period, an aspect that has been observed for both social class and income (Bengtsson and Dribe 2011; Bengtsson et al. 2020; Debiasi et al. 2023; see also Chapter 9), making Landskrona a relevant context for testing the AIH as well. This in turn makes it relevant to test the IIH in the Landskrona setting.

Theory

Economic inequality in Landskrona changed markedly over just a few decades in the mid-twentieth century. The analysis in Chapter 3 suggests that inequality significantly declined between 1930 and 1950, followed by almost no changes until the early 1990s. Can such a development have had an impact on people's health and well-being? And what would be the possible explanations for such a relationship? Below we discuss three parallel hypotheses[3] and their related mechanisms that are compatible with a negative association between income inequality and health.

The Income Inequality Hypothesis (IIH)

One explanation for why inequality might vary with health is that every individual suffers when there is an increase in income inequality, regardless of where they stand on the income ladder. This explanatory model is traditionally referred to as the "income inequality hypothesis." Several mechanisms may explain the observed relationship between income inequality and health: social structures, psychological phenomena, monetary factors, and political processes. These mechanisms primarily work at the micro level—among individuals or households—through either individual experience or interpersonal connections. Other mechanisms generally operate at the macro level, where societal structures related to the healthcare system, economic growth, and redistribution of resources matter.

A first possible mechanism relates to trust and social cohesion. Research has demonstrated that societies with high income inequality are often characterized by low levels of trust and confidence between people and by minimal involvement in civic society and social networks (see Jordahl 2007; Putnam 2000). Some believe that significant income differences reduce trust. The reasons are that inequality can be interpreted as a sign that some individuals in society act in unreliable ways and entrench their position at the expense of others, and experimental research also shows that we tend to trust others who are relatively similar to ourselves in terms of, say, income (Coleman 1990; Fukuyama 1995). The link to health is mainly based on psychosocial mechanisms. Trust can increase the individual's sense of security. Access to social networks can affect health when the individual is offered social support in a stressful situation and given access to health-related knowledge (Baum 1999; Kawachi et al. 2008).

A second possible mechanism that may allow income inequality to affect health is that societies with large income disparities often have problems with crime and violence. According to sociological theory, high crime rates go hand in hand with income inequality as those who feel permanently locked into their economic situation experience frustration and alienation. Over time, this feeling of alienation eventually breaks down societal values and results in greater levels of crime (Merton 1968). Economic theory also predicts a positive relationship between economic inequality and property crime. Large income disparities can encourage the view that the expected returns from crime are generally greater than the returns from legal activities (Becker 1968; Ehrlich 1973). Crime and violence can in turn have direct negative health effects on victims of crime as well as trigger mental health problems in others out of fear and concern that they, too, or their loved ones will be exposed to crime and violence (Demombynes and Ozler 2005; Green and Grimsley 2002).

A third possible mechanism relates to policy and the supply of public goods. When high income means greater political power as well, the self-interests of elite groups may dictate which political reforms are implemented (Krugman 1996). In this scenario, tax cuts and the setting of priorities in public healthcare may be more detrimental to the poor than the rich, which may in turn be more detrimental to population health. Even in the context of a democratic political process, healthcare expenditures and the funding of the healthcare system may be related to economic inequality. For example, the richer and poorer may have conflicts of interest regarding how public resources should be used (Alesina et al. 1999; Zweifel et al. 2009).

In summary, the aggregation level of inequality can be crucial for identifying the mechanisms we believe may be at work for the IIH. In our setting, where we examined neighborhood income inequality and its relevance for adult mortality, the most likely mechanisms are the two that mirror either trust and social cohesion or crime and violence. Our assumption is that the political mechanism must be less relevant in this setting since there was surely no large variation in terms of access to public goods or differences in taxation across neighborhoods in Landskrona during the period of our study.

The Relative Income Hypothesis (RIH)

A somewhat different starting point as to why inequality matters for our well-being and health is that people make social comparisons and assess their lives by comparing their social status to that of others. From an economic perspective, we can think of social status in monetary terms and the fact that individuals perceive their place in the "social hierarchy" to be relative to others in the income distribution. The greater the income differences in a society, the more aware people presumably are of their social status in this respect. The social comparisons we make to others who have greater (more visible) economic resources may cause chronic stress, which could in turn give rise to poor physical health over time and consequently also affect mortality. For example, people with a lower income may feel lower self-esteem and greater shame when comparing themselves to wealthier individuals living in the same neighborhood (Wilkinson and Pickett 2009). Social status comparisons could also cause stress by making the individual feel that they are not in control of their life (Marmot et al. 1991).

Consequently, a relative income effect on health may exist, which is referred to in the literature as the "relative income hypothesis." Essential here for individual health and well-being is the difference between an individual's income and the income of a reference group; that is, the individual's income is seen in relation to the average income of others and used by the individual for comparison. According to this hypothesis, an individual who feels that everyone else is becoming better off in terms of their income and economic position while his or her own is unchanged will consequently feel worse off.[4] Hirschman (1973) compared this to a situation in which a driver who is stuck in traffic and sees the cars in the other lanes starting to move forward will become frustrated. The argument that making social comparisons will in turn affect the individual's general health refers to a body of literature on primate health (see, e.g., Sapolsky et al. 1997 on subordinate baboons having higher stress levels than their superiors) and also to experimental research on how the stimulation of anger and frustration gives rise to stress, which in turn has physiological effects.

The RIH is consistent with a negative relationship between income inequality and population health (Wagstaff and van Doorslaer 2000). Thus, the RIH is a competing hypothesis to the IIH and should be tested in parallel. Since the RIH thesis concerns the relationship between an individual's economic position and that of their peers, an appropriate test of the RIH is to see how the average income of the individual's neighborhood affects their health or longevity while also controlling for individual income. Such a test will show how the average income in a neighborhood affects individual health when everyone else, but not the individual him- or herself, on average gets economically better off.

The Absolute Income Hypothesis (AIH)

If health depends on economic resources and if this relationship is nonlinear, then the level of absolute income provides another possible explanation for the negative relationship between inequality and population health. There are several reasons why income matters for health and well-being. First, those with a low income probably cannot afford certain goods that are important for health or, to a lesser extent, cannot consume health services (Deaton 2002). Second, the quality of medical treatment may depend on the ability to pay. Third, income can be relevant to health when a low-paid job is associated with more health risks (e.g., jobs with higher danger or negative exposures). And, last, there may be differences in health-related behaviors between rich and poor, such as smoking, alcohol consumption, diet, and exercise (Östling et al. 2020). It is also likely that health returns to income, regardless of the mechanisms that are driving the relationship, diminish with a rise in income. In other words, one extra dollar given to a deprived individual will increase their health status more than the same extra dollar spent on a rich individual.

Notably, health and well-being may also affect earnings. Individuals with poor health face reduced work opportunities and lower earnings when they are able to work. This is, for example, illustrated in research revealing that hospitalizations among adults lead to subsequent declines in earnings (Dobkin et al. 2018). Moreover, it is crucial to acknowledge that various factors can contribute to both good health and higher income. For instance, self-control or better knowledge of the health production function is a potential third factor that may be associated with income, and more affluent parents may be more inclined to invest in the healthcare of their children while also striving to ensure their economic prosperity. Taken together, it is a difficult task to make causal statements about the relationship between income and health, and systematic empirical evaluations suggest causal effects of income appear to vary over time, space, and context (Lleras-Muney 2022).

To sum up, three parallel hypotheses are compatible with a negative association between income inequality and population health. This implies that they should be tested simultaneously, including all three factors in the same empirical model.

Data and Methods

Data

We used the Scanian Economic-Demographic Database (SEDD) with individual-level longitudinal data for Landskrona (Bengtsson et al. 2021; see also Chapter 1). The database includes annual information on income, occupation, and mortality for all individuals and their families in Landskrona during 1939–1967. For the same period, we also have geocoded the residential histories of the entire population of Landskrona at the address level (Hedefalk and Dribe 2020). Because each move has been traced within the city boundaries, we have continuous information about an individual's place of residence at a very detailed geographic level (Figure 10.1). In addition, individuals have been linked with accuracy to the buildings where they resided because the start and end dates of the buildings and streets in Landskrona are known.[5]

Our first step was to describe the pattern and development of spatial inequality over time in Landskrona. Next, we tested the three hypotheses regarding income, income inequality, and mortality (the AIH, RIH, IIH). To do so, we focused on two mortality outcomes: early-adulthood death (dying before age 50) and dying before the life expectancy of the cohorts studied (age 70) (see Dribe and Eriksson 2023). We observed and followed the individuals who were present in Landskrona between 1939 and 1967 and aged between 18 and 70 years.

We used total annual income at the family level, which was derived as the equivalized family income for each family j in a given year t. This method of equivalence follows the guidelines of the Organisation for Economic Co-operation and Development (OECD) adopted in most studies dealing with family poverty and economic inequality and helps us understand how much income a family has available to meet their basic needs (Brea-Martinez et al., 2023). It considers the family's size and income accordingly so we can compare the financial situations of different families more accurately (OECD 2011).

$$\text{Equivalized family income}_{jt} = \Sigma(income)_{jt} / \sqrt{\left[\Sigma(size)_{jt}\right]} \qquad (10.1)$$

The descriptive results display Landskrona's evolving demographic and economic spatial patterns for the study period (see Table 10.1). We present three indicators by 250 m² grids for 6 benchmark years covering (1) neighborhood population density, (2) average family income per neighborhood, and (3) the annual within-neighborhood Gini coefficient.[6]

We analyzed the adult long-term exposure to inequality by using the income information in two ways. First, to study mortality before age 50, we followed

Table 10.1 Descriptive statistics of the variables used in the logistic regressions.

Sample P(mortality before age 50): exposure ages 18–50

Variables	N	Mean	SD	Min	Max
Deaths before age 50 (percent)	9,337	5		0	100
Ln average family inc.	9,088	9.84	0.74	3.5	12.68
Ln average grid income	9,337	9.78	0.51	6.49	11.49
Average grid Gini	9,337	0.33	0.05	0.01	0.66
Women (percent)	9,337	50		0	100
Birth year	9,337	1904	8.54	1888	1947
Maximum HISCLASS	9,337	3.85	1.81	1	7
Born in Landskrona (percent)	9,337	42		0	100
N of observations	9,337	13.74	7.86	1	29

Sample P(mortality before age 70): exposure ages 18–70

Variables	N	Mean	SD	Min	Max
Deaths before age 70 (percent)	6,103	33		0	100
Ln average family inc.	5,843	9.63	0.83	5.7	12.83
Ln average grid income	6,103	9.82	0.46	6.77	11.73
Average grid Gini	6,103	0.33	0.05	0.02	0.62
Women (percent)	6,103	52		0	100
Birth year	6,103	1889	12.03	1868	1947
Maximum HISCLASS	6,103	4.17	1.94	1	7
Born in Landskrona (percent)	6,103	38		0	100
N of observations	6,103	15.17	7.77	1	29

Source: Own calculations based on Scanian Economic-Demographic Database (SEDD) (Bengtsson et al. 2021).

those individuals living in Landskrona between 1939 and 1967 from age 18 either until death before age 50 or until they were censored from our study on turning 50. We then repeated the procedure for individuals aged 18–70.

In examining the AIH, we averaged the annual family income for each individual studied over the period of observation (aged 18–49 or 18–69). In addition, we averaged the annual family income by neighborhood to examine the RIH. We averaged the income of all neighborhoods in which the individual resided during the period of observation. Finally, we examined the IIH by calculating the within-municipality Gini coefficient for each year and averaged this for the individual's period of observation by the neighborhood in which they lived.

In the regressions we used basic demographic and socioeconomic controls. The control variables were gender, year of birth, the total number of observations of the individual, the highest social class achieved in the period of observation (using HISCLASS), and whether the individual was born in Landskrona. Table 10.1 presents the descriptive statistics for all variables.

We were interested in the individual's long-term and cumulative exposure to income inequality at the neighborhood level, so the data used has a pooled format that merges all individuals' observations into only one, averaging all the characteristics from individuals. In this regard, we can capture the cumulative health exposure of people across their adult life. We used logistic regressions to model the probability of dying before ages 50 and 70, respectively. We display the results in terms of average marginal effects to make correct comparisons across subsamples (Mood 2010). The modeling strategy has been done stepwise. First, we included a regression model with sociodemographic controls and the averaged family income (for testing AIH). Next, we added the average neighborhood income (for testing RIH), and finally, we included the averaged neighborhood annual Gini coefficient (for testing IIH). We estimated the models for both men and women together and separately to capture possible gender differences in the association between income, relative income, income inequality, and health.

Results

Descriptive Results

Figure 10.1 displays the evolving population density by neighborhood in Landskrona for 6 benchmark years (1940, 1945, 1950, 1955, 1960, and 1965). The colors scaled from light (lower levels) to dark (higher levels) were classified using sextiles and represent each neighborhood's population density over time. Moreover, the maps show reference points for the city's main square, secondary

INCOME, INEQUALITY, AND GEOGRAPHY 317

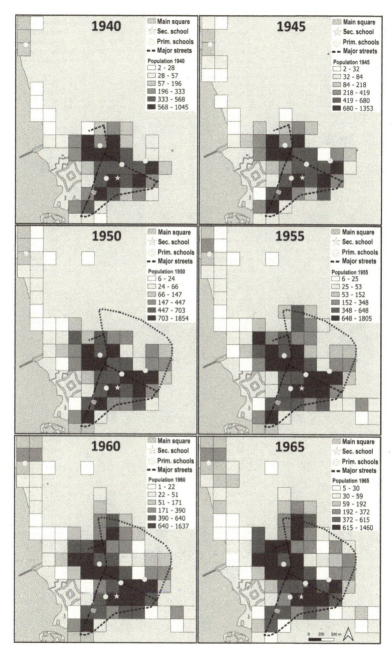

Figure 10.1 Population in Landskrona by 250 m² grids in six different years (1940–1965).
Quantiles (sextiles) are used to group the population values. Only populated grid-cells are shown in the maps.
Source: Own calculations based on Scanian Economic-Demographic Database (SEDD) (Bengtsson et al. 2021).

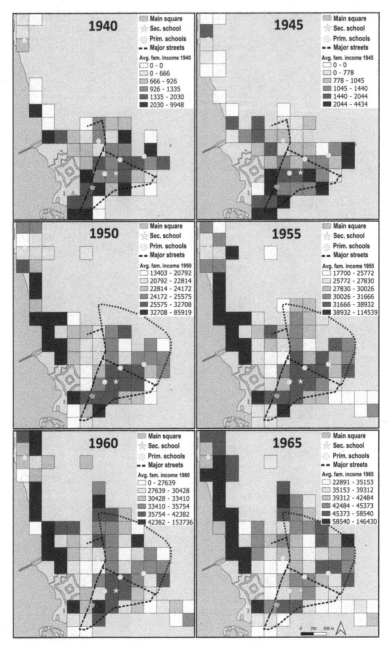

Figure 10.2 Mean family income in Landskrona by 250 m² grids in six different years (1940–1965).
Quantiles (sextiles) are used to group the mean family income values. Only populated grid-cells are shown in the maps.

Source: Own calculations based on Scanian Economic-Demographic Database (SEDD) (Bengtsson et al. 2021).

INCOME, INEQUALITY, AND GEOGRAPHY 319

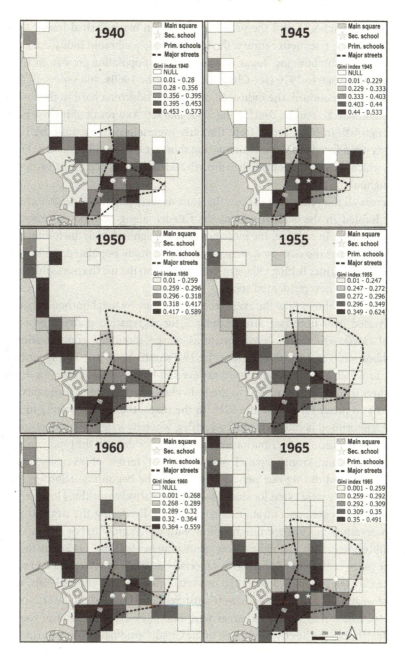

Figure 10.3 Gini index in Landskrona by 250 m² grids in six different years (1940–1965).
Quantiles (quintiles) are used to group the Gini coefficients. Populated grid cells that have a missing Gini index (due zero mean family income) belong to the NULL group.
Source: Own calculations based on Scanian Economic-Demographic Database (SEDD) (Bengtsson et al. 2021).

and primary schools, and the principal streets (in black dashed lines). In the first half of the twentieth century, the town experienced rapid industrialization connected to shipbuilding, sugar, and textiles. The population grew from 13,000 in 1900 to 30,000 in 1970 (see Chapter 2). From the 1960s, and especially from the mid-1970s onward, the industrial crisis hit Landskrona hard in the form of population decline and a contracting labor market. As a result of intense population growth in Landskrona from the early twentieth century until the 1970s, the city often faced problems with housing shortages. This is illustrated in Figure 10.1, which shows both rapid urban growth and high levels of population density throughout the period.

Across all the years under study, the most densely populated neighborhoods were located in the eastern part of the Citadel, along or near the main city thoroughfares. In contrast, the more peripheral neighborhoods, including those that emerged as the city grew, were usually less densely populated. An example of this is the former fishing village of Borstahusen on the north coast, which over time became a new residential area.

Figure 10.2 shows how the average family income by neighborhood changed and varied over time (see also Chapter 5 for segregation patterns based on social class). The figure reveals patterns of the economic concentration of neighborhoods in Landskrona from the 1940s until 1970. The average income level to which the inhabitants were exposed in their own neighborhoods and in others is intrinsically related to the individual's perception of inequality and works as a proxy for testing the RIH. In the maps, the average family income by neighborhood is categorized into sextiles, whereby a light color denotes the bottom of the income distribution and a darker color denotes the top.

Overall, Landskrona's spatial segregation in terms of average income levels increased during our period of study. In the beginning, relatively poor neighborhoods were often located close to the relatively wealthy. However, the pattern of income concentration changed gradually during the near 30 years of observation and was seemingly in line with urban growth. For instance, the neighborhoods with the highest average income in 1940 and 1945 were located in the more central areas of the city, especially near the main square and south of the Citadel. However, from 1950 onward, and especially in the 1960s, most of the wealthiest neighborhoods were clustered near the coast and north of the Citadel, where new residential areas were built. The concentration of wealthy neighborhoods in the city center east of the Citadel gradually shrank during this period.

In contrast, the poorer areas followed the opposite trend. They were initially clustered on the north coast near the fishing village of Borstahusen in the 1940s, but, by the 1960s, the poorest neighborhoods were increasingly found in the city center and the outskirts southwest of Landskrona.

Finally, we illustrate spatial inequality in Landskrona using Gini coefficients for the years under study. Figure 10.3 illustrates the Gini trend shown in quintiles and labeled by intensity, with a light color representing low inequality and a dark color higher income disparity. The figure shows important within-city inequality variation as the Gini coefficients are almost four times higher in some neighborhoods than others. This variation follows a marked spatial and temporal pattern. We can see a particular change in the concentration of low and high income inequality neighborhoods from the 1940s to the 1960s.

Figure 10.3 also indicates the overall pattern of income inequality in the city during this period (see Chapter 3). For instance, almost all neighborhoods in 1940 and 1945 are dark colors, when the Gini coefficient measure for overall inequality in Landskrona was about 0.4. Conversely, we see neighborhoods in light colors, from 1950 onward, that denote lower within-neighborhood inequality, and this was at a time when inequality in the city overall was below 0.3. More specifically, in 1940 and 1945, within-neighborhood inequality was usually concentrated at higher levels (with the Gini above 0.3) in the city center, an area also characterized by higher mean income. At the same time, areas further away from the city center show a low concentration of within-neighborhood disparity, with Gini coefficients below 0.25.

It is notable that, for the years 1960 and 1965, we observe how the pattern of within-neighborhood inequality, one that was initially high, started to vary as income inequality increased in areas where it had previously been low. This change may be explained in part by the new residential areas built in the north of the city from the end of the 1950s, and by the new socioeconomic configuration, which progressively changed from being an area of low inequality to one with a much more mixed pattern.

When we relate Figure 10.3 to Figure 10.2, we observe two compositions of high-inequality grids. On the one hand, several neighborhoods with high income inequality also had a relatively high average income, an aspect one might expect since within-neighborhood inequality tends to be high among relatively wealthy groups. On the other hand, some neighborhoods representing the lowest average income group also had relatively high income inequality.

Regression Results

We now move on to the regression results. We estimated three regression models to examine the association between adult mortality and long-term exposure to inequality at the neighborhood level and the relative economic position of individuals in comparison to peers in their neighborhood, as well as their absolute income. Table 10.2 displays the marginal effects for the three main variables

Table 10.2 Marginal effects for variables of interest from all models.

	Mortality age 50 (1)			Mortality age 70 (2)		
	Model 1	Model 2	Model 3	Model 1	Model 2	Model 3
All: exposure since age 18 (A)						
Ln average family income	−0.03***	−0.01***	−0.01***	−0.05***	0.01	0.01*
Ln average grid income		−0.08***	−0.08***		−0.39***	−0.38***
Standardized average grid Gini			0.01***			0.05***
Men: exposure since age 18 (B)						
Ln average family income	−0.04***	−0.01**	−0.01**	−0.05***	0.03*	0.03**
Ln average grid income		−0.11***	−0.10***		−0.41***	−0.40***
Standardized average grid Gini			0.01***			0.05***
Women: exposure since age 18 (C)						
Ln average family income	−0.02***	−0.01***	−0.01***	−0.05***	0	0
Ln average grid income		−0.06***	−0.06***		−0.36***	−0.35***
Standardized average grid Gini			0.01***			0.05***
All–exposure since 10 years before; age 40 (1) and age 60 (2) (D)						
Ln average family income	−0.01***	−0.01***	−0.01**	0.01	0.03***	0.03***
Ln average grid income		−0.03***	−0.03***		−0.13***	−0.14***
Standardized average grid Gini			0			0.02***

Note: ***p < 0.01, **p < 0.05, *p < 0.1.
Source: Own calculations based on Scanian Economic-Demographic Database (SEDD) (Bengtsson et al. 2021).

of interest; namely, the logarithm of the mean family income, neighborhood mean income, and mean within-neighborhood inequality to which individuals were exposed over time based on the neighborhood in which they resided over the years. We present the marginal effects for both our main outcomes: mortality before ages 50 and 70.

Panel A at the top of Table 10.2 presents the results for the full sample regarding long-term exposure (averaged information from age 18). Model 1 includes mean family income for the individual, which shows a slightly negative association with mortality; the increase in the long-term family income reduced the probability of dying before age 50 or 70 by 3–5 percentage points. Model 2 includes the mean neighborhood income for all individuals. Here we note contrasting magnitudes for the two outcomes studied. For individuals dying before age 50, an increase in the mean neighborhood income is associated with a decrease of 0.08 in the probability of dying, whereas for those dying before age 70, the increase is associated with a decrease of almost 40 percentage points.

Model 3 includes the within-neighborhood inequality exposure. Once again, we find negative and statistically significant associations for mean family income, in line with the AIH, and a negative relationship for mean neighborhood income. The result for average Gini exposure indicates a positive and statistically significant association, in line with the IIH stating that inequality is bad for individual health over and above one's absolute level of income. Each unit increase by one standard deviation in the average Gini coefficient increases the probability of dying before ages 50 and 70 by 0.01 and 0.05, respectively, a relatively big increase given the small number of individuals dying before these ages.

Panels B and C present estimation results by gender. Overall, these results suggest similar patterns for both men and women and for that observed in Panel A for the pooled sample, with only some difference in magnitudes. For example, we note slightly lower magnitudes for women, especially regarding the impact of mean neighborhood income and within-neighborhood inequality on mortality at ages 50 and 70.

We also see similar patterns in the baseline regression when restricting the span of observation for the individual's exposure from age 18 up to 10 years before the cut-off points (i.e., up to ages 40 and 60 on the probability of dying before ages 50 and 70, respectively; Panel D). One main difference between the results of the two models concerns magnitudes, which are generally lower in this specification and explore more recent exposure compared to the baseline. Similarly, the neighborhood inequality estimate is lower in Panel D than in Panel A. This finding gives an indication of the relevance of accurately capturing long-term exposure in studying the role between relative income and income inequality and health and well-being.

In all specifications, the marginal effects for the control variables are in line with what we expected based on theory and previous empirical work (see Tables A10.1–A10.6 for full specifications). Notably, men had a higher probability of dying than women, and, similarly, individuals born in the city of Landskrona had a higher probability of dying than those born outside of the city.

As a final test of sensitivity, we ran the models without adding information on social class. In Table A10.7, we see that, by excluding HISCLASS for likely disparities in the risk of dying, all three variables of interest (family income, neighborhood income, and the neighborhood Gini) still show the same associations noted in the baseline setting. Finally, by adding the squared term of the Gini index in Table 10.1 we conclude that the relationship between income inequality and the risk of dying before ages 50 and 70 is still weak and mainly linear.

Conclusion

This chapter provides insights into the spatial development of income inequality in an industrial city in Sweden over a period when overall income disparities decreased and there was rapid expansion of the welfare state. Despite the notable overall decline in income inequality, we find remarkable spatial differences in income concentration and distribution across neighborhoods in Landskrona. In our empirical analysis, we explore this variation in order to understand the possible health effects in relation to such economic inequalities.

We tested three hypotheses linking income inequality and mortality and focusing particularly on long-term exposure and the role of local neighborhood influences. The results from our full regression models show that exposure to high mean neighborhood incomes can increase survival. This association between relative income (RIH) and mortality is stronger in the case of mortality before age 70 than in that of mortality before age 50. One should bear in mind here that the incidence of early-adult deaths before age 50 was low in our sample (around 3 percent).

Taken together, we find no support for the RIH as stated in the literature, which finds other people's average income, conditioned on own income, to be harmful for one's own health and well-being (Daly et al. 2013; Eibner and Evans 2005; Jones and Wildman 2008). Instead, our results align with what Hirschman (1973) called a "signaling effect" when he likened this to a situation where an individual who is stuck in traffic sees the cars in the other lanes starting to move forward. If the individual interprets this as meaning that he or she, too, will soon start rolling, then this inequality could actually reduce stress and increase well-being and health. Similarly, knowing that the neighbors have a higher income or have been given a pay raise might also improve health and well-being if this is interpreted as: "If she can do it, so can I" or "Soon it will be my turn to receive a higher income." Given that individuals in the neighborhood are quite similar, our testing of the RIH on this very local geographical level partially relates to studies considering reference groups based on common characteristics other than just geographical proximity. Miller and Paxson (2006) suggest that the RIH should be tested with reference to average income within the subgroup of the population to which the individual belongs. Their study, focusing on the United States, uncovers no support for the notion that residing in close proximity to prosperous neighbors leads to heightened mortality, but they find evidence that certain age cohorts experience a decrease in mortality risks when residing in communities with relatively affluent neighbors.[7] Interestingly, our results also align with research that focuses on the role of contemporary relative income in Swedish municipalities, finding a positive RIH effect of mortality (Gerdtham and Johannesson 2004).

Regarding the question of whether income inequality is detrimental to individual health in the case of long-term exposure and when disparities are measured at the local level, we find support for the IIH. As noted in reviews of the literature and in a meta-analysis (Wilkinson and Pickett 2006; Kondo et al. 2014), the literature on inequality and health has found more evidence in support of the IIH at relatively high geographic scales. Our results show that, in the case of long-term exposure, we may also find support for the hypothesis at a lower geographic aggregation, such as the neighborhood level, even if income inequality in small areas may be affected by the residential segregation of rich and poor—segregation that serves to increase inequality between areas and diminish inequality within them.

A main contribution of this chapter in relation to the existing literature is that we focus on long-term inequality exposure. If it takes time for the health effects of income inequality to manifest themselves, approaches that use near simultaneous measures of income inequality and health will underestimate the long-term effects. Our results suggest that temporality and cessation of exposure matter, and estimated magnitudes across the different empirical models indicate that long exposure in adulthood to income inequality is more detrimental to individual health than is more recent exposure. Our study thus confirms previous research that claims that the association between health outcomes and exposure to inequality over a span of up to 15 years holds greater significance compared to the association between health and immediate levels of inequality (Blakely et al. 2000; Kondo et al. 2012; Zheng 2012).

We cannot test possible mechanisms, but the level of aggregation used for the period of exposure in our study suggests that the positive relationship between income inequality and mortality is channeled through either (1) trust and social cohesion, or (2) crime and violence, or both. Theoretically, the positive relationship between income inequality and adult mortality could also be explained by public policy decisions on issues such as healthcare and educational expenditure taken at the city rather than the neighborhood level. The results are thus consistent with growing evidence that certain social outcomes associated with disadvantage in society are more common in contexts with greater inequality between rich and poor (Pickett and Wilkinson 2015).

Finally, when comparing all three of the main variables studied, we find mixed evidence for the AIH. This is interesting when seen in relation to—and possibly also explained in part by—the fact that the socioeconomic gradient in health in Sweden only seems to appear near the end of the study period.

Taken together, factors such as own family income, living in wealthier neighborhoods for a long time, and exposure to more unequal neighborhoods can all impact individual health and survival. It is worth noting that the association between relative income and income inequality with mortality moves in opposite directions when mortality is measured at the neighborhood level. This suggests that the health effects of a person's relative position in the income distribution, compared to their peers, can differ from the health effects of income inequality in the broader neighborhood context.

Appendix

Table A10.1 Full model marginal effects for the probability of dying before age 50.

	Model 1	Model 2	Model 3
Women (Men ref.)	−0.02***	−0.02***	−0.02***
	(0.00)	(0.00)	(0.00)
Birth year	0.01***	0.01***	0.01***
	(0.00)	(0.00)	(0.00)
Low skilled (ref)			
Higher managers	−0.01	−0.00	−0.01
	(0.01)	(0.01)	(0.01)
Lower managers	−0.00	−0.00	−0.00
	(0.00)	(0.00)	(0.00)
Skilled workers	−0.01	−0.01	−0.01
	(0.01)	(0.00)	(0.00)
Unskilled workers	−0.01	−0.01	−0.01
	(0.01)	(0.01)	(0.01)
NA	0.01	0.02	0.02
	(0.01)	(0.01)	(0.01)
Born in Landskrona	0.03***	0.02***	0.02***
	(0.00)	(0.00)	(0.00)
N of observations	−0.00***	−0.00***	−0.00***
	(0.00)	(0.00)	(0.00)
Ln of average family income	−0.03***	−0.01***	−0.01***
	(0.00)	(0.00)	(0.00)
Ln of average grid income		−0.08***	−0.08***
		(0.01)	(0.01)
Average Gini (standardized)			0.01***
			(0.00)
N	9,088	9,088	9,088

Note: ***p < 0.01, **p < 0.05, *p < 0.1.
Source: Own calculations based on Scanian Economic-Demographic Database (SEDD) (Bengtsson et al. 2021).

Table A10.2 Marginal effects of the full logistic regression models on the probability of dying before age 70 in Landskrona, 1939–1967.

	Model 1	Model 2	Model 3
Women (Men ref.)	−0.02***	−0.02***	−0.02***
	(0.00)	(0.00)	(0.00)
Birth year	0.01***	0.01***	0.01***
	(0.00)	(0.00)	(0.00)
Low skilled (ref)			
Higher managers	−0.01	−0.00	−0.01
	(0.01)	(0.01)	(0.01)
Lower managers	−0.00	−0.00	−0.00
	(0.00)	(0.00)	(0.00)
Skilled workers	−0.01	−0.01	−0.01
	(0.01)	(0.00)	(0.00)
Unskilled workers	−0.01	−0.01	−0.01
	(0.01)	(0.01)	(0.01)
NA	0.01	0.02	0.02
	(0.01)	(0.01)	(0.01)
Born in Landskrona	0.03***	0.02***	0.02***
	(0.00)	(0.00)	(0.00)
N of observations	−0.00***	−0.00***	−0.00***
	(0.00)	(0.00)	(0.00)
Ln of average family income	−0.03***	−0.01***	−0.01***
	(0.00)	(0.00)	(0.00)
Ln of average grid income		−0.08***	−0.08***
		(0.01)	(0.01)
Average Gini (standardized)			0.01***
			(0.00)
N	9,088	9,088	9,088

Note: ***p < 0.01, **p < 0.05, *p < 0.1

Source: Own calculations based on Scanian Economic-Demographic Database (SEDD) (Bengtsson et al. 2021).

Table A10.3 Marginal effects of the full logistic regression models on the probability of dying before age 50 with exposure measured on ages 40–50 in Landskrona, 1939–1967.

	Model 1	Model 2	Model 3
Women (Men ref.)	−0.02***	−0.02***	−0.02***
	(0.00)	(0.00)	(0.00)
Birth year	0.00***	0.01***	0.01***
	(0.00)	(0.00)	(0.00)
Low skilled (ref)			
Higher managers	−0.01*	−0.01	−0.01
	(0.01)	(0.01)	(0.01)
Lower managers	−0.01	−0.00	−0.00
	(0.00)	(0.00)	(0.00)
Skilled workers	−0.01	−0.01	−0.01
	(0.00)	(0.00)	(0.00)
Unskilled workers	−0.01	−0.01	−0.01
	(0.01)	(0.01)	(0.01)
NA	0.01	0.01	0.01
	(0.01)	(0.01)	(0.01)
Born in Landskrona	0.02***	0.02***	0.02***
	(0.00)	(0.00)	(0.00)
N of observations	−0.01***	−0.01***	−0.01***
	(0.00)	(0.00)	(0.00)
Ln of average family income	−0.01***	−0.01***	−0.01**
	(0.00)	(0.00)	(0.00)
Ln of average grid income		−0.03***	−0.03***
		(0.00)	(0.00)
Average Gini (standardized)			0.00
			(0.00)
N	8,873	8,873	8,873

Note: ***$p < 0.01$, **$p < 0.05$, *$p < 0.1$.

Source: Own calculations based on Scanian Economic-Demographic Database (SEDD) (Bengtsson et al. 2021).

Table A10.4 Marginal effects of the full logistic regression models on the probability of dying before age 70 with exposure measured on ages 60–70 in Landskrona, 1939–1967.

	Model 1	Model 2	Model 3
Women (Men ref.)	−0.04***	−0.03***	−0.04***
	(0.01)	(0.01)	(0.01)
Birth year	0.01***	0.02***	0.02***
	(0.00)	(0.00)	(0.00)
Low skilled (ref)			
Higher managers	−0.01	−0.01	−0.02
	(0.02)	(0.02)	(0.02)
Lower managers	−0.01	−0.00	−0.01
	(0.01)	(0.01)	(0.01)
Skilled workers	−0.03*	−0.03*	−0.03*
	(0.01)	(0.01)	(0.01)
Unskilled workers	−0.00	−0.00	−0.00
	(0.02)	(0.02)	(0.02)
NA	−0.05***	−0.05***	−0.05***
	(0.01)	(0.01)	(0.01)
Born in Landskrona	0.03**	0.02**	0.02**
	(0.01)	(0.01)	(0.01)
N of observations	−0.04***	−0.04***	−0.04***
	(0.00)	(0.00)	(0.00)
Ln of average family income	0.01	0.03***	0.03***
	(0.01)	(0.01)	(0.01)
Ln of average grid income		−0.13***	−0.14***
		(0.02)	(0.02)
Average Gini (standardized)			0.02***
			(0.00)
N	4,839	4,839	4,839

Note: ***$p < 0.01$, **$p < 0.05$, *$p < 0.1$.

Source: Own calculations based on Scanian Economic-Demographic Database (SEDD) (Bengtsson et al. 2021).

Table A10.5 Marginal effects of the full logistic regression models on the probability of dying before age 50 in Landskrona, 1939–1967, by gender.

	Model 1: Men	Model 1: Women	Model 2: Men	Model 2: Women	Model 3: Men	Model 3: Women
Birth year	0.01***	0.01***	0.01***	0.01***	0.01***	0.01***
	(0.00)	(0.00)	(0.00)	(0.00)	(0.00)	(0.00)
Low skilled (ref)						
Higher managers	−0.00	0.00	0.00	0.00	−0.00	0.00
	(0.01)	(0.00)	(0.01)	(0.00)	(0.01)	(0.00)
Lower managers	−0.00	−0.00	0.00	0.00	−0.00	−0.00
	(0.01)	(0.01)	(0.01)	(0.01)	(0.01)	(0.01)
Skilled workers	−0.00	−0.01*	−0.00	−0.01*	−0.00	−0.01*
	(0.01)	(0.01)	(0.01)	(0.01)	(0.01)	(0.01)
Unskilled workers	−0.01	−0.02*	−0.00	−0.01*	−0.00	−0.01
	(0.01)	(0.01)	(0.01)	(0.01)	(0.01)	(0.01)
NA	0.06	−0.00	0.09	0.01	0.08	0.01
	(0.07)	(0.01)	(0.07)	(0.01)	(0.07)	(0.01)
Born in Landskrona	0.03***	0.02***	0.02**	0.01**	0.02**	0.01**
	(0.01)	(0.01)	(0.01)	(0.01)	(0.01)	(0.01)
N of observations	−0.00**	−0.00***	−0.00***	−0.00***	−0.00**	−0.00***
	(0.00)	(0.00)	(0.00)	(0.00)	(0.00)	(0.00)
Ln of average family income	−0.04**	−0.02***	−0.01**	−0.01***	−0.01**	−0.01***
	(0.00)	(0.00)	(0.00)	(0.00)	(0.00)	(0.00)
Ln of average grid income			−0.11***	−0.06***	−0.10***	−0.06***
			(0.01)	(0.01)	(0.01)	(0.01)
Average Gini (standardized)					0.01***	0.01***
					(0.00)	(0.00)
N	4,524	4,450	4,524	4,450	4,524	4,450

Note: ***$p < 0.01$, **$p < 0.05$, *$p < 0.1$.

Source: Own calculations based on Scanian Economic-Demographic Database (SEDD) (Bengtsson et al. 2021).

Table A10.6 Marginal effects of the full logistic regression models on the probability of dying before age 70 in Landskrona, 1939–1967, by gender.

	Model 1: Men	Model 1: Women	Model 2: Men	Model 2: Women	Model 3: Men	Model 3: Women
Birth year	0.03***	0.03***	0.04***	0.04***	0.05***	0.04***
	(0.00)	(0.00)	(0.00)	(0.00)	(0.00)	(0.00)
Low skilled (ref)						
Higher managers	0.03	0.09*	0.05	0.08	0.00	0.03
	(0.03)	(0.04)	(0.03)	(0.04)	(0.02)	(0.04)
Lower managers	−0.01	−0.01	−0.00	0.01	−0.01	−0.01
	(0.02)	(0.02)	(0.02)	(0.02)	(0.02)	(0.02)
Skilled workers	−0.01	−0.05**	−0.01	−0.04*	−0.01	−0.03*
	(0.02)	(0.02)	(0.02)	(0.02)	(0.02)	(0.02)
Unskilled workers	−0.04	0.01	−0.01	−0.01	−0.01	−0.01
	(0.02)	(0.03)	(0.02)	(0.02)	(0.02)	(0.02)
NA	−0.23***	−0.03	−0.16**	−0.02	−0.16**	−0.02
	(0.06)	(0.02)	(0.05)	(0.01)	(0.05)	(0.01)
Born in Landskrona	0.05***	0.02	0.04**	0.01	0.03**	0.01
	(0.01)	(0.01)	(0.01)	(0.01)	(0.01)	(0.01)
N of observations	−0.02***	−0.01***	−0.02***	−0.02***	−0.02***	−0.02***
	(0.00)	(0.00)	(0.00)	(0.00)	(0.00)	(0.00)
Ln of average family income	−0.05***	−0.05***	0.03*	−0.00	0.03**	0.00
	(0.01)	(0.01)	(0.01)	(0.01)	(0.01)	(0.01)
Ln of average grid income			−0.41***	−0.36***	−0.40***	−0.35***
			(0.02)	(0.02)	(0.02)	(0.02)
Average Gini (standardized)					0.05***	0.05***
					(0.00)	(0.01)
N	2,851	2,992	2,851	2,992	2,851	2,992

Note: ***$p < 0.01$, **$p < 0.05$, *$p < 0.1$.

Source: Own calculations based on Scanian Economic-Demographic Database (SEDD) (Bengtsson et al. 2021).

Table A10.7 Marginal effects of the full logistic regression models on the probability of dying before age 50 and 70 without HISCLASS in Landskrona, 1939–1967.

	Age 50	Age 70
Women (Men ref.)	−0.01***	−0.04***
	(0.00)	(0.01)
Birth year	0.01***	0.04***
	(0.00)	(0.00)
Born in Landskrona	0.02***	0.02**
	(0.00)	(0.01)
N of observations	−0.00***	−0.02***
	(0.00)	(0.00)
ln Family Income	−0.01***	0.02**
	(0.00)	(0.01)
ln Grid Income	−0.08***	−0.40***
	(0.01)	(0.01)
Grid Gini	0.01***	0.05***
	(0.00)	(0.00)
N	9,015	5,843

Note: ***p < 0.01, **p < 0.05, *p < 0.1.

Source: Own calculations based on Scanian Economic-Demographic Database (SEDD) (Bengtsson et al. 2021).

Table A10.8 Marginal effects of the full logistic regression models on the probability of dying before age 50 and 70 in Landskrona 1939–1967, adding Gini and squared Gini terms for controlling for non-linear associations.

	Age 50	Age 70
Women (Men ref.)	−0.02***	−0.04***
	(0.00)	(0.01)
Birth year	0.01***	0.04***
	(0.00)	(0.00)
Low skilled (ref)		
Higher managers	−0.01	0.01
	(0.01)	(0.02)
Lower managers	−0.00	−0.01
	(0.00)	(0.01)
Skilled workers	−0.01	−0.02
	(0.00)	(0.01)
Unskilled workers	−0.01	−0.01
	(0.01)	(0.01)
NA	0.02	−0.03*
	(0.01)	(0.01)
Born in Landskrona	0.02***	0.02*
	(0.00)	(0.01)
N of observations	−0.00***	−0.02***
	(0.00)	(0.00)
Ln of average family income	−0.01***	0.01*
	(0.00)	(0.01)
Ln of average grid income	−0.08***	−0.40***
	(0.01)	(0.01)
Average Gini (standardized)	0.01***	0.04***
	(0.00)	(0.00)
Average Gini ^2 (standardized)	−0.00	0.01***
	(0.00)	(0.00)
N	9,015	5,843

Note: ***p < 0.01, **p < 0.05, *p < 0.1

Source: Own calculations based on Scanian Economic-Demographic Database (SEDD) (Bengtsson et al. 2021).

Notes

1. The income inequality hypothesis was given impetus early on by the Whitehall Studies for the United Kingdom and by parallel studies for France (Desplanques 1976) and the United States (Kitagawa and Hauser 1973), which showed that social position mattered for death patterns despite the existence of a well-developed welfare state. A dominant idea before the publication of these studies was that socioeconomic health differences were a remnant of the past and would completely disappear in the mature welfare state and with the introduction of medical innovations that made a significant difference in healthcare (cf. Bengtsson and van Poppel 2011).
2. The problem is that we may have an *ecological fallacy* when drawing conclusions about individuals based on aggregate data on population health. An ecological fallacy occurs when correlations found in aggregate observations differ from the correlations in the underlying individual observations (Robinson 1950). In the specific case of the income inequality hypothesis, an ecological fallacy is likely to occur because the relationship between individual income and health tends to be nonlinear (Karlsson et al. 2010).
3. The three hypotheses are parallel and interconnected in the sense that it is in fact possible to find support for all of them at the same time when using individual-level data. This also means that a negative relationship between income inequality and population health (i.e., one at the aggregate rather than the individual level) is compatible with all three hypotheses in that it is not possible to distinguish whether inequality or relative or absolute income explains a noted relationship at this aggregation.
4. It is, however, unclear to whom individuals primarily compare themselves. Do income differences within society matter, or do we primarily compare ourselves to people who are of the same age, who do the same kind of work, who are at the same workplace, who live in our neighborhood, or who are our closest friends? See Deaton (2008) for an elaborate discussion on the difficulty of defining appropriate reference groups.
5. See Hedefalk and Dribe (2020) and Hedefalk et al. (2023) for more details on the geocoding and its match rate. For the purposes of this chapter, we used grids of 250 m^2 to spatially analyze the neighborhoods.
6. The Gini coefficients are calculated using yearly equivalized family incomes, whereby each family is regarded as one unit per year. This is a different approach to that used in Chapter 3, where Gini coefficients were computed by individual income at an active age. Despite these differences, the overall trends and levels in income inequality are highly similar.
7. However, there is evidence that other outcomes are affected by such relative deprivation. For example, the risk of teenage childbearing has shown to be especially high for individuals residing in poor neighborhoods surrounded by more affluent neighborhoods (South and Crowder 2010).

References

Alesina, A., R. Baqir, and W. Easterly. 1999. "Public Goods and Ethnic Divisions." *Quarterly Journal of Economics* 114 (4): 1243–1284.

Baum, F. 1999. "Social Capital: Is It Good for Your Health? Issues for a Public Health Agenda." *Journal of Epidemiology and Community Health* 53 (4): 195–196.

Becker, G. S. 1968. "Crime and Punishment: An Economic Approach." *Journal of Political Economy* 76 (2): 169–217.

Beckfield, J., S. Olafsdottir, and E. Bakhtiari. 2013. "Health Inequalities in Global Context." *American Behavioral Scientist* 57 (8): 101–439.

Bengtsson, T., and M. Dribe. 2011. "The Late Emergence of Socioeconomic Mortality Den Differentials: A Micro-Level Study of Adult Mortality in Southern Sweden 1815–1968." *Explorations in Economic History* 48 (Suppl): 389–400.

Bengtsson, T., M. Dribe, and J. Helgertz. 2020. "When Did the Health Gradient Emerge? Social Class and Adult Mortality in Southern Sweden, 1813–2015." *Demography* 57 (3): 953–977.

Bengtsson, T., M. Dribe, L. Quaranta, and P. Svensson. 2021. "The Scanian Economic Demographic Database, Version 7.2 (Machine-readable database)." Lund: Lund University, Centre for Economic Demography.

Bengtsson, T., and F. van Poppel. 2011. "Socioeconomic Inequalities in Death from Past to Present: An Introduction." *Explorations in Economic History* 48 (Suppl): 343–356.

Bergh, A. 2021. *kapitalistiska välfärdsstaten* [The Capitalistic Welfare State]. Lund: Studentlitteratur.

Bergh, A., T. Nilsson, and D. Waldenström. 2016. *Sick of Inequality? An Introduction to the Relationship Between Inequality and Health*. Cheltenham, UK: Edward Elgar Publishing.

Blakely, T. A., B. P. Kennedy, R. Glass, and I. Kawachi. 2000. "What Is the Lag Time Between Income Inequality and Health Status?" *Journal of Epidemiology and Community Health* 54 (4): 318–319.

Blakely, T. A., K. Lochner, and I. Kawachi. 2002. "Metropolitan Area Income Inequality and Self-Rated Health: A Multi-Level Study." *Social Science & Medicine* 54 (1): 65–77.

Brea-Martinez, G., M. Dribe, and M. Stanfors. 2023. "The Price of Poverty: The Association Between Childhood Poverty and Adult Income and Education in Sweden, 1947–2015." *Economic History Review* 76 (4): 1281–1304.

Chen, Z., and C. A. Crawford. 2012. "The Role of Geographic Scale in Testing the Income Inequality Hypothesis as an Explanation of Health Disparities." *Social Science & Medicine* 75 (6): 1022–1031.

Chetty, R., M. Stepner, S. Abraham, et al. 2016. "The Association Between Income and Life Expectancy in the United States, 2001–2014." *Journal of the American Medical Association* 315 (16): 1750–1766.

Coleman, J. S. 1990. *The Foundations of Social Theory*, Cambridge, MA: Harvard University Press: 300–321.

Daly, M. C., D. J. Wilson, and N. J. Johnson. 2013. "Relative Status and Well-Being: Evidence from US Suicide Deaths." *Review of Economics and Statistics* 95 (5): 1480–1500.

Deaton, A. 2002. "Policy Implications of the Gradient of Health and Wealth." *Health Affairs* 21 (2): 13–30.

Deaton, A. 2008. "Income, Health, and Well-Being Around the World: Evidence from the Gallup World Poll." *Journal of Economic Perspectives* 22 (2): 53–72.

Debiasi, E., M. Dribe, and G. Brea-Martinez. 2023. "Has It Always Paid to be Rich? Income and Cause-Specific Mortality in Southern Sweden 1905–2014. *Population Studies* 1–21.

Demombynes, G., and B. Özler. 2005. "Crime and local inequality in South Africa." *Journal of Development Economics* 76 (2): 265–292.

Desplanques, G. 1976. *La mortalité des adultes suivant le milieu social 1955–1971*. Paris: INSEE.

Dobkin, C., A. Finkelstein, R. Kluender, and M. J. Notowidigdo. 2018. "The Economic Consequences of Hospital Admissions," *American Economic Review* 108: 308–352.

Dribe, M., and B. Eriksson. 2023. "Socioeconomic Status and Adult Lifespan 1881–2020: New Estimates from Swedish Death Registers and Full-Count Census Data." Lund Papers in Economic Demography 2023: 3.

Du, H., R. B. King, and P. Chi. 2019. "Income Inequality Is Detrimental to Long-Term Well-Being: A Large-Scale Longitudinal Investigation in China." *Social Science & Medicine* 232 (1): 120–128.

Ehrlich, I. 1973. "Participation in Illegitimate Activities: A Theoretical and Empirical Investigation." *Journal of Political Economy* 81 (3): 521–565.

Eibner, C., and W. N. Evans. 2005. "Relative Deprivation, Poor Health Habits, and Mortality." *Journal of Human Resources* 40 (3): 591–620.

Fukuyama, F. 1995. *Trust: the Social Virtues and the Creation of Prosperity.* New York: Free Press.

Gerdtham, U., and M. Johannesson. 2004. "Absolute Income, Relative Income, Income Inequality, and Mortality." *Journal of Human Resources* 39 (1): 228–247.

Green, G., and Gilbertson J. M., & Grimsley, M. F., 2002. Fear of crime and health in residential tower blocks: A case study in Liverpool, UK. The European Journal of Public Health, 12 (1), 10–15.

Grönqvist, H., P. Johansson, and S. Niknami. 2012. "Income Inequality and Health: Lessons from a Refugee Residential Assignment Program." *Journal of Health Economics* 31 (4): 617–629.

Hedefalk, F., and M. Dribe. 2020. "The Social Context of Nearest Neighbors Shapes Educational Attainment Regardless of Class Origin." *Proceedings of the National Academy of Sciences* 117 (26): 14918–14925.

Hedefalk, F., I. K. van Dijk, and M. Dribe. 2023. "Childhood Neighborhoods and Cause-Specific Adult Mortality in Sweden 1939–2015." *Health & Place* 84: 103–137.

Hederos, K., M. Jäntti, L. Lindahl, and J. Torssander. 2018. "Trends in Life Expectancy by Income and the Role of Specific Causes of Death." *Economica* 85 (339): 606–625.

Hirschman, A. O. 1973. "The Changing Tolerance for Income Inequality in the Course of Economic Development." *World Development* 1(12): 29–36.

Jen, M. H., K. Jones, and R. Johnston. 2009. "Global Variations in Health: Evaluating Wilkinson's Income Inequality Hypothesis using the World Values Survey." *Social Science & Medicine* 68 (4): 643–653.

Jones, A. M., and J. Wildman. 2008. "Health, Income and Relative Deprivation: Evidence from the BHPS." *Journal of Health Economics* 27 (2): 308–324.

Jordahl, H. 2007. "Inequality and Trust." *Research Institute of Industrial Economics (IFN)* working paper 715.

Karlsson, M., T. Nilsson, C. H. Lyttkens, and G. Leeson. 2010. "Income Inequality and Health: Importance of a Cross-Country Perspective." *Social Science & Medicine* 70 (6): 875–885.

Kawachi, I., S. V. Subramanian, D., and D. Kim. 2008. *Social Capital and Health: A Decade of Progress and Beyond.* New York: Springer.

Kitagawa, E. M., and P. M. Hauser. 1973. *Differential Mortality in the United States: A Study in Socioeconomic Epidemiology.* Cambridge, MA: Harvard University Press.

Kondo, N., M. Rostila, and M. Å. Yngwe. 2014. "Rising Inequality in Mortality among Working-Age Men and Women in Sweden: A National Registry-Based Repeated Cohort Study, 1990–2007." *Journal of Epidemiology and Community Health* 68 (12): 1145–1150.

Krugman, P. 1996. "The Spiral of Inequality." *Mother Jones*, 21: 44–49.

Lleras-Muney, A. 2022. "Education and Income Gradients in Longevity: The Role of Policy." *Canadian Journal of Economics* 55 (1): 5–37.
Mackenbach, J. P. 2019. *Health Inequalities: Persistence and Change in Modern Welfare States*. Oxford: Oxford University Press.
Marmot, M. G., S. Stansfeld, C. Patel, F. North, J. Head, I. White, ... and G. D. Smith. 1991. "Health Inequalities among British Civil Servants: The Whitehall II Study." *The Lancet* 337 (8754): 1387–1393.
Merton, R. K. 1957. *Social Theory and Social Structure*. Glencoe, IL: Free Press.
Miller, D. L., and C. Paxson. 2006. "Relative Income, Race, and Mortality." *Journal of Health Economics* 25 (5): 979–1003.
Mood, C. 2010. "Logistic Regression: Why We Cannot Do What We Think We can Do, and What We can Do About It." *European Sociological Review* 26 (1): 67–82.
Organisation of Economic Cooperation and Development (OECD). 2011. *Divided We Stand: Why Inequality Keeps Rising*. Paris: OECD Publishing.
Östling, R., D. Cesarini, and E. Lindqvist. 2020. "Association Between Lottery Prize Size and Self-Reported Health Habits in Swedish Lottery Players." *JAMA Network Open* 3 (3): e1919713.
Pickett, K. E., and R. G. Wilkinson. 2015. "Income Inequality and Health: A Causal Review." *Social Science & Medicine* 128 (1): 316–326.
Putnam, R. D. 2000. *Bowling Alone: The Collapse and Revival of American Community*. New York: Simon and Schuster.
Robinson, W. S. 1950. "Ecological Correlations and the Behavior of Individuals." *American Sociological Review* 15 (3): 351–357.
Rostila, M., M. L. Kölegård, and J. Fritzell. 2012. "Income Inequality and Self-Rated Health in Stockholm, Sweden: A Test of the 'Income Inequality Hypothesis' on Two Levels of Aggregation." *Social Science & Medicine* 74 (7): 1091–1098.
Sapolsky, R. M., S. C. Alberts, and J. Altmann. 1997. "Hypercortisolism Associated with Social Subordinance or Social Isolation Among Wild Baboons." *Archives of General Psychiatry* 54 (12): 1137–1143.
South, S. J., and K. Crowder. 2010. "Neighborhood Poverty and Nonmarital Fertility: Spatial and Temporal Dimensions." *Journal of Marriage and Family* 72 (1): 89–104.
Tibber, M. S., F. Walji, J. B. Kirkbride, and V. Huddy. 2022. "The Association Between Income Inequality and Adult Mental Health at the Subnational Level: A Systematic Review." *Social Psychiatry and Psychiatric Epidemiology* 57 (1): 1–24.
Vågerö, D., and O. Lundberg. 1989. "Health Inequalities in Britain and Sweden." *The Lancet* 334 (8653): 35–36.
Wagstaff, A., and E. Van Doorslaer. 2000. "Income Inequality and Health: What Does the Literature Tell Us?". *Annual Review of Public Health* 21 (1): 543–567.
Wilkinson, R. G. 2001. *Mind the Gap: Hierarchies, Health and Human Evolution*. New Haven: Yale University Press.
Wilkinson, R., and K. Pickett. 2009. *The Spirit Level: Why Equality Is Better for Everyone*. London: Penguin.
Zagorski, K., M. D. R Evans, J. Kelley, and K. Piotrowska. 2014. "Does National Income Inequality Affect Individuals' Quality of Life in Europe? Inequality, Happiness, Finances, and Health." *Social Indicators Research* 117 (3): 1089–1110.
Zheng, H. 2012. "Do People Die from Income Inequality of a Decade Ago?" *Social Science & Medicine* 75 (1): 36–45.
Zweifel, P., F. Breyer, and M. Kifmann. 2009. *Health Economics*. Heidelberg, Berlin: Springer-Verlag.

11
The Industrial City and Its People
Summary and Conclusion

Martin Dribe, Therese Nilsson, and Anna Tegunimataka

This volume is about how individuals and families lived their lives in an industrial city during much of the twentieth century and the beginning of the twenty-first. It was a period of major societal transformations, related initially to the Second Industrial Revolution and the final phases of the demographic transition, and later to the emergence and development of the modern Scandinavian welfare state. Throughout this period, Western societies experienced unprecedented gains in material welfare and living standards, although these gains were not always equally distributed. From 1900 to 1980, the ratio of average incomes in the top 10 percent and the bottom 50 percent dropped from 19 to 7 in Europe and from 14 to 9 in North America (Chancel and Piketty 2021). In the late nineteenth century, Sweden ranked among the most unequal countries in Europe, but even here a substantial reduction in economic inequalities took place in parallel with a rapid increase in average incomes, making Sweden one of the most equal countries in the world by 1980 in terms of income (Chancel et al. 2022; Roine and Waldenström 2008, 2009; Schön 2010). These trends, however, saw a reversal after 1980, when Western countries experienced growing disparities, with income and wealth becoming increasingly unequally distributed (Piketty 2018; see also DeLong 2022). The Nordic countries—Sweden included—also experienced very similar trends (Roine and Waldenström 2008, 2009; Schön 2010) despite the stronger involvement of the state in the economy and well-developed welfare systems. Still, the Nordic countries remain among the most equal Western countries in terms of income, although Sweden is the most unequal of the Nordics (World Bank 2020).

The course of the demographic transition and the post-transition demographic development followed a similar course across the Western world. Mortality, which had already started to decline in Sweden in the late eighteenth century, continued to decline in the twentieth century, increasing life expectancy at birth from about 55 years for men and 57 years for women in the first decade of the twentieth century to 80 and 84 years, respectively, in 2015.

After the end of the fertility transition in the 1930s, when the total fertility rate was less than two children per woman, there was an increase in marriage and marital fertility during the baby boom of the 1940s and 1950s (Van Bavel and Reher 2013), followed by a long-term decline in fertility to the subreplacement levels (e.g. Sobotka 2017) that have become a major concern of the early twenty-first century as Western populations are aging (United Nations 2023). Sweden has shown a somewhat deviant pattern, with more pronounced fertility variations than most other Western countries (Hoem and Hoem 1996)—variations that to a large extent have been related to economic cycles affecting the labor market for both men and women (Stanfors 2003). Nonetheless, the trend toward lower fertility has taken place in Sweden, as well as in the other Nordic countries, and the most recent decline—since 2010—would appear more difficult to link to changes in family policy, gender equality, or economic growth (Hellstrand et al. 2021; Ohlsson-Wijk and Andersson 2020).

This volume fills a gap in the narrative of twentieth-century demographic, social, and economic history by focusing on the individual—or micro—level as a complement to the more standard macro-level perspective. This approach has rarely been taken in previous research over such a long period of time due to a lack of high-quality micro-level data. To apply a micro-level perspective, we would prefer to have information similar to that available in contemporary administrative registers in many Western countries. But no country has had comprehensive digitized registers of demographic, social, and economic conditions of its entire population until the late 1960s—and most are often much later than that. Instead we have focused on an industrial city—Landskrona—and its rural hinterland in a region of southern Sweden, where we have a unique opportunity to analyze interactions between demography and socioeconomic conditions at the individual and family levels for the entire period 1905–2015. The different chapters of this volume present analyses that are based on data from the Scanian Economic-Demographic Database (SEDD), and, taken together, they give a nuanced picture of the demographic and socioeconomic development of families and individuals undergoing the fundamental societal changes of the twentieth century.

Landskrona constitutes a fair representation of a Swedish industrial city during this period. History and statistics reveal the city to be a good lens through which to observe the processes of industrial expansion and decline during the twentieth century. Its story is similar to former industrial hubs across Europe and North America, even though Landskrona, by international comparison, is a rather small industrial city. At the same time, it is important to keep in mind that, in some aspects, Sweden differed from most other Western countries in that the population was very homogenous throughout almost the entire period, the extension of suffrage came late and then happened very quickly, the country was neutral in both World War I and World War II, and institutions of exceptionally high quality were established (Bergh 2022). Notwithstanding, the findings based on individual and family data provide invaluable insights and impart lessons applicable to other contexts.

The overview presented in Chapter 2 shows that Landskrona followed the same trends and variations as other Swedish cities in economic and demographic terms, but that, in some cases, the city was at the lower end of the distribution, such as in terms of earnings and education. The Social Democratic party—whose ideological view was that collective social provision is a productive investment and a condition for growth, central to the inception and development of the universal Swedish welfare state (Andersson 2006)—came into political power in the city in 1919 and stayed there until the 1990s.

Within 150 years the city of Landskrona was transformed into an industrial center, with periods of boom and crisis followed by de-industrialization. Major transformations, including industrial expansion and decline, changing labor market conditions, in-migration from the countryside and from abroad, changing family patterns and gender relations, and also progressive solutions to problems such as the lack of social security, can generate fundamental socioeconomic change, shaping economic inequality and conditions for social mobility (cf. Birdsall et al. 2001; Deaton 2013; Galor 2022).

As demonstrated in Chapter 3, economic inequality in Landskrona showed a clear U-shaped long-term trend, coinciding with the similar development in Sweden as a whole. Notably, the microdata also showed a U-shaped pattern for the development of intergenerational income persistence over time, recalling the negative association between inequality and intergenerational mobility as envisaged by the "Great Gatsby curve" (cf. Blanden 2013; Chetty et al. 2014; Corak 2013). A small literature on long-run mobility trends based on brother comparisons suggests income mobility improved for the cohorts of 1930–1955, in parallel with the introduction of the modern welfare state and also the reductions in income inequality noted in Finland and Norway, and this was followed by stagnation and declines in mobility for the cohorts of 1955–1970 (Markussen and Roed 2017; Pekkala and Lucas 2007; Pekkarinen et al. 2017). Moreover, findings for the United Kingdom (Blanden et al. 2004) and France (Nicoletti and Ermisch 2007) suggest that the role of family background mattered more for individuals born in 1950–1970 compared to earlier cohorts, and this was mirrored by increasing income persistence across generations. Thanks to the micro-level income data across multiple generations, and for both sons and daughters, the case of Landskrona shows us that the decline in income persistence started before 1930 and that daughters acquired an income level closer to that of their fathers as women increasingly entered the labor force. Turning to absolute upward mobility, the share of individuals earning more than their parents has decreased in recent decades, suggesting that the development of economic inequality might be an obstacle to equal opportunities.

The industrial city of the twentieth century rested on migration, whereby streams of people moving in and out of it defined its changing character over time. Overall, as shown in Chapter 4, the net migration to Landskrona was positive throughout this time except for two distinct periods involving industrial crises in the 1920s and the 1970s, and, similarly, the economic crisis in the early 1990s initially meant negative net migration. Still, for most years, the majority of the city's inhabitants were not born in the city, thus pointing to the city's role in offering job opportunities and the importance of the labor market and to the role of economic development as a pull factor for migration (see Lee 1966; Massey et al. 1993; Massey et al. 2005; Piore 1979). In the early twentieth century, migrants came from rural or other urban contexts in Sweden, but, over time, the city included a larger share of migrants from other countries, and, in the last decades, they came increasingly from non-European origins. Notably these migration patterns might partially explain the marked development in income persistence across generations in Landskrona (Chapter 3). A long-standing hypothesis is that intergenerational mobility may surge during periods of rapid economic transformation and high migration, particularly migration induced by spatial differences in economic development (Abramitzky et al. 2021; Lipset and Bendix 1959; Long 2005; Ward 2022). Evidence for Swedish municipalities in the late nineteenth century shows that migrant brothers were more likely to transition out of their father's occupation compared to brothers who did not move (Berger et al. 2023). During the period of our study, moving may at times have also enabled the individual to exploit the advantages of city living over rural living, and the city provided opportunity, too, in terms of higher economic growth and greater occupational and income mobility. On the other hand, the industrial crises of the 1920s and 1970s meant poorer employment opportunities and lower wages. There is both theoretical and empirical support for the idea that the labor market conditions encountered upon arrival matter for migrants' long-term earnings and employment (Åslund and Rooth 2007; Holmstrom and Milgrom 1987; Oreopoulos et al. 2012).

The large and more or less continuous inflow of individuals and families to Landskrona, together with the changing character of the in- and out-migrants, make it pertinent to examine the spatial distribution of households and how this evolved. The role of residential segregation is relevant because high levels can raise concerns regarding social sustainability and reduce the status of urban areas as places of opportunity with equal chances and prospects for all (Van Ham et al. 2021). A large interdisciplinary literature also shows that socioeconomic segregation can affect the life chances of many (e.g., Chetty et al. 2014; Hedefalk and Dribe 2020), and segregation of the urban housing market interacts with high rates of poverty and results in geographically concentrated poverty, with the lower social classes residing in geographically isolated, homogeneous neighborhoods. Segregation patterns and their development are generally determined not only by demographic trends but also by macro-structural factors, including economic policy (Alba and Foner 2014; Koopmans 2010), as well as by local factors such as housing, housing tenure, and labor markets (Musterd et al. 2017).

Despite considerable previous research in this field, we have limited insights into whether and how segregation changed over time when measured at the local level. The analysis in Chapter 5 used geocoded information at the block level to show an emergent spatial pattern of social class segregation from 1940, after which the city developed from a pre-industrial and compact conurbation with socially mixed neighborhoods to a more segregated urban area that experienced suburbanization of the upper social classes. These findings mirror research on contemporary European cities showing that residential segregation between high- and low-income groups has increased in recent decades (Fujita and Maloutas 2016; Musterd et al. 2017; Tammaru et al. 2020). Available time series on segregation within cities cover only short periods, whereas residential segregation is likely to be a long-term process. Factors affecting social class segregation of this kind may have long time lags, and the processes that shape residential segregation (e.g., housing and income policy) are equally long.

Both industrialization and the demographic transition have had a far-reaching impact on individuals and families by fundamentally altering social relations within the family. These changes, together with increased female labor force participation, have revolutionized the productive role of women (Davis 1945; Demeny 1968; Notestein 1945). In the first half of the twentieth century, married women chose to add occasional paid employment to their role set but with little or no impact on men's involvement in household work. The post-World War II period witnessed a striking change in the economic role and position of women and also in terms of gender relations both within and outside the family (e.g., Jonung and Persson 1994; Stanfors 2007; Stanfors and Goldscheider 2017). In the 1970s, this was followed by family demographic changes, including delayed entry into marriage and parenthood, increased union instability, the rise of nonmarital cohabitation and childbearing, and greatly reduced total fertility. These trends, referred to as the "second demographic transition," are often linked with rising female independence and labor force participation (Lesthaeghe 1983, 2010; Van de Kaa 1987).

The analysis in Chapter 6 shows that trends in family formation (i.e., marriage and fertility) and in union dissolution through death or divorce developed in parallel with economic and institutional change, most notably the expansion of the welfare state, over the twentieth century. Few married women worked at the beginning of the period, but unmarried women, mostly active in agriculture and domestic roles, were more likely to be employed. A key shift occurred around 1970, when more than half of married women joined the labor force, with childcare, government jobs, and female skill upgrade facilitating this change (Bhalotra et al. 2022; Fischer et al. 2020). This shift, boosting female labor force participation rates to very high levels by international standards at the time (Grönlund et al. 2017), broke traditional gender roles, impacting family dynamics by making family choices more voluntary and enabling divorce. During the 1970s and 1980s, women's economic independence improved. Despite concerns of a weakening of the family as an institution in the 1960s, families remained strong. By 1990, the labor force participation of married and cohabiting women was higher than for single women, indicating a dual-earner norm. The development in Landskrona signifies a regional gender revolution over the twentieth century, altering family dynamics and roles significantly.

While traditional analyses of the benefits of marriage have generally emphasized the economic gains, contemporary research also shows that married people on average tend to have better health (Aizer et al. 2013; Hu and Goldman 1990; Rendall et al. 2011). In the light of Gary Becker's theoretical work (Becker 1973, 1974), marriage can be viewed as a partnership for joint production, consumption, and risk-sharing that is in many ways beneficial for both parties. Having a partner and related social support can benefit individual physical health and emotional well-being and may also follow on from the increased likelihood of the healthy to marry or from a relationship between disease and divorce (Goldman et al. 1995; Lillard and Panis 1996).

Health differences by marital status existed in historical societies (Grundy and Tomassini 2010; Mineau et al. 2002), but there is limited knowledge about the long-term development of such differences and their interaction with gender and social class. Interestingly, the analysis in Chapter 7 demonstrates that the health gains of marriage increased after 1950, in conjunction with fundamental societal improvements and changes regarding family and demographic behavior. Possible explanations for the widening differentials are the decline in baseline mortality, the change in selection into single living, the increased importance of lifestyle differences between the married and the single, and possibly the greater emotional stress of singlehood.

The noted falling marital fertility in the first decades of the twentieth century and concerns about population decline fueled by high maternal and infant mortality laid the foundations of an international infant welfare movement (Fildes et al. 2013). In the early 1890s, public health strategies such as *gouttes de lait* (milk stations) to provide babies of poorer families with clean, sterilized or pasteurized milk had begun in France before traveling to Great Britain and the United States (Meckel 1998). For many countries, the losses of World War coupled with the continued decline in the birth rate placed an even greater emphasis on the importance of preserving infant lives (Dwork 1987). While the debate on the need and desire to save the lives of mothers and young children was international, the solutions in Sweden were in part unique (Bhalotra et al. 2022). During the period 1920–1950, a number of welfare schemes focusing on preventive health measures for children and their mothers was implemented across the country, of which all were universal and of which several constituted significant steps in the development of the modern welfare state. Both city dwellers and rural inhabitants benefited from the modernization of healthcare and medical progress, as shown in Chapter 8. These findings have the potential to influence current global health priorities (cf. World Health Organization [WHO]/UNICEF 2022) by highlighting that large gains in infant health may be achieved by relatively low-cost and scalable interventions, and they also have wider contemporary relevance, as shown by a number of recent programs targeting high-risk mothers and their children in, for example, the United Kingdom, Chile, and India (Bhalotra et al. 2017; Cattan et al. 2019; Clarke et al. 2018; Dhamija and Gitanjali 2021).[1]

Institutional and medical developments played a role in infant survival chances and thus partly explain the large gains in infant health and life expectancy during the period studied. Life expectancy in Sweden has increased from 40 years in 1840 to more than 80 years today, which is an increase of almost 3 months per year over the course of the study period. At the same time, we have become taller, stronger, and more productive (Floud et al. 2011; Öberg 2014), and the decisive role of infectious disease in determining length of life has been replaced by cardiovascular disease and cancer.

In the 1950s and 1960s, it was assumed that not only would mortality further decline with the development of the modern welfare state, economic growth, and medical progress, but also socioeconomic differences in mortality would converge and possibly even disappear (Antonovsky 1967, 1980). However, recent evidence suggests that the health gaps between rich and poor have increased in most industrialized countries—Sweden included—from 1970 onward (Fors et al. 2021; Hederos 2018; Mackenbach 2019; Marmot 2004). Research has questioned the convergence hypothesis and argued that class differences in mortality have always existed and have stayed more or less constant over time (e.g., Cassel 1976; Deaton 2016; Elo 2009). The analysis in Chapter 9 shows that the social class gradient in adult mortality appeared as late as the mid-twentieth century (see also Bengtsson and Dribe 2011; Bengtsson et al. 2020) but that it was also more pronounced in urban than in rural areas. Moreover, the findings suggest that the urban mortality penalty lasted considerably longer than has previously been found at an aggregated level in Sweden. A possible mechanism behind the greater mortality difference in urban areas is that the urban environment was unable to provide the means to compensate for an inherently more stressful lifestyle, one known to have more adverse health effects on individuals from the lower classes than on those from the higher classes. Another mechanism could be that work conditions were unhealthier and more dangerous in the factories in the city than were conditions in the countryside.

There are many theories regarding how health inequalities arise and why they persist in modern welfare states (see Mackenbach 2019 for a comprehensive review). While some theories emphasize the role of social selection and the fact that individuals have certain characteristics beneficial for both socioeconomic status and health resulting in the noted gradient (Batty et al. 2006; Mackenbach 2010; West 1991), other theories emphasize the role of absolute and relative resources respectively (i.e., that individual income and/or average income in society at large as well as income distribution matter for our health; Wilkinson and Pickett 2009). In Chapter 10, a descriptive analysis using geocoded data on the neighborhood level describes changes and persistence in spatial income inequality in Landskrona from 1940 to 1970, and, in a second-step regression analysis, shows that own family income, long-term exposure to wealthier neighborhoods, and also long-term exposure to a more unequal income distribution in the neighborhood of residence were important for individual survival. The analysis not only brings to the literature examining the role of income dispersion for health and well-being insights regarding the role of local inequality, but also complements research on how neighborhoods influence the outcomes of children (see, e.g., Ainsworth 2002; Chetty et al. 2014, 2016; Donnelly et al. 2017). The historical and longitudinal study of a medium-sized city beyond the US context provides a more comprehensive understanding of how neighborhoods impact individual outcomes across a diverse context and also shows that such effects are not only a contemporary phenomenon.

In conclusion, the chapters in this volume present a wide range of research on the interaction between economic, social, and demographic factors at the individual level. It is based on a unique data infrastructure whereby individuals and families can be followed longitudinally over the twentieth and early twenty-first centuries. Thus, the research is able to close the gap between historical studies based on parish records and contemporary research based on full-count registers or detailed surveys.

The findings show how the behavior of individuals and families was conditioned by the larger societal transformations of the twentieth century; transformations associated with industrialization and deindustrialization. The rise and fall of the industrial city had far-reaching implications on some patterns of behavior while leaving few traces in others. The life events in Landskrona offer a prism through which we can view individual life courses during these times of profound social change. Even though the study population was not statistically representative of the Swedish population, the societal transformations of the twentieth century affected it in the same way as it did the populations of other cities and areas. The long-term patterns of social, economic, and demographic interactions revealed in the different chapters are therefore likely to be of broad relevance far beyond Landskrona and its hinterland. From the 1970s onward, when we have national comprehensive registers that also allow us to compare the differences in demographic outcomes across groups, the patterns are quite similar in the study area to Sweden as a whole, which further underlines this conclusion. Taken together, the volume provides a novel micro-based understanding of urban life and its developments in Sweden during the twentieth century. This knowledge is highly relevant in itself, and it also offers important insights into contemporary policy considerations as well as the development of theoretical frameworks.

Note

1. Regarding the role of economic versus social investments for population health across countries and time, see Riley (2007). For countries like Japan, Mexico, and Sri Lanka he states that dissemination of information about health risks and their avoidance, rather than investments in healthcare, explains much of the significant improvements in health and life expectancy.

References

Abramitzky, R., L. Boustan, E. Jácome, and S. Pérez. 2021. "Intergenerational Mobility of Immigrants in the United States Over Two Centuries." *American Economic Review* 111 (2): 580–608.

Ainsworth, J. W. 2002. "Why Does It Take a Village? The Mediation of Neighborhood Effects on Educational Achievement." *Social Forces* 81 (1): 117–152.

Aizer, A. A., M.-H. Ming-Hui Chen, E. P. McCarthy, et al. 2013. "Marital Status and Survival in Patients with Cancer." *Journal of Clinical Oncology* 31 (31): 3869–3876.

Alba, R., and N. Foner. 2014. "Comparing Immigrant Integration in North America and Western Europe: How Much do the Grand Narratives Tell Us?" *International Migration Review* 48 (1 Suppl): 263–291.

Andersson, J. 2006. *Between Growth and Security: Swedish Social Democracy from a Strong Society to a Third Way.* Manchester: Manchester University Press.

Antonovsky, A. 1967. "Social Class, Life Expectancy and Overall Mortality." *Milbank Memorial Fund Quarterly* 45 (2, Part 1): 31–73.

Antonovsky, A. 1980. "Implications of Socio-Economic Differentials in Mortality for the Health System." *Population Bulletin* 13: 42–52.

Åslund, O., and D.-O. Rooth. 2007. "Do When and Where Matter? Initial Labour Market Conditions and Immigrant Earnings." *Economic Journal* 117 (518): 422–448.

Batty, G. D., G. Der, S. Macintyre, and I. J. Deary. 2006. "Does IQ Explain Socioeconomic Inequalities in Health? Evidence From a Population Based Cohort Study in the West of Scotland." *British Medical Journal* 332: 580–584.

Becker, G. 1973. "A Theory of Marriage: Part I." *Journal of Political Economy* 81 (4): 813–846.

Becker, G. 1974. "A Theory of Marriage: Part II." *Journal of Political Economy* 82 (2): S11–S26.

Bengtsson, T., and M. Dribe. 2011. "The Late Emergence of Socioeconomic Mortality Differentials: A Micro-Level Study of Adult Mortality in Southern Sweden 1815–1968." *Explorations in Economic History* 48 (Suppl): 389–400.

Bengtsson, T., M. Dribe, and J. Helgertz. 2020. "When Did the Health Gradient Emerge? Social Class and Adult Mortality in Southern Sweden, 1813–2015." *Demography* 57 (3): 953–977.

Berger, T., P. Engzell, B. Eriksson, and J. Molinder. 2023. "Social Mobility in Sweden Before the Welfare State." *Journal of Economic History* 83 (2): 431–463.

Bergh, A. 2022. *Den kapitalistiska välfärdsstaten* [The Capitalist Welfare State]. Lund: Studentlitteratur.

Bhalotra, S., M. Karlsson, and T. Nilsson. 2017. "Infant Health and Longevity: Evidence From a Historical Intervention in Sweden." *Journal of the European Economic Association* 15 (5): 1101–1157.

Bhalotra, S., M. Karlsson, T. Nilsson, and N. Schwarz. 2022. "Infant Health, Cognitive Performance and Earnings: Evidence from Inception of the Welfare State in Sweden." *Review of Economics and Statistics* 104 (6): 1138–1156.

Birdsall, N., A. C. Kelley, and S. Sinding (eds.). 2001. *Population Matters: Demographic Change, Economic Growth, and Poverty in the Developing World*. Oxford: Oxford University Press.

Blanden, J. 2013. "Cross-Country Rankings in Intergenerational Mobility: A Comparison of Approaches from Economics and Sociology." *Journal of Economic Surveys* 27 (1): 38–73.

Blanden, J., A. Goodman, P. Gregg, and S. Machin. 2004. "Changes in Intergenerational Mobility in Britain." In *Generational Income Mobility in North America and Europe*, edited by M. Corak, 122–146. Cambridge: Cambridge University Press.

Cassel, J. 1976. "The Contribution of the Social Environment to Host Resistance: The Fourth Wade Hampton Frost Lecture." *American Journal of Epidemiology* 104 (2): 107–123.

Cattan, S., D. A. Kamhöfer, M. Karlsson, and T. Nilsson. 2017. "The Short- and Long-Term Effects of Student Absence: Evidence From Sweden." IZA Discussion Paper No. 10995.

Chancel, L., and T. Piketty. 2021. "Global Income Inequality, 1820–2020: The Persistence and Mutation of Extreme Inequality." *Journal of the European Economic Association* 19 (6): 3025–3062.

Chancel, L., T. Piketty, E. Saez, and G. Zucman (eds.). 2022. *World Inequality Report 2022*. Cambridge, MA: Harvard University Press.

Chetty, R., N. Hendren, and L. F. Katz. 2016. "The Effects of Exposure to Better Neighborhoods on Children: New Evidence from the Moving to Opportunity Experiment." *American Economic Review* 106 (4): 855–902.

Chetty, R., N. Hendren, P. Kline, and E. Saez. 2014. "Where Is the Land of Opportunity? The Geography of Intergenerational Mobility in the United States." *Quarterly Journal of Economics* 129 (4): 1553–1623.

Clarke, D., G. Cortés Méndez, and D. Vergara Sepúlveda. 2018. "Growing Together: Assessing Equity and Efficiency in an Early-Life Health Program in Chile." IZA Discussion Paper No. 11847.

Corak, M. 2013. "Income Inequality, Equality of Opportunity, and Intergenerational Mobility." *Journal of Economic Perspectives* 27 (3): 79–102.

Davis, K. 1945. "The World Demographic Transition." *Annals of the American Academy of Political and Social Science* 237 (1): 1–11.

Deaton, A. 2013. *The Great Escape. Health, Wealth, and the Origins of Inequality*. Princeton: Princeton University Press.

Deaton, A. 2016. "On Death and Money: History, Facts, and Expectations." *Journal of the American Medical Association* 315 (16) 1703–1705.

DeLong, J. B. 2022. *Slouching Towards Utopia: An Economic History of the Twentieth Century*. London: Basic Books.

Demeny, P. 1968. "Early Fertility Decline in Austria-Hungary: A Lesson in Demographic Transition." *Daedalus* 97 (2): 502–522.

Dhamija, G., and S. Gitanjali. 2021. "Lasting Impact of Early Life Interventions: Evidence from India's Integrated Child Development Services." *Journal of Development Studies* 57 (1): 106–138.

Donnelly, L., I. Garfinkel, J. Brooks-Gunn, B. G. Wagner, et al. 2017. "Geography of Intergenerational Mobility and Child Development." *Proceedings of the National Academy of Sciences* 114 (35): 9320–9325.

Dwork, D. 1987. *War Is Good for Babies and Other Young Children: A History of the Infant and Child Welfare Movement in England, 1898–1918*. London: Tavistock Publications.

Elo, I. T. 2009. "Social Class Differentials in Health and Mortality: Patterns and Explanations in Comparative Perspective." *Annual Review of Sociology* 35 (1): 553–572.

Fildes, V., L. Marks, and H. Marland. 2013. *Women and Children First (Routledge Revivals): International Maternal and Infant Welfare, 1870–1945*. London: Routledge.

Fischer, M., M. Karlsson, T. Nilsson, and N. Schwarz. 2020. "The Long-Term Effects of Long Terms: Compulsory Schooling Reforms in Sweden." *Journal of the European Economic Association* 18 (6): 2776–2823.

Floud, R., R. Fogel, B. Harris, and S. Hong. 2011. *The Changing Body: Health, Nutrition, and Human Development in the Western World since 1700*. Cambridge: Cambridge University Press.

Fors, S., J. W. Wastesson, and L. Morin. 2021. "Growing Income-Based Inequalities in Old-Age Life Expectancy in Sweden, 2006–2015." *Demography* 58 (6): 2117–2138.

Fujita K., and T. Maloutas (eds.). 2016. *Residential Segregation in Comparative Perspective: Making Sense of Contextual Diversity*. London: Routledge.

Galor, O. 2022. *The Journey of Humanity. The Origins of Wealth and Inequality*. London: The Bodley Head.

Goldman, N., S. Korenman, and R. Weinstein. 1995. "Marital Status and Health Among the Elderly." *Social Science & Medicine* 40 (12): 1717–1730.

Grönlund, A., K. Halldén, and C. Magnusson. 2017. "A Scandinavian Success Story? Women's Labour Market Outcomes in Denmark, Finland, Norway and Sweden." *Acta Sociologica* 60 (2): 97–119.

Grundy, E. M., and C. Tomassini. 2010. "Marital History, Health and Mortality Among Older Men and Women in England and Wales." *BMC Public Health* 10 (1): 554.

Hedefalk, F., and M. Dribe. 2020. "The Social Context of Nearest Neighbors Shape Educational Attainment Regardless of Class Origin." *Proceedings of the National Academy of Sciences* 117 (26): 14918–14925.

Hederos, K., M. Jäntti, L. Lindahl, and J. Torssander. 2018. "Trends in Life Expectancy by Income and the Role of Specific Causes of Death." *Economica* 85 (339): 606–625.

Hellstrand J., J. Nisén, V. Miranda, et al. 2021. "Not Just Later, but Fewer: Novel Trends in Cohort Fertility in the Nordic Countries." *Demography* 58 (4): pp.1373–1399.

Hoem, B., and J. Hoem. 1996. "Sweden's Family Policies and Roller Coaster Fertility." *Journal of Population Problems* 52 (3-4): 1–22.

Holmstrom, B., and P. Milgrom. 1987. "Aggregation and Linearity in the Provision of Intertemporal Incentives." *Econometrica* 55 (2): 303–328.

Hu, Y., and N. Goldman. 1990. "Mortality Differentials by Marital Status: An International Comparison." *Demography* 27 (2): 233–250.

Jonung, C., and I. Persson. 1994. "Combining Market Work and Family." In *Population, Economy and Welfare in Sweden*, edited by T. Bengtsson, 37–64. Heidelberg: Springer.

Koopmans, R. 2010. "Trade-Offs Between Equality and Difference: Immigrant Integration, Multiculturalism and the Welfare State in Cross-National Perspective." *Journal of Ethnic and Migration Studies* 36 (1): 1–26.

Lee, E. S. 1966. "A Theory of Migration." *Demography* 3 (1): 47–57.

Lesthaeghe, R. 1983. "A Century of Demographic and Cultural Change in Western Europe." *Population and Development Review* 9 (3): 411–435.

Lesthaeghe, R. 2010. "The Unfolding Story of the Second Demographic Transition." *Population and Development Review* 36 (2): 211–251.

Lillard, L. A., and C. W. A. Panis. 1996. "Marital Status and Mortality: The Role of Health." *Demography* 33 (3): 313–327.

Lipset, S. M., and R. Bendix. 1959. *Social Mobility in Industrial Society*. Berkeley: University of California Press.

Long, J. 2005. "Rural-Urban Migration and Socioeconomic Mobility in Victorian Britain." *Journal of Economic History* 65 (1): 1–35.

Mackenbach, J. P. 2010. "New Trends in Health Inequalities Research: Now It's Personal." *Lancet* 376 (9744): 854–855.

Mackenbach, J. P. 2019. *Health Inequalities: Persistence and Change in European Welfare States*. Oxford: Oxford University Press.

Markussen, S., and K. Røed. 2017. "Egalitarianism Under Pressure: Toward Lower Economic Mobility in the Knowledge Economy?" IZA Discussion Papers 10664.

Marmot, M. 2004. *The Status Syndrome: How Social Status Affects our Health and Longevity*. London: Bloomsbury Press.

Massey, D. S., J. Arango, G. Hugo, et al. 1993. "Theories of International Migration: A Review and Appraisal." *Population and Development Review* 19 (3): 431–466.

Massey, D. S., J. Durand, and N. J. Malone. 2005. "Principles of Operation: Theories of International Migration." In *The New Immigration: An Interdisciplinary Reader*, edited by C. Suarez-Orozco, M. Suarez-Orozco, and D. B. Qin-Hilliard, 21–33. New York: Routledge.

Meckel, R. A. 1998. *Save the Babies: American Public Health Reform and the Prevention of Infant Mortality, 1850–1929*. Ann Arbor: University of Michigan Press.

Mineau, G. P., K. R. Smith, and L. L. Bean. 2002. "Historical Trends of Survival Among Widows and Widowers." *Social Science & Medicine* 54 (2): 245–254.

Musterd S., S. Marcinczak, M. van Ham, and T. Tammaru. 2017. "Socioeconomic Segregation in European Capital Cities: Increasing Separation Between Poor and Rich." *Urban Geography* 38 (7): 1062–1083.

Nicoletti, C., and J. Ermisch. 2007. "Intergenerational Earnings Mobility: Changes Across Cohorts in Britain" *B. E. Journal of Economic Analysis & Policy* 7 (2).

Notestein, F. W. 1945. "Population: The Long View." In *Food for the World*, edited by T. W. Schultz, 36–57. Chicago: University of Chicago Press.

Ohlsson-Wijk, S., and G. Andersson. 2020. "Disentangling the Swedish Fertility Decline of the 2010s." *Demographic Research* 47 (12): 345–358.

Öberg, S. 2014. *Social Bodies: Family and Community Level Influences on Height and Weight, Southern Sweden 1818–1968*. PhD Dissertation, University of Gothenburg, Department of Economic History.

Oreopoulos, P., T. von Wachter, and A. Heisz. 2012. "The Short- and Long-Term Career Effects of Graduating in a Recession." *American Economic Journal: Applied Economics* 4 (1): 1–29.

Pekkala, S., and R. E. B. Lucas. 2007. "Differences Across Cohorts in Finnish Intergenerational Income Mobility" *Industrial Relations: A Journal of Economy and Society* 46 (1): 81–111.

Pekkarinen, T., K. G. Salvanes, and M. Sarvimäki. 2017. "The Evolution of Social Mobility: Norway During the Twentieth Century." *Scandinavian Journal of Economics* 119 (1): 5–33.

Piketty, T. 2018. *Capital in the Twenty-First Century*. Cambridge, MA: Belknap.

Piore, M. P. 1979. *Birds of Passage: Migrant Labour and Industrial Societies*. Cambridge: Cambridge University Press.

Rendall, M. S., M. M. Weden, M. M. Favreault, and H. Waldron. 2011. "The Protective Effect of Marriage for Survival: A Review and Update." *Demography* 48 (2): 481–506.

Riley, J. C. 2007. *Low Income, Social Growth, and Good Health: A History of Twelve Countries*. Berkeley: University of California Press.

Roine, J., and D. Waldenström. 2008. "The Evolution of Top Incomes in an Egalitarian Society: Sweden, 1903–2004." *Journal of Public Economics* 92 (1–2): 366–387.

Roine, J., and D. Waldenström. 2009. "Wealth Concentration Over the Path of Development: Sweden, 1873–2006." *Scandinavian Journal of Economics* 111 (1): 151–187.

Schön, L. 2010. *Sweden's Road to Modernity. An Economic History*. Stockholm: SNS.

Sobotka, T. 2017. "Post-Transitional Fertility: The Role of Childbearing Postponement in Fuelling the Shift to Low and Unstable Fertility Levels." *Journal of Biosocial Science* 49 (Suppl.): 20–45.

Stanfors, M. 2003. *Education, Labor Force Participation and Changing Fertility Patterns: A Study of Women and Socioeconomic Change in Twentieth Century Sweden*. Stockholm: Almqvist & Wiksell International.

Stanfors, M. 2007. *Mellan arbete och familj. Ett dilemma för kvinnor i 1900-talets Sverige* [Between Work and Family. A Dilemma for Women in Twentieth-Century Sweden]. Stockholm: SNS.

Stanfors, M., and F. Goldscheider. 2017. "The Forest and the Trees: Industrialization, Demographic Change, and the Ongoing Gender Revolution in Sweden and the United States, 1870–2010." *Demographic Research* 36 (6): 173–226.

Tammaru, T., S. Marcinczak, R. Aunap, et al. 2020. "Relationship Between Income Inequality and Residential Segregation of Socioeconomic Groups." *Regional Studies* 54 (4): 450–461.

United Nations. 2023. *Leaving No One Behind in an Ageing World: World Social Report 2023*. New York: United Nations.

Van Bavel, J., and D. S. Reher. 2013. "The Baby Boom and Its Causes: What We Know and What We Need to Know." *Population and Development Review* 39 (2): 257–288.

Van de Kaa, D. J. 1987. "Europe's Second Demographic Transition." *Population Bulletin* 42: 1–59.

Van Ham, M., T. Tammaru, R. Ubarevičienė, and H. Janssen. 2021. *Urban Socioeconomic Segregation and Income Inequality: A Global Perspective*. Cham, Switzerland: Springer.

Ward, Z. 2022. "Internal Migration, Education, and Intergenerational Mobility: Evidence from American History." *Journal of Human Resources* 57 (6): 1981–2011.

West, P. 1991. "Rethinking the Selection Explanation for Health Inequalities." *Social Science & Medicine* 32 (4): 373–384.

Wilkinson, R. G., and K. Pickett. 2009. *The Spirit Level: Why More Equal Societies Almost Always Do Better*. London: Allen Lane.

World Bank. 2020. *Reversals of Fortune. Poverty and Shared Prosperity 2020*. Washington DC: The World Bank.

World Health Organization (WHO) and the United Nations Children's Fund (UNICEF). 2022. *Protect the Promise: 2022 Progress Report, Every Woman Every Child. Global Strategy for Women's, Children's and Adolescents' Health (2016-2030)*. Geneva: WHO/UNICEF.

Index

For the benefit of digital users, indexed terms that span two pages (e.g., 52–53) may, on occasion, appear on only one of those pages.

Tables, figures, and boxes are indicated by *t*, *f*, and *b* following the page number

AB Förenade Superfosfatfabriker, 46
absolute income hypothesis (AIH), 309, 313–14, 316, 326
adult mortality
   absolute mortality differentials and, 287–88
   age trends and, 30, 31–32, 76*t*, 200, 230, 230*t*, 287–88, 292, 294*t*
   alcohol consumption and, 231
   divorce trends and, 239*t*
   early life conditions and, 283–84, 285
   in "five parishes," 218*t*, 222–26, 225*t*, 238*t*, 239*t*, 290–92, 291*t*, 294*t*, 302*t*
   fundamental causes theory and, 281–82
   gender and, 222–27, 225*t*, 229*t*, 230*t*, 231–32, 235–36, 236*t*, 238*t*, 284, 285, 288, 289*f*, 290, 291*t*, 292, 293*t*, 294*t*, 296
   hazard ratios on, 222–26, 228*t*, 230*t*, 291*t*, 293*t*, 294*t*, 302*t*
   infectious diseases and, 6, 215, 273, 283, 345
   in Landskrona, 56, 58*f*, 71, 76*t*, 218*t*, 222–26, 225*t*, 236*t*, 238*t*, 239*t*, 286, 288, 290–92, 291*t*, 294*t*, 302*t*
   marriage trends and, 213–14, 215, 222–30, 225*t*, 229*t*, 230*t*, 232–35, 236*t*, 239*t*, 298*t*
   nutrition and, 283–84, 285
   overall improvements in, 6, 236, 288, 339, 344
   pollution and, 283, 285–86
   regional differences and, 231
   relative mortality differentials and, 290–92
   segregation and, 146
   smoking and, 231, 296
   social class and, 213–14, 227–28, 229*t*, 230, 232, 235–36, 238*t*
   socioeconomic gradient and, 281–82, 283, 284–85, 288, 289*f*, 290–92, 291*t*, 293*t*, 294*t*, 296, 298*t*, 302*t*, 307
   urban-rural disparities and, 125, 285, 288, 289*f*, 292, 293*t*, 296–97, 298*t*, 345–46
African migrant population in Landskrona, 34*t*, 35, 133*t*, 134, 135*t*, 136, 137*t*, 138*t*, 140*t*, 141*t*
age structure of population, 2, 30–32, 60–61, 73*t*, 287–88

agriculture. *See also* farmers
   circular migration and, 127–28
   decline in employment in, 5–6, 82, 119–20, 129
   economic downturns in, 119
   occupational structure and, 82
   rationalization and, 8–9, 43–44, 119–20, 121, 126–27
   supply industries serving, 37, 46
alcohol consumption, 214, 234, 282, 284–85, 313
Alter, George, 17
antenatal care, 54, 244, 252–53, 254–55, 255*b*, 257–58, 273
antibiotics, 243–45, 250–51, 263, 266, 270
antiseptic methods, 243, 246, 247, 273–74
ASEA, 46
Asian migrant population in Landskrona, 34*t*, 35, 123, 131, 133*t*, 134, 135*t*, 136, 138*t*
ASSA ABLOY, 46
Asylen, 61–62
Austrian migrants in Landskrona, 34*t*, 130–31

baby boom, 7, 60–61, 62–63, 180, 189, 219, 340
Balkan Wars refugees (1990s), 27, 35
Barnavärn, 255*b*, 257–58
Becker, Gary S., 172–73
Bergsöe, 46
Bernadotte, Folke, 35
BESAM, 46
Borås (Sweden)
   age structure of population in, 31*t*, 32*t*
   female labor-force participation in, 47*f*, 47
   industrial structure of, 38*f*, 50
   map of, 28*f*
   mean income for male workers in, 48*t*, 50
   percentage of workforce in industry in, 35–36
   poor relief in, 65*t*
   sex ratios at birth in, 33*t*
   textile industry in, 37, 47
Borstahusen (Sweden), 157–61, 162–63, 164, 320

Bosnian refugees, 35
Bourdieu, Pierre, 83
Bruces shipyard, 42

Canada, 235–36
cancer, 213, 233, 282, 345
cardiovascular disease, 233, 282, 345
Carl Emond clothing company, 45
CEBE, 46
Center Party, 69*f*, 69
child allowance policies, 8
childbearing
  average hospital stay following, 254
  cesarean deliveries and, 251
  childbirth allowance policies and, 248–49
  cohabitation and, 187–88
  crude birth rates and, 60*f*, 60–61
  delivery rooms and, 253–55
  home births and, 244, 247–49, 253
  hospital births and, 244, 248–50, 251, 255–57, 274
  hygiene and, 248
  institutionalization of, 248, 273–74
  maternity hospitals and, 248, 249–50, 253–54, 255*b*
  maternity wards and, 248–50
  medicalization of, 243–44, 247
  modernization of, 253–57
  nurses and, 248
  out-of-wedlock births and, 170–71, 187–88
childcare
  female labor-force participation and, 11, 205–6, 207
  government subsidy support for, 12
  Landskrona Women's Organization and, 61–62
  Nordic countries and, 11
child mortality, 2, 56, 57*f*, 244, 254–55, 285
children's healthcare center (*barnavårdscentral*; BVC), 249*b*, 254–55, 255*b*, 257–58, 267–68, 270, 271*t*
Chile, 344–45
Christian Democratic Party, 69*f*, 69
circular migration, 127–28, 142, 143
circulatory diseases, 284–85
Cityvarvet AB, 42
cohabitation
  childbearing and, 187–88
  female labor-force participation and, 343–44
  health outcomes and, 227
  longitudinal data on, 217–19
  overall increase in, 2, 170–71, 172–73, 178, 188, 217–19
  parenthood and, 174
Conservative Party (Moderaterna), 69*f*, 69

county hospitals (länslasarett), 27, 53–54, 253–55, 255*b*, 257–58
  Cox proportional hazards model and, 175, 176, 188, 193, 196*t*, 197*t*, 198*t*, 217, 290
crime, 150, 311–12, 325–26
crude birth rates (CBR), 60*f*, 60–61
crude death rates (CDR), 54–55, 55*f*, 258–59, 259*f*
cultural capital, 83
Czechoslovakian migrants in Landskrona, 34*t*, 35

Danish migrants in Landskrona, 34*t*, 35, 44–45, 130–31, 134
deindustrialization
  housing oversupply and, 27
  income inequality and, 83–84, 92–94, 105
  knowledge economy and, 3
  in Landskrona, 3–4, 10, 35–36
  oil crisis of 1973 and, 10
  out-migration and, 27
  service sector and, 3
  unemployment and, 27, 105
dementia, 233–34
Denmark, 36–37, 251–52, 296. *See also* Danish migrants in Landskrona
diarrheal diseases, 55–56, 251–52, 285
Diet of the Four Estates (*Ståndsriksdagen*), 66–68
diphtheria, 55–56
divorce
  age trends and, 200, 201*t*
  economic growth and, 199
  female labor-force participation and, 199
  gender and, 201*t*, 202*f*, 220*f*, 224*f*, 231–32
  health outcomes and, 214–15, 227
  longitudinal data on, 217–19
  mortality trends and, 239*t*
  no-fault divorce and, 195–99, 203–4, 216
  overall increase in levels of, 173–74, 195–99, 203–4
  rates of, 173–74, 195, 202–4, 219, 221*f*
  risk ratios regarding, 200–1, 202*f*, 203*f*, 203–4
  social acceptance of, 2
  social class and, 173–74, 204–5, 219
  Sweden's legal reforms regarding, 195–99
  women's economic independence and, 199, 204–6, 219
Durkheim, Émile, 172, 231–32

earnings. *See also* wages
  health outcomes and, 313
  mean income levels and, 49*f*, 50
  median income for male workers and, 48*t*, 50
  Scanian Economic-Demographic Database and, 15

eclampsia, 257–58
economic crises in Sweden
　early 1920s and, 41–42, 44, 71, 94, 104, 119, 126, 142, 342–43
　financial crisis of early 1990s and, 10–11, 99–101, 105, 342
　Great Depression and, 5–6, 7, 104, 142
　industrial crisis of 1970s and, 28–29, 40, 42, 44, 45, 71–72, 104–5, 125, 142, 143, 232–33, 316–20, 342
　oil crisis of 1973 and, 10, 104–5
economic inequality. *See* income inequality
education outcomes
　gender and, 103, 110*f*, 207
　income inequality and, 110*f*
　industrialization of early twentieth century and, 6
　introduction of compulsory education system in Sweden (1842) and, 8, 19n.2, 64–65
　knowledge economy and, 10
　public sector investment and, 9–10
　social mobility and, 82
Egnahemsrörelsen (Own Home movement), 52
EGP class scheme, 16–17
elections in Sweden, 68–69
electrification, 5–6, 120, 142
Emil Emond clothing company, 45
England, 235–36. *See also* United Kingdom
Erlander, Tage, 10
Estonian migrants in Landskrona, 34*t*, 35
ethnic enclaves, 151, 165n.2
European Union, 10–11

family
　baby boom and, 7
　family change and, 19, 170–73, 205–7, 208
　family formation and, 2, 62–63, 171–73, 175–95, 205–6, 343–44
　family policy and, 8, 11, 340
　female labor-force participation and, 173, 205–6
　fertility decline and, 170–71
　gender revolution and, 171–72, 174, 175
　industrialization and, 170, 173–74, 343
　migration and, 117
　nuclear family structure and, 173
　Scanian Economic-Demographic Database and, 14–15
　Second Demographic Transition and, 171
　separate spheres and, 177
　sizes of, 2, 172–73
farmers. *See also* agriculture
　fertility trends among, 193, 196*t*

　in "five parishes," 86
　heterogeneity among, 16
　Historical International Social Class Scheme coding and, 16
　migration patterns among, 133*t*, 135*t*, 137*t*, 138*t*, 140*t*, 141*t*, 185*t*
　mortality trends among, 229*t*, 291*t*, 293*t*, 294*t*, 298*t*, 302*t*
female labor-force participation
　brush factories and, 46–47, 48
　chemical industry and, 48
　childcare and, 11, 205–6, 207
　cohabitation and, 343–44
　divorce and, 199
　family and, 173, 205–6
　fertility decline and, 2, 170–71
　food industry and, 48
　gender revolution and, 9–10, 171, 174
　geographical breakdown of, 47*f*
　"glass ceiling" and, 105–6
　income inequality and, 105–6
　increase in overall levels of, 205–6
　industrialization and, 171, 343
　Industrial Revolution and, 170
　intergenerational income mobility and, 103
　lower-skilled workers and, 86, 87*t*, 91
　male breadwinner model and, 6
　marriage and, 172–73, 208, 343
　mechanical workshops and, 48
　paper and pulp industry and, 48
　post–World War II workforce expansion and, 27
　public sector employment and, 205–6
　school teachers and, 65, 86–91, 87*t*
　Second Demographic Transition and, 174
　skilled workers and, 87*t*, 91
　sugar industry and, 46–47, 48
　textile industry and, 46–48
　tobacco industry and, 46–48
　unskilled workers and, 87*t*, 91
　white-collar workers and, 86–91, 87*t*
fertility
　age at first birth and, 189, 192*f*
　age structure of population and, 30–31
　average intervals between births and, 193, 194*f*
　baby boom and, 7, 60–61, 62–63, 180, 189, 219, 340
　crude birth rates and, 60–61, 60*f*
　female labor-force participation and, 2, 170–71
　fertility decline and, 2, 6, 30–31, 60–61, 154, 170–71, 174, 176–77, 188–89, 199, 206–7, 340

fertility (*cont.*)
  fertility transition and, 60, 170, 188–89, 193, 340
  general fertility rate and, 61, 61*f*
  marriage and, 62–63, 187–95, 196*t*, 197*t*, 198*t*, 340, 344–45
  social class and, 173–74, 189, 191*f*, 193–95, 196*t*, 197*t*, 198*t*
  total fertility rates and, 60, 188–93, 190*f*, 191*f*, 340
  total marital fertility rates and, 188
  urban *versus* rural trends in, 189
Finland, 9–10, 34*t*, 35, 130–31, 296, 341–42
First Industrial Revolution, 119, 121
Fitzgerald, F. Scott, 83
"five parishes." *See also* Halmstad (Skåne County, Sweden), Hög (Sweden); Kågeröd (Sweden); Kävlinge (Sweden); Sireköpinge (Sweden)
  adult mortality in, 218*t*, 222–26, 225*t*, 238*t*, 239*t*, 290–92, 291*t*, 294*t*, 302*t*
  divorce in, 199–200, 201*t*, 202*f*, 203*f*, 204*t*, 220*f*, 221*f*
  fertility in, 187–89, 190*f*, 191*f*, 192*f*, 193–95, 194*f*, 196*t*, 198*t*
  geography of, 13–14
  income inequality in, 92, 93*f*, 96–99, 98*f*
  infant health in, 244–45, 258–61, 260*f*, 262*f*, 263*f*, 264*t*, 265, 265*f*, 267–68, 269*t*, 272*t*, 273–74
  map of, 13*f*
  marriage in, 178–87, 179*f*, 181*f*, 182*f*, 183*f*, 201*t*, 220*f*, 221*f*, 225*t*
  maternal health in, 244–45, 258, 267–68
  maternity ward births in, 256*f*
  mean income levels in, 108*t*
  population levels in, 12–13
  social-class structure in, 85*f*, 86, 218*t*, 287
  social mobility and, 83, 108*t*
  unskilled workers in, 86, 96–99
  widowhood trends in, 201*t*, 202*f*, 203*f*, 204*t*, 220*f*, 228*t*, 237*t*
Fordism, 7, 104, 119–20
foreign-born population in Landskrona, 34*t*, 35, 96, 98*f*, 105–6, 130–31, 217, 287. *See also* migration
Former Yugoslavia, migration from, 32–35, 34*t*, 96
France, 195, 235–36, 251, 341–42, 344–45

Gävle (Sweden)
  age structure of population in, 31*t*, 32*t*
  female labor-force participation and, 47*f*
  industrial structure of, 28*f*
  map of, 28*f*
  mean income for male workers in, 48*t*
  poor relief in, 65*t*
  population levels in, 29–30
  sex ratios in, 32, 33*t*
gender
  adult mortality and, 222–27, 225*t*, 229*t*, 230*t*, 231–32, 235–36, 236*t*, 238*t*, 284, 285, 288, 289*f*, 290, 291*t*, 292, 293*t*, 294*t*, 296
  divorce and, 201*t*, 202*f*, 220*f*, 224*f*, 231–32
  educational outcomes and, 103, 110*f*
  gender equality and, 12, 171, 174, 340
  gender gap in lifetime income and, 94, 95*f*, 105–6
  gender roles and, 170–72, 343–44
  income inequality and, 83–84, 92, 94–96, 95*f*, 97*f*, 105–6
  intergenerational income mobility and, 99–103, 100*t*, 101*t*, 106, 109*f*
  marriage and, 171, 175, 177, 179*f*, 180–87, 185*t*, 201*t*, 220*f*, 224*f*, 225*t*, 229*t*, 230*t*
  mean income levels and, 107*t*, 108*t*
  Second Demographic Transition and, 171
  "separate spheres" and, 170, 171, 177, 205–6, 208n.1
  widowhood and, 178, 201*t*, 202*f*, 219–22, 220*f*, 223*f*, 224*f*, 228–29, 228*t*, 231–32, 237*t*
gender revolution
  childcare and, 12
  divorce and, 171
  family change and, 171–72, 174, 175
  female labor-force participation and, 9–10, 171, 174
  industrialization and, 171–72, 205
  men's engagement in household responsibility and, 174
  modernization and, 173, 177, 178, 195–99
gentrification, 151
geocoded data, 14, 148, 152, 309, 346
Germany
  migration from, 34*t*, 35, 41, 130–31
  Swedish metal industry and, 44
germ theory of disease, 245–46
GHH, 44
Gini coefficient
  calculation of, 111n.2
  in "five parishes," 93*f*
  as income inequality measure, 83–84, 91–92
  in Landskrona, 92–94, 93*f*, 104–5, 310, 319*f*, 321
  in Sweden, 93*f*, 104–5
glass ceiling, 94, 105–6

INDEX   357

Goldscheider, Frances, 9–10, 174
Goode, William, 172, 173–74, 204–5
Götaverken shipyard (Göteborg), 42
Göteborg (Sweden)
    age structure of population in, 31*t*, 32*t*
    children's hospital in, 250
    female labor-force participation in, 47*f*
    industrial structure of, 38*f*
    map of, 28*f*
    mean income for male workers in, 48*t*, 50
    native population share in, 126
    poor relief in, 65*t*
    population levels in, 29, 30*f*
    sex ratios in, 33*t*
    voter turnout levels in, 70–71
gouttes de lait (milk stations in France), 251, 344–45
Gråen reef (Sweden), 46
Great Depression, 5–6, 104, 142
Great Gatsby curve, 83, 106, 341–42
Greece, migration from, 130–31
Green Party, 69, 69*f*
gross domestic product (GDP) in Sweden, 5–6, 41–42

Halmstad (Halland County, Sweden)
    age structure of population in, 31*t*, 32*t*
    female labor-force participation in, 47*f*
    industrial structure of, 38*f*
    map of, 28*f*
    mean income for male workers in, 48*t*, 50
    poor relief in, 65*t*
    population levels in, 29–30
    sex ratios in, 33*t*
    total migration rates and, 123
Halmstad (Skåne County, Sweden), 291*t*, 294*t*, 298*t*, *See also* "five parishes"
healthcare. *See also* health outcomes
    children's healthcare centers and, 249*b*, 254–55, 255*b*, 257–58, 267–68, 270, 271*t*
    collective health insurance schemes and, 246–47
    government investment in, 104
    modernization in, 244, 253–57, 274–75
    public sector investment in, 9–10
health outcomes
    absolute income hypothesis and, 309, 313–14, 316, 326
    air pollution and, 283
    alcohol consumption and, 214, 234, 313
    cohabitation and, 227
    divorce trends and, 214–15, 227
    education and, 307
    food inspection and, 283
    marriage and, 213–15, 344
    migration status and, 217
    neighborhood influences on, 346
    nutrition and, 307
    regression analysis of, 315*t*, 316, 321–24, 322*t*, 327*t*, 328*t*, 329*t*, 330*t*, 331*t*, 332*t*, 333*t*, 334*t*
    relative income hypothesis and, 312–13, 314, 316, 324–25
    smoking and, 214, 313
    social class and, 216
    social networks and, 234–35, 311
    social support and, 214, 231, 234–35
    survival analysis and, 217
    urban penalty and, 283, 288, 292
    widowhood trends and, 214–15, 227
Helsingborg (Sweden), 126, 132, 136, 137*t*, 138*t*
Hirschman, Albert O., 312, 324–25
Historical International Social Class Scheme (HISCLASS), 16–17, 84, 176
Historical International Standard Classification of Occupations (HISCO), 15–16, 84, 176
Hög (Sweden), 12, 13–14, 290–92, 291*t*, 294*t*, 298*f*, *See also* "five parishes"
home visits for children's health, 8, 251–52, 257
homophily, 148, 150, 164
hospitals
    childbirth at, 244, 248–50, 251, 255–57, 274
    children's hospitals and, 54, 250, 254–55, 255*b*, 257–58
    county hospital (*länslasarett*) and, 27, 53–54, 253–55, 255*b*, 257–58
    maternity hospital (*barnbördshuset*) and, 248, 249–50, 253–54, 255*b*
housing
    apartment houses and, 52
    baby boom and, 7
    cooperative housing associations (HSB) and, 52
    deindustrialization and oversupply in, 27
    foreign-born population and, 35
    housing policy and, 147
    industrialization and demand for, 52
    million homes program (*miljonprogrammet*) and, 9–10, 53
    Own Home movement (*Egnahemsrörelsen*) and, 52
    public funding for, 9–10, 104–5
    rental associations (*hyresgästföreningar*) and, 52
    shipyard industry and, 52, 121–22
Hungary, migration from, 34*t*, 35, 130–31

hygiene, 1–2, 244, 246–47, 248, 296–97
hyresgästföreningar (rental associations), 52

income and taxation registers, 15, 84, 176
income inequality. *See also* income inequality hypothesis (IIH)
   crime and, 311–12, 325–26
   education outcomes and, 110*f*
   elite policy preferences and, 311
   financial crisis of early 1990s and, 105
   in "five parishes," 92, 93*f*, 96–99, 98*f*
   foreign-born populations and, 96, 98*f*, 105–6
   gender and, 83–84, 92, 94–96, 95*f*, 97*f*, 105–6
   Gini coefficient measures of, 83–84, 91–92
   income concentration and, 92–94, 320, 324
   industrialization and, 83–84, 104
   in Landskrona, 83–84, 92–96, 93*f*, 95*f*, 97*f*, 98*f*, 104–6, 321, 324, 339
   longitudinal data and, 310
   long-term exposure to, 315–16, 324, 325
   oil crisis of 1973 and, 92–94
   public goods and, 311–12
   social class and, 83–84, 96, 97*f*, 98*f*, 104, 105
   social trust levels and, 311, 312, 325–26
   spatial inequality and, 309, 314, 321
   in Sweden, 92–94, 93*f*, 104–5, 339
   top 1 percent of earners and measures of, 83–84, 91–92, 94, 95*f*, 104
   violence and, 311–12, 325–26
income inequality hypothesis (IIH)
   geocoded data and, 309
   health outcomes and, 307
   individual level data and, 307–8, 309
   neighborhood-level data and, 309, 315, 321–23, 325
incubators, 248, 250
India, 344–45
industrial city
   Landskrona as, 26, 27, 36–37, 40, 340–41, 346–47
   manufacturing and, 35–36, 36*f*
   migration and, 115–18, 139, 342
industrialization
   education outcomes and, 6
   families and, 170, 173–74, 343
   gross domestic product growth and, 5–6
   housing demand and, 52
   income inequality and, 83–84, 104
   living standards and, 1–2
   migration and, 2–3, 118–19, 122
   occupational structure and, 82
   poor relief and, 63–64
   rural industry and, 37
   social mobility and, 82, 83
   urbanization and, 1–2, 6, 37, 118–19
Industrial Revolution
   female labor-force participation and, 170
   First Industrial Revolution and, 119, 121
   longevity and, 170
   Second Industrial Revolution and, 5–6, 119, 121, 339
   Third Industrial Revolution and, 10
industrial society, 3, 10, 83
infant health
   antenatal care and, 252–53
   antibiotics and, 243–45, 250–51, 263, 266, 270
   antiseptic techniques and, 243, 246, 247, 273–74
   clean water and, 243–44
   congenital or perinatal problems and, 263, 264*t*, 273
   epidemic disease outbreaks and, 55–56
   home visit programs and, 251–52
   hospital improvements and, 243–44
   incubators and, 248, 250
   infant welfare movement and, 8, 344–45
   infectious disease and, 245–46, 263, 264*t*
   intervention analysis and, 266–70, 267*f*, 271*t*, 272*t*
   maternity wards and, 268
   midwife training and, 247–48
   nutrition and, 251–52, 273–74
   overall improvements in, 2, 55–56, 56*f*
   penicillin and, 267–68, 273–74
   population decline concerns and, 344–45
   postpartum stays and, 250
   preventive care and, 251–53
   rural-urban discrepancies and, 265
   sex ratio at birth and, 253, 258–59, 261, 262*f*, 271*t*, 272*t*
   social class and, 274
   stillbirths and, 244–45, 248–49, 258–61, 260*f*, 266, 268–70, 269*t*, 271*t*, 272*t*, 273–74
   sulfa drugs and, 250–51, 263, 266–68, 270–74, 272*t*
   infant mortality and, 245–46, 261–65, 263*f*, 264*t*, 265*f*, 268, 271*t*, 272*t*, 273, 344–45
infectious diseases
   antibiotics and, 250–51
   child mortality and, 285
   infant health and, 245–46, 263, 264*t*
   migration and, 283
   mortality rates and, 6, 215, 273, 283, 345
   sulfa drugs and, 250–51
   urbanization and, 283

INDEX 359

in-migration
  age and, 133*t*, 136, 137*t*, 140*t*, 142
  agricultural rationalization and, 119–20
  economic crisis of 1920s and, 119
  gender and, 126–27, 133*t*, 136, 137*t*, 142
  industrialization and, 120
  Landskrona and, 32–35, 33*f*, 75*t*, 115–16, 121, 124*f*, 125*f*, 126–28, 129*t*, 132–34
  marital status and, 137*t*, 140*t*
  Nordic countries and, 123
  rural areas and, 139, 141*t*, 142
  rural *versus* urban regions and, 129*t*
  social class and, 132–34, 133*t*, 136, 137*t*, 140*t*, 142
  urbanization and, 9–10, 115, 125
  World War II and, 127
intergenerational income mobility, 83–84, 99–103, 100*t*, 106, 341–42
intergenerational rank-rank association, 99–101, 100*t*, 101*t*, 102*t*
international trade during World War I and World War II, 5
iron industry, 37, 39
ISCO-88, 16
Italy, migration from, 34*t*, 130–31

Järnkonst, 46

Kågeröd (Sweden), 12, 13–14, 291*t*, 294*t*, 298*t*, *See also* "five parishes"
Kävlinge (Sweden), 12–14, 286, 290–92, 291*t*, 294*t*, 298*t*, *See also* "five parishes"
Keynesian economic policy, 8, 10–11
knowledge economy, 3, 10
Kockums, 44
Kosovo, refugees from, 35
Kreuger, Alan, 83
Kreuger, Ivar ("Kreuger crash"), 7, 19n.1, 104

Landskrona (Sweden)
  adult mortality in, 56, 58*f*, 71, 76*t*, 218*t*, 222–26, 225*t*, 236*t*, 238*t*, 239*t*, 286, 288, 290–92, 291*t*, 294*t*, 302*t*
  age structure of population in, 30–31, 31*t*, 32*t*, 60–61
  antenatal and postnatal care in, 257–58
  average income by family in, 318*f*, 320
  brush factories in, 39–40, 46–47, 48, 50–51
  chemical industry in, 39–40, 46, 48, 71, 74*t*
  child mortality in, 56, 57*f*
  Citadel in, 320
  crude birth rates in, 60, 60*f*
  crude death rates in, 54–55, 55*f*
  crude marriage rates in, 62–63, 63*f*
  deindustrialization in, 3–4, 10, 35–36
  divorce trends in, 199–200, 201*t*, 202–5, 202*f*, 203*f*, 204*t*, 219, 220*f*, 221*f*
  educational achievement levels in, 66, 67*f*
  female-headed households and, 156, 157*f*
  female labor-force participation in, 47–48, 47*f*
  fertility trends in, 60, 61, 61*f*, 187–89, 190*f*, 191*f*, 192*f*, 193–95, 194*f*, 196*t*, 197*t*
  food industry in, 37, 40, 71, 74*t*, 121
  foreign-born population in, 34*t*, 35, 96, 98*f*, 105–6, 130–31, 217, 287
  founding (1413) of, 3–4, 26
  Gini coefficient in, 92–94, 93*f*, 104–5, 310, 319*f*, 321
  hospitals in, 53–54, 244, 254–55
  housing in, 9–10, 52–53, 71, 316–20
  income inequality and health outcomes in, 309, 310
  income inequality in, 83–84, 92–96, 93*f*, 95*f*, 97*f*, 98*f*, 104–6, 321, 324, 339
  individuals without a registered income in, 84
  as industrial city, 26, 27, 36–37, 40, 340–41, 346–47
  industrialization in, 6, 7, 40, 71
  industrial structure of, 37–46, 38*f*, 50, 74*t*, 123
  infant health in, 244–45, 258–61, 260*f*, 262*f*, 263*f*, 264*t*, 265, 265*f*, 267–68, 269*t*, 270, 271*t*, 272*t*
  infant mortality in, 55–56, 56*f*, 76*t*, 243
  in-migration and, 32–35, 33*f*, 75*t*, 115–16, 121, 124*f*, 125*f*, 126–28, 129*t*, 132–34
  intergenerational income mobility in, 99–101, 103*f*, 106
  intergenerational rank-rank association in, 100*t*, 101*t*, 102*t*
  landskommmuner (rural municipalities) incorporated into, 26
  leather tanneries in, 39–40
  locations of factories and industries in, 50–52, 51*f*
  maps of, 13*f*, 28*f*, 51*f*
  marriage trends in, 178–87, 179*f*, 181*f*, 182*f*, 183*f*, 201*t*, 219, 220*f*, 221*f*, 225*t*, 236*t*
  maternal health in, 243, 244–45, 258, 267–68
  maternity care in, 253
  maternity ward births in, 256*f*
  mean age of family head by block in, 155, 155*f*, 163–64
  mean family size by block in, 154*f*, 163–64
  mean income for male workers during 1920s in, 48*t*, 50
  mean income levels in, 49*f*, 50, 107*t*

Landskrona (Sweden) (*cont.*)
    medium-skilled workers in, 84–86, 87*t*
    metal industry in, 37, 39, 40, 44, 71, 74*t*
    migration flows and, 131–39
    net migration and, 127, 128*f*, 130*t*, 342
    nursing homes in, 53
    old-age mortality in, 59*f*, 76*t*
    out-migration and, 35, 71, 121, 123, 124*f*, 125*f*, 126, 127, 134–36, 135*t*, 138*t*, 139
    paper and pulp industry in, 40, 48, 74*t*
    percentage of workers in industry in, 35–37, 36*f*
    poor relief in, 64, 65*t*
    population density by neighborhood in, 316–20, 317*f*
    population levels in, 3–4, 12–13, 26, 28–29, 29*f*, 71, 122–23, 316–20
    port of, 26, 36–37, 41, 71
    public bathhouses in, 54
    public sector employment in, 36–37
    refugees in, 116
    retail sector in, 36–37
    right-wing political parties in, 69–70
    schools in, 27, 65–66, 71
    segregation in, 11–12, 27, 154–56, 320
    service sector in, 11–12
    sewerage and, 244, 283
    sex ratios in, 32, 33*t*
    share of children by block in, 155, 156*f*, 163–64
    shipyard industry in, 9, 26, 39–40, 41–42, 50–52, 71, 73*t*, 94, 104–5, 121
    social-class structure in, 85*f*, 86, 107*t*, 108*t*, 157, 218*t*, 287
    social mobility in, 83–91, 100*t*, 101*t*, 102*t*, 104
    Spanish flu epidemic (1918) in, 54–55, 71
    sugar industry in, 9, 26, 37–40, 43–44, 50–52, 71, 73*t*
    textile industry in, 9, 10, 37–39, 40, 44–45, 46–47, 48, 50–51, 71, 74*t*, 104–5, 121
    tobacco industry in, 39–40, 46–47
    total migration rates and, 125*f*
    total mortality in, 55
    transport sector in, 36–37, 121
    voter turnout levels in, 70–71
    water systems in, 54, 244, 283
    widowhood trends in, 201*t*, 202–3, 202*f*, 203*f*, 204*t*, 220*f*, 228*t*, 237*t*
    women elected to public office in, 69–70, 70*f*
    World War I and food shortages in, 54
Landskronahem, 53
Landskrona Nya Mekaniska Verkstad, 44, 48

Landskronas fruntimmersförening (Landskrona Women's Organization), 61–62
Landskrona Warfsaktiebolag shipyard, 41
Landsorganisationen (LO), 6–7
Landsverk, 44
länslasarett (county hospital), 27, 53–54, 253–55, 255*b*, 257–58
Lebanon, immigrants from, 35
Lee, Everett, 116–17
Left Party, 69
Liberal Party, 12, 69, 69*f*
lifetime income
    gender gap in, 94, 95*f*, 105–6
    intergenerational income mobility and, 99–103, 103*f*, 106, 109*f*
Linköping (Sweden), 126
longevity, 2, 170, 231, 234–36, 308–9, 313
lower-skilled workers
    female labor-force participation and, 86, 87*t*, 91
    fertility trends among, 191*f*, 193–95, 196*t*, 197*t*, 198*t*
    health gradient and, 283
    Historical International Social Class Scheme coding and, 16
    income inequality and, 96, 104
    in Landskrona, 84–86, 87*t*, 91
    marriage trends among, 184–87, 185*t*
    migration patterns among, 132, 133*t*
    mortality patterns and, 289*f*, 293*t*, 294*t*, 298*t*
    residential patterns among, 156–57, 159*f*, 162–63
Lund (Sweden), 132, 136, 137*t*, 138*t*

male breadwinner model, 6, 9–10, 105–6, 233
Malmö (Sweden)
    age structure of population in, 31*t*, 32*t*
    female labor-force participation in, 47*f*
    industrial structure of, 38*f*
    Landskrona and, 132, 136
    map of, 13*f*
    mean income for male workers in, 48*t*, 50
    native population share in, 126
    poor relief in, 65*t*
    population levels in, 29, 30*f*
    railway from Göteborg to, 13–14
    re-emergence as industrial city after 1995 of, 5
    sex ratios in, 33*t*
    voter turnout levels in, 70–71
Mandemakers, Kees, 17

marriage
  age trends and, 178–80, 183f, 200, 201t, 230t
  average duration of, 199, 200, 201t
  companionate marriage and, 177, 199
  decline in social importance of, 2
  delay in entry to, 170–71, 172–73, 174, 184, 343
  female labor-force participation and, 172–73, 208, 343
  fertility trends and, 62–63, 187–95, 196t, 197t, 198t, 340, 344–45
  gender and, 171, 175, 177, 179f, 180–87, 185t, 201t, 220f, 224f, 225t, 229t, 230t
  happiness and, 234–35
  health outcomes and, 213–15, 344
  institutional marriage and, 177
  life expectancy and, 199
  longitudinal data on, 217–19
  marriage boom, 62–63, 180–87, 189, 219
  marriage rates and, 62–63, 62f, 63f, 180, 181f, 182f, 215, 219
  mortality trends and, 213–14, 215, 222–30, 225t, 229t, 230t, 232–35, 236f, 239t, 298t
  remarriage trends and, 180
  same-sex marriage and, 177, 216
  social class and, 17, 180, 184–87, 185t
  Western European Marriage Pattern and, 176–77, 215, 216
maternal health
  antenatal care and, 252–53
  antibiotics and, 244–45, 266, 270
  antiseptic methods and, 246, 247, 254–55, 273–74
  clean water and, 243–44
  home visit programs and, 251
  maternal mortality and, 231, 243–44, 247, 258–59, 259f, 273, 344–45
  maternal trauma, 250
  maternity care and, 253
  midwife training and, 248, 258–59
  penicillin and, 246, 251, 267–68
  postpartum stays and, 250
  preventive care and, 251–53
  sulfa drugs and, 246, 266–68, 270–73
maternity hospital *(barnbördshuset)*, 248, 249–50, 253–54, 255b
maternity leave, 8, 10
maternity wards, 54, 248–50, 256f, 268, 269t, 273
measles, 55–56, 285
medical innovations, 244–45, 248, 249b, 250–51, 257
Medicinalstyrelsen, 54

medium-skilled workers
  fertility trends among, 189, 191f, 196t, 197t, 198t
  in Landskrona, 84–86, 87t
  marriage trends among, 184–87, 185t
  residential patterns among, 157, 158f
metal industry
  auto and aircraft manufacturing and, 45, 71
  economic crisis of early 1920s and, 44
  electrical goods industry and, 46
  industrial crisis of 1970s and, 44, 71–72
  in-migration and, 127
  in Landskrona, 37, 39, 40, 44, 71, 74t
  skilled workers and, 87t, 91
  workforce in, 44
middle class, 37, 82–83
midwifery
  home births and, 243–44
  hygienist movement and, 246–47
  obstetrical instruments and, 247
  professionalization and training in, 243, 244, 247–48, 258–59, 273–74
  public sector employment and, 253
migration. *See also* in-migration; out-migration
  age as selection mechanism for, 117, 122, 132, 133t
  circular migration and, 127–28, 142
  economic development and, 3, 115, 116, 117, 118–22
  family decision-making and, 117
  financial crisis of early 1990s and, 342
  gender and, 133t
  industrial cities and, 115–18, 139, 342
  industrial crisis of 1970s and, 125
  industrialization and, 2–3, 118–19, 122
  innovation and, 3
  international migration, 3, 18, 129, 130–31, 142
  labor migration and, 12, 119–20, 130–31, 134
  marital status and, 133t, 134
  migration flows and, 2–3, 116, 122–39
  net migration and, 121, 127, 128f, 129, 130t, 142, 342
  networks of, 118
  push and pull framework of, 2–3, 116–17, 118, 139, 342
  rationalization and, 116
  social class and, 132
  Sweden's policies regarding, 2–3, 131
  total migration rates and, 123
  wages and, 116–17, 118, 119
miljonprogrammet (million homes program), 9–10, 53

milk depots (United Kingdom), 251
Moderaterna (Conservative Party), 69, 69*f*
  multinomial logit regression, 200, 202–3, 204*t*

Neolithic Revolution, 1–2
neonatal health
  neonatal intensive care units (NICUs) and, 244–45, 249*b*, 250, 266, 268–70, 269*t*, 273–74
  neonatal mortality and, 244, 246, 261, 263*f*, 265, 271*t*, 272*t*, 273–74, 275*t*
  preventive care programs and, 251–52
  social class and, 244
Netherlands, 195, 252–53, 281–82
Nordic countries. *See also specific countries*
  childcare and, 11
  fertility trends in, 171, 340
  gender equality and, 171
  income inequality levels in, 339
  intergenerational income mobility in, 99–101
  migration patterns from, 35, 123, 133*t*, 134, 135*t*, 136, 137*t*, 138*t*, 141*t*
  Second Demographic Transition and, 206
  state intervention in the economy in, 339
  welfare state in, 339
Norrköping (Sweden)
  age structure of population in, 31*t*, 32*t*
  female labor-force participation in, 47, 47*f*
  industrial structure of, 38*f*
  map of, 28*f*
  mean income for male workers in, 48*t*, 50
  native population share in, 126
  sex ratios in, 33*t*
  textile industry in, 47
North America, 1–3, 6, 34*t*, 339, 340–41. *See also* Canada; United States
Norway, 34*t*, 36–37, 214, 235–36, 251–52, 341–42
NYK, 16
Nyköping (Sweden), 52

odds ratios, 18, 133*t*, 135*t*, 137*t*, 138*t*, 140*t*, 141*t*
oil crisis of 1973, 10, 27, 92–94, 104–5
old-age mortality, 56, 59*f*, 76*t*
Öresundvarvet shipyard (Landskrona), 41–42, 46, 52, 64
out-migration
  age and, 134–36, 135*t*, 138*t*, 139, 141*t*, 143
  agricultural rationalization and, 121
  automobiles and, 121–22
  commuter towns and, 121–22
  deindustrialization and, 27
  gender and, 135*t*, 138*t*, 141*t*
  Landskrona and, 35, 71, 121, 123, 124*f*, 125*f*, 126, 127, 134–36, 135*t*, 138*t*, 139

marital status and, 135*t*, 136, 138*t*, 141*t*
rural areas and, 139, 141*t*, 143
social class and, 121–22, 134, 135*t*, 139, 141*t*, 143
Own Home movement (*Egnahemsrörelsen*), 52

parental leave, 10, 11, 207
Paris (France), 281–82
Parsons, Talcott, 172
penicillin, 246, 249*b*, 250–51, 267–68, 270, 272*t*, 273–74
pension system in Sweden, 6–7, 9–10
Petterson & Ohlsen, 44
pneumonia, 249*b*, 250–52, 266, 270, 285
Poland, migration from, 34*t*, 35
pollution, 283, 285–86
poor relief, 26, 63–64, 65*t*
population stagnation, 32–35
post-industrialization, 4, 139
postnatal care, 244, 255–57, 255*b*, 273
predictive mean matching methods (PMM), 111n.1
prenatal care, 252–53
Providence (Rhode Island), 281–82
public health, 244, 245–47, 266, 273–74, 283, 311, 344–45

rationalization
  agriculture and, 8–9, 43–44, 119–20, 121, 126–27
  competition and, 119–20
  economic growth and, 5, 10
  Fordism and, 119–20
  gender balance of workers and, 127
  Great Depression and, 5–6
  industrial structure and, 120
  migration and, 116
  sugar industry and, 5, 9, 43–44, 127
  Taylorism and, 119–20
  textile industry and, 5, 8–9, 127
Ravenstein, Ernst George, 116–17
Red Cross, 35
refugees, 35, 71, 116, 122
relative income hypothesis (RIH), 312–13, 314, 316, 324–25
rental associations (*hyresgästföreningar*), 52
residential segregation. *See* segregation
respiratory disease, 233
Romanian immigrants in Landskrona, 35
rubber industry, 37, 51–52

Säbyholm (Sweden), 43, 44
Saltsjöbaden agreement, 7
Sandvången housing development (Landskrona), 44–45, 53, 155, 157–60, 162–63

Sankt Ibb (Sweden), 26
Scandinavia, 151, 244, 251, 339. *See also specific countries*
Scanian Economic-Demographic Database (SEDD)
　continuous population registers and, 14–15
　divorce data and, 175
　fertility data and, 175
　geocoded date in, 14
　income and taxation registers and, 15
　income inequality data and, 314
　individual-level data in, 14
　infant health data in, 244–45
　Intermediate Data Structure and, 17
　longitudinal nature of, 4, 14, 17
　marriage data and, 175, 216
　maternal health data in, 244–45
　micro-level demography in, 340
　occupational data in, 176
　occupational notations in, 16
　segregation and, 152
　social mobility and, 84
Scania region (Sweden), 12, 26, 128–29, 129t, 130t, 215, 244, 245–46. *See also* Scanian Economic-Demographic Database (SEDD)
Schelling model of segregation, 150, 151
Schlasbergs, 44–45, 48
Schön, Lennart, 5
Second Demographic Transition (SDT), 11, 170–71, 174, 177, 195, 199–200, 206, 343
Second Industrial Revolution, 5–6, 119, 121, 339
segregation
　adult mortality and, 146
　building-level measures of, 164
　Chicago School research and, 148
　constraint models and, 148, 164
　definition of, 146
　discrimination and, 149, 150–51
　dissimilarity indicies and, 165
　educational achievement levels and, 148–49
　educational outcomes and, 146–47
　ethnicity and, 27, 146–47, 149–50, 151
　geocoded data and, 147, 148, 152, 343
　homophily and, 148, 150, 164
　housing policy and, 147
　Isolation Index and, 147–48, 153, 160–62, 161f, 162f, 164, 165
　labor market outcomes and, 146
　in Landskrona, 11–12, 27, 154–56, 320
　longitudinal data on, 147
　migrant populations and, 149, 163–64
　mortgage industry and, 149
　place stratification theory and, 148, 149, 164
　residential preference models and, 148, 150, 164
　Schelling model of, 150, 151
　social class and, 146–47, 148–49, 151, 156–63, 158f, 159f, 160f, 164, 165, 342–43
　spatial assimilation and, 148–49, 164
　in the United States, 149, 150–51
　welfare state and, 151
service sector, 11–12, 115, 120–21, 122
sewerage, 6, 87t, 244, 245–46, 283
shipyard industry
　economic crisis of early 1920s and, 41–42, 71, 94, 126
　in Göteborg, 41–42
　housing and, 52, 121–22
　industrial crisis of 1970s and, 9, 10, 40, 42, 44, 71–72, 104–5, 127
　in-migration and, 127
　international competition in, 42
　in Landskrona, 9, 26, 39–40, 41–42, 50–52, 71, 73t, 94, 104–5, 121
　in Malmö, 41–42
　Öresundsvarvet shipyard and, 41–42, 46, 52, 64
　white-collar workers in, 86–91, 87t
　workforce in, 41–42, 73t, 155
Shorter, Edward, 177
singlehood and single living, 172–73, 178, 214, 215–16, 233–34, 236, 344
Sireköpinge (Sweden), 12, 13–14, 291t, 294t, 298t, *See also* "five parishes"
Skånska sockerfabriksaktiebolaget, 43
skilled workers
　carpentry and, 87t, 91
　Historical International Social Class Scheme coding and, 16
　income inequality and, 96
　in Landskrona, 87t, 91
　metal industry and, 87t, 91
　migration patterns among, 132, 133t, 135t, 137t, 138t, 140t, 141t
　mortality patterns among, 288, 289f, 291t, 293t, 294t, 298t, 302t
smallpox, 285
smoking, 214, 282, 284–85, 296, 313
social class. *See also* socioeconomic status (SES)
　child mortality and, 244
　classification systems and, 16–17
　fertility trends and, 173–74, 189, 191f, 193–95, 196t, 197t, 198t
　income inequality and, 83–84, 96, 97f, 98f, 104, 105
　in-migration and, 132–34, 133t, 136, 137t, 140t, 142

social class (*cont.*)
  in Landskrona, 85*f*, 86, 107*t*, 108*t*, 157, 218*t*, 287
  marriage and, 17, 180, 184–87, 185*t*
  mean income levels and, 107*t*, 108*t*
  measures of, 286–87
  mortality trends and, 213–14, 227–28, 229*t*, 230, 232, 235–36, 238*t*
  occupation and, 15
  segregation and, 146–47, 148–49, 151, 156–63, 158*f*, 159*f*, 160*f*, 164, 165, 342–43
Social Democratic Party, 6–7, 8, 12, 27, 68*f*, 68–69, 69*f*, 71
  changes in government coalitions (1976-2006) and, 10–11, 12
  founding (1889) of, 6–7
  hegemony in parliament (1932-1976) of, 8, 10, 68
  in Landskrona, 6–7, 8, 12, 27, 68*f*, 68–69, 69*f*, 71
  rental associations and, 52
  vote share achieved by, 68*f*
  welfare state and, 341
social mobility
  absolute social mobility levels and, 82
  absolute upward income mobility and, 101–2
  ascription and, 82
  cultural capital and, 83
  economic inequality and, 83
  higher education and, 82
  industrialization and, 82, 83
  intergenerational income mobility and, 83, 99–103, 106, 109*f*
  intergenerational rank-rank association and, 99–101, 100*t*, 101*t*, 102*t*
  in Landskrona, 83–91, 100*t*, 101*t*, 102*t*, 104
  occupational structure and, 82
social policy, 6–7, 10, 104. *See also* welfare state
social stratification, 16–17, 84–91, 157–60
socioeconomic status (SES). *See also* social class
  adult mortality gradient and, 281–82, 283, 284–85, 288, 289*f*, 290–92, 291*t*, 293*t*, 294*t*, 296, 298*t*, 302*t*, 307
  child mortality and, 285
  divorce trends and, 173–74
  measures of, 176
  nutrition and, 307
  as proxy for economic independence, 171–72
  socioeconomic segregation and, 146–47, 148–49, 160, 165, 342–43
  working conditions and, 283
Solidar, 54
South Africa, 149

Spanish flu epidemic (1918), 54–55, 71
SSYK, 16
Ståndsriksdagen (Diet of the Four Estates), 66–68
Statistics Sweden, 40
steel industry, 10
stillbirths. *See under* infant health
Stinson, 45
Stockholm (Sweden)
  adult mortality in, 56
  age structure of population in, 31*t*, 32*t*
  female labor-force participation in, 47*f*
  income inequality and health outcomes and, 309
  industrial structure of, 38*f*
  map of, 28*f*
  mean income for male workers in, 48*t*, 50
  native population share in, 126
  poor relief in, 65*t*
  population size in, 9–10, 29, 30*f*
  sex ratios in, 33*t*
structural crises in Sweden, 5–6, 10, 142
structural transformation, 10, 115, 118, 119–20
suffrage, 6–7, 27, 68, 69–70, 340–41
sugar industry
  cartelization in, 43
  female labor force participation in, 46–47, 48
  in-migration and, 127
  in Landskrona, 9, 26, 37–40, 43–44, 50–52, 71, 73*t*
  rationalization in, 5, 9, 43–44, 127
  workforce in, 43, 46–47, 73*t*
sulfa drugs, 246, 249*b*, 250–51, 263, 266–68, 270–74, 272*t*
Sundsvall (Sweden)
  age structure of population in, 31*t*, 32*t*
  female workforce participation in, 47*f*
  industrial structure of, 38*f*
  map of, 28*f*
  maternity hospital in, 249–50
  mean income for male workers in, 48*t*
  poor relief in, 64, 65*t*
  population levels in, 29–30
  sex ratios in, 33*t*
Supra, 45, 46
Svenska sockerfabriks AB, 43
Svenska varv, 42
Sweden
  absolute income mobility and, 101–2
  adult mortality trends in, 296
  age structure of population in, 30–31, 31*t*, 32*t*
  divorce law reform in, 195–99
  divorce trends in, 195–99, 221*f*

emigration to North America from, 2–3, 6
European Union membership (1994) of, 10–11
fertility trends in, 188–89, 340
gender equality and, 171
"golden age" of economic performance (1950-1970) in, 2–3, 8–9
Great Depression and, 7, 104
home visit healthcare programs in, 251–52
income inequality levels in, 92–94, 93f, 104–5, 339
infant mortality in, 243
intergenerational income mobility in, 99–101
life expectancy in, 345
marriage rates in, 221f
migration policies in, 2–3, 131
national health statute (1874) in, 283
Second Demographic Transition and, 206
sex ratios at birth in, 33t
socioeconomic gradient in health in, 310
urbanization levels in, 3–4
voter turnout levels in, 70–71
Sweden Democratic Party, 69f, 69
Swedish Federation of Employers (Svenska arbetsgivareföreningen), 7
Swedish Parliament, 6–7, 42, 66–68
Syrian migrants in Landskrona, 35

Taylorism, 119–20
technological change, 5–6, 11, 105, 121–22
textile industry
  in Borås, 37, 47
  female workforce participation in, 46–48
  financial crisis of early 1990s and, 10
  industrial crisis of 1970s and, 40, 45, 71–72, 104–5
  industrialization of Sweden and, 37
  in-migration and, 127
  international competition in, 45
  in Landskrona, 9, 10, 37–39, 40, 44–45, 46–47, 48, 50–51, 71, 74t, 104–5, 121
  rationalization in, 5, 8–9, 127
  workforce in, 44–45
Third Industrial Revolution, 10, 105
Thulin, Enoch, 45
Thulinverken, 45, 46
tobacco industry, 39–40, 46–48
Trelleborg (Sweden)
  age structure of population in, 31t, 32t
  female labor-force participation in, 47f, 47, 48
  industrial structure of, 38f
  map of, 28f
  mean income for male workers in, 48t

poor relief in, 65t
right-wing parties in, 69–70
rubber industry in, 37
sex ratios in, 32, 33t
tuberculosis, 285
Turkey, migrants in Landskrona from, 35, 130–31

Uddevalla (Sweden)
  age structure of population in, 31t, 32t
  female workforce participation in, 47f
  industrial structure of, 38f
  map of, 28f
  mean income for male workers in, 48t, 50
  poor relief in, 65t
  sex ratios in, 32, 33t
unemployment
  during 1990s, 9–10
  deindustrialization and, 27, 105
  economic crisis of early 1920s and, 42
  Great Depression and, 7
  industrial crisis of 1970s and, 42
  in Landskrona, 11–12
United Kingdom, 195, 251, 341–42, 344–45
United States
  absolute upward income mobility and, 101–2
  divorce trends in, 195
  Great Depression and, 7
  income inequality and mortality risks and, 324–25
  obstretric and pediatric care in, 252–53
  segregation in, 149, 150–51
  urbanization in, 6
unskilled workers
  decline in overall importance of, 84–86
  female labor force participation and, 87t, 91
  fertility trends among, 189, 191f, 196t, 197t, 198t
  in "five parishes," 86, 96–99
  Historical International Social Class Scheme coding and, 16–17
  income inequality and, 96–99, 104
  in Landskrona, 84–86, 87t, 91, 96–99
  marriage trends among, 185t
  migration patterns among, 133t, 135t, 137t, 138t, 140t, 141t, 142
  mortality trends among, 288, 289f, 290, 291t, 293t, 294t, 302t
  residential patterns among, 157–60, 159f
urbanization
  density of social interaction and, 118
  industrialization and, 1–2, 6, 37, 118–19
  infectious diseases and, 283

urbanization (*cont.*)
  in-migration and, 9–10, 115, 125
  poverty and, 6
  segregation and, 152
  social networks and, 234
  wages and, 121
  water infrastructure and, 6, 283
  work conditions and, 345–46

vaccines, 6
Västerås (Sweden), 52
Ven island (Sweden), 26
Vita bandets mjölkdroppe, 62
VME Industries, 44

wages. *See also* earnings
  economic crisis of 1920s and, 119
  "golden years" (1950-1970) and, 8–9
  during industrial expansion (1890-1930), 5–6
  migration and, 116–17, 118, 119
  in rural *versus* urban areas, 37
  urbanization and, 121
Wales, 235–36
water, 6, 54, 243–44, 245–46
Weibull, Annie, 62
welfare state
  childcare and, 232–33
  child health and, 344–45
  elder care and, 64
  expansion after World War II of, 104–5
  family formation and, 343–44
  labor movement and, 1–2
  maternal health and, 344–45
  mortality improvements and, 345–46
  pensions and, 232–33
  poverty reduction and, 232–33
  Social Democratic Party and, 341
  social mobility and, 341–42
  women's economic independence and, 205
white-collar workers
  diversification of occupations among, 87*t*, 91
  education industry and, 86–91

  fertility trends among, 189, 191*f*, 196*t*, 197*t*, 198*t*
  higher white-collar workers, 16–17, 86–91, 92, 96, 142, 157–62, 164, 165
  Historical International Social Class Scheme coding and, 16
  income inequality and, 96, 97*f*
  in Landskrona, 86–91, 87*t*
  lower white-collar workers, 16, 84–86, 96, 134, 142–43, 156–57, 158*f*, 161, 176
  marriage trends among, 184–87, 185*t*
  migration patterns among, 132, 133*t*, 135*t*, 137*t*, 138*t*, 140*t*, 141*t*, 142
  mortality trends among, 229*t*, 288, 289*f*, 290–92, 291*t*, 293*t*, 294*t*, 298*t*, 302*t*
  overall increase after World War II in number of, 105
  public sector jobs for, 9–10
  residential patterns among, 157, 158*f*, 160*f*, 161–62, 164
  shipyard industry and, 86–91, 87*t*
Whitehall studies, 283, 335n.1
whooping cough, 285
widowhood
  age trends and, 201*t*, 202–3
  dementia and, 233–34
  gender and, 178, 201*t*, 202*f*, 219–22, 220*f*, 223*f*, 224*f*, 228–29, 228*t*, 231–32, 237*t*
  health outcomes and, 214–15, 227
  longitudinal data on, 217–19
  mortality trends and, 203–4, 214–15, 216, 227, 228–29, 231–32, 235, 237*t*, 239*t*
  social class and, 204–5
  social networks and, 234
  spousal age gaps and, 216
  "widowhood penalty" and, 228–29, 235
women's economic independence, 170–72, 199, 204–6, 207–8
World War I, 5, 8, 54, 92, 340–41
World War II, 5, 127, 340–41

Yara, 46
Yugoslavia. *See* Former Yugoslavia, migration from